Last Chance in Manchuria

Last Chance in Manchuria

THE DIARY OF CHANG KIA-NGAU

Edited by and with an introduction by

Donald G. Gillin and Ramon H. Myers

Translated by Dolores Zen,
with the assistance of Donald G. Gillin

HOOVER INSTITUTION PRESS

Stanford University, Stanford, California

Hoover Press Publication 379

First printing, 1989
Manufactured in the United States of America
Printed on acid-free paper

95 94 93 92 91 90 89   9 8 7 6 5 4 3 2 1

Library of Congress Cataloging in Publication Data
Chang, Kia-ngau, 1889–1979.
Last chance in Manchuria.
(Hoover press publication ; 379)
Translation based on the original handwritten diary entitled: Tung-pei chieh shou chiao she jih chi.
Includes index.
1. Chang, Kia-ngau, 1889–1979—Chronology.
2. Bankers—China—Biography. I. Gillin, Donald G.
II. Myers, Ramon Hawley, 1929–   . III. Title.
IV. Title: Tung-pei chieh shou chiao she jih chi.
HG1552.C43A3 1988   332.1'092'4 [B]   88-8352
ISBN 0-8179-8791-6

Design by P. Kelley Baker

Contents

Contents

Editors' Commentary

The editors have deleted those parts of the diary that, in our judgment, contain irrelevant details or appear repetitive. We have tried to render the Russian names transliterated by Chinese characters to approximate their phonetic sound, but errors likely exist. All place names in Manchuria have been spelled according to their citation in *Webster's New Geographical Dictionary*. Where place names could not be found in *Webster's*, we romanized according to the Wade-Giles system. We attempted to make spellings and usage consistent but retained Chang Kia-ngau's anomalies. We romanized Chang Kung-ch'uan (his courtesy name) as Chang Kia-ngau, which he preferred when writing in English. Chang Chia-ao is his literary name.

The editors also have prepared a brief summary of the major events and insights for each month of the diary as a guide for those readers who wish to study specific events.

Finally, we would like to especially thank Professor Yin-lien Chin of Vassar College for her assistance with respect to the translation. It has been invaluable and we, along with the translator, are most grateful.

China and the Northeast circa 1945

Harbin
Ch'ang-ch'un
Mukden
Antung
Dairen
Hu-lu-tao
Port Arthur
Peiping
Tientsin
Nanking
Shanghai
Chungking

Introduction

THE BACKGROUND OF THE CHANG KIA-NGAU DIARY

Events in Manchuria, the northeastern region of China, have probably exerted more influence on modern Chinese history than those in any other area. From Manchuria came the Manchu invaders, who invaded China, defeated the Ming dynasty, and established the Ch'ing dynasty in 1644. Russia and Japan, competing for access to Manchuria's rich resources, fought a war there in 1904–1905. Having won that war, Japan spent the next three decades steadily enlarging its power in Manchuria; in 1931, the so-called Kwantung Army, based in Manchuria, seized the entire Northeast and set up a puppet regime under P'u-yi, the former Manchu emperor. Japan's action was designed to keep Manchuria out of the hands of the new Chinese central government established at Nanking in 1927 by Chiang Kai-shek and his Nationalist party (Kuomintang).

Chiang's government coveted Manchuria not only because of its claim to sovereignty over all of China but also because of Manchuria's potential as the industrial heartland of East Asia. Far from being the remote, cold wasteland many Westerners imagine, Manchuria has abundant coal, iron, timber, and other resources that are necessary to an industrial infrastructure. As Chiang was keenly aware, a Chinese government deprived of the Northeast would be unable to transform China into a modern industrial state. Until their surrender in August 1945, however, it was the Japanese who, at the expense of their domestic economy, controlled and built Manchuria into the largest and most modern industrial region in Asia.[1]

According to General Alexander von Falkenhausen, perhaps Chiang's closest foreign friend, during the 1930s Chiang was determined to prevent the Japanese from permanently controlling the natural resources of the Northeast. Alarmed by this sentiment and by Chiang's growing strength, the Japanese invaded China Proper in 1937. Japan used Manchuria as a base of operations in China and as the locus of the industries that sustained the Japanese war effort. As a consequence of that occupation, Chiang's government was obsessed with gaining control of Manchuria after the Allied powers defeated Japan in August 1945, for ceding Manchuria to any other power would make a mockery of China's wartime losses, annul its victory over Japan, and belie its new, internationally recognized status as a great power.

Nevertheless, foreign troops occupied Manchuria during the days immediately before Japan's surrender as part of the Yalta Agreement between the United States and the Soviet Union. Not only had China not been a party to those discussions, but the United States had deliberately concealed any knowledge of those talks and their likely implications for China from Chiang. When Dean Acheson transmitted the State Department's White Paper on China to President Harry Truman, he tried to justify that devious course as follows:

> For reasons of military security, and for those only, it was considered too dangerous for the United States to consult with the Nationalist government regarding the Yalta Agreement or to communicate its terms at once to Chungking [Chiang's wartime capital]. We were then in the midst of the Pacific War. It was felt that there was grave risk that secret information transmitted to the Nationalist capital at that time would become available to the Japanese almost immediately. Under no circumstances, therefore, would we have been justified in incurring the security risks involved. It was not until June 15, 1945, that General [Patrick J.] Hurley was authorized to inform Chiang Kai-shek of the agreement.[2]

And what an agreement it was. To begin with, the Yalta Agreement totally ignored Chinese sovereignty over Manchuria. The area had always belonged to China, but during the late nineteenth century foreign pressures compelled Peking to grant territorial concessions first to Russia and then to Japan. In effect, the Yalta Agreement yielded to the Soviet Union the same territorial rights that tsarist Russia had enjoyed before its defeat in the Russo-Japanese War of 1904–1905. The agreement specified that Dairen would become an international port and that the Soviet Union would be guaranteed priority in its use, that the naval base at Port Arthur would still be rented to the Soviets, that the Chinese Eastern Railroad and the South Manchuria Railway would be managed by a joint Sino-Soviet company, and that the remainder of Manchuria would revert to Chinese sovereignty.

When it learned of the Soviet-American agreement, Chiang's government hastily signed a treaty with Moscow dealing with the Northeast and other territorial issues. The Sino-Soviet Treaty of Friendship and Alliance, confirming the Yalta Agreement, was signed on August 14, 1945, the very day Japan surrendered. Considering that the United States had always cited military reasons to justify the Yalta Agreement and its legitimation of Soviet claims in Manchuria, the timing of the Sino-Soviet pact can only be called ironic. The United States acceded to the Yalta Agreement to pay Stalin for Soviet participation in the war against Japan, but why did the Republic of China (ROC) enter into a treaty confirming that accord at a time when the Japanese threat to China no longer existed? The answer lies in the growing uncertainties of the relationship between China and the United States and the expanding threat from the Chinese Communists.

In 1943 the ROC enjoyed a remarkable popularity in the United States, largely due to its long and heroic resistance to Japan and to Madame Chiang Kai-shek's masterful depictions of Chinese sacrifice. But public enthusiasm for Chiang's cause was not universally shared by important figures in the State Department and the army. Some individuals were keenly aware that Chiang's government had sustained numerous defeats by the Japanese and that its subsequent exile to the backwaters of China had decimated morale and paved the way for corruption and ineptitude. Others of Chiang's U.S. opponents admired the Chinese Communists and wanted the United States to support them, at least to the extent of forcing Chiang to share power with them. Having worked with the Communists, however, Chiang was convinced that any power they gained would be used to undermine his own regime and further the communist goal of acquiring totalitarian control over all of China, which he felt would be tantamount to Russian domination of China. His resistance to U.S. pressure to cooperate with the Communists, along with other factors, brought him into conflict with General Joseph Stilwell, commander of all U.S. ground forces in China and nominally Chiang's chief of staff.

Even while Stilwell was building the *Yüan-cheng chün* (expeditionary force)—several divisions of Americanized Nationalist troops who became perhaps the best army in Chinese history—he concealed neither his intense dislike of Chiang nor his admiration for the Chinese Communists. Stilwell insisted that Chiang's other armies' many faults would prevent them from effectively resisting a major Japanese offensive in China. When such an offensive took place in 1944, Stilwell's opinions were vindicated: the Nationalist forces fell back in disarray, allowing the Japanese to occupy or destroy all the U.S. air bases in South China; only the Expeditionary Force prevented the Japanese from reaching Chungking. Stilwell pressed his advantage in Washington to insist that the United States force Chiang to share power with the Communists.

Chiang admired Stilwell's qualities as a general and cherished the troops he had trained, but Chiang, who could not allow his authority to be flouted in China urged Washington to have Stilwell removed from his command. Nevertheless, Stilwell's criticisms, coupled with the recent defeat of most of Chiang's armies by the Japanese, convinced Franklin Roosevelt's and later Truman's administrations that Chiang's government was a weak, unreliable ally, incapable of playing a major role in the war against Japan.

Other important Americans dissented from that point of view. Among them were General Claire Chennault, commander of the United States Air Force in China, who bitterly opposed Stilwell's proposal to use Chinese communist troops; Admiral Nelson Miles, whose naval mission to China helped the ROC organize guerrilla units for use against both the Japanese and the Communists; and Stilwell's successor as commander of U.S. ground forces in China, General Albert C. Wedemeyer. Although aware of its failings, Wedemeyer staunchly supported Chiang's government as the only alternative to a communist regime that he felt would inevitably be pro-Russian and anti-American. He believed that, if trained along the lines Stilwell had employed, most Nationalist troops could be turned into first-rate soldiers able to stand up to and even defeat the Japanese.

In Washington, however, Stilwell's doubts about the reliability of Chiang's government prevailed, perhaps because of the influence of Stilwell's patron and close friend, General George C. Marshall, the United States Army's chief of staff. Consequently, although Washington decided not to join forces with the Communists, the Nationalists were discounted as a significant ally against Japan. Implicit in that attitude was the assumption that only the Soviets could be counted on to hold down U.S. casualties in the ferocious last-ditch resistance of Japanese forces in China. But Russia would not embark on a war against Japan without a substantial reward, which the United States ceded in the Yalta Agreement.

The United States expected Chiang's government to ratify the Yalta Agreement by incorporating its provisions into its own separate treaty with the Soviet Union. Chiang attached too much importance to his alliance with the United States to refuse that demand, particularly in view of the strains of the Stilwell incident. Thus, on being formally notified of the Yalta Agreement, Chiang immediately began to negotiate such a treaty with the Russians.

This raises the question of why those negotiations continued after Japan's surrender made the avowed purpose of the Yalta Agreement meaningless. Chiang evidently did not dare enrage the Soviets by rejecting the pact because, presumably, the United States would not support him if he did.

Furthermore, the Russian army had quickly overwhelmed the Japanese forces in Manchuria and taken possession of that territory by the time of the Japanese surrender on August 14, 1945. Unable to count on U.S. military or diplomatic intervention on his behalf, Chiang had no way to secure a Russian withdrawal from the Northeast except by bargaining with the Soviets, which began with Chinese ratification of a treaty accepting the Yalta Agreement.

Another factor was the Chinese Communist Party, the Kuomintang's rival for almost a quarter century. Under the leadership of Mao Tse-tung and Chiang Kai-shek, the two parties had become so militarized that they were little more than two armies with different political programs. The Communists drew their support almost entirely from the poorer peasantry, the rural underclass, and radically alienated intellectuals. The sources of Nationalist support were more varied and included the emerging urban business class, the younger members of the rural elite, the less impoverished peasantry, and those military officers and intellectuals who favored evolutionary rather than revolutionary change as the answer to China's problems.

Each party forged pragmatic alliances with warlords and occasionally with each other, one of which lasted from 1921 to 1927 and another, from 1937 to 1945. The savage battles they waged in the interim came to a temporary halt in 1935 with the almost total defeat of the Communists, who were saved from destruction by Japan's invasion of China in 1937. That incursion, which preoccupied Chiang's armies and soon all but annihilated them, along with the loss of the urban bases that were the chief source of Kuomintang power, shattered and demoralized the Nationalists. The Communists, meanwhile, had retained most of their military strength largely by avoiding serious encounters with the Japanese. The disruption and depredations of the Japanese army impoverished much of the population of North China and swelled the numbers of people susceptible to the appeal of the revolutionary egalitarianism preached by the Communists, who, until the war ended, shrewdly tempered their doctrine to also attract the less destitute peasantry.

Hampered by their urban orientation and their commitment to a less radical ideology, the Nationalists, unable to compete for peasant support and reduced to apathy and despair by the numerous Japanese victories, gave way to self-indulgence and corruption that worsened with the influx of massive U.S. financial and military aid into Nationalist-held areas. Free of those difficulties, the Communists flourished, to the growing dismay of their rivals, who lashed out in 1941 and repudiated their former "united front" against the Japanese. Chiang may have contemplated escalating that repudiation into a full-scale offensive against the Communists, but Japan's attack on Pearl Harbor intervened. Thereafter, Chiang did not dare renew the civil war while Japan remained undefeated for fear of alienating the growing American presence in China.

Japan's sudden surrender in 1945 appeared to remove that restraint, but Chiang then had to contend with the probability that the Soviet Union would give Manchuria and large parts of Soviet-occupied northwestern China to the Chinese Communists. The newly appointed U.S. ambassador to China, Patrick J. Hurley, discounted that probability after talks in Moscow with Stalin and other Soviet leaders in early 1945. Hurley believed that fear of U.S. retaliation would block an open alliance between Russia and the Chinese Communists. Feeling that the Soviets, at least for the time being, considered the Nationalists militarily far superior to the Communists, Hurley believed that the Soviets would be reluctant to commit themselves to the Chinese Communists. On the basis of his conversations in Moscow, Hurley also questioned whether the Russians really wanted a potentially formidable, albeit communist, regime in China and suggested that they might prefer a weaker, more accommodating, noncommunist state.[3]

Hurley, a staunch anticommunist, enjoyed Chiang's confidence, and Chiang was likely influenced by Hurley's views on Soviet apprehensions about the situation in China. At any rate, when Chiang's negotiators raised the question of Russian relations with the Chinese Communists, the latter were doubtless surprised and dismayed by the Soviets' pledge in their treaty with Chiang that they would not aid any parties or groups in China that opposed Chiang's government, which they recognized as the only legitimate Chinese government.

This was not the first time the Russians had overlooked their differences with Chiang to pursue a mutually advantageous policy in China at the expense of the Chinese Communists. In 1923, only two years after the formation of the Chinese Communist Party (CCP), the Soviets, for the sake of a more effective united front against Western and Japanese imperialism in China, forced the CCP to submit to the Kuomintang of Sun Yat-sen and Chiang Kai-shek. Although the Communists initially benefited from that unwanted alliance, it ultimately resulted in their virtual annihilation by Chiang and his warlord allies.

For his part, Chiang spent four months in the Soviet Union studying Russian methods of organization and warfare. After his return to China, he frequently expressed his admiration for the Soviets, and in 1925 sent his eldest son, Chiang Ching-kuo, to study in Russia, where he remained for the next twelve years, becoming fluent in Russian and well-versed in Soviet affairs. But Chiang broke with the Soviets in 1927 only because they insisted on promoting communism in China. The Soviets continued to proselytize during the 1930s, while Chiang was battling the resurgent communist movement of Mao Tse-tung and preparing for war with Japan.

By 1936, however, Mao's army had been almost annihilated, and it was increasingly evident that Chiang Kai-shek, having destroyed the chief domes-

tic threat to his rule, intended to resist the Japanese, whose growing aggres-
siveness also menaced the Soviet Union. Stalin, therefore, once again pressured the Chinese Communists to subordinate themselves to the Nationalists,
this time in the war against Japan. Late in 1936, when a disaffected warlord in
league with the Communists seized Chiang Kai-shek at Sian in northwestern
China, the Soviets pressured Mao into releasing Chiang to head a Chinese
alliance against Japan in which the Communists would be very junior partners. After 1937, when that alliance provoked the Japanese into invading
China and attacking the Nationalist armies, the Soviets gave Chiang's government large amounts of military aid. During China's long war with Japan the
Soviets, despite their subsequent neutrality pact with the Japanese, frequently indicated their abiding sympathy with Chiang's cause and did not
even hint that the Chinese Communists were a significant component of the
Chinese war effort.

All this explains why when Japan surrendered, the leadership of the
Soviet Union did not immediately commit itself to the communist side in
China's imminent civil war. Even before Japan's surrender the Russians had
begun to dismantle and remove most of the machinery in Manchuria's factories to the Soviet Union, which might have been an effort to help the
Chinese Communists by depriving Chiang's government of the economic
and military advantages of the northeastern industry. However, in Professor
Steven Levine's book *Anvil of Victory* (1987), which describes and analyzes
events in Manchuria between 1945 and 1949, he suggests that the stripping
of Manchuria's factories had less to do with Russian attitudes toward the
Kuomintang-CCP conflict than it did with a single-minded policy of using
the resources in Russian-occupied areas to reconstruct those parts of the
Soviet industrial complex that had been destroyed by the invading Germans.[4] In that case, ransacking Manchurian factories did not signify Soviet
contempt for their pledge not to assist Chiang's enemies in China.

Whether the Russians would actually honor that pledge, however,
greatly depended on the reliability of U.S. support for Chiang's regime, the
military balance between the Communists and the Nationalists, and Chiang's
willingness to make concessions to the Soviets beyond those embodied in the
Yalta Agreement and the Kuomintang's subsequent treaty with the Soviets.
The urgency of such concessions was underscored by the speed with which
tens of thousands of Chinese communist soldiers and cadres made their way
into Soviet-occupied Manchuria from their bases in northern and northwestern China. Chiang's government thus had to persuade the Russians to leave
Manchuria as soon as possible and in such a way that control of that region
would pass to the Nationalists instead of the Communists. Chiang, therefore,
proposed further negotiations with the Russians.

The Soviets welcomed his offer and invited him to send a special diplomatic mission to the former Manchurian capital of Ch'ang-ch'un, now the headquarters of the Soviet Army occupying Manchuria, to discuss with Marshal Rodion Malinovsky, the commander of that army, what the Russians wanted from Chiang's government in return for control of the Northeast. Malinovsky, a much-decorated hero of the Russian victory over Nazi Germany, was Moscow's de facto proconsul in East Asia and one of the highest-ranking members of the Soviet hierarchy. He was assisted in his negotiations with the Chinese by another distinguished Soviet official, later a deputy foreign minister, M. I. Sladkovsky of the Far Eastern Department of the Ministry of Foreign Trade. It appears that Stalin himself took a personal interest in the negotiations.

The Chinese side, which Chiang optimistically called the Commission for the Recovery of Manchuria, was led by its highest-ranking member, General Hsiung Shih-hui, chairman of the Nationalist Military Affairs Commission for Manchuria. Hsiung also headed a branch of Chiang's own headquarters and, together with General Tung Yen-p'ing, a vice-chief of staff of the Nationalist Army, was responsible for maintaining liaison with the Soviet Army. The most important members of the mission, however, were Chiang Ching-kuo, selected not only because he was Chiang Kai-shek's son but also because of his fluency in Russian and his familiarity with the Soviet Union, and the highly respected economist, banker, and official Chang Kia-ngau, chairman of the Northeast Economic Commission.

From the time of his appointment to the mission on September 8, 1945, Chang Kia-ngau was acutely sensitive to the importance of his mission. Accustomed to keeping a diary,[5] he began writing a detailed account of his daily experiences before he arrived in Manchuria. Chang Kia-ngau's diary spans the period from October 12, 1945, through April 30, 1946, when he was either in Ch'ang-ch'un negotiating with the Russians or conferring with Chiang Kai-shek and other leaders in Chungking or Nanking, which became China's capital in 1946. General Tung Yen-p'ing took Chang Kia-ngau's place during his absence.

The unusual candor, spontaneity, and sincerity of Chang's account of these negotiations and the events surrounding them make it historically valuable. Chang wrote for his eyes alone, as evidenced by the diary's language, which is often terse, even telegraphic.

THE HISTORY OF CHANG KIA-NGAU
AND THE PUBLICATION OF HIS DIARY

Chang Kia-ngau, also known by his courtesy name of Chang Kung-ch'uan, was born on October 21, 1889, in Chia-ting, the county seat of Kiangsu province, not far from Shanghai. The fourth son in a family of eight boys and four girls, he was traditionally educated, being tutored at home and having read the Confucian Four Books by the age of nine.[6] He made a comment a few years before his death to suggest he was considered precocious.[7] When he was fourteen, his family sent him to Shanghai to study foreign languages but within a year transferred him to a Chinese school in the city of Pao-shan, where he was again tutored.

When he was seventeen, he moved to Peking to study under a special tutor, T'ang Wen-chih, and to prepare for the imperial examinations necessary to become an official. At T'ang's urging, however, Chang left for Tokyo in 1906 to enroll in the premier Industrial High School to learn Japanese and prepare for university entrance exams. At first Chang thought he might study shipbuilding, but after entering Keiō University he began to concentrate on economics. He took courses in finance from Enok H. Wickers, a visiting Harvard professor, and various Japanese professors taught him about Western liberalism.[8] He became very interested in the state policies that Japan's leaders used to promote rapid economic development during the Meiji period and was particularly inspired by the fiscal reforms of Matsukata Masayoshi, Japan's great financial minister of the 1880s. Chang vowed that when he returned to China he would devote his life to its economic modernization.[9]

After graduating from Keiō he returned to Peking and entered the newly established Board of Posts and Communications in 1909. When the 1911 revolution broke out, he moved to Chekiang, where he served as secretary to Chu Jui, the provincial governor. He returned to Peking as chief secretary in the Senate of the new republic's Parliament. By then he had had enough of politics, viewing it as a complex, uncertain vocation, and in 1913 became the assistant manager of the Shanghai branch of the Central Bank of China, an institution that had always interested him and that he viewed as an appropriate vehicle for modernizing China. When, on May 11, 1916, his bank received an order from Yuan Shih-k'ai to cease redeeming bank notes to customers on demand, Chang met with bank officials to discuss what action to take. On his initiative they agreed to disobey Yuan's order and continue to redeem all bank notes. Chang, acting on the belief that the integrity of the nation's banking system depended on modern banks honoring the rightful claims of their customers, incurred Yuan's wrath. When Chang learned of orders for his arrest, he took temporary refuge in the foreign settlement in Shanghai. His brave action brought him instant public recognition.[10]

On May 30, 1917, Chang set up the *Bankers' Weekly* in Shanghai, which soon became the leading financial organ for Chinese and foreign businessmen. During the 1920s Chang began hiring foreign-educated Chinese, diversifying the bank's investments by making loans for railroads like the Lunghai Railway in 1924, and developing the bank's capabilities to handle foreign exchange. Chang played a leading role in modernizing the Central Bank of China and made it an instrument for facilitating the expansion of China's modern economic sector.

According to H. H. K'ung, who later headed the Bank of China, Chiang Kai-shek greatly admired Chang Kia-ngau and wanted the Central Bank of China to serve as the new Nationalist government's central bank of issue.[11] However, because of the tumultuous military and political conditions in what was still essentially warlord China, Chang hesitated to commit his bank to a new regime whose future was very much in doubt. Therefore, Chiang took over the Central Bank of China and placed it under the direction of T. V. Soong, his brother-in-law and one of the few men in the Nationalist government whose financial expertise was comparable to Chang's. Although Chang initially stayed on as his assistant director, he found it impossible to work with the temperamental Soong and finally retired from the bank entirely. Nevertheless, his relationship with Chiang, who continued to hold him in high regard, remained cordial. In 1935, Chiang appointed Chang minister of railways in his new cabinet; under Chang's stewardship, railway construction expanded rapidly. Chang was also made minister of communications in 1937, but he resigned because of poor health in 1942 and went to the United States to study how China could quickly resume economic development after the war.

When Chang returned to China in late 1945, after Chiang Kai-shek appointed him chairman of the Northeast Economic Commission, he conducted his government's negotiations with the Russians until the end of April 1946, when he resigned to go into mourning following the death of his first wife. In March 1947, however, he was recalled to government service and appointed governor of the Bank of China, a post he held until May 1948. During that time he proposed a plan for a national currency reform that would use gold and silver (China's traditional unit of account before 1936) to restore currency stability and allow the government time to cut its budget deficits and reverse the hyperinflation then under way.[12] His proposal most likely came too late, and it certainly never received the U.S. support and financial assistance needed to make it work.

Following his resignation from government service, Chang left China to spend three years in Australia lecturing on economic conditions in Asia. He moved to Los Angeles in 1953 and spent the next sixteen years teaching at Loyola University. He spent the last decade of his life as a senior research fellow at Stanford University's Hoover Institution on War, Revolution and Peace participating in seminars and conferences, corresponding with friends and fellow researchers, and continuing his scholarly writings. In addition to his diary and public papers, Chang Kia-ngau produced two important books on the Chinese economy: *China's Struggle for Railroad Development* (1943) and *The Inflationary Spiral: The Experience in China, 1939–1950* (1958).

Chang died on October 18, 1979, just three days short of his 90th birthday. A Confucian scholar who had received a Western-style education in Japan and was fluent in both Japanese and English, Chang was a leading member of that first generation of twentieth-century Chinese technocrats and leaders who did so much to lay the foundations of China's modern economy. His many remarkable achievements included founding the Central Bank of China, serving as minister of railroads and minister of communication in the Chinese government, subsequently working as a diplomat for that government, and numerous writings and publications. In everything he accomplished, Chang proved, as his diary amply demonstrates, an exemplary man: intelligent and perceptive, hardworking and responsible, loyal but not a sycophant, well-informed, realistic, and completely devoted to his country's interests as he discerned them.

THE DIARY'S ORGANIZATION

The first section of Chang's handwritten diary contains daily accounts of his meetings with Chinese leaders and Soviet officials, discussions with other members of the Chinese mission, and communications with Chungking, a number of them with Chiang Kai-shek himself. Telegrams—most of them secret and encoded—between Chang and his aides in Ch'ang-ch'un, particularly Tung Yen-p'ing, make up a large part of the second section of the diary. That same section includes daily narratives of key events in Chungking related to the recovery of Manchuria, as well as to the conflict between the Nationalists and the Communists.

Chang strove to faithfully record day-to-day events as they occurred. He was interested in recording and, from time to time, analyzing events, not in embellishing them. He tells us what people said and did but not, as a rule, what they were like, how they dressed, or how they impressed him. This was true even of close colleagues like Chiang Ching-kuo and Hsiung Shih-hui, as well as Malinovsky and Sladkovsky. In Chang's diary, these important actors come and go like shadows; instead, Chang's concern was with events, which he scrupulously placed in the order of their occurrence. He frequently relies on his secretary's notes of conversations with Malinovsky and Sladkovsky. Complete telegram texts sometimes form a day's entry; other days' accounts include newspaper references.

Chang sometimes interrupts himself to interpret events or to speculate about the Soviets' real motives. As the diary unfolds there is a sense of drama: Will the Soviets and the Nationalists be able to work out an arrangement acceptable to both sides? At times they seem to approach an accord, but then events force the two parties apart. The diary is also pervaded by a sense of impending disaster, for Chang realizes that as long as the Soviets delay their withdrawal from Manchuria, conditions there can only become more unfavorable to the Nationalists. The longer the Soviets stall, the less likely it is that Chiang's government will gain control of the Northeast.

Chang probably never rewrote, emended, or even reread his diary in its entirety because that brief period of history contained too many painful memories. Before he died in 1979 he deposited his diary and other personal papers and books in the archives of the Hoover Institution, stipulating that the diary not be opened until ten years after his death. In 1980, however, about a third of the diary appeared in the pages of an ROC magazine, *Chüan-chi wen-hsüeh* (Biographical Literature), and Steven Levine cited that material to help demonstrate the Soviet role in developing a communist base in Manchuria after Japan's surrender. In 1982, the publishers of *Chüan-chi wen-hsüeh* produced, in Chinese, a two-volume, year-by-year chronology of Chang Kia-ngau's life, including the diary he kept during his involvement with Manchuria.

To the best of our knowledge no studies to date refer to this publication. There was thus a pressing need for an English translation of Chang's diary, and in the summer of 1984 his widow authorized translation and publication of the manuscript. We believe that this complete translation of Chang Kia-ngau's Manchurian diary will help scholars interpret the complex events in Manchuria during the first six months after the end of World War II—events that, as Levine has shown, likely determined the outcome of China's civil war and the speed with which it ended. Chang's diary is a detailed account of the meetings between the Chinese mission in Manchuria and the Soviet military commanders and their advisers and also describes high-level meetings of Nationalist leaders wherein Chinese policy was formulated. An insider's account of the efforts of Chiang Kai-shek's government to take control of Manchuria, this diary offers an entirely new interpretation of why that attempt failed.

Before discussing the importance of the diary itself, we will present the major historical interpretations of how the Soviet occupation of Manchuria influenced the civil war, for only by considering the historical context, as it is presently understood, can we evaluate the information the diary provides and thus lay the foundation for a reinterpretation of some key events in China during those years.

CURRENT HISTORICAL INTERPRETATIONS

There were critical factors and subsidiary factors that interacted to determine the outcome of the civil war, although interpretations vary as to why the

Chinese Nationalists lost. Franz Michael and George Taylor hold that "the civil war was primarily a military conflict; it was decided by strategy and generalship in a few major battles."[13] Their interpretation places primary importance on conventional warfare, arguing that economic and political considerations aggravated the general conditions under which the war was fought but were not decisive. As for the most important theater of military conflict, it was Manchuria. "Manchuria became the decisive theater of the war, for it was here that Chiang's best armies, trained and equipped by the United States during the closing years of the war, were committed."[14]

Because the Nationalist strategy was based on occupying cities—in essence, a stationary war—Chiang Kai-shek's armies eventually suffered serious supply shortages and morale problems due to the difficulties of transport and geographic isolation. The ROC stumbled into this predicament partly because of bad decisions by the Nationalist leadership and partly because of the failure of the ROC to recover Manchuria before the Chinese Communists could install their forces there and establish intelligence and support facilities. Again, this interpretation places great importance on the Soviet occupation of Manchuria.

> When the government armies were ready to move, the Russian occupation forces denied them the use of Dairen and its railway communications and permitted the harbor of Ying-k'ou to fall into Chinese communist hands. Government troops had to fight their way into Manchuria, where the fighting continued. The Soviet Union respected its agreements and surrendered the main cities and railroad lines to Nationalist forces but permitted the Chinese Communists to obtain the arms and equipment surrendered by the Japanese, thus providing them with a vast stock of artillery and heavy equipment. With this equipment the Communists were able to change from small-scale guerrilla warfare to field battles in which they could match the artillery strength of the Nationalist armies, if not their air force.[15]

Although fighting would continue in Manchuria for almost two years longer, the communist forces eventually won several key battles that decided the fate of the Northeast. Those victories profoundly affected the outcome of China's civil war because they isolated and later destroyed Chiang's best, Americanized armies, freeing the communist armies in Manchuria for use against the other Nationalist forces in North China.

Historian Immanuel C. Y. Hsü, instead of stressing the primacy of military activity, attributes the Nationalist defeat largely to the eight years of the Second Sino-Japanese War, which enfeebled Chiang Kai-shek's government to the extent that it was impotent to unify the nation and initiate postwar reconstruction.[16] Hsü blames the fate of Chiang's cause after 1945 on the Nationalist strategy of committing its best troops to Manchuria in a winner-take-all gamble, as well as economic decline from inflation, loss of public support, weak socioeconomic reforms, and failure of U.S. mediation and aid.[17] But Hsü also agrees with Michael and Taylor's interpretation that the Soviets delayed the arrival of Nationalist troops in Manchuria long enough to facilitate "the movement of the Chinese communist army, equipping it with captured Japanese arms and allowing it to absorb puppet military units." According to Hsü, "Three times the Soviet troops delayed their withdrawal under various pretexts, and when they finally did leave in May 1946, Manchuria was all but in the hands of the Chinese Communists."[18]

In 1956 Chiang Kai-shek wrote his last book, *Soviet Russia in China: A Summing Up at Seventy*. His explanation of why the Nationalists failed to unify China is complex and considers many, not always carefully connected factors. In particular, though, Chiang blamed the Soviet Union's bad faith in negotiations for preventing the entry of Nationalist forces into Manchuria.[19] He also saw the Soviets' post–World War II strategy as targeting China for the expansion of international communism. He did, however, take personal blame for "committing the best government troops to the northeastern provinces only to be bogged down there. When these provinces fell, the government had to evacuate North China. By that time, the entire situation had deteriorated beyond control."[20]

Chiang admitted that the Nationalists "should have canceled the take-over operations" in the northeastern provinces at the outset—late 1945 and early 1946.[21] By concentrating its best armed forces in the Peiping-Tientsin area, Chiang contended, his government could have held the corridor at Shan-hai-kuan, which led into Manchuria, and used Chin-chou, just north of the Manchurian border, as a forward base. The Nationalists would then have had sufficient military control south of the Great Wall to govern all of North China, and the Soviet activities on behalf of the Communists in Manchuria would have alerted the rest of the world to Russia's designs on the Northeast. It is problematic whether world opinion would have shifted in favor of the Nationalists, but Chiang blamed the defeat of his best armies in Manchuria not only on his own government's poor policies but also on the duplicity of the Soviet Union, which, ignoring its pledge not to support his enemies, gave the Communists the help they needed to build a powerful field army in the Northeast.

However, another interpretation, The White Paper on China, August 1949, has probably shaped the public's view of the civil war period more than any other single piece of writing. In his explanatory letter to President Truman that outlined the central argument of that report, Dean Acheson gave the basic view of the U.S. State Department as to why the ROC lost the civil war:

The reasons for the failures of the Chinese Nationalist government appear in some detail in the attached record. They do not stem from any inadequacy of American aid. Our military observers on the spot have reported that the Nationalist armies did not lose a single battle during the crucial year of 1948 through lack of arms or ammunition. The fact was that the decay which our observers had detected in Chungking early in the war had fatally sapped the powers of resistance of the Kuomintang. Its leaders had proved incapable of meeting the crisis confronting them, its troops had lost the will to fight, and its government had lost popular support. The Communists, on the other hand, through a ruthless discipline and fanatical zeal, attempted to sell themselves as guardians and liberators of the people. The Nationalist armies did not have to be defeated; they disintegrated. History has proved again and again that a regime without faith in itself and an army without morale cannot survive the test of battle.[22]

This statement covers the overall picture, but what does the White Paper say about Manchuria specifically?

The U.S. State Department was informed on September 10, 1945, by its Moscow embassy that the Sino-Soviet friendship pact, signed on August 14, 1945, would not prevent the Russians from helping the Chinese Communists gain a foothold in Manchuria and that Russian willingness to withdraw its forces and admit Chinese (Nationalists) to civil affairs control reflected mature statesmanship on the part of Stalin and his Moscow advisers.[23] The White Paper also admitted that the Russians had refused Chinese government forces the use of Dairen, the most important nonmilitary port in the Northeast, and had blocked their advance into the region. "This delay also had the effect of giving the Chinese Communists time to build up their forces in Manchuria, which had apparently been reinforced by the movement of hastily organized or reinforced units from Chahar and Jehol provinces [on the northwestern border of Manchuria]."[24] Moreover, the "Chinese Communists were enabled to take over and put into use among their troops stores of weapons and military supplies possessed by the Japanese at the time of their surrender and made available directly or indirectly by the Russians." Therefore, the civil war rapidly spread into Manchuria and could not be contained any longer. When communist forces seized Ch'ang-ch'un on April 18, 1946, several days after Russian troops had withdrawn, that victory made the communist generals "overconfident and less amenable to compromise."[25] At the same time this new development encouraged "the ultrareaction groups in the [Nationalist] government, which were then in a position to say that the [Chinese] Communists had demonstrated that they never intended to carry out their agreements."[26] With all hopes of containing the civil war now dashed and with fighting rapidly spreading into Manchuria, Chiang committed the bulk of his best troops to the Northeast, despite the advice of General Albert C. Wedemeyer and other U.S. military advisers to keep those troops south of the Great Wall.[27] These factors, according to the White Paper, determined the course of events in Manchuria and eventually the Nationalist military defeat there.

From the above interpretations we see how the Nationalists lost the civil war and how the role of Manchuria, and its occupation by Soviet troops, greatly influenced the Nationalist-communist conflict in China. The White Paper also mentions the Russian removal of "considerable Japanese-owned industry and equipment from Manchuria."[28] But neither this source nor the other accounts cited above discuss in any detail the negotiations that took place between the Soviets and the Nationalists. A work that does so is Tang Tsou's *America's Failure in China, 1941–1950*, which although offering no concise explanation of the role Manchuria played in the civil war, by relying heavily on Chinese materials published in 1952 in Taipei, particularly the account by Tung Yen-p'ing, Chang Kia-ngau's top aide, provides one of the best accounts of the occupation of the region.

In early October 1945, according to Tang Tsou, the Soviets informed Chungking that they could not send troops to Dairen to recover the Northeast because Dairen was "a commercial port" and not for military troops.[29] The Nationalists next tried to land at Hu-lu-tao and Ying-k'ou on October 29, but communist New Fourth Army troops already had occupied the area. The Soviets then informed the Nationalists that irregular units there made it impossible to guarantee a safe Nationalist landing, even though they had promised some weeks before to render assistance.[30] Government troops then slowly began to enter Manchuria through the Shan-kai-kuan corridor; they occupied Chin-chou on November 26, five weeks after being denied entry into Dairen.[31]

Meanwhile, communist troops rapidly entered Manchuria and fanned out through the countryside, chiefly because of "the freedom of action granted, and assistance given, by the Soviet occupation forces."[32] Negotiations for the withdrawal of Soviet troops and the entry of Nationalist troops continued. Soviet withdrawal from Manchuria was postponed three times: the November 30 agreement was postponed until January 3, 1946, again until February 1, 1946, and yet again until the end of April 1946.[33] The Soviets left Manchuria in May.

On November 24, 1945, Sladkovsky, Marshal Malinovsky's top economic adviser, presented Chang Kia-ngau with a proposal for Sino-Soviet economic cooperation in 80 percent of Manchuria's heavy industry.[34] The Nationalists would not agree to the proposal until all Soviet troops had left the region. Discussions on troop withdrawal and economic cooperation continued but to little avail. On February 7, 1946, the U.S. State Department informed both Moscow and Chungking that it would not accept exclusive Sino-Soviet control over industry in Manchuria because this would be contrary to America's traditional Open Door policy, which insisted on equal rights for all foreign powers throughout China.

Chiang Kai-shek faced a serious dilemma. The right wing of his Nationalist party already had stirred up violent anti-Soviet and anti–Chinese communist feelings, instigating student demonstrations in many large cities. The public's image of the Nationalist party had greatly improved, but if Chiang had agreed to the terms of the economic discussions with the Soviets, there may have been a negative backlash against the government and the Kuomintang. Meanwhile, Nationalist negotiators in Manchuria "had gained the impression that, if the Chinese government agreed to the Soviet demands, the Soviet government would not allow the Chinese Communists to play an open part in Manchuria, while permitting them to operate as a purely local force."[35] Chang Kia-ngau even urged Chiang Kai-shek to "approve a list of ten to twenty jointly managed enterprises so that, to use the words of Mr. Chang's brother, 'economic cooperation between Soviet Russia and China could be established to serve as a foundation for friendly relations between the two countries.' "[36] Chiang Kai-shek agonized but eventually decided not to go ahead with the arrangement.

The Soviets prolonged their occupation of Manchuria, not leaving Ch'ang-ch'un until April 14; on April 19 communist troops entered the city and took it over. The ensuing battle between Nationalists and Communists resulted in a full-scale war throughout Manchuria and ended any possibility of an unobstructed Nationalist takeover of the Northeast. Tang Tsou concludes that the Soviet Union rendered great aid to the Chinese Communists by preventing the Nationalists from gaining control of Manchuria and is critical of Patrick Hurley's optimistic assessment in early 1945 that the Russians might support Chiang Kai-shek's government. Tang argues instead that, as might be expected, Soviet policy toward China was "fundamentally one of hostility toward the Nationalists and support for the Communists"[37] and maintains that this was borne out by events in the first half of 1946.

Steven I. Levine's 1987 account of how the Communists defeated the Nationalist troops and seized Manchuria in late 1948 is the most authoritative work on the outcome of the civil war.[38] His theses are that the war really was decided in Manchuria, that conventional warfare determined the outcome of the conflict, and that the communists' two-track strategy of mobilizing men and matériel in both villages and important urban centers in northern Manchuria enabled them to defeat the Nationalist forces in the field. That strategy of land reform and mobilization policies in the countryside, as well as targeting and seizing key cities in northern Manchuria that could serve as new staging platforms for the large field army under Lin Piao, finally defeated the Nationalists. Levine's argument is that communist policies in both the villages and cities eventually paid off.

Levine also argues that Soviet delays in withdrawing their troops gave the Communists enough time to send political and military cadres, as well as troops, from northern China into the Northeast, enabling them, by the spring of 1946, to take over Ch'ang-ch'un. The Communists, Levine continues, would still require at least another two years to build their base areas and to train a sufficiently large conventional army to defeat the Nationalists in several critical, major battles. Arguing that it was time that allowed the Communists to become entrenched in the northeastern countryside, Levine cites portions of Chang Kia-ngau's diary.

Levine's use of the early section of the diary, along with Soviet materials, enables him to argue that the Soviet Union adopted a two-track policy toward the Chinese. The first component of that strategy involved the pursuit of Soviet interests in keeping the United States out of Manchuria (and China as a whole) and establishing a sphere of economic influence in the Northeast. Levine attributes Stalin's decision to his desire "to reduce the threat of a hostile coalition forming against him by withdrawing his forces from Manchuria and Iran, the dangerously exposed salients of his political position."[39] But at the same time, Levine contends, the Soviets gave the Communists considerable assistance and the time to become entrenched in the countryside before allowing the Nationalists to take over the cities along the central railway.

Levine's work offers a detailed account of probably the most important theater of action during the civil war: Manchuria. Although his study focuses chiefly on how the Communists organized their base in Manchuria and how they built a large-scale army capable of waging conventional war, it also documents the crucial Soviet role in that region during the first half year after World War II. Levine referred to only part of Chang Kia-ngau's diary, but he recognized its overall importance for elucidating Soviet aims in Manchuria in particular and toward China in general. Let us now look at the diary itself.

HISTORICAL SIGNIFICANCE OF THE DIARY

We see four major themes running through the diary: the persistence of foreign imperialism, Sino-Soviet economic negotiations and their meaning, Soviet policy toward China, and ROC domestic politics and the art of secret negotiations.

Foreign Imperialism in China and Chiang Kai-shek's Reaction

A preoccupation with national sovereignty pervades Chang Kia-ngau's diary. In an early passage, he notes sardonically that the United States did not obtain the Chinese government's consent to the concessions made to the Soviet Union in the Yalta Agreement, which, he observes, forced China to enter into the Sino-Soviet Treaty of Friendship and Alliance on August 14, 1945. "Undoubtedly," he states, "when the Chinese people as a whole read about this agreement, they will be enraged."

As soon as the treaty was signed, Chang and the other members of the Chinese mission in Manchuria had to concern themselves with what they regarded as a blatant Russian violation of China's sovereignty there, which had serious military and political implications for Chiang Kai-shek's government. In a supplemental agreement to the Sino-Soviet agreement, Dairen, one of Manchuria's largest and most strategically located ports, was declared "a free port open to the commerce and shipping of all nations."[40] Chiang's government took this to mean that Nationalist troops would be free to land at Dairen and proceed inland to Manchuria, which was important to the Nationalists because no other means would allow them to occupy the Northeast so swiftly and effectively. Therefore, according to Chang Kia-ngau's diary, when Hsiung Shih-hui first met with Malinovsky on October 13, 1945, Hsiung informed the Soviet side that the Nationalists wanted to land troops at Dairen, as well as at the less important ports of Ying-k'ou, Antung, and Hu-lu-tao, and hoped for Soviet assistance in so doing, Chang reports Malinovsky's response:

> With respect to the Nationalists landing at Dairen, the issue should be settled between the two governments. As for the Nationalist troops landing in the Antung region, the Soviets are unable to express an opinion about this, since this is not under their jurisdiction. There is no problem concerning our [Nationalists] landing at Ying-k'ou and Hu-lu-tao. He also expressed the opinion that we should transport our troops into the Northeast by rail. As for our setting up air traffic control stations in Mukden, Ch'ang-ch'un, Dairen, and Harbin, he first must ask for instructions from Moscow.

The diary relates that on October 17, in their second meeting with Malinovsky, the Nationalists again asked to land troops in Dairen in early November. Malinovsky replied that the Soviets would withdraw their troops to the Mukden region during November 15–20 and to the Ch'ang-ch'un area between November 20 and 30 and that by December 3 "at the latest they will withdraw into the Soviet Union." Malinovsky went on to say that "besides Dairen, there also are Hu-lu-tao, Ying-k'ou, and Antung" where Nationalist troops could land.

But the diary entry for October 21 reports the reply of Major General Pavlovsky, vice-chief of staff of the Soviet Army, to the various requests made by the Nationalist side. Stated Pavlovsky, "The Sino-Soviet treaty designates Dairen as a free commercial port. Permitting our [Nationalist] troops to land there would be a violation of the treaty. Second, in the same vein, consent cannot be given to our setting up an air traffic direction station at Dairen." Pavlovsky went on to deny most of the requests made by the Nationalists and to lay down stringent conditions for the few requests that were granted.

It was clear to Chang Kia-ngau that the Soviet side "had resolutely rejected our proposal to land at Dairen." Within ten days after his arrival in Ch'ang-ch'un, Chang realized that the Soviet military also had no intention of allowing the Nationalist government to send its troops into Manchuria to recover that region. Chang recognized these Soviet intentions from the very outset of the negotiations: "Their intention was all too clear. Why hadn't our foreign affairs officials given this their attention?" The Nationalist team then met to deal with the new crisis and decided to submit a written protest, claiming that the Sino-Soviet friendship treaty guaranteed Chinese troops the right to land anywhere in Manchuria and urging that the two governments' foreign ministries clear up the dispute. The conflict was never resolved to Chungking's satisfaction, and the Nationalists were forced to continue to negotiate from a position of great weakness.

Chang Kia-ngau's diary clearly indicates that the Chinese mission's concern with China's national sovereignty in the Northeast reflected Chiang Kai-shek's own preoccupations. In a most personal and moving communication with Chang, Chiang strongly hints that he agrees with Chang on the necessity of negotiating with the Russians but says that he is "restricted by considerations of sovereignty as well as theories of legality and reason." In another communication with Chang, Chiang stressed the great value the Chinese attach to their country's natural resources as a reason for rejecting the Soviet Union's claim to "war booty" in the Northeast, which not only implies a great regard for national sovereignty but is very much in keeping with the legacy of Sun Yat-sen, who repeatedly castigated the Manchu dynasty for mortgaging China's natural resources to foreign powers.

Chiang Kai-shek's attention to the subject of Manchuria's natural resources and, by implication, its industrial potential raises interesting questions about Chang Kia-ngau's survey of the industrial economy that Japan had developed in the Northeast. Chang conducted this survey immediately after arriving in Manchuria to disprove the Soviet claim that Manchuria's industries existed chiefly to support the Japanese war effort and were, therefore, legitimate "war booty" of the Soviet army, which was under no obligation to turn those resources over to China. Chang consulted not only Chinese employed in

Manchuria's Japanese-run industries but also the Japanese managers of those enterprises, whom, for reasons that should be explored, the Russians had allowed to stay on in Manchuria. Chang's work, completed in early 1946, was an unusually informed and detailed survey that must have been the most authoritative evaluation of Manchuria's economy then available.

Did this survey make Chiang Kai-shek and other Nationalist officials determined to possess the Northeast at any cost, notwithstanding the warnings of General Wedemeyer and other U.S. military advisers that such a campaign would necessitate a dangerous overextension of Nationalist military resources? Manchuria had been bombed by Allied planes only three times, and damage to its industrial complex had been minimal.[41] Thus, by August 1945, following the destruction of German and Japanese industrial capacity, the economy of Manchuria constituted the world's fourth-largest industrial complex (one: the United States, two: the Soviet Union, and three: Great Britain), and Chang Kia-ngau's confirmation of that may have been an important event in China's civil war. To be sure, the Russians had carried off all the machinery in Manchuria's factories, but the railroads, dams, power plants, telegraph lines, and the rest of Manchuria's industrial infrastructure were still intact. Chiang's ally, the United States, could have easily replaced the machinery. Thus, the prize at stake was enormous, and Chiang Kai-shek could not relinquish the potential industrial heartland of China to the Communists because it would make them industrially and, therefore, militarily superior to the Nationalists.

Chiang Kai-shek did not think the Chinese Communists were either able or willing to defend China's national sovereignty in the Northeast against the Russians. On the contrary, Chang Kia-ngau notes that Chiang contemptuously referred to the Communists in the Northeast as "puppets" of the Russians, and the diary suggests that there was some justification for this accusation. For example, as a result of Russian and communist efforts to intimidate its personnel, Chiang Kai-shek withdrew most of the Chinese mission from Ch'ang-ch'un on November 17, 1945, which was tantamount to telling the Soviets that the Nationalist government would not negotiate with them until they adopted more favorable policies in the Northeast. Anxious to resume the negotiations and, at least in part, fearful that this public display of Chiang's anger would provoke U.S. intervention, the Russians made a number of important concessions, including promises to protect the personnel of the Chinese mission's headquarters, to eradicate all "mob action" against them, and to stop the increasingly inflammatory anti-Nationalist propaganda in Ch'ang-ch'un. At the same time, the Nationalists would be allowed to take over both the municipal government and the public security bureau. The Soviet negotiators would ask Moscow whether the Nationalists could organize their own internal security forces for the Northeast, and the Russians would step up their efforts to disarm "irregular" (largely communist) military forces. Furthermore, the Soviets agreed to let Chiang Kai-shek airlift 50,000 Nationalist troops into Ch'ang-ch'un and promised not to let the Communists obstruct railway transportation of another two divisions of Nationalist troops between China Proper and Mukden, the industrial center of Manchuria.

All this was a substantial setback for the Chinese Communists in Manchuria, especially because it occurred, according to Levine,[42] before they were fully entrenched in the countryside. In fact, Chang Kia-ngau, elated by the Soviet promises to the Nationalists and convinced of their sincerity, presented Tung Pi-wu, the chief Chinese communist representative in Ch'ang-ch'un, with an ultimatum demanding that the Communists withdraw altogether from the critical rail corridor between China Proper and Mukden. To Chang's delight, Tung, after consulting with his superiors, affirmed that the communist Eighth Route Army would evacuate the rail corridor on the condition that advancing Nationalist units refrain from attacking it during the pullback. The Communists were obviously heeding the orders of the Russians, whose supreme commander, Malinovsky, told Chang Kia-ngau about that time, "In the final analysis, our aim is to assist the Chinese government in establishing its political power in the Northeast." Elated, Chang spoke of the Nationalists acquiring "an unhindered political position" in Manchuria. By January 5, 1946, the Nationalists were airlifting their troops into Mukden at the rate of ten planeloads a day. In Chang's opinion, his government was unlikely to encounter any Soviet resistance to its taking control of all the major cities of Manchuria, at least for the time being.

Such control also would have placed the Nationalists in possession of Manchuria's industrial complex, which, as previously noted, could easily have been restored with U.S. help. For that matter if, as Chang Kia-ngau was convinced, the Russians sincerely wanted to manage that complex jointly with the Chinese, the Russians would have to return all the Japanese machinery and provide substantial capital and technical assistance of their own; they had, in fact, proposed this several times in their talks with Chang Kia-ngau. This course, more than any military concession to the Nationalists, could have been catastrophic for the communist cause in the Northeast and throughout China.

Nevertheless, it suited Russian interests to ignore such considerations, and Moscow seems to have been unconcerned about the impact of its actions on the fortunes of the Chinese Communists. Certainly, as Chang's diary recounts, Stalin's remarks to Chiang Ching-kuo during the course of a six-hour conversation with him in Moscow in early January 1946 indicated that Stalin more or less dismissed the Chinese Communists as a force whose chief value was to keep the Nationalists "honest," although he added that they might win out in China if the Nationalists proved ineffectual. It is possible, of course, that

Stalin was insincere and meant to mislead Chiang Ching-kuo about the importance the Soviets attached to their involvement with the Chinese Communists. However, the diary offers another, more direct piece of evidence suggesting that the Chinese Communists in Manchuria acted essentially at the beck and call of the Russians. Writing on February 24, 1946, Chang Kia-ngau describes a visit by Tung Pi-wu and Wang Jo-fei, another communist leader, who asked him when, if ever, the Soviets would withdraw their army from Manchuria and expressed fears that the Communists would "remain under their wing, unable to establish independent political power in Manchuria" until they did so. Chang concluded that the Russians still had not indicated to the Chinese Communist Party either its scope of influence in the Northeast or its area of occupation, which suggests that the Chinese Communists in Manchuria were almost totally subordinate to the Russians and placed Soviet interests ahead of their own, not to mention China's. This would explain their utter silence about the behavior of Russian troops in Manchuria. The diary does not go into this subject, but a number of other informed sources agree that the Russians treated the Manchurian population abominably. The virtually undisciplined Russian soldiers' drunken binges led to widespread looting, rape, and even murder, until most Manchurians feared and hated the Russians far more than they had ever loathed the Japanese.[43]

In addition, the Russian dismemberment of Manchurian industry had devastated the economy of the Northeast. According to Levine, Manchuria's "expanding economy in the [first half of] the twentieth century created a growing demand for labor."[44] However, following Russia's occupation, industrial production in southern Manchuria, where most industry was concentrated, "virtually collapsed."[45] This decline resulted in massive unemployment among Manchurian industrial workers as well as the suffering of millions of other Manchurians, including the peasants, whose livelihood was tied to Manchurian industry. Yet not once did the Chinese Communists publicly protest against Soviet depredations in Manchuria; indeed they probably welcomed the dismantling of Manchurian industry because, in addition to rendering its productive capacity useless to the Nationalists, it served communist interests by creating widespread poverty, misery, and anguish.

Consequently, the Nationalists had to defend Chinese interests in the Northeast against the Russians, and the diary shows how almost painfully preoccupied the Nationalists were with denying the Soviets any legal basis for acquiring in Manchuria anything comparable to the previous dominance of the Japanese. Chou En-lai was indeed correct when he stated some decades later that "General Chiang Kai-shek has a sense of national respect,"[46] but no evidence exists that the Chinese Communists shared that sense during the Russian occupation of Manchuria. On the contrary, as noted above, the diary shows that they often acted as the Russians' junior partners, which may account for some of Chang Kia-ngau's personal contempt for them, as evidenced by his frequent references to them as *kung-fei* (communist bandits).[47]

If considerations of national sovereignty were important factors in Chiang Kai-shek's attitude toward the Manchurian situation, his attitude was also profoundly influenced by his relationship with the United States. From the very inception of Chang Kia-ngau's mission, the U.S. State Department took an intense interest in his negotiations with the Russians. As Levine points out, the State Department, under the guise of promoting America's traditional Open Door policy, was actually bent on advancing U.S. strategic interests in Manchuria as part of America's worldwide struggle with the Soviet Union. Evidently the State Department concluded that those interests would not be served by giving the Russians anything in Manchuria that the Yalta Agreement and Chiang's subsequent treaty had not already granted them—even if Chiang felt his government would benefit by making additional concessions to the Soviets. Chang Kia-ngau deplored Washington's repeated warnings to China not to damage U.S. rights in Manchuria and considered those warnings to be a thinly veiled effort to undermine and invalidate his negotiations with the Russians.

Unless he was willing to dissolve his alliance with the United States, however, Chiang was obliged to defer to U.S. wishes. Repudiating them was unthinkable not only because of the enormously valuable material (chiefly military) advantages Chiang's government enjoyed as a result of the alliance but also because of the ethos of modernity to which the Nationalists subscribed, which was inextricably associated with the United States. That paradigm, a quintessentially urban and potentially middle-class, pluralistic, even democratic concept of modernization, was modeled after the United States and at odds with anything else being promoted in China. This is amply illustrated by several entries in the diary of Chang Kia-ngau, who, as his government's representative, emphasized the importance to Manchuria of private enterprise, a market economy, and light industry capable of manufacturing consumer goods. The contrast between this model and the Chinese Communists' suffusive Russian-style collectivism and preoccupation with heavy industry is striking and highlights a vitally important but often overlooked difference between the Nationalists and their communist enemies.

Undoubtedly, breaking with the United States on an important issue like negotiations with the Russians was rendered even more unthinkable for the Nationalists by America's defeat of Japan in World War II, which, although less militarily and strategically important than Russia's destruction of Hitler's army, must still have been awesome to the Chinese Nationalists, whose own forces had, as late as the summer of 1944, been overwhelmed by the Japanese. Alienating an ally like the United States must have seemed tantamount to insanity to Ch'en Ch'eng, most of Chiang Kai-shek's other generals, and especially U.S.-oriented and -educated Nationalist leaders like T. V. Soong, whom Chang Kia-ngau obviously considered a formidable obstacle to negotiations with the Soviets. Significantly, the Nationalist officials who favored negotiating with the Soviets on Manchuria—figures like Chang Kia-ngau, Chiang Ching-kuo, Hsiung Shih-hui, and even Chiang Kai-shek— were not U.S.-oriented but had received Chinese, Russian, or Japanese educations.[48]

T. V. Soong's role is especially intriguing, for it seems probable that someone privy to the negotiations kept Washington unusually well informed. Could this have been Soong? He had represented his government in Washington for several years and formed close friendships with a number of important U.S. officials. Certainly, he was a likely source of information for the United States about Chiang Kai-shek's negotiations with the Russians, which may explain why the U.S. State Department often seemed to move almost in tandem with Soong and other Chinese officials opposed to those negotiations. For example, Chang Kia-ngau noted that only one day after Soong told him negotiations with the Soviets were bound to be fruitless and should be shelved, Secretary of State James F. Byrnes warned China not to sign any Manchurian agreement with the Russians that violated the Open Door policy. Byrnes also set down other conditions certain to be unacceptable to the Russians. Chang wrote despondently that this would encourage those who wanted to "adopt a rigid attitude" toward the Soviets and who felt that "we can resist the Soviet Union by relying on American support." He further speculated that when the Soviets learned of this new U.S. revelation, they would suspect that the Nationalists were resisting Soviet demands because they were dependent on the United States. Consequently, it would be more difficult for Chiang Kai-shek's government to reach an agreement with the Russians.

The kind of thinking Chang Kia-ngau deplored seems to have been particularly characteristic of Foreign Minister Wang Hsüeh-t'ing, who, like Soong, was unenthusiastic about negotiating with the Russians. Chang noted Wang's elation at the resolutions passed by the conference of Allied foreign ministers held in Moscow in late December 1945. Those resolutions convinced Wang that the Soviets could not act independently or temperately, a conclusion that prompted Chang's scorn for the naive assumption that China no longer had to make concessions to the Russians because the Americans would restrain them. Surely, this almost coordinated opposition by both the United States and many of Chiang Kai-shek's most trusted subordinates was very much in his mind when, in a January 16 letter to Chang Kia-ngau, Chiang first indicated that the Nationalists should make whatever concessions were necessary to obtain an immediate agreement with the Russians about Manchuria and then rejected that policy on the grounds that "I have no alternative."

By rejecting a potentially beneficial agreement with the Russians and opting instead for total reliance on the United States, Chiang Kai-shek broke with a tradition of evenhandedness in dealing with rival foreign powers that had been characteristic of Chinese foreign policy since the 1850s and that he had employed with considerable success in the 1920s and 1930s. What did Chiang and his cause receive in return for this policy of "leaning to one side"? The answer, at least in Manchuria, must be nothing at all. Not once did Washington even hint that the Soviets risked a military confrontation with the United States by violating both the Yalta Agreement and their own treaty with the Nationalists, by helping the Communists in Manchuria, or by intimidating the Nationalists and making demands on them that encroached on China's sovereignty in the Northeast. On the contrary, when confronted with gunfire from communist troops who had entrenched themselves near the port of Ying-k'ou, U.S. naval vessels refused to land Nationalist troops, even though their commander, General Tu Yü-ming, was confident that his crack Americanized forces could storm ashore with only artillery support from the warships and no other U.S. involvement in the fighting.[49]

By withholding any possibility of armed intervention on behalf of Nationalist interests in Manchuria, Washington avoided a Russo-U.S. military confrontation but prevented Chiang Kai-shek from coping with the Russians in Manchuria except by offering them extraordinary concessions. Yet, as Chang Kia-ngau bitterly observes, when Chiang contemplated making those concessions, the Americans objected and interfered in his negotiations in such a way as to render them futile. This left Chiang hamstrung and without effective means to handle the situation in Manchuria.

The diary, moreover, contains abundant evidence that General George C. Marshall's mission to China significantly reduced Nationalist chances of gaining control of Manchuria. As the civil war escalated in late 1945, with the Nationalists on the offensive and the Communists offering ferocious resistance, the Truman administration came to fear that, unless stopped, the conflict might provoke the Soviet Union to intervene on behalf of the Communists. That, in turn, could necessitate a U.S. counterintervention in support of the Nationalists, resulting in a Russo-U.S. confrontation in China and, perhaps, the outbreak of a third world war. Consequently, the U.S. State Department instructed Ambassador Hurley to try to induce the Nationalists and the Communists to lay down their weapons and form a coalition government to rule China. But Hurley was too committed to the Nationalist cause to succeed. He envisioned a coalition regime completely dominated by Chiang Kai-shek, a situation the Communists found unacceptable. Thus, the fighting continued, and Hurley eventually resigned his post, charging that the Communists were being encouraged to defy him by sympathizers in the State Department.

Hurley was replaced by General Marshall, who had retired from active duty in the United States Army. This appointment was a triumph for Hurley's opponents because, as Levine puts it, "During the war, Marshall, as chief of staff, had been a strong supporter of General Joseph Stilwell . . . and he was sympathetic to Stilwell's caustic view of Chiang Kai-shek and the Nationalist war effort. He had few illusions and little respect for the Nationalist leader."[50]

Marshall, however, was under orders to do nothing that might undermine Chiang Kai-shek's government, and he left Washington determined to see that Nationalist troops occupied Manchuria, fearing that the Russians would acquire permanent control of the Northeast. But after arriving in China and meeting with Chou En-lai, the Chinese communist envoy, Marshall quickly concluded that Hurley had been wrong and that Chiang Kai-shek was the chief obstacle to a peaceful resolution of China's civil war. He demanded, therefore, that Chiang accept both an immediate cease-fire and a coalition government in which the Communists would have substantial power.

For reasons already mentioned, Chiang remained unwilling to share power with the Communists. Moreover, he did not want a truce when his armies were still advancing, albeit with increasing difficulty. Such a respite would give the communist armies time to rest, regroup, and strengthen their defenses. But Marshall was President Truman's personal representative and had the authority to cut off all U.S. military and economic assistance to the Nationalists, and Chiang felt he could not do without that aid, especially because his best, Americanized troops, poised to advance into Manchuria, were dependent on the United States for ammunition, fuel, and spare parts for their U.S.-made weapons and equipment.

As a result, Chiang gave in to Marshall's demands and—very reluctantly—entered into negotiations with the Communists to form a coalition government. He also grudgingly accepted the Marshall Truce that, beginning in January 1946, halted all military operations and troop movements in northern and northeastern China, but he adamantly refused to apply that truce in Manchuria on the grounds that China's national sovereignty demanded that Nationalist troops occupy the Northeast as soon as the Russians withdrew. Equally grudgingly, the Communists agreed not to obstruct that occupation.

From his vantage point in Ch'ang-ch'un, Chang Kia-ngau was able to assess the impact on the Northeast of both the truce and the negotiations between Chiang Kai-shek's government and the Chinese Communists, which he found devastating to the Nationalist cause in Manchuria. Between mid-

November 1945 and mid-January 1946 when the Marshall Truce actually took effect in northern China, the Russians made many concessions to the Nationalists respecting Manchuria. The Soviets must have felt it imperative during this period to come to terms with Chiang's Kai-shek's government because, as already noted, many of those concessions were of substantive military value and, undoubtedly, most unwelcome to the Chinese communist forces in Manchuria. Levine contends that after Chiang publicly expressed his exasperation with the Russians by withdrawing most of the Chinese mission from Ch'ang-ch'un, the Soviets feared angering the United States if they persisted in helping the Communists obstruct the Nationalist takeover of Manchuria.

However, there was probably another equally important reason for Moscow's actions. The Russian presence in Manchuria was almost exclusively military, and, as already demonstrated, Soviet interests there were largely strategic. The Russians consequently were bound to take an intense interest in the struggle between the Chinese communist and Chinese Nationalist armies in northern and northwestern China, which began almost immediately after Japan's surrender in August 1945 and continued until the imposition of the Marshall Truce in January 1946. During those months, the Russian army occupied parts of several of China's northwestern provinces, and thus Soviet military observers were excellently positioned to evaluate that conflict. They evidently concluded that the Nationalists were winning and would ultimately defeat the communist armies; it is improbable that Stalin, on advice from Malinovsky's militarily oriented headquarters, would otherwise have made so many concessions to the Nationalists before the imposition of the Marshall Truce. If the Soviets drew such a conclusion, it utterly contradicted that of General Marshall, who, shortly after his arrival in China, predicted a debacle for the Nationalists if the fighting in North China continued. Thus, Marshall's orders from Washington to support Chiang Kai-shek's government compelled him to insist on a truce in North China.[51]

Chiang Kai-shek opposed such a truce, and if subsequent Russian actions in Manchuria are any measure of the Marshall Truce's impact on the military situation in northern China, with solid reasons. As we have noted, communist forces there had been driven back by Nationalist advances, but when the truce ended those advances, the Soviets, according to the diary, immediately stopped trying to conciliate the Nationalists in Manchuria and instead imposed fewer and fewer restraints on the Communists in the Northeast. On the very day the truce was promulgated, thousands of communist troops attacked the Nationalist garrison at Ying-k'ou with what Chang Kiangau regarded as open Russian support. At noon that day the Russians fired on Nationalist soldiers entering Mukden, and in Kirin the next day they disarmed and imprisoned five thousand men that the Nationalists had organized into a local security force.

The Soviets repeatedly cited the Marshall Truce and its chief instrument, the Political Consultative Conference, as justification for reneging on concessions they had made to the Nationalists and for taking actions favorable to the Communists. For example, again on the day the truce was promulgated, the Russians retracted their promise to help the Nationalists take over a mining zone occupied by communist irregulars on the grounds that Chiang Kai-shek and the Chinese Communist Party had ordered both sides to end their clashes and that it was Soviet policy not to become involved in China's civil war. Chang Kia-ngau noted that this was the first occasion that the Soviets used the term *Chinese Communist Party* to refer to the communist presence in Manchuria, which, in his opinion, made the communist irregulars there "an accepted fact." In his own words, "the Political Consultative Conference has become a shelter for the Eighth Route Army in the Northeast, and other irregulars can exist there under the shelter of the Eighth Route Army." Soon the Communists were accusing the Nationalists of violating the truce agreement by sending Nationalist troops into Manchuria instead of relying on "local troops" and "the people's armed forces" to maintain order.

Chang Kia-ngau, feeling that Marshall's intervention had legitimized the communist forces in Manchuria, observed that as a result of the truce the Communists had begun to demand a share in the civil administration of the Northeast through local governments chosen by so-called popular elections. Levine has shown that such governments were not "elected" and "democratic," as the Communists claimed, but were imposed by communist party organizations and the communist armies.[52] Nevertheless, wrote Chang Kia-ngau, the Communists now had "the truce agreement and the Political Consultative Conference to back them up."

None of this was in keeping with Marshall's truce, which specifically exempted Manchuria from its provisions so that, presumably, the Nationalists could take over there without hindrance. But, as the diary shows, the truce actually helped the Russians and the Chinese Communists obstruct that takeover. Both of whom felt that the United States was wavering in its support for Chiang Kai-shek, that the United States looked on the Communists as legitimate contenders for power in China, and that nothing they might do there was likely to provoke U.S. intervention on Chiang's behalf. The behavior of General Marshall, as revealed in the diary, was not calculated to counteract this impression. Chang implies that Marshall was impressed by the assurances about communist intentions given him by Chou En-lai, who, as Nationalist armies advanced into the Northeast, finally demanded an immediate cease-fire. Marshall endorsed that demand on April 24 and in a conversation with Chang Kia-ngau's brother the next day reiterated that endorsement, saying that although the Communists had acted wrongly by violating the truce agreement and obstructing the entry of Nationalist troops into Manchuria, "the central government also has committed many mistakes." Apparently that vague, unsubstantiated indictment of the Nationalists was intended to justify Marshall's repudiation of an important part of his own truce agreement. Meanwhile, several of his tripartite truce teams entered Manchuria, where their presence must have further strengthened the communist party since, as the diary relates, they behaved as if both sides were entitled to be present in the Northeast. Perhaps this is why, according to Chang, the Russians, who initially rejected the idea of the teams, welcomed them.

Thus, critics of the U.S. State Department's subsequent White Paper on China may have been correct in holding Marshall responsible for many of the misfortunes that overtook Chiang Kai-shek's government in the crucial year of 1946. This also tends to support the contention of Yen Hsi-shan, the Nationalist premier and former warlord, that the Nationalists might have been more effective in their postwar struggle with the Communists if they had foregone the material benefits of their alliance with, and distanced themselves from, the United States.[53]

Sino-Soviet Economic Negotiations

Accounts of the Sino-Soviet negotiations on economic cooperation in Manchuria probably take up half the diary. Chang Kia-ngau's initial assignments were to expedite the transfer of Japanese assets to Chiang Kai-shek's government, supervise the services necessary to restore economic activity, and represent the government in the Sino-Soviet management of Manchuria's central railway, sanctioned by the Yalta Agreement. The Soviets, however, had a very different view of how Japanese assets should be handled.

In a second meeting with Malinovsky on October 17, 1945, the Nationalists were informed that "all factories formerly operated by the Japanese should be regarded as war booty belonging to the Soviet Army." The same day, immediately after the meeting, Special Envoy Chiang Ching-kuo told Chang Kia-ngau that, during the negotiation of the Sino-Soviet friendship treaty, T. V. Soong had informed Stalin that all Manchuria's industries "should be owned by China." Stalin replied that the "enterprises in Manchuria belonging to special company organizations shall be regarded as war booty and owned by the Soviets. Those belonging to private Japanese individuals could be handed back to China to compensate for the war losses of the Chinese people." Chiang Kai-shek's ministers never pursued the matter with Stalin, and therefore the disposition of Japanese wealth was still undecided in mid-August. Chang Kia-ngau apparently felt that this diplomatic oversight was disastrous for the Nationalists.

As already indicated, Japan's contribution to Manchuria's economic development had been great, although Chiang Kai-shek's government probably had no idea how great until Chang Kia-ngau completed his postwar survey of Manchuria's economy. They did know that in 1943 Manchuria produced at least half of China's output of certain key items (see following table).

On October 20, Chang Kia-ngau reported to President Chiang that the Soviets had begun carrying away Japanese machines from Manchuria's factories. He asked the president to immediately initiate government-level talks on the "war booty" issue to urge the Chinese government to save as much of Manchuria's industry as possible. Chang suggested that Japanese assets be used to compensate the people but did not specify whether people denoted both Russians and Chinese or merely the latter. He warned that if joint management with the Soviets came to pass, it could produce future difficulties in attracting foreign capital into the region and said that the Nationalists should keep the Fu-shun mines and not allow them to be managed by the Sino-Soviet enterprise that was to supervise the Ch'ang-ch'un railway between Harbin and Dairen. Chang glumly concluded that "because of constraints imposed by the existing situation, militarily and politically we are in a disadvantageous position in the Northeast. If, in addition, we achieve nothing there economically, then indeed our presence there will be purely nominal."

Sladkovsky and Chang first met on October 27 to arrange an agenda. Chang led off, saying he had come to Manchuria "for the purpose of promoting Chinese and Soviet economic cooperation." The two representatives appeared to establish some degree of trust over the issues of what scope of industry might be considered as compensation to the Soviets and what industries the two sides might manage jointly. On November 13 Chang learned that the Soviets were trying to persuade leading officials in the largest Japanese enterprises to write letters expressing their willingness to "voluntarily hand over those enterprises to the Soviet Union, the reason advanced for this transfer being that the above enterprises had both aided the enemy during the war." Chang realized "how concerned the Soviets are with the industry and mines of Manchuria and how much they desire to have a share in these." He proceeds to enumerate:

This is an important reason for their efforts to make impossible the penetration of American influence into Manchuria and for obstructing the dispatch of our troops into the Northeast. First, the Soviets schemed to snatch from the Japanese as war booty the industries and mines of Manchuria. Meanwhile, fearing that their scheme might not succeed, they dismantled important machinery in Manchuria and transferred it into their own possession.

COMPARATIVE PRODUCTION OF
THE NORTHEAST AND CHINA, 1943

Commodities	China	Northeast	The Northeast's Share of China's Production (%)
Coal	51,299	25,320	49.4
(Thousand metric tons)			
Iron ore	12,607	5,408	42.9
(Thousand metric tons)			
Steel	1,941	1,702	87.7
(Thousand metric tons)			
Steel products	534	495	92.7
(Thousand metric tons)			
Electric power	2,520	2,098	83.3
(Thousand kilowatt-hours)			

SOURCE: Tung-pei wu-tzu t'iao-ch'a wei-yuan-hui yen-chiu-tsu [The Research Group of the Northeast Resource Survey Commission], ed., *Tung-pei ching-chi hsiao-tsung-shu: tzu-yuan chi ch'an-yeh* [A Small Compendium on the Economy of the Northeast: Resources and Industry] (1946), vol. 1, part 2, pp. 2–3. This survey is in twenty volumes.

By now it is all too clear that there is no way to resolve the problem of the takeover of the Northeast without first solving the economic problem. Now I can discern the significance of Marshal Malinovsky's statement on November 7 that "hereafter, the work of the first stage of the takeover will be Your Excellency's."

Chang also learned that the Soviets had given one million yuan in army scrip to their Far Eastern Trading Company to purchase property. These and other actions convinced Chang that the Soviets had long-term economic interests in Manchuria and that they wanted to work out an arrangement with the Nationalist government to achieve those interests.

On November 16 Chang and Sladkovsky held another long exchange during which Chang informed Sladkovsky that the Nationalists were moving their headquarters from Ch'ang-ch'un to Shan-hai-kuan and were going to allow the Soviet Grain Company to operate its own air transport services. Discussion then shifted to the type of large-scale organization the two sides could use to jointly manage various enterprises in Manchuria and which Japanese enterprises should fall under the control of this organization. Sladkovsky preferred to use the old Heavy Industry Company, a huge conglomerate the Japanese had formed in 1937, but Chang opposed that idea because such a plan would continue Japanese imperialist policies. The two sides agreed to draw up a list of industries that Soviets and Chinese might manage jointly. After his long session with Sladkovsky, Chang Kia-ngau offered the following reaction to the day's discussion:

> The fact that Counselor Sladkovsky has revealed to me Soviet hopes indicates that, because we are withdrawing our headquarters, the Soviet side is anxious to settle the economic question so that they can take a step further and resolve the issue of our takeover. This demonstrates fully that the economic question is the key factor . . . Sladkovsky's remark that the opinions I raised indeed could serve as a basis for genuine cooperation between the two nations seems to indicate that there is room for negotiation.

On November 20 Sladkovsky and Chang met again, this time considering the details of how the Soviets and the Chinese might jointly manage various enterprises. They decided to leave the matter of defining economic cooperation to the ministers of their respective governments. On November 23 Chang met with Malinovsky and learned that the Soviets did not object to airlifting Chinese troops into Mukden and Ch'ang-ch'un. Malinovsky again expressed his interest in cooperating with the Chinese to manage Japanese enterprises and stated that "the Soviet government is willing to cooperate with China on the principle of each country having an equal share. In other words, the capital owned by the Soviets is not to exceed 50 percent. This will demonstrate fully the friendly spirit of the Soviets." Chang left for Chungking on November 24 to confer with top Chinese officials.

On November 28 Chang met with Foreign Minister Wang Hsüeh-t'ing, President T. V. Soong of the Executive Yuan, Chiang Ching-kuo, and Hsiung Shih-hui for discussions on how to deal with the Manchurian problem. Wang, adopting a legalistic view, stated that the matter of disposing of Japanese assets in Manchuria would have to be decided by the Allied Control Council in Japan, while Soong argued that political difficulties between the Soviet Union and the ROC had to be resolved before economic cooperation could be discussed. Apparently Chang Kia-ngau did not agree with this argument, as his diary indicates:

> In the evening, I saw President Soong of the Executive Yuan. He repeated his previously stated view that, certainly at present, the issue of Sino-Soviet economic cooperation cannot be discussed. Therefore, the opinion of Messrs. Soong and Wang is directly opposed to Malinovsky's expectations. Indeed, the views of Soong and Wang are correct, both from a legal angle and from the point of view of reason. But Marshal Malinovsky is anxious that we settle the economic question before Soviet troops withdraw. Actually, I think it would have been all right to discuss the economic question simultaneously. But Messrs. Soong and Wang are both deeply worried that even after they obtain the right of economic cooperation the Soviets will not allow

us to accomplish our takeover without hindrance, so that our government will have assumed too great a responsibility. Moreover, the various obstructions created by the Soviets have made it impossible for us to trust them. However, based on impressions I received from my contacts with the Soviets, while I dare not say that a settlement of the economic question will result in our takeover being unhindered, I still believe such a settlement will solve the greater part of the problem. But today, since responsible officials of the government have such views, I can only act in accordance with them.

Chang had probably argued that accepting economic cooperation with the Soviets was essential before the Nationalists could take over Manchuria. The diary strongly indicates that Chiang Ching-kuo completely supported Chang Kia-ngau, but ultimately he must have deferred to Soong and Wang, even though he believed them to be wrong. Thereafter, Chang Kia-ngau complied with the Foreign Ministry's rigid conduct of the negotiations with the Soviets over Manchuria but repeatedly expressed his frustrations with this erroneous policy as he noted the expansion of Chinese communist military power in the region.

Chang Kia-ngau, then, opted to advise the Soviets that detailed discussions about "measures for economic cooperation" would take place after their withdrawal and to draw up a Plan for Early-Stage Economic Reconstruction that would demonstrate that the "Chinese government will try its best to cooperate with the Soviets"—a compromise policy that he hoped both sides might accept. The Chungking government seems to have adopted Chang Kia-ngau's strategy, but to what extent it negotiated with the Soviet Foreign Ministry to implement that strategy cannot be ascertained until Sino-Soviet foreign relations documents are made public. The diary sheds little light except to mention that negotiations were continuing.

Chang Kia-ngau returned on December 4 from Chungking to Ch'ang-ch'un and met the following day with Marshal Malinovsky and Chiang Ching-kuo. The Soviets raised no objection to airlifting Nationalist troops into Ch'ang-ch'un or to transporting them to Mukden by rail. Malinovsky revealed January 3 as the new deadline for the withdrawal of Soviet troops but was primarily interested in the issue of economic cooperation. Chiang Ching-kuo and Chang Kia-ngau reported their discussions to Chungking. Chang's inference was that

Two major discrepancies exist between the views of our central government and those of the Soviets. One: The Soviets insist that we settle the question of economic cooperation before they will discuss our taking over the Northeast. Initially, they will allow us to take over Dairen, Mukden, Ch'ang-ch'un, and Harbin, since these lie along the Ch'ang-ch'un Railroad. But it seems we will still have to wait before taking over the various provinces. However, officials of our central government like President Soong and Foreign Minister Wang insist that we take over first and then discuss the economic question.

Chang goes on to point out that the Soviets have tried to "demonstrate their spirit of adhering to the Sino-Soviety treaty" and have wanted to give Chiang Kai-shek's government "ample time for discussing the economic question." Chang expresses admiration for Soviet "sharp-witted diplomacy." He complains that the Chinese "only know how to adhere to principles, but do not know how to adapt our methods in order to implement those principles." Chang singles out T. V. Soong in particular for this failing. "He feels that we can accomplish nothing in our negotiations with the Soviets and that this will result in our efforts being in vain. On the other hand, Foreign Minister Wang is discreet and careful. He always bases his ideas on legality and reason." Chang Kia-ngau concludes, "I am deeply worried that Sino-Soviet negotiations may end in failure."

Although Chang Kia-ngau and Sladkovsky continued to meet and discuss the details of economic cooperation, Sino-Soviet negotiations remained stalled while their respective foreign ministers wrangled over whether economic cooperation talks should begin before or after the total withdrawal of Soviet troops from Manchuria. Chungking never budged from its position, even though there were times when it seemed that if the Nationalist side had conceded to Soviet demands, economic cooperation might have been arranged. Only President Chiang Kai-shek had the power to break the impasse between the ROC and Soviet foreign ministries, but he chose not to exercise it. The Soviets' irritation at Chiang's rejection of their terms mounted, and when Madame Chiang Kai-shek visited Manchuria on January 22, 1946, to express gratitude to Soviet troops for the liberation of Manchuria from Japan and to meet with top Soviet commanders, Marshal Malinovsky found an excuse to be absent. On January 25 Sladkovsky toughened his negotiating stance with Chang Kia-ngau.

Meanwhile, unanticipated events made it difficult for President Chiang Kai-shek to consider compromising with the Soviets or establishing economic cooperation with them before they withdrew their troops. Political consultations between the Nationalists and the Chinese Communists on the issue of how the two sides would establish their authority in Manchuria motivated Chang to make the following entry for January 31:

Tomorrow, the date for the withdrawal of Soviet troops will already have arrived, but the Soviet army still shows no sign of withdrawing northward from Ch'ang-ch'un. Moreover, there has been no progress at all with respect to our taking over administration of the various provinces. This last month has passed quickly. In my view, since the Political Consultative Conference began on January 10, Sino-Soviet relations with respect to the Northeast have been encumbered by the relationship between the Nationalists and the Communists. If we had reached a settlement with the Soviets before the tenth, political issues between the Nationalists and the Communists might never have become involved. Despite secret Soviet speculations that the irregular armed forces they have nurtured here must inevitably reflect Soviet political interests, this problem would not have been able to surface.

After returning to Chungking on February 4, Chang held further discussions with President Chiang on how to break the impasse with the Soviets. Chang outlined his concerns and ideas about how the government should deal with the current crisis and predicted that U.S.-Soviet rivalry would intensify and that the Soviets would continue to allow the Chinese Communists to become entrenched in the region. He suggested two options: (1) break off discussions with the Soviets entirely or (2) offer them major concessions. Obviously preferring the latter course, Chang hinted that diplomatic talks might take place in Peiping or Chungking. President Chiang replied that he would consider his advice and get back to him.

Three days later, at his residence, Chiang Kai-shek held a top-level dinner meeting where it was decided "to allow the addition to the list of jointly managed enterprises of the An-shan Iron and Steel Works and the He-kang Coal Mines, as the Soviets wished." The Chinese would also approve joint management of the Civil Aviation Company in Manchuria. As the following remarks suggest, Chang Kia-ngau, because of the time required to obtain a positive agreement, despaired of a positive outcome.

> These will be our final concessions. In my opinion, reason dictates that under such exceedingly urgent circumstances we should use the quickest way of beginning talks with the Soviets, because, as long as we are paying the price of adding the An-shan Iron and Steel Works and the He-kang Coal Mines, we may as well notify the Soviets of our decision as soon as possible, with the aim of retrieving the situation—however minuscule the possibility of actually succeeding. Indeed, we should not still go through the various procedures of first formulating a plan, then discussing it and finally submitting for approval and instructions. But in my capacity as chairman of the Economic Commission, how can I go beyond the limits of my power and deal with matters under the jurisdiction of other people? In my innermost heart there is only a burning anxiety.

Chang felt he had limited authority and sensed that further delays would add new troubles to the ROC's burdens.

On February 15 Chang mentioned that people from Manchuria living in Chungking were demonstrating in the streets for more vigorous government action to recover their homeland. He feared that the recovery issue would soon become politicized and made the following prediction in his February 20 entry:

> Subsequently, people in the Northeast and the so-called nationalists will definitely start attacking us. Not only will they revile those in charge of the negotiations, but, moreover, it will certainly be difficult to carry out the negotiations and reach an agreement. This is because, only a month ago, the Northeast question involved only negotiating with the Soviets; today, however, military and political questions concerning the Chinese Communists have become part of the picture. A situation has already been created that leaves no means of settling the matter.

What Chang feared soon came to pass. On February 22 huge demonstrations, organized by students demanding that all Soviet troops withdraw from Manchuria, broke out in the streets. The demonstrators also protested the murder on January 28, 1946, of Chang Hsing-fu, one of China's most prominent mining engineers, whom the Nationalist government had sent, along with other mining engineers, to Manchuria to explore the possibility of reopening the Fu-shun mines. The diary vividly describes how Chang and his party, supposedly under the protection of the Soviet Army, were butchered by Chinese communist soldiers and records the outraged anguish of Chang Kia-ngau who, having accepted Russian assurances of the party's safety, felt personally responsible for their deaths. Because those murders coincided with the beginning of the Marshall Truce, Russian complicity in them must be regarded as part of the Soviet response to that truce. (The truce, as already noted, meant the Soviets no longer had to conciliate the Nationalists in Manchuria but were free to oppose them.)

Once the Soviets decided to stop restraining the Communists, such murders were inevitable because, according to Levine and others, the Chinese Communists were recruiting soldiers and militiamen from Manchuria's rural underclass, which was made up of criminals and delinquents.[54] These people, consumed by hatred of anyone more fortunate than themselves, could easily turn murderous. There was no need to kill Chang Hsing-fu and the engineers who accompanied him; simply detaining them would have accomplished any communist military objective. The skills possessed by those engineers proved that they were educationally and, therefore, economically advantaged, which made them "class enemies" and, consequently, appropriate targets for murder. In his assessment of the incident Chang Kia-ngau emphasized that Chang Hsing-fu was a distinguished engineer whose services were desperately needed by his economically underdeveloped country, which suggests that Chang perceived implications more terrible than those normally associated with political killings. In retrospect, those murders were a chilling omen of the future, when the Communists would exterminate much of China's educated population.

The Second Congress of the Nationalist Party Central Committee convened on March 1, 1946. During that congress various political factions attacked government officials who were involved in the recovery of the Northeast. Chang Kia-ngau's worst fears were realized; the Nationalist failure to work out a Soviet withdrawal had become a political issue dividing the Kuomintang. On March 6 the congress even debated the Sino-Soviet friendship treaty, which certain groups demanded be revised.

Despite these new developments, the Soviets kept the door open for a possible agreement with the Nationalists on the cooperative management of various enterprises. On March 27 Ambassador I. Petrov presented an eight-part proposal for economic cooperation to the ROC Foreign Ministry, but Foreign Minister Wang would only discuss the terms for the Nationalist takeover of Manchuria and Soviet assistance in that operation. Meanwhile, Chang Kia-ngau, communicating by telegram with Vice-Chief of Staff Tung Yen-p'ing in Ch'ang-ch'un, urged him to save the negotiations for economic cooperation. On April 8 Chang submitted the draft of an alternative for such cooperation that listed the various enterprises both sides might be prepared to manage jointly. Later that same day he delivered his plan to Foreign Minister Wang and recorded the following:[55]

> He [Wang] still insists that we should begin discussions with the Soviets only after we receive a reply concerning whether they will assist our troops to advance northward to replace the defense of the Northeast. He does not know that the key to whether the Soviets will assist us to advance northward to replace that defense is whether or not the two sides reach an agreement on economic cooperation. Moreover, the Soviets long ago completed arrangements for obstructing, in a variety of ways, the northward advance of our troops. Now they are quietly awaiting the outcome of the negotiations about economic cooperation, and they will manipulate the situation accordingly. Yet Foreign Minister Wang still does not perceive this. I really am deeply worried about the future of our country.

On April 9 President Chiang invited Chang Kia-ngau, Foreign Minister Wang, and several other top officials to a private meeting. Here is how Chang summed up the talks:

> During our discussion, President Chiang maintained that, in order to quickly replace the defense along the Chinese–Ch'ang-ch'un rail line, we

should begin talks with the Soviets soon. But Foreign Minister Wang thought we should wait, first, for Vice-President of the Executive Yuan Wong's return to Chungking and, second, for the Soviet ambassador's reply concerning the question of the Soviets assisting us in replacing the defense of the Northeast. My view was that we might as well begin talks and discuss with the Soviets, simultaneously, the questions of economic cooperation and their assisting us in replacing the defense of the Northeast. In this way, both matters could proceed at the same time. In the end, President Chiang instructed the Ministries of Foreign Affairs and Economics to each assign one vice-minister to the negotiations. He also instructed me to assist them from the sidelines.

Discussions between the two sides continued in the same halfhearted way until the Soviets withdrew from Manchuria in May with neither side obtaining what it really wanted.

From these diary entries it is clear that the ROC vacillated between negotiating with the Soviets over cooperative management of former Japanese enterprises and demanding that such negotiations begin in earnest only after the Soviets had withdrawn from Manchuria. Contrary to Tang Tsou's account, President Chiang Kai-shek never completely terminated the negotiations but was persuaded by his foreign minister and other top officials to demand that the Soviets withdraw and to alter the economic negotiations by interjecting new demands. As Chang Kia-ngau repeatedly pointed out, this strategy was bound to fail. Rather than making firm concessions to motivate the Soviets to make a deal on the management of former Japanese enterprises or breaking off discussions altogether, the ROC took the middle course. In so doing, they left the Soviets no other course but to help the Chinese communist forces establish a base in Manchuria.

Soviet Policy Toward China

What was the Soviet Union's policy toward China in the months after World War II? The diary provides some fascinating insights into Moscow's great concern with keeping the United States out of Manchuria (and, for that matter, China) and with giving itself, if at all possible, a sphere of influence in northeastern China. At the important October 29, 1945, meeting, Malinovsky complained about a U.S. warship in Dairen, its captain even going ashore to make an inspection. After that meeting, Chang Kia-ngau noted Malinovsky's "dissatisfaction with our reliance on American forces to send our troops into the Northeast and, even more, the reluctance of the Soviet Union to see American influence penetrate into the Northeast" and made similar observations after meeting with Malinovsky on November 5:

The Soviets are unwilling to have us rely on the United States to transport our troops. In other words, they are unwilling to have the United States acquire a foothold in the Northeast. The landing at Dairen of personnel from an American warship to inspect conditions there aroused resentment on the part of the Soviets. On October 29 during the fourth talk, Malinovsky's tone and countenance were stern when he mentioned the landing of personnel from this American warship. On October 29 Vice-Chief of Staff Tung notified the Soviets that we had decided to borrow American transports to send our troops to Hu-lu-tao and Ying-k'ou. This, too, must have caused the Soviets dissatisfaction. Therefore, postwar antagonism between the United States and the Soviet Union and the fact that we must rely on the United States may be important factors obstructing the entry of our troops into the Northeast.

Indeed, Soviet-U.S. rivalry would prove to be a formidable factor in restricting the ROC's ability to bargain with the Soviets for the withdrawal of their troops.

On January 9, 1946, Chang noted the Soviet reaction to a press announcement that General Wedemeyer had offered U.S. assistance in transporting General Tu Yü-ming's troops into Manchuria.

This will provoke the Soviets and make them apprehensive about American influence penetrating the Northeast. General Wedemeyer did not know that, when we met him for the first time, Marshal Malinovsky had already hinted at his anger over an American warship sailing into Dairen harbor in October of last year to inspect matters there, and its captain going ashore. Nor did General Wedemeyer know that Marshal Malinovsky explicitly stated to me that he was unwilling to see American political influence infiltrate the Northeast by means of the American dollar. After today, when General Wedemeyer further expressed America's intention of fostering China's military strength in the Northeast, Soviet suspicion and jealousy are bound to increase further.

Stalin and Malinovsky not only wanted to keep the United States out of Manchuria but were equally anxious to preserve Soviet influence in the region. The diary gives examples of the Soviets' flexibility in disposing of Japanese assets. After first claiming that all Japanese assets were war booty and hence Russian property, the Soviets modified their stand, conceding that, for all practical purposes, only those assets "run up for military purposes" would be considered (November 13 entry). After making up a list of such enterprises, the Soviets expressed their willingness to consider Sino-Soviet management of them. Negotiations continued for many months thereafter over which enterprises should be jointly managed and which should be Chinese-owned and -operated.

On January 26 Sladkovsky and Chang held a long discussion on the issue of Japanese assets. Sladkovsky began by pointing out the concessions the Soviet side had already made and expressing his fear "that today the Chinese have chosen to obliterate and ignore this fundamental Soviet spirit." His example was the Chinese side agreeing to joint enterprise management of mines whose output was small "and their equipment, inadequate" but omitting the giant An-shan iron mine, which was tantamount "to refusing to manage jointly with the Soviet Union the iron and steel enterprises of the Northeast." Sladkovsky named other important enterprises that had not been considered for joint management and urged the Chinese to stop procrastinating and make a sincere effort to reach an accord on economic cooperation. Chang reported that after the meeting Sladkovsky had given him to understand that "the reason the Soviets wish to enter into intimate economic cooperation with us is that they do not want a third nation to enter the Northeast. It does not mean that the Soviets want to monopolize the advantages there."

On February 1 Malinovsky reiterated that the Chinese had excluded too many important enterprises from joint management. He also defended Soviet demands for economic cooperation and urged Chang to work out a better arrangement when he returned to Chungking. But the discussions in Chungking on economic cooperation between Ambassador Petrov and Foreign Minister Wang were halfhearted at best. On March 12 Sladkovsky telegraphed Chang that he hoped economic negotiations could be concluded and hinted at further Soviet concessions. Chang's diary suggests that the Soviets had made a genuine effort for five months to share Japanese assets in Manchuria with the Nationalists, with the goal of creating a sphere of economic influence in Manchuria and excluding U.S. influence.

But if Manchuria was important to the Soviets' national interests, what of their presumably more important goal of advancing the triumph of Chinese communism? Here the diary reveals that the Soviets had, in essence, a two-track Chinese policy. The first track sought to neutralize U.S. influence in China and expand Soviet influence in the Northeast. But if that policy failed, they would shift to track two and help the Chinese communist forces establish a revolutionary base in Manchuria.

There was little doubt in Chang Kia-ngau's mind that the Soviets had held that two-track policy from the beginning of their occupation of Manchuria. On track one, they had expressed interest in an economic accord with the ROC (although allowing Chinese communist cadres and troops to enter the region). As prospects for economic cooperation gradually dimmed, however, they switched to track two and began providing the Chinese Communists with more help. As early as October and November, the Soviets provided only moderate assistance to the Chinese Communists yet allowed Mao Tse-tung's troops to move into the area around Ying-k'ou to hold off Nationalist troops attempting to land there. Other incidents during those same months convinced Chang Kia-ngau that the Soviets were rendering assistance to the Communists while negotiating an economic accord with the Nationalists.

On March 17, 1946, a wire from Tung Yen-p'ing provided Chang with evidence that the Soviets hoped that their aid would enable the Communists to hang onto their newly established revolutionary base. Tung's cable read as follows:

> On the ninth and thirteenth of this month, a certain Soviet colonel convened a meeting of Chinese and Japanese Communists at the former Railroad Bureau in Ch'ang-ch'un. He issued an important statement to the effect that (1) In order to deal with the questions of the Near East, the Soviet Army will no longer be able to station troops in China's Northeast; the question of the Northeast will have to be settled through diplomatic channels. (2) Besides adherence to the Sino-Soviet treaty, the Soviets also demand the right of joint control of power plants, the iron and steel industries, and mining enterprises, etc., in the Northeast; but in the event that the United Nations adopts a rigid attitude, the Soviets can withdraw those demands. (3) The Soviets hope that the Chinese and Japanese Communists in the Northeast will maintain themselves by relying on their own efforts. The Soviets will not be able to give them direct assistance. And so on. I think these disclosures are very significant.

Tung's cable confirms Levine's point that the changing international situation, particularly a Soviet confrontation with Britain and the United States over control of Iran, compelled Stalin to withdraw Soviet troops from Manchuria.[56] The Soviets told the Chinese Communists candidly that they had tried to negotiate economic cooperation with the Nationalists, that they intended to honor the Sino-Soviet treaty, and that they hoped the aid they had rendered so far would enable the local Communists to carry on their revolutionary activities.

But the Soviets were still pursuing economic negotiations with the ROC. On March 27 Foreign Minister Wang invited Chang to the ministry, where he was given a note by Ambassador Petrov. In his diary, Chang quotes from Petrov's note:[57]

> Largely on the basis of my repeated discussions with Counselor Sladkovsky in January and my talk with Marshal Malinovsky on February 1, the sum-

mary results proposed a minimum number of enterprises for economic cooperation, along with those that, except for the Fu-shun coal mines, the Soviets anticipate we will agree on. The Soviets are unwilling "to lose the enterprises they may have obtained for joint management simply because the withdrawal of their troops is not accompanied by a formal replacement by Nationalist defenses." They also anticipate that, when we have defeated the Communists, the Soviets can continue to negotiate and reach an agreement with us. I really admire their farsightedness.

Late in the afternoon of April 17, Chang visited Petrov to inform him of Chang's earlier efforts to negotiate an arrangement with the Soviets and to express his hope that Petrov could "make great efforts to retrieve the situation there." Petrov replied that the Soviets had negotiated in good faith and that joint Soviet-Nationalist management of the agreed-upon enterprises was feasible. By then, however, fierce fighting had already broken out between Nationalist and Communist forces around Ch'ang-ch'un. Chang expressed concern that if the Nationalists could not get their troops into Ch'ang-ch'un and Harbin to defend those cities, it would be "difficult to continue discussions about the economic question on a satisfactory basis." Petrov wondered why the truce team could not get the Nationalists and the Communists to negotiate a cease-fire. Chang observed,

> Judging from the aforementioned tone of the Soviet ambassador's remarks, the situation in Ch'ang-ch'un may still be retrieved through the work of the tripartite truce team—if we settle the economic question with the Soviets immediately. My observations suggest that the Soviets are still inclined to let us replace the defenses in Ch'ang-ch'un and Harbin. But, owing to their growing armed strength, the Chinese Communists are liable to demand a united regime. I have held from the beginning, however, that the Soviet Union cherishes different views with regard to southern and northern Manchuria. In southern Manchuria, it still respects our government as the host; in northern Manchuria, it is letting Communists from Yen-an, as well as communist elements nurtured by the Soviets, share political power.

Thus, Chang suggests that the Soviet two-track policy was still operational but in a Manchuria divided into Nationalists and Communists. Until May 1946, when the Soviets finally pulled their troops out of Manchuria, they kept the door open for discussion with the Nationalists about cooperative management of former Japanese assets. A full-fledged civil war erupted in Manchuria after the Soviets left, and peace was not restored or economic reconstruction begun until the civil war was over.

Nationalist Domestic Policies and Secret Negotiations

Could the Nationalists have negotiated their way into Manchuria sooner than they did, as the diary would seem to suggest? Before we discuss this issue, let us say a word about the conduct of Nationalist negotiations. Discussions with the Soviets were carried out at two levels. First, government representatives negotiated in Chungking, with an occasional meeting in Moscow, as when Chiang Ching-kuo went to Russia to confer with Stalin. Second, the two sides negotiated in Ch'ang-ch'un. Even after Chang Kia-ngau returned to Chungking on February 4, he communicated with the Soviet High Command in Manchuria through Tung Yen-p'ing. Soviet strategy was thus defined by Stalin and coordinated by Petrov in Chungking and Malinovsky in Ch'ang-ch'un, both of whom had carte blanche to negotiate Stalin's two-China policy in the field and, if problems arose, would quickly consult with Moscow.

On the Chinese side the situation was different. Government representatives consulted with each other to formulate policies for recovering the Northeast from the Soviets. The diary frequently mentions disagreements that arose in the course of these consultations. Chang Kia-ngau and unnamed others urged greater Nationalist concessions to resolve the issue of economic cooperation and clear the way for prompt political and military decisions about the recovery of Manchuria. T. V. Soong and Wang Hsüeh-t'ing demanded a political settlement first and economic discussions afterward. President Chiang, vacillating between these two positions, tried to achieve both at the same time.

The result was a delay of seven months before Nationalist troops were allowed to take over the central railway line and Mukden, Ch'ang-ch'un, and Harbin, the principal cities along it. The communist troops that occupied Ch'ang-ch'un in May would eventually be driven out, but the seven months' delay gave them time to deploy their troops and cadres in the Northeast and to mobilize an army equal to that of the Nationalists for the first time.

The Nationalists conducted these negotiations in secret between October 1945 and February 1946, but by March the issue of Manchuria's recovery had been politicized within the Kuomintang, exacerbating the existing factionalism in Chiang Kai-shek's party. The subject was openly debated during the Second Congress of the party's Central Committee. T. V. Soong and Wang Hsüeh-t'ing's opposition to the negotiations has already been described. But in the Second Congress Chiang Kai-shek confronted another dilemma that, as the diary relates, bedeviled his efforts to negotiate an agreement with the Russians. Chiang's devoted followers, including the influential Ch'en Li-fu, felt strongly that the Chinese Communists were vulnerable because of Russian abuses of the population in Manchuria and the looting of Manchurian industry. Chiang's adherents wanted to publicize such Soviet actions and—to counteract increasingly successful Chinese communist efforts to portray the Nationalists as lackeys of an imperialist United States—indict the Communists for their collaboration with the Russians.

Chiang Kai-shek was sympathetic to this strategy but even more convinced that economic concessions to the Russians in the Northeast were necessary to acquire effective military and political control of that region. He tried, therefore, to restrain Ch'en Li-fu and the other Kuomintang "nationalists," as Chang Kia-ngau called them (which suggests that Chang considered their nationalism both more fervent and narrower than the patriotism of other Kuomintang elements). Chang Kia-ngau and Chiang Kai-shek feared that if these nationalists were not restrained they would antagonize the Soviet Union and make an acceptable agreement on the Northeast impossible. Chang Kia-ngau notes that Chiang Kai-shek personally rebuked Ch'en Li-fu for organizing a demonstration of Chungking students against the Soviet presence in Manchuria. This raises the question of whether negotiations with the Soviets prevented Chiang's government from capitalizing on an important communist weakness.

Chang Kia-ngau, however, also describes the nationalists' strident demands at the Kuomintang party congress that the government break off negotiations with the Soviets. These nationalists attacked Chang and others in charge of the talks, despite Chiang Kai-shek's plea to the delegates to refrain from irresponsible attacks on his appointees. Undoubtedly, the intensity and extent of those attacks by his closest followers influenced Chiang's decision not to make the concessions necessary to an economic agreement with the Russians in the Northeast. Thus, because of the contradiction between two sensible approaches to the Russian occupation of Manchuria, Chiang Kai-shek's government derived little benefit from either.

In this instance, as in others, Chang Kia-ngau's diary provides significant insights into Chiang Kai-shek's character and the nature of his relationship with his subordinates during the immediate postwar period. Certainly, Chiang does not look like a despot; on the contrary, it appears that his authority within both the Chinese government and his own political party was very circumscribed. This is amply illustrated by his failure to bend Soong, Wang, and the dissident nationalists to his will with respect to an agreement with the Russians. Moreover, his letters to Chang Kia-ngau contain nothing dictatorial or autocratic; nor were those qualities characteristic of his behavior, as described in the diary. As for negotiations with the Russians, Chiang solicited advice from all quarters and did not flinch at the criticism that bombarded him at the Kuomintang party congress in 1946.

Chang Kia-ngau regretted Chiang Kai-shek's inability to impose his will on the government and the Kuomintang and quotes with approval Chiang's advice to the delegates at the congress that (evidently because of Russian and, therefore, U.S. involvement) in the future the Nationalists would have to resolve their problems politically rather than militarily and "employ political deftness as well as behave with forbearance." Chang says later that Chiang's "viewpoint with respect to the question of the Northeast is more profound than that of any other responsible authority in the government." These and other references to Chiang indicate Chang Kia-ngau's deep respect for him and for his son, Chiang Ching-kuo. It would appear that this feeling was fully reciprocated and that Chang Kia-ngau was highly thought of by everyone with whom he associated, including Malinovsky, Sladkovsky, and even the communist leaders Tung Pi-wu and Chou En-lai.

Beyond being an important intragovernmental and intraparty issue, the Northeast question had also become a subject in the truce negotiations between the Nationalists and the Communists. The recovery of Manchuria was further complicated by U.S. pressure for equal rights in Manchuria, and these difficulties, in turn, delayed negotiations with the Soviets. The Nationalists were constrained by U.S. pressure, by emerging domestic political pressures, and by the recalcitrant Russians, who delayed their departure from Manchuria to wring economic concessions from the Nationalists. As the changing world scene forced Stalin to withdraw Soviet troops in April and May 1946, the Chinese Communists became bolder and more aggressive. Just as the Soviets withdrew, the Communists attacked, forcing President Chiang to dispatch his best-trained troops to Manchuria to recover the cities that had fallen into communist hands.

Chang Kia-ngau summed up his feelings of despair after reading on April 20 that communist troops had seized the cities of Ssu-p'ing and Ch'ang-ch'un.

> For more than five months, I have earnestly and with great anxiety trotted back and forth between Chungking and Ch'ang-ch'un. Either in the snowbound Northeast, or in high-flying airplanes, I gave up thinking about my own life, and yet I have achieved a result like this! I do not know whether the policy adhered to by our authorities presages disaster or good fortune. Add to this the spectacle of the Second Congress, where the nationalists flaunted their biased, narrow viewpoints, and others chimed in to take advantage of the situation to wage personal vendettas. This has created today's irretrievable situation. Will the result be darkness or light? So now I know that great affairs of state are like a heavy weight hanging by a single hair. I fear that, instead of introspectively examining themselves, those responsible for the current situation still pride themselves on having settled on a correct policy.

The diary ends soon after this entry. The civil war had shifted to Manchuria, and the outcome there would determine the outcome of the war.

CONCLUSION

The conventional explanations as to why the Nationalists lost the civil war are based primarily on the U.S. State Department's White Paper and on journalistic accounts like Theodore White's *Thunder Out of China*, which claim that the Nationalists were not as successful as the Chinese Communists at mobilizing men and matériel for their war effort.

The Nationalists, positioned in the cities, capable of tapping urban wealth, and able to obtain U.S. military aid, believed that, after World War II, they could absorb and control ever-larger concentric rings of the countryside and eventually envelop the entire country. That strategy had worked from 1928 to 1937, even without U.S. military aid. During that decade, Chiang Kai-shek's government had been preoccupied with creating an army powerful enough to defeat both the warlords and the Communists, who were disrupting China's national unity, and to fight Japan. Whatever economic resources the government did not devote to the military, it used for urban industrial development, presuming this would result in economic development of the countryside. By the time of the Japanese invasion in 1937, the Nationalists had created modern institutions, including banks and communications and transportation networks, to service both industry and agriculture. Urban centers like Shanghai linked many regions in prosperous economic exchanges. Had war not intervened, the urban economic development of the 1930s would have begun to modernize China's agricultural economy. But all this ended with Japan's invasion. Thereafter, for reasons already noted, those parts of China still under Nationalist rule deteriorated economically, and, at the same time, the Nationalists could not or would not pursue policies needed to mobilize popular support.

Meanwhile, the Communists developed their own policies to mobilize rural manpower and materials for their administrative networks and army. Their first principle was "party control based on indoctrination of cadres and enforcement of discipline."[58] The second principle was to "find out what the peasant[s] wanted and give it to them"[59] (making the life of rural people better, rapidly building a new military to defend them, and fighting the Japanese). After the war, those same principles would be used to fight the Nationalists.

A new element of this strategy, in both northern China and Manchuria in 1946–1947 was land reform, a tactic embodying violent means designed to eliminate the rural elite who controlled and ran village and country affairs and to redistribute their wealth to poorer households. The Communists thus replaced the traditional rural elite with their own cadres and local supporters, established new networks of town and village control, and mobilized popular support for the party's activities and goals. By constantly perfecting this strategy and its component policies after Japan's surrender, the Communists did not have to rely on Japanese wealth in the territories formerly held by the army. But their acquisition of such assets was a windfall that enabled them to field, especially in Manchuria, far more powerful armies than would otherwise have been possible.

Viewing the competing strategies of the Kuomintang and the Communists from the perspective of the diary, we offer another explanation of why the civil war ended as quickly as it did, with a communist victory. The Nationalists and the Communists employed quite different strategies to mobilize manpower and matériel for their armies. The Nationalist strategy was to quickly occupy the urban centers in areas formerly held by the Japanese and then use the resources of those centers to extend the Nationalist administration into the countryside through the traditional town and village elites. This, it was hoped, would quickly restore economic exchange between the countryside and the cities, which would lead to swift economic reconstruction. In northern China, with U.S. aid, the Nationalists accomplished such an occupation, but in Manchuria, as the diary shows, the Soviets used the concessions of Yalta and the Sino-Soviet treaty to prevent a Nationalist occupation. Still, as the diary indicates, the Russians were willing to reverse that policy and let the Nationalists occupy Manchuria's cities immediately if Chiang Kai-shek's government made one additional, sweeping concession: joint control of Manchuria's industrial economy. When the Nationalists wavered, the Soviets allowed the Chinese Communists to send large numbers of troops and cadres into the Northeast, which not only put pressure on the Nationalists to meet Soviet demands regarding that region but also ensured that, if Soviet negotiations with the Nationalists failed, the Chinese Communists would be able to set up their own regime in Manchuria—one presumably friendly, if not actually subordinate, to the Soviet Union. By pursuing this two-track policy, the Russians managed to exclude the United States from the Northeast and, at the same time, keep out of China's civil war.

The diary argues that if the Nationalists had made major concessions to the Soviets to reach an early accord on economic cooperation, Nationalist troops might have been able to occupy Manchuria's cities as early as January or early February 1946 and in sufficient force to establish Nationalist control before the civil war flared up. But by late February, with no accord in sight and communist forces firmly entrenched in Manchuria, Chang Kia-ngau believed the situation was irremediable. He offered these words after receiving a cable from Chiang Kai-shek on February 20:

> Personally, I feel that, although their claim to war booty is a legal and rational necessity for the Soviets, we have, after all, promised to replace it with a compensatory sum. The discrepancy, therefore, exists only in words;

in actual practice there is no difference. What really matters is the expansion of Chinese communist forces in the Northeast. During the past month, Chinese communist forces have already acquired a foundation in the Northeast. Thus, even if we can negotiate an agreement with the Soviets, we will still have to resort to armed force to take over the areas outside the various major cities. It follows from this that, although we have already made great concessions to the Soviets, we are still unable to take over most areas. Subsequently, people in the Northeast and the so-called nationalists will definitely start attacking us. Not only will they revile those in charge of the negotiations, but, moreover, it will certainly be difficult to carry out the negotiations and reach an agreement. This is because, only a month ago, the Northeast question involved only negotiating with the Soviets; today, however, military and political questions concerning the Chinese Communists have become part of the picture. A situation has already been created that leaves no means of settling the matter.

Because Chiang Kai-shek's government had to fight a civil war in Manchuria before it could establish an urban power base there, it had little chance to implement its strategy of developing the urban sector of the economy, utilizing Japanese assets to initiate rapid overall economic recovery, and thus guaranteeing Nationalist control of the countryside.

The diary also confirms Levine's thesis about the communist defeat of Chiang's best troops and the undermining of his government's capacity to replace them but clearly implies that if the Soviets had allowed Nationalist forces to enter Manchuria by 1945 or early 1946, their occupation of the cities and their economic cooperation with the Soviets might have produced an economic recovery that could have spread throughout China. That prospect was a distinct possibility, for the diary shows that the Soviets definitely sought economic accords with the Nationalists.

Rather than opt for that strategy or make substantive economic concessions to the Soviets for joint management of certain Manchurian enterprises, the Nationalists continued to negotiate economic cooperation while demanding that the Soviets withdraw. This policy failed. By the time the Soviets left Manchuria, the civil war theater had shifted to the Northeast, with Chinese communist power nearly equivalent to the Nationalists.

For the Nationalists this was a devastating catastrophe and one that Chang Kia-ngau predicted in his last diary entries. During the following months, however, it appeared that Chang had been overly pessimistic about Nationalist chances of defeating the Communists in the Northeast. To be sure, as Chang records in his diary, Lin Piao, by hastily recruiting an army of Eighth Route Army veterans and former Manchurian puppet soldiers, initially imposed a series of military setbacks on the slowly advancing Nationalist forces. But he failed to reckon with the high morale, greater firepower, and vastly superior training of the Americanized troops of the Nationalist New First and New Sixth armies, all veterans of the long, successful campaign against the Japanese in Burma, who by May were relentlessly bearing down on Lin Piao's troops. A U.S. military observer noted that, in spite of their initial successes, Lin Piao and the other communist commanders in Manchuria were engaged in a kind of warfare unfamiliar to them that they were ill-equipped to wage.[60] Nevertheless, Lin Piao decided to risk everything on the defense of Ssu-p'ing, a crucial rail junction just south of Ch'ang-ch'un, where he concentrated the bulk of his army in hopes of not only halting the Nationalists but also destroying most of their forces.[61] Meanwhile, Chou En-lai said in effect that a Nationalist breakthrough at Ssu-p'ing would imperil the entire communist situation in Manchuria.

Following a protracted artillery exchange that reduced the city of Ssu-p'ing to rubble, the Communists mounted one "human sea" assault after another against the Nationalists, who retaliated with their considerable fire-power. As Lin Piao's casualties soared into the thousands and tens of thousands, he became desperate. According to the Nationalists, he finally threw into the battle 100,000 unemployed factory workers from Ch'ang-ch'un.[62] A communist participant had this to say about the battle:

> In order to stop the Kuomintang . . . [the communist party] . . . used all its noncombatant political working staff, its local comrades and even high school students. They literally just threw them at the Kuomintang's crack troops. It was a massacre; more than five thousand noncombatants, who had never had any military training, were killed or wounded.[63]

By May 18 nearly 40,000 communist troops, at least half of Lin Piao's army, were dead, while others were surrendering to the Nationalists by the thousands,[64] including Lin Piao's chief of operations, which suggests the dimensions of the communist defeat.[65] Meanwhile, another Nationalist force, after destroying communist troops garrisoning the city of Fu-shun, was threatening Lin Piao's flank. Consequently, during the night of May 18 Lin Piao withdrew what was left of his army and fled north, closely pursued by Nationalist forces who advanced at the rate of 30 miles day, just about as fast as they could move.[66] A neutral Chinese reporter who was in daily communication with Chou En-lai and other communist leaders said they were panic-stricken by what had happened at Ssu-p'ing,[67] and Chou En-lai told General Marshall that the Communists would evacuate Ch'ang-ch'un if the Nationalists stopped at that city.[68] They did not, but the Communists evacuated it anyway, in considerable panic. The Nationalists had advanced almost one hundred miles in only three days.[69] So impressed were the Russians by the strength of Chiang's armies in Manchuria that they renewed their overtures to his government.[70] Meanwhile, Lin Piao's retreating army showed signs of disintegrating, as evidenced by the massive surrender of its soldiers.[71] So rapid and overpowering was the Nationalist advance that the Communists surrendered cities without a fight and even failed to destroy an important railroad bridge across the Sungari River. By June the Nationalists had advanced another two hundred miles and were within striking distance of Harbin, the only major Manchurian city still in communist hands, which, according to a U.S. authority, Lin Piao was on the verge of evacuating.[72] Its loss would compel Lin Piao to withdraw his army into the Soviet Union and leave the Nationalists in possession of Manchuria except those parts of the countryside the Communists could hold onto.

After defecting to the Nationalists, a member of Lin Piao's staff said that Lin was depressed by what happened to his army at Ssu-p'ing.[73] At a subsequent press conference, Lin appeared utterly dejected and vowed that he would never fight that way again.[74] In a booklet he wrote about this time, he advised communist commanders to have at least a 500 to 600 percent superiority in manpower before trying to stand up to the superior firepower of the Nationalists.[75] Mao Tse-tung acknowledged the magnitude of the disaster by removing P'eng Chen, his chief political commissar in Manchuria, and by warning against the tactics employed by Lin Piao.[76]

On June 6, Chiang Kai-shek, with his troops poised for the assault on Harbin less than twenty miles away, suddenly halted their advance and agreed to observe a fifteen-day truce, later extended to nearly one month.[77] When his incredulous commanders begged him to reconsider, telling him that Harbin in Nationalist hands ensured a total victory over communist military forces in Manchuria, he became very angry. To Tu Yü-ming, his supreme commander in Manchuria, Chiang said, "You say that taking the city will be easy, but if you knew the reasons why we can't take it, then you would understand why taking it is not easy at all!"[78]

Not only Tu, but Li Tsung-jen, the respected Kwangsi army commander nominally in charge of Chiang's headquarters in Peiping, was aghast at Chiang's decision.[79] Subsequently, Chiang called this decision the worst mistake he ever made in dealing with the Communists.[80] In his memoirs he blamed himself; however, there is abundant evidence that General Marshall was responsible for Chiang's forfeit of his victory in Manchuria.[81] Throughout the Nationalist advance in Manchuria, the Communists bitterly assailed Marshall, charging that his truce in North China was a hoax to safeguard Nationalist supply lines there while Chiang's forces destroyed Lin Piao's army in Manchuria, and used this as an excuse for resuming their own military activities in northern China. As his efforts to prevent civil war in China crumbled, Marshall seized on a communist promise to end hostilities in northern China if Chiang halted the advance of his troops in Manchuria. According to Levine,

> Implicitly admonishing Marshall for sheltering the faltering enemy, Chiang asserted that the CCP would accept the harsh terms he now offered them if only Marshall supported the government's position. Marshall was adamant, however, and threatened to withdraw his services as mediator if Chiang's military offensive continued. Behind Marshall's threat stood the possible loss of American military assistance and economic aid that Chiang needed badly.[82]

The result was Chiang's order to his commanders in Manchuria to halt their offensive and, for the time being, to end the fighting there because Marshall at once extended the truce in northern China to Manchuria. The Communists were elated and warmly welcomed Marshall's representative to Harbin, where he had been sent as head of a tripartite truce team to ensure that the fighting in Manchuria ended.[83] As for the Nationalists, even Ch'en Ch'eng, Chiang's chief of staff, whom Marshall regarded as friendlier than most of Chiang's generals, observed that "it was a hell of a poor way to fight a war."[84] Another Nationalist general in charge of a province in Manchuria was more explicit: "If I fight the Communists I might lose half my province," he observed, "but in this peace I will lose it all."[85]

The end of the Nationalist drive on Harbin represented the beginning of the "falling action" for Chiang's forces in Manchuria. Although fighting there began again in a few months and continued for two more years, the Nationalist armies in Manchuria never regained anything approaching the advantage they enjoyed early in the summer of 1946. Ultimately, what happened there during that summer not only cost them a military victory in Manchuria but resulted in their utter defeat there and in the rest of China.[86]

DONALD G. GILLIN AND RAMON H. MYERS

NOTES

1. Ramon H. Myers, *The Japanese Economic Development of Manchuria 1932–1945* (New York and London: Garland Publishing, Inc., 1982).

2. U.S. Department of State, *The White Paper on China (August 1949)*, vol. 1 (Stanford, California: Stanford University Press, 1967), p. ix.

3. Tang Tsou, *America's Failure in China, 1941–1950*, vol. 1 (Chicago: University of Chicago Press, 1967), pp. 338–40.

4. Steven I. Levine, *Anvil of Victory: The Communist Revolution in Manchuria, 1945–1948* (New York: Columbia University Press, 1987), pp. 69–70.

5. After President Chiang Kai-shek assigned Chang Kia-ngau to head the economic committee (a component of the Nationalist government's commission to recover the Northeast from occupation by the Soviet Union), Chang Kia-ngau began keeping a detailed diary. This diary recorded his observations and activities during the period he was involved with the central government to recover northeastern China from the control of the Soviet Union. Chang gave his diary to the Hoover Institution, along with other personal papers and materials, on July 29, 1974. He asked that the Hoover Institution Archives impose a ten-year restriction whereby the diary would not be revealed to anyone. The translation appearing in this volume is based on that original, handwritten diary, which has the title *Tung-pei chieh-shou chiao-she jih-chi: i-chiu ssu-wu, pa, ehr-shih-san ch'-i-chiu ssu-liu, ssu, san-shih chih* [My Diary of the Negotiations to Recover Northeast China: August 23, 1945–April 30, 1946]. It seems that Chang began keeping a fragmentary journal in 1917 at age 29. In fact, the journal that Chang kept throughout his life, as well as a copy of the diary contained in the Hoover Institution Archives, has been published in Yang Sung-ling, ed., *Chang Kung-ch'uan hsien-sheng nien-p'u ch'u-kao* [First Draft of a Yearly Chronology for Mr. Chang Kung-ch'uan], vol. 1 (Taipei: Biographical Literature Press, 1982). We do not know how Mr. Yang acquired a copy of the original diary. Chang's journal continues up to his death, a few days short of 90, on October 18, 1979; the last entry is dated September 1, 1979. See Yang Sung-ling, *Chang Kung-ch'uan*, vol. 2, p. 1373. (That source will be cited hereafter as *NP*, with appropriate volume and page references.)

6. *NP*, vol. 1, p. 32.

7. Ibid., vol. 2, p. 1345.

8. *NP*, vol. 1, pp. 11–12.

9. Ibid., vol. 2, p. 1345.

10. Howard L. Boorman and Richard C. Howard (eds.), *Biographical Dictionary of Republican China*, vol. 1 (New York: Columbia University Press, 1967), p. 27. Also *NP*, vol. 1, p. 27.

11. This insight is contrary to the interpretation given by Sterling Seagrave in his best-selling book *The Soong Dynasty*. Seagrave would have his readers think that Chiang and Chang became lifelong enemies, an assumption the diary proves false. Further evidence of this was provided by Mr. L. K. K'ung on the basis of a conversation with his father, who was well informed concerning the relationship between Chang Kia-ngau and T. V. Soong. His remarks make far more sense than anything Seagrave has to say. See also Donald G. Gillin, *Falsifying China's History: The Case of Sterling Seagrave's "The Soong Dynasty"* (Stanford: Hoover Institution Press, 1986), pp. 8–9.

12. See Chang Kia-ngau's currency reform plan in *NP*, vol. 2, pp. 1412–26. Scholars seeking to understand the complex conditions of China's postwar monetary and financial world in 1947 are advised to consult Chang's diary; see *NP*, vol. 2, pp. 783–938 in particular.

13. Franz H. Michael and George E. Taylor, *The Far East in the Modern World*, rev. ed. (New York: Holt, Rinehart and Winston, 1964), pp. 444–45.

14. Ibid., p. 445.

15. Michael and Taylor, *The Far East*, p. 440.

16. Immanuel C. Y. Hsü, *The Rise of Modern China* (New York: Oxford University Press, 1970), p. 734.

17. Ibid., pp. 734–38.

18. Hsü, *The Rise of Modern China*, p. 721.

19. Chiang Chung-cheng (Chiang Kai-shek), *Soviet Russia in China: A Summing-Up at Seventy* (Taipei: China Publishing Company, 1969), pp. 234–35.

20. Ibid., p. 246. Chiang felt in retrospect that the Nationalists should not have tried to take over Manchuria in the first place.

21. Chiang, *Soviet Russia in China*, pp. 245–46.

22. U.S. Department of State, *The White Paper on China*, vol. 1, p. xlv.

23. Ibid., p. 122.

24. U.S. Department of State, *White Paper*, vol. 1, p. 147.

25. Ibid.

26. U.S. Department of State, *White Paper*, vol. 1, p. 149.

27. Ibid., p. 131.

28. U.S. Department of State, *White Paper*, vol. 1, p. 122.

29. Tang Tsou, *America's Failure in China* (Chicago: University of Chicago Press, 1963), vol. 1, p. 328.

30. Ibid., p. 329.

31. Tang, *America's Failure in China*, vol. 1, p. 330.

32. Ibid., p. 331.

33. Tang, *America's Failure in China*, vol. 1, p. 333.

34. Ibid., pp. 335–36.

35. Tang, *America's Failure in China*, vol. 1, p. 337.

36. Ibid.

37. Tang, *America's Failure in China*, vol. 1, p. 338.

38. Levine, *Anvil of Victory*.

39. Ibid., p. 79.

40. U.S. Department of State, *White Paper* (August 1949), vol. 2, p. 589.

41. George Moorad, *Lost Peace in China* (New York, 1949), pp. 137–38 and p. 161 and O. Borisov, *The Soviet Union and the Manchurian Revolutionary Base* (Moscow, 1975), pp. 70–71 and p. 254.

42. See Levine, *Anvil of Victory*, chap. 6.

43. Keith Eiler (ed.), *Wedemeyer on War and Peace* (Stanford: Hoover Institution Press, 1987), pp. 147; Moorad, *Lost Peace in China*, pp. 160–61; *Newsweek*, March 18, 1946, p. 51; *New Yorker*, December 8, 1951, p. 110; *Time*, December 3, 1965, p.

3; and Chin Tien-jung, *Ta-lu i-chiu* [Memories of the Mainland], *T'ien-wen t'ai* [Observatory Review], February 2, 1965, p. 3 and February 6, 1965, p. 3.

44. Levine, *Anvil of Victory*, p. 151.

45. Ibid., p. 182.

46. *New York Times*, August 10, 1971, p. 15:8.

47. The translator translated these references as "Communists" because she felt Chang Kia-ngau's term was needlessly pejorative.

48. It should be noted that, on the basis of one diary entry, an exception to this would be the American-educated son of Sun Yat-sen, Sun Fo, the leader of the legislative branch of the Nationalist government, who expressed to Chang Kia-ngau his unreserved support for the effort to negotiate an agreement with the Russians. But in no respect was he as influential as Soong; in fact, the diary mentions him only once.

49. Ray Huang, Memoirs, vol. 12, pp. 8–9. Huang was adjutant to General Cheng Tung-kuo, one of the Nationalist commanders, but his memoirs have not been published.

50. Levine, *Anvil of Victory*, p. 54.

51. See the diary entry for April 25; Lyman P. Van Slyke (ed.), *Marshall's Mission to China* (Arlington, Va.: University Publications of America, 1976), p. xxix; and a September, 1986 interview with General Albert C. Wedemeyer, who commanded U.S. troops in China for nearly two years before Marshall's arrival. Wedemeyer, who maintained close liaison with the Nationalist armies, feels that in 1945–1946 neither he, Marshall, nor any other U.S. officer in China had sufficient knowledge of the military situation there to venture an informed assessment of its future course.

52. Levine, *Anvil of Victory*, pp. 112–13.

53. Brian Crozier, *The Man Who Lost China* (New York: C. Scribner, 1976), p. 339.

54. Levine, *Anvil of Victory*, pp. 223, 263; and Chao Chia-hsiang, *Chao Chia-hsiang chiang-chün shih wen-chi* [Poetry and Essays of General Chao Chia-hsiang] (Taipei, 1960), p. 63. (General Chao was perhaps the most respected Manchurian general attached to the Chinese mission in Ch'ang-ch'un.)

55. In his entry for April 8, Chang included his lengthy plan on where and in what industries economic cooperation would apply and the principles underlying that cooperation.

56. Levine, *Anvil of Victory*, p. 79.

57. The words *when we have defeated the Communists* in this paragraph are puzzling. It is likely that Chang meant *if we defeat the Communists*, but even this implies that, as late as the end of March, the Soviets felt the Nationalists might still vanquish the communist armies. In Manchuria, this is what happened, with an almost decisive Nationalist victory over the Communists at Ssu-p'ing in June 1946. Significantly, although the Nationalists had broken off negotiations with the Russians after the Chinese Communists seized Ch'ang-ch'un in April, the Soviets proposed resuming those talks immediately after the Nationalist victory at Ssu-p'ing, a course

Chiang Kai-shek refused to take. See Chiang, *Soviet Russia in China*, pp. 147–48; and William Whitson, *The Chinese High Command* (New York: Praeger, 1973), pp. 84–85.

58. John K. Fairbank, *The Great Chinese Revolution, 1800–1985* (New York: Harper & Row, 1986), p. 246.

59. Ibid.

60. Robert Rigg, *Red China's Fighting Hordes* (Harrisburg, Pa.: Military Service Publishing, 1951), p 191.

61. Liu Pai-yü, *Li-shih te pao feng-yü* [Historic Upheavals] (Shanghai: Shanghai Magazine Company, 1949), p. 8.

62. John Beal, *Marshall in China* (Toronto, Canada: Doubleday, 1970), p. 66.

63. Liu Shaw Tong, *Out of Red China* (New York: Duell, Sloan and Pearce, 1953), pp. 122–23.

64. Rigg, *Red China's Fighting Hordes*, p. 190; Chiang Kai-shek, *Soviet Russia in China* (New York: Farrar, Straus and Giroux, 1976), p. 177; and Ray Huang, "Some Observations on Manchuria in the Balance, Early 1946," *Pacific Historical Review*, May 1958, p. 166.

65. Beal, *Marshall in China*, pp. 66–67 and interview with Ray Huang, April 1968. Huang interviewed Lin Piao's chief of operations after his surrender.

66. Liu Mien, *Lun Nan Pei Ch'ao* [On the Northern and Southern Dynasties] (Hong Kong: Free Literature Press, 1947?), p. 4 and Huang, Memoirs, vol. 12, p. 25.

67. Beal, *Marshall in China*, p. 162. (The reporter was Eric Chou, of the relatively independent newspaper *Ta Kung Pao*.)

68. See ibid., p. 65.

69. Huang, Memoirs, vol. 12, p. 30; *Hung-ch'i p'iao-p'iao* [The Red Flag Waves], vol. 14 (China Youth Publishing Co.), pp. 133–36; Liu Pai-yü, *Ying-hsiung te chi-lu* [Reminiscences of Heroes] (Harbin: Harbin Northeastern Bookstore, 1947), pp. 4–8; General Ch'en Po-chun, *Ping-lin ch'eng-hsia: hui-yi chie-fang Pei-ping* [The Seige—Recollections of the Liberation of Peiping].

70. Chiang, *Soviet Russia in China*, pp. 147–48 and Whitson, *Chinese High Command*, pp. 84–85.

71. Huang, Memoirs, vol. 12, p. 31.

72. Whitson, *Chinese High Command*, p. 304.

73. Huang, "Some Observations on Manchuria," p. 166.

74. Rigg, *Red China's Fighting Hordes*, p. 192.

75. Ibid., p. 202.

76. "Chairman Mao's Successor—Deputy Commander Lin Piao," *Current Background*, no. 894, p. 17 and Edward Rice, *Mao's Way* (Berkeley: University of California Press, 1974), p. 117.

77. Rice, *Mao's Way*, p. 117; Tang, *America's Failure in China*, p. 427; and James Harrison, *The Long March to Power: A History of the Chinese Communist Party* (New York: Praeger, 1972), p. 402.

78. Chin Tien-jung, "Chiu-i ta-lu" [Remembering the Mainland], *T'ien-wen t'ai* [The Observatory Review], December 14, 1965. Chin served as chief of logistics for the Nationalist armies in Manchuria during much of the civil war. Also Huang, Memoirs, vol. 12, p. 35.

79. Tong Te-kong, "Report on Supplementary Research on the Memoirs of Li Tsung-jen" (New York: Columbia University East Asian Institute, 1965, mimeo), p. 1.

80. Chiang, *Soviet Russia in China*, p. 177.

81. For example, see Chao Chia-hsiang, *Chiang-chün shih wen-chi* [Historical Works of the General] (Taipei: Committee for the Posthumous Publication of General Chao's Works, 1960), p. 3. (Chao was a general attached to Chiang Kai-shek's headquarters in Ch'ang-ch'un.) Beal, *Marshall in China*, pp. 158–59 and Christopher Rand, writing in the *New York Herald Tribune*, reproduced in *Catholic World*, March 1949, p. 425.

82. Levine, *Anvil of Victory*, p. 84. Levine's source is the *Foreign Relations Papers of the United States for 1946*, Washington, D.C.: Government Printing Office.

83. Chou Erh-fu, *Tung-pei heng-tuan-mien* [Expedition to the Northeast] (Chinjih: Current Press, 1946), pp. 155–57.

84. Beal, *Marshall in China*, pp. 176 and 158.

85. Anna Louise Strong, *The Chinese Conquer China* (Garden City, N.J.: Doubleday, 1949), p. 72.

86. The degree to which the revelations in Chang Kia-ngau's diary alter our previous understanding of what happened in Manchuria in 1945 and 1946 is best seen by contrasting them with the account of those events on pages 726 to 734 of the recently published thirteenth volume, part two, of *The Cambridge History of China: Republican China 1912–1949* (Cambridge, Eng.: Cambridge University Press, 1986). This account strongly emphasizes the role of the United States in Nationalist efforts to establish themselves in Manchuria while it was occupied by the Russians; however, the diary shows that, except for airlifting a few thousand Nationalist troops into Soviet-held Ch'ang-ch'un and landing a few thousand more at the remote seaport of Ying-k'ou, U.S. assistance played no role whatsoever in these efforts. Far more important is the omission from the *Cambridge History* of any mention of the prolonged negotiations between Chiang Kai-shek's government and the Soviet Union's over joint management of Manchuria's industrial economy, which, as the diary amply demonstrates, was a principal concern of both governments. The account in the *Cambridge History* fails to assess the significance of the Soviet stance in these negotiations, which would indicate that, until Marshall imposed his truce in January 1946, the Russians were convinced that the Nationalists were winning the civil war in North China. There is also no mention of the effect of that truce or of any of Marshall's other actions in China on the Russian attitude toward the Nationalists' situation in Manchuria. The diary shows that this had a devastating impact on Chiang Kai-shek's government. Moreover, despite a paucity of information on the happenings in Manchuria during 1945 and early 1946, the *Cambridge History* makes much of Nationalist reluctance to have Marshall's truce teams enter Manchuria. The diary, however,

shows how the activities of those teams in the Northeast tended to legitimize the presence of the Chinese Communists there and reflected Marshall's bias against the Nationalists in their struggle with the Communists. Finally, when describing events in Manchuria immediately following the conclusion of the diary, the account in the *Cambridge History* underemphasizes the military importance of the Nationalist victory over the Communists at Ssu-p'ing, as well as Marshall's role in denying Chiang Kai-shek's government the fruits of that victory.

THE DIARY OF CHANG KIA-NGAU

Preparing for Manchuria

Chang Kia-ngau, while representing the Republic of China (ROC) at an international conference in Canada in mid-August 1945, is recalled to Chungking, the wartime capital of the ROC, to become chairman of the newly established northeastern Economic Commission. The ROC government created this commission to study the economic resources of Manchuria and to facilitate the Nationalist recovery of China's three eastern provinces (Manchuria, called Manchukuo under Japanese rule) from the troops of the Soviet Union. Soviet troops had just occupied that large region of China when the Soviet Union declared war against Japan on August 15, 1945.

Before returning to China on September 8, 1945, Chang Kia-ngau confers with leading U.S. government officials in Washington, D.C., about China's postwar economic recovery, particularly Manchuria's.

After arriving in Chungking on September 14, Chang Kia-ngau meets with leading ROC officials about the Soviet military occupation of Manchuria and the recent negotiations between Nationalist China and the Soviet Union. Chang learns that the ROC and the Soviet Union have not come to any agreement on how the Chinese government will recover Manchuria from Soviet troop occupation. The Ministry of Foreign Affairs informs Chang of a Soviet memorandum announcing that Soviet troops would be withdrawn from Manchuria during the last half of October 1945 and that Marshal Rodion Malinovsky is in charge of all Soviet military and civilian personnel.

On October 20 Chang Kia-ngau consults with President Chiang Kai-shek and submits his list of the nine officials he wants to serve on the northeastern Economic Commission. President Chiang approves the list. Chang Kia-ngau leaves for Ch'ang-ch'un, Manchuria, on October 10.

+ + + + + + +

On August 23, 1945, while I was representing the government at the International Civil Aviation Conference being held in Canada I received a communication from General Secretary Wang Hsüeh-t'ing conveying President Chiang's request that I speedily return. Meanwhile, I had received a wire from Chang Yueh-chün also requesting that I return at once. I did not know what mission awaited me. On September 1 Ch'ien I-li came to tell me that the government had designated me chairman of the northeastern Economic Commission. On September 8 I left the United States by plane, crossing the Atlantic, and returned to China via Casablanca, Cairo, Karachi, and Calcutta. I found that the newspapers already had published the news that I was to be chairman of the board of directors of the Ch'ang-ch'un Railroad, as well as chairman of the northeastern Economic Commission. I arrived in Chungking on September 14. On the fifteenth President Chiang invited me for lunch. He told me that he had had the appointments published without first consulting me. This had placed me in a very embarrassing situation. He said the positions carried with them heavy responsibilities, that it had not been easy for him to find a suitable person, and urged me to accept. I asked to be given time for consideration. Immediately after, I wrote a summary of the economic policies that should be pursued following the takeover of the Northeast and an outline for the organization of the Economic Commission. I also stated that I was willing to hold these positions only until after the takeover was accomplished.

This I submitted to the president on September 19. On the twentieth President Chiang again invited me for lunch and I reiterated that I would hold the positions only temporarily. I requested that, following the completion of the takeover, he appoint other persons. After learning on September 1 that I would be given a mission in the Northeast, in order to better prepare myself, I had exchanged views with different persons in the United States government. On September 6 at 12:30 P.M. Secretary of the Treasury Fred Vinson talked with me at the Treasury Department. Our discussion concerned questions having to do with China's finances and economy. The general tenor of his words was,

America's aim in the future is to maintain peace, prosperity, and security in the world. It is our hope that the various nations will jointly contribute to this goal. The United States government is anxious to aid friendly nations; however, at present we are constrained by the political situation. Our own expenditures are vast and complicated, so that everything must be approved by the Congress. We hope for an early stabilization of the Chinese political situation.

He inquired about the future situation in China. I replied that the following were of the greatest importance: (1) regulation of the currency (2) economic construction (3) with respect to foreign relations, the establishment of good economic relationships. His response was "The most important thing is still the regulation of the currency. Until this is done economic life cannot return to normal. As for economic construction, let it develop gradually instead of rampantly, like mushrooms." Finally I told him that I did not yet know what kind of task I would be assuming in the future and that I might need to consult him from time to time. Vinson's answer was "I'll be glad to help at any time."

On September 5 at 9:30 A.M. Secretary of Commerce Henry A. Wallace talked with me at the Commerce Department. In response to my inquiry about his opinions concerning the Northeast Wallace said,

The essence of the Sino-Soviet treaty signed by China is basically the same as that I discussed with President Chiang while I was in Chungking and that President Roosevelt told President Chiang about twelve months ago. What is most important is to help the peasants improve their agricultural techniques so that their living standards can be maintained and raised. Then the people in the Northeast naturally will support the central government. Otherwise, like the people in Outer Mongolia, they will gradually lean toward the Soviet Union because of their gratitude for various kinds of Soviet help. To sum up the situation, whether the government now can recover entirely in the Northeast depends on the soundness and wisdom of the administrative measures that the government puts into effect there.

On September 6 at 4:00 P.M. Under Secretary of State Dean Acheson talked with me at the State Department. There also were present two persons in charge of economics: Thorp, assistant to Under Secretary Clayton, and Sumner, an economic adviser. I proposed that when the United States government re-established its consulate in the Northeast it also dispatch there three specialists: one in the field of agriculture, one in industry, and one in finance. This would make possible timely consultations with respect to agriculture, industry, and finance. Acheson fully endorsed my suggestion. I then talked privately with Thorp. He was deeply worried about the fact that industry in the Northeast was under the control of the Natural Resources Commission. This meant that such industry was state-owned, creating a situation that by contradicting the U.S. policy of encouraging private enterprise would make it difficult to attract foreign capital. He expressed the hope that the central government would give this issue its attention. He also asked whether we had entered into any treaty with the Soviets concerning the joint management of industry.

On September 4 at 4:00 P.M. John Carter Vincent, chief of the Far Eastern Division of the State Department, talked with me at the department. I first asked him whether the United States regarded the Northeast as part of the Soviet sphere of influence. He replied,

> I attended the Potsdam Conference and know that we absolutely did not agree to such a situation. The United States does not regard the Northeast as part of either the Soviet sphere of influence or the American sphere of influence. We hope that with respect to its decrees and measures having to do with the economy of the Northeast the central government will take into consideration local conditions. When called for, special treatment may be necessary to some extent, but it must not be allowed to foster disunity. In other words, within the framework of unity room must be left for special considerations but divisiveness must be avoided.

He then added that the U.S. consulate in the Northeast soon would be established.

On September 5 at 3:00 P.M. Harry D. White, assistant under secretary of the Treasury, talked with me at the Treasury Department. When I asked him for his views concerning the currency of the Northeast he replied,

> If the currency circulating in Manchuria is higher in value than the national currency you can only, for the time being, continue to use the currency in circulation and wait for the reform of the Chinese currency to take place before withdrawing the present currency from circulation. But a ratio must be fixed between the currency now in circulation and the national currency so that the national currency is somewhat devalued. For example, if 1 yuan of Manchurian currency is valued at 50 yuan of national currency, then the ratio should be fixed at 25 yuan for 1 yuan. As for Japanese deposits, these must be liquidated without exception but without interfering with trade. Concerning the question of the Chinese currency, the essential point is to resolve the conflict with the communist party, since as long as civil strife continues goods cannot flow freely, foreign capital cannot enter, and therefore the value of the currency cannot be stabilized.

Irving Friedman, a specialist in currency in the Treasury Department, had studied Chinese finance. Therefore, I took advantage of this occasion to talk with him. He said that if China chose to impose strict foreign exchange controls, then, because at present its foreign exchange reserves already are sizeable, these would be sufficient to support the currency in circulation. However, if it chose to relax its foreign exchange controls it must give first priority to balancing its international accounts, while at the same time improving China's taxation system for the purpose of avoiding an excessive budget deficit.

On September 6 at 2:45 P.M. I talked with Hudson, under secretary of Agriculture, and Moore, head of the Foreign Cooperation Bureau, at the Department of Agriculture. I first asked Mr. Hudson whether it would be possible for the Department of Agriculture to assign a specialist to the staff of the U.S. consulate so that when we encountered problems concerning agriculture we might obtain timely advice of a nonofficial character. Hudson replied that it would be difficult for someone at the same time to both perform consular duties and also advise the Chinese government. On the other hand, Moore fully approved of my idea and said that there existed precedents for this in Central and South America.

On September 4 at 10:00 A.M. I spoke with Charles Moser, chief of the Far Eastern Unit of the Department of Commerce, at the Department of Commerce. Moser said that the commercial and industrial enterprises in the Northeast should be owned by the people because any other arrangement would conflict with traditional U.S. policy. When I asked if the United States was still maintaining an Open Door policy, Moser said that, of course, U.S. businessmen certainly would return and revive the enterprises they had owned in the Northeast before the war. As for long-term U.S. investment in the Northeast, this would have to be determined by China's economic policies and what safeguards such investment would enjoy. He added that Manchuria was known for its agricultural wealth and that if it proved difficult to export certain products, they might first be processed and then marketed.

On September 5 at 11:00 A.M. I talked with Wayne Taylor, president of the Import and Export Bank, at the bank. In response to my question about the principles concerning loans to the Northeast, he said that the first condition was that there be guarantees that both the principal and the interest (of all loans) be paid in foreign exchange. The second condition was the practicality of the plan, and the third was that there must be a guarantor. He said that since the Bank of China had a branch in America, that branch should be the organization to issue a guarantee.

On September 14, after arriving in Chungking, I began inquiring among the authorities there concerned with foreign affairs whether, since the signing of the Sino-Soviet treaty, there had been discussions with the Soviets about specific takeover procedures. I then learned that there had been only an exchange of documents with respect to two issues: the withdrawal of Soviet troops and the replacement of the Soviet garrison by our troops.

There had been no agreement about how our troops were going to enter Manchuria, how our officials will take over and establish the government's authority, or how the economic enterprises will be transferred to us. The government had presumed that all problems would naturally be resolved once our troops had arrived in the Northeast. In September, the Chinese Foreign Ministry received a Soviet memorandum, delivered by the Soviet ambassador to China, stating that (1) The Soviet High Command already had begun a partial withdrawal of Soviet troops from the three northeastern provinces. (2) The bulk of the Soviet Army will begin to withdraw from the three northeastern provinces during the latter half of October of this year so as to complete the withdrawal by the end of November of the same year. (3) The Soviet government already has appointed Marshal Malinovsky to be its delegate plenipotentiary in the negotiations over the withdrawal of Soviet troops from the Northeast. Between October 10 and October 15 Marshal Malinovsky will discuss this same issue in Ch'ang-ch'un with the properly appointed delegate plenipotentiary of the Chinese High Command. The Foreign Ministry responded by notifying the Soviet ambassador that the Chinese government had appointed General Hsiung Shih-hui to be chairman of the Military Affairs Commission in Manchuria and head of its northeastern headquarters—i.e., the representative of the Chinese national government in the Northeast. On October 3 Vice-Minister of Foreign Affairs Kan Chieh-hou further notified the Soviet ambassador that Chairman Hsiung would be able to reach Ch'ang-ch'un on or around the tenth of this month and requested that Soviet troops begin gradually to withdraw as soon as our troops arrived in the Northeast to replace the Soviet garrison.

During the three weeks between September 19, when I submitted my summary to President Chiang, and October 10, when I left Chungking for the Northeast, there were two joint conferences of the Administrative and Economic commissions. One was held on the 22 of September and the other, on September 28. Both conferences dealt with measures for taking over the Northeast, but no instructions were known to have been issued by the foreign affairs authorities concerning how the Soviet Union was going to transfer political power or how it was going to hand over to us economic enterprises in its possession. Most likely, our foreign affairs authorities, as well as Chairman Hsiung, assumed that there would be no problem at all concerning the withdrawal of Soviet troops and did not make an intensive study of the phrase, contained in the Soviet ambassador's summary: "Negotiations about the question of the withdrawal of Soviet troops from the three northeastern provinces."

I was not well informed about the past history of Sino-Soviet negotiations. I only acquired a certain amount of indirect knowledge from the following persons:

Shen Ch'eng-chang, who took part in the conference on the Sino-Soviet treaty in Moscow. When I called on him on September 25, he told me that during the discussions for the Sino-Soviet treaty the leader of our delegation was so eager for the conference to succeed that he did not make a careful study of the various details. He especially was totally unprepared to present our views with respect to how the boundary line with Outer Mongolia should be drawn.

Petrov, the Soviet ambassador to China. On September 25 the head of the Northeast Headquarters, Hsiung Shih-hui, gave a banquet for Ambassador Petrov. After getting acquainted, I called on Petrov at 3:00 P.M. the next day and we talked for about an hour. He told me that,

> On September 24 the Soviet command in the Northeast began issuing its own military currency. They have been forced to do so because while he was in the Soviet Union discussing the Sino-Soviet treaty, T.V. Soong, the president of the Executive Yuan of the Chinese national government, rejected Stalin's proposal that the Chinese government assume the expenses of the Soviet occupation forces. As for fixing the ratio between this military currency and the Chinese national currency, this is being negotiated with the Chinese Ministry of Finance.

Upon my hearing this, a question arose in my mind: were the Soviet troops really going to withdraw immediately? Because if the takeover could begin immediately after our arrival, the time required would only be two or three weeks. Then why was it necessary to issue military currency? Therefore, I inquired at the Foreign Ministry. The ministry then prepared and sent me a summary of the proceedings which, briefly, were as follows:

> On August 9 of this year Chinese ambassador to the Soviet Union Fu sent a message saying that the Soviet Foreign Ministry personally had notified him that by now the Soviet troops had been in Manchuria for three weeks and constantly were in need of cash to purchase grain for the army and for other things. The Soviet government has now instructed the Red Army command in Manchuria to issue bank notes for use in China. Their form and color are to differ slightly from those of the national currency, and their amount is to be sufficient for the needs of the Red Army for three months. They are to be recalled by China in the future and replaced through payments from Japanese indemnities, etc. We then submitted this message to the president for approval and also wired Ambassador Fu, asking him to find out from the Soviet Foreign Ministry the amount of currency that the Red Army command intended to issue. On September 1 Minister of Foreign Affairs Wang also personally notified the Soviet ambassador of this. On September 15 Ambassador Fu again wired, saying that the Soviet government had appointed Petrov, its ambassador to China, as delegate plenipotentiary to

discuss and formulate with our government an agreement on ways in which China and the Soviet Union would meet the expenses of the Red Army on Chinese soil. On the same day Miklashevsky, a counselor in the Soviet embassy, delivered to this ministry in person a draft of a financial agreement that had been formulated by the Soviets. We have signed it and submitted to the president a request that Minister of Finance Yü be appointed a delegate to enter into discussions with the Soviets.

Upon reading the words "to be sufficient for the needs of the Red Army for three months" I felt relieved.

During our talk on the same day, Ambassador Petrov also mentioned that, in accordance with the Sino-Soviet treaty, regulations concerning the joint management of the Ch'ang-ch'un Railroad should be discussed together by three delegates from each side, within one month after the signing of the treaty, and then submitted to both governments for their endorsement within two months. As for which assets of the Ch'ang-ch'un Railroad should belong to the jointly managed company, this likewise should be discussed by three delegates from each side. A decision should be reached within three months and submitted to both governments for their endorsement. Both committees must meet in Chungking. "We hope that China will act according to the treaty." Then he added "The chairman of the board of directors of the Ch'ang-ch'un Railroad will shoulder heavy responsibilities having to do with politics and economics. I hope Your Excellency will enjoy great success." The tone of his words implied that the Soviets regarded the chairman of the board of directors of the Ch'ang-ch'un Railroad as comparable to the general manager of the Manchurian railroads under the Japanese. All political and economic concerns of China and the Soviet Union concerning the Northeast are thrust on the chairman of the board of directors alone, suggesting that the Soviets regard the future Northeast just as the Japanese had regarded the three northeastern provinces before the creation of Manchukuo. Taking over does not mean that we're going to get back the Northeast.

Words of Chiang Ching-kuo, special envoy of the Ministry of Foreign Affairs: At 5:00 P.M. on September 20 Special Envoy Chiang came and said that the period for Sino-Soviet joint management of the Ch'ang-ch'un Railroad clearly had been designated as 30 years but that control of the railroad might very well pass to China before the end of that period. This will depend on whether we can adequately tackle the responsibility. Future development of industry in the Northeast must be considered as part of the industry of the entire country, and planning for it must not be done independently. Ching-kuo took part in the conference on the Sino-Soviet treaty. I inferred from his tone that he attached great importance to the Sino-Soviet relationship in the future.

On the question of the northeastern currency, the Soviet Army already has issued its own bank notes and there was bound to be a discrepancy in value between these bank notes and the national currency. The economic and financial situation in the Northeast necessarily must differ from that in China Proper; in the Northeast the issuing of bank notes is best done independently until measures governing the regulation of the national currency have been formulated by the government. Consequently, on September 29, after discussing this matter with Finance Minister Yü Hung-chün, I obtained his approval. On October 7 I also consulted T.V. Soong, president of the Executive Yuan, and also obtained his approval. We decided to issue a special kind of bank note to be used alongside the paper bank notes currently circulating in the Northeast.

Concerning decisions made about the list of candidates for the Economic Commission of the Northeast Headquarters as well as the board of directors and board of supervisors of the Ch'ang-ch'un Railroad: On October 20 I saw President Chiang and gave him the following list of designated candidates which he approved:

Ho Lien, delegate of the Ministry of Economics

Ling Hung-hsün, delegate of the Ministry of Communications

Ch'ien T'ien-ho, delegate of the Ministry of Agriculture and Forestry

P'ang Sung-chou, delegate of the Grain Ministry

Huo Ya-min, delegate of the general office for the Four Ministries

Chang Chen-lu, Chi Shih-ying, Wang Chia-chen, and Ma Yi, representatives of the northeastern population.

The above are to be members of the Economic Commission.

In Ch'ang-ch'un, Manchuria

OCTOBER 12–31, 1945

On October 12 the Republic of China (ROC) delegation arrives by plane in Ch'ang-ch'un and is met by Soviet officers and troops led by Major General Pavlovsky. Chang Kia-ngau learns that the Soviet Army has terminated the activities of the ROC's Bank of China and Bank of Communication in Manchuria and that the Chinese delegates have no way to pay their expenses. He also learns that the Soviet Army has been collecting industrial equipment, vehicles, and even furniture to ship to the Soviet Union.

On October 13 Chairman Hsiung Shih-hui, Chang Kia-ngau, and other delegates confer with Marshal Malinovsky to discuss how soon ROC troops can move into Manchuria to take over the region from Soviet military occupation. Malinovsky is unable to offer the Chinese army any Soviet assistance, but he states that on November 20 Soviet troops in southern Manchuria will move north to Mukden and then withdraw to Harbin on November 25. ROC troops can land at Ying-k'ou but not at Dairen until both governments agree on the status of Dairen. Soviet troops also have imposed martial law and decreed that secret organizations in Manchuria should cease their activities.

Chang Kia-ngau later confides to his diary that the Soviets have concocted excuses to delay Nationalist troops from entering to recover Manchuria. In the subsequent days and weeks Chang Kia-ngau reports his meetings with local Chinese officials and learns how economic conditions have *deteriorated: there is rampant inflation and an acute shortage of energy, raw materials, and equipment.*

On October 17 the Chinese delegation again meets with Malinovsky to present its plan for the entry of Nationalist troops into Manchuria and their takeover of industries managed by Manchukuo and Japan. Malinovsky neither approves nor rejects this plan but reiterates the position he set forth at the previous meeting. He then states that all factories formerly operated by the Japanese or with the Chinese are war booty and belong to the Soviet Army. Malinovsky also urges the ROC delegation to send experts to restore postal services and communications.

Chang Kia-ngau later confides to his diary that the Soviets are still trying to prevent Nationalist troops from entering Manchuria. Chang also learns from Chiang Ching-kuo that during the negotiations of the Sino-Soviet friendship treaty, Stalin informed T. V. Soong that all special state enterprises in Manchuria should be Soviet war booty and that private Japanese firms should be returned to the Chinese. At that time Soong made no attempt to resolve this issue with Stalin.

The Chinese delegation now realizes that settling the disposition of Japanese-Manchukuo enterprises with the Soviet Union is a thorny issue that might delay the Nationalist recovery of Manchuria.

On October 21 Major General Pavlovsky meets with the Chinese team and informs the delegates that Nationalist troops cannot land at Dairen because that would violate the Sino-Soviet friendship treaty, which stipulates that Dairen is a free commercial port. But the Nationalists are free to land their troops anywhere else in southern Manchuria.

Chang Kia-ngau learns that Soviet troops have confiscated all documents belonging to the Kuomintang (KMT) party branch headquarters in Ch'ang-ch'un and have terminated that unit's activities. Soviet officials then complain to the ROC delegation that anti-Soviet activities flourish throughout Manchuria's large cities. Meanwhile, with U.S. assistance, Nationalist troops plan to land at Ying-k'ou.

On October 27 Chang Kia-ngau holds exploratory talks with M. I. Sladkovsky, the leading economic expert on the Soviet side, to discuss the disposition of Japanese economic assets. Nationalist troops try to land at Hu-lu-tao, but they are repulsed by "bandit troops" on shore.

On October 29 the Chinese delegation again meets with Malinovsky to decide how Nationalist troops can enter Manchuria, but there is still no clear resolution. Malinovsky complains of anti-Soviet activities in the large cities and hints that KMT organs are behind them. He also strongly complains about the recent entry of a U.S. warship into Dairen. Chiang Kia-ngau interprets Malinovsky's remarks to mean that fear of the Americans extend-

ing their influence into Manchuria is causing the Soviets to deliberately prevent Nationalist troops from entering Manchuria.

+ + + + + + +

One hundred and fourteen days elapsed between October 12, 1945, when I arrived in Ch'ang-ch'un, and February 2, 1946, when I returned to Chungking because of the breakdown of the Sino-Soviet negotiations. I stayed in Ch'ang-ch'un for 77 days. Altogether, it was 190 days from beginning to end. Now, I shall make a copy of my diary, kept from day to day, to be referred to by future historians.

OCTOBER 12.   This was the embarrassing situation when I arrived in Ch'ang-ch'un: On October 10 I left Chungking for Ch'ang-ch'un. At 9 the plane took off. Traveling with me were Chairman of the headquarters Hsiung Shih-hui, Foreign Affairs Special Envoy Chiang Ching-kuo, and Mo Te-hui, a member of the Political Committee of the headquarters. At 3:00 P.M. we arrived in Peiping, where we stayed two nights. At 10:30 A.M. on the twelfth we left Peiping and at 3:00 P.M. our plane arrived in Ch'ang-ch'un. As we arrived I looked down at the airport from the plane and saw that it was filled with Soviet officers and soldiers; there were few Chinese around. There to meet us on behalf of Malinovsky (commander in chief of the occupation army) was Major General Pavlovsky (vice-chief of staff of the general headquarters of the Soviet Army). Chairman Hsiung and I were lodged at the residence of the former Manchurian puppet official Ting Chien-hsiu. The place also served as our temporary office. Both our cook and bodyguard were assigned by the Soviet Army command. Since the mayor of Ch'ang-ch'un, Ts'ao Chao-yuan, and the head of its public security bureau both recently were appointed by the Soviet Army, naturally freedom of action will be difficult; neither do we know how to get in touch with local industrial and commercial circles and the personnel of various economic enterprises and organizations. It was like finding ourselves in a foreign country.

Then we found that we cannot use the national currency. Only after arriving in Ch'ang-ch'un did I learn that the Soviet Army had ordered the former Bank of China and Bank of Communications to cease business. The Northeast Headquarters, not having a cent in its pocket, has no way of obtaining funds to take care of its expenses. Although Tung Yen-p'ing, vice-chief of staff of the headquarters, was charged with the task of making all necessary arrangements prior to the stationing of the headquarters in Ch'ang-ch'un, he had arrived in Ch'ang-ch'un only three days before and, naturally, had had no time to report to the central government about actual conditions existing in Ch'ang-ch'un. Concerned ministries of the central government, especially its Foreign Affairs Ministry, still had no experience in dealing with such big issues as the taking over of lost territories. They cannot be expected to make careful and comprehensive preparations ahead of time. As a result, the takeover personnel have encountered this embarrassing situation.

On the same day I received a report saying the Soviet Army was plundering industrial equipment. At the Feng-man Large Power Plant they already have taken away six of the eight generators. In Fu-shun they already have dismantled and taken away two furnaces. They are in the process of dismantling and taking away broadcasting equipment. They also have totally removed and shipped away the furniture and automobiles belonging to various organizations. Prices in Ch'ang-ch'un are rather low, but there is a shortage of goods. The highest price for [the name of the commodity has been left out] ordinary household use is approximately one thousand yuan [dollars] in army bank notes.

On the same evening the three of us, Chairman Hsiung, Special Envoy Chiang, and I, formulated the procedure for negotiating with the Soviets:

1. We shall request that communications be speedily restored, that we be given means of transportation, and that the safety of the personnel of the headquarters be guaranteed.

2. They should provide us with a number of military planes and a number of army uniforms.

3. We should be given accommodations for air transportation in the Northeast.

OCTOBER 13.　　At 3:00 P.M., together with Vice-Chief of Staff Tung Yen-p'ing, Chairman Hsiung, and Special Envoy Chiang, I went to the general headquarters of the Soviet Army to call on Marshal Malinovsky. This was our first talk. First, Chairman Hsiung stated that the headquarters is in charge of the takeover of political and economic affairs in the Northeast. He expressed the hope that the Soviets would give us friendly assistance. He also brought up the following five items:

1. He inquired about Soviet procedures for evacuating their troops.

2. He informed them that we shall transport troops to the Northeast by sea to take over the defense there. We intend to land these troops at Dairen, Ying-k'ou, Antung, and Hu-lu-tao and request that the Soviets assist us. We also are preparing to airlift a small force of troops to Mukden, Ch'ang-ch'un, etc., and we need to set up air traffic control stations in these places. We also request Soviet assistance in this.

3. We hope that communications in the Northeast soon can be restored so that, after their arrival, our troops can be transported to various places and our administrative personnel reach such places to take over.

4. Our administrative personnel for various provinces and cities in the Northeast are already arriving. They will be going to these provinces and cities to take over administrative organizations there. We request Soviet assistance in this.

5. We request that the Soviets lend us trains, airplanes, and ships for the transportation of Chinese troops and that they also allocate to us for use by our headquarters personnel a portion of the motor vehicles left behind by the Japanese.

Malinovsky replied as follows:

1. With respect to the issue of evacuating Soviet troops, this could not be accomplished speedily because railroad rolling stock either was damaged by the Japanese or shipped by them to Korea, while the highways have been damaged. But we have decided on a general procedure, as follows: Beginning on November 20 troops stationed in southern Manchuria will be evacuated northward to Mukden. On the twenty-fifth they will be evacuated from Mukden to Harbin. On the thirtieth they will be withdrawn beyond the Chinese national border.

2. With respect to our landing at Dairen, the issue should be settled between the two governments. As for our landing in the Antung region, the Soviets are unable to express an opinion since this is not under their jurisdiction. There is no problem concerning our landing at Ying-k'ou and Hu-lu-tao. He also expressed the opinion that we should transport our troops into the Northeast by rail. As for our setting up air traffic control stations in Mukden, Ch'ang-ch'un, Dairen, and Harbin, he first must ask for instructions from Moscow.

3. Currently, railroads everywhere in the Northeast are busy transporting Soviet troops. Furthermore, plague has been discovered in Po-ke-na and K'o-erh-ch'in-yu-i-ch'ien-ch'i so that passenger trains cannot pass through.

4. Concerning the question of our taking over administrative organizations in various places, martial law has obliged the Soviet Army to take charge of such administration. Moreover, former administrative personnel in various places have fled or have been dismissed and replaced by the Soviet Army because their actions were not in the interests of the Soviet Army. Mukden and Jehol are examples. As a result, he also must

ask Moscow for instructions concerning our taking over administrative power in various places.

5. With regard to the Soviets providing us with vehicles for transportation, the Soviets always have been short of seagoing vessels, so they are in no position to help us. As for Soviet transport planes, these all were bought from the United States and are limited in number, so that it is difficult for the Soviets to spare any. But this issue can be negotiated between the two governments on the basis of the Sino-Soviet treaty. Very few automobiles were left behind by the enemy.

He gave extremely muddled answers concerning the three issues about economics that I raised:

1. In response to our request that he allocate to us a portion of the bank notes issued by the Manchurian Central Bank and left behind by the enemy, Malinovsky said that we should state in writing the sum we needed. Then they will consider and deal with the matter.

2. In response to our request that he permit the Bank of China and the Commercial Bank to resume business in various places, Malinovsky said that he must seek instructions from his superiors.

3. When I requested that he allow us to take over the Manchurian puppet regime's printing bureau, Malinovsky replied that he also must seek instructions from his superiors.

Last, Malinovsky issued a warning to our delegation, saying that our secret organizations in the Northeast must cease their activities; if not, severe measures would be taken against them.

My Analysis of the First Talk with Malinovsky

The Soviets have no intention of actively supporting the transportation of our troops into the Northeast. Moreover, they want us to transport our troops by rail, knowing that communist troops at Shan-hai-kuan have cut rail communication between Manchuria and China Proper. Implicit here is an unwillingness to have us send a large number of troops into the Northeast.

The Soviets have devised excuses to delay our taking over local administrative organizations. They also say communications are still being obstructed in various places. It seems that the Soviets are still engaging in activities or arrangements in various places that they do not want us to know about. The plague that has been discovered in Po-ke-na and K'o-erh-ch'in-yu-i-ch'ien-ch'i, as well as the dismissal and replacement of administrative personnel in Jehol, makes me wonder whether the Soviets have other plans for Inner Mongolia and Jehol.

The restrictions that the Soviets have placed on our secret organizations seem to indicate that until Soviet troops evacuate the Northeast politically and militarily, we will not be allowed the least bit of freedom of action there. Does their clear-cut announcement of the dates for the evacuation of their troops mean that the Soviets already have definite plans and are going to implement these before they leave?

Note: Malinovsky was born in Odessa. During World War I he voluntarily joined the army. Afterward he graduated from the Frunze Military Academy. During World War II, for a time he was commander of the Byelorussian army, commanding it during its retreat from the Germans. Later, he defeated the enemy near T'e-na-pu-lo-pien-t'o-lo-fu-ssu-k'e. Then, as an army commander, he took part in the great battle of Stalingrad. Furthermore, on the Romanian front he broke through into Central Europe and defeated the Germans in Hungary and Czechoslovakia. For this he was promoted to marshal and subsequently became commander of the First Front Army in Chai-pai-ko-erh in Siberia. He directed the battles against the Japanese army in Manchuria.

OCTOBER 14.　　In a report to President Chiang I summarized various reports as well as my own previously mentioned feelings and thoughts. Generally, this said,

> The Soviets have recalled all Manchurian puppet bank notes and have closed the printing bureau. The market has completely ceased to function. The gauge of the railroad track north of Harbin has been widened to that used in the Soviet Union. For the most part, machinery in the factories has been dismantled and removed, including part of the generators in the power plants. The Soviets also have dismantled and removed communications equipment and even taken away furniture belonging to organizations. The city now is empty. It seems that the Soviets are preparing to create in Inner Mongolia, Jehol, and Chahar a special regime that will completely surround the nine northeastern provinces. I'm afraid even the Manchurian coastline is in danger of being blockaded. When the Northeast has been entirely surrounded in this way, the jointly managed Chinese–Ch'ang-ch'un Railroad will be like a dagger piercing our heart. Moreover, with blood having been drained from the entire body, the Northeast is bound to become a sitting duck for the Soviet Union.

In the morning I saw Wu Chin-ch'uan, head of the Investigation Section of the Manchurian Central Bank, as well as Meng Ch'ing-en and Kai Wan-chung, who serve in the Ministry of Economics. They were recommended by Ke Tsu-lan, manager of the Bank of China in Ch'ang-ch'un. I asked them to gather data on finance and economics in the Northeast. I also received Tung Kuo-liang, Sung Li-sheng, Chiang Yen-wei, and Liu P'eng-yi, underground workers in Ch'ang-ch'un.

OCTOBER 15.   Special Envoy Chiang Ching-kuo came to tell me that today he saw Malinovsky, who brought to his attention three points:

1. Chinese who have been in the service of the Japanese now are offering their services to the national government.

2. Since the Northeast has been separated from the central government for 30 years, there exist all kinds of peculiar conditions that merit special attention.

3. Hereafter, like Germany after World War I, Japan is likely to re-emerge as a world power, so it is necessary to take precautions.

I gathered that his intention was to tell us that we no longer should employ any civil or military personnel who had worked for the Manchurian enemy regime and that in the future the national government probably cannot extend to the Northeast policies it employs in China Proper. In addition, he hints that China also must do its best to cooperate with the Soviet Union in order to prevent Japan from re-emerging.

    Li Mo-chiu, vice-chairman of the Merchants' Guild of the city of Ch'ang-ch'un, Liu Jun-feng, manager of the Yü-chang-yuan Brewery, and Liu Yung-tien, its vice-manager, came to report on local market conditions in Ch'ang-ch'un. According to them, for four or five years the people in the Northeast have not had cotton cloth. Also in short supply are medicines and daily necessities. Compared to 1938, the current price of commodities has risen from ten to one hundred times, or even more. For example, the price of rice has risen from 1 yuan per catty [about 1.1 pound] to 15 yuan per catty. Meat has gone from 20 or 30 cents a catty to 30 yuan a catty, while wood for fuel has risen from 5 to 6 yuan per hundred pieces to 60 yuan.

    Tung Yü-shu, chairman of the board of directors of the Northeastern Electric Communications and Telephone Company; Wang Chia-tung, counselor as well as head of Ch'ang-ch'un Control Bureau; Tung Min-shu, head of the Ch'ang-ch'un Postal Control Bureau; and Cheng Chin-jung, a director of the Manchurian Electric Company came to see me. Each of them reported on current conditions in their organizations.

OCTOBER 16.   Hsü Shao-ch'ing, assistant general director of the Manchurian Central Bank, came to report that the bank originally had issued bank notes amounting to approximately 80 billion yuan. Before evacuating, the Japanese gave to the staffs of various organizations sums amounting to approximately 40 billion yuan to meet the expenses of disbanding their personnel. The Soviet Army then withdrew approximately two or three billion yuan. At present, only two or three million yuan remain in storage. Former bank notes invalidated total more than one billion yuan. Aside from these, because of the recent adoption of a new format we are in the process of printing more bank notes. The printing is not yet completed. At present, there is in storage approximately 50 tons of bank note paper, which can be used to print bank notes amounting to twenty billion yuan. There is a printing bureau behind the bank that can print the bank notes.

Chin Tzu-kang of the Hsing-nung Bank came to see me. He brought one million yuan in bank notes issued by the Manchurian Central Bank. He said this was the sum left by the Japanese to meet the expense of disbanding personnel and specified that this was being given to the headquarters to meet its expenses.

Shih Shu-lin, associate research fellow at the Continental Science Academy, came to report that the Soviet Army had taken away all of the raw materials stored in the four experimental factories attached to the academy. It also took part of the apparatus in the laboratories, but, generally speaking, the laboratories were quite intact.

Wang Chia-ting of the Forest Products Commune came to see me. Ma Tzu-yuan, formerly assistant manager of the Bank of China in Harbin, arrived from Harbin on a Soviet airplane and came to see me. According to his report, the gauge of the railroad north of Harbin has been changed from the standard gauge of 4 feet, 8.5 inches, to a wide gauge of 5 feet, so that now these rails are the same as those in the Soviet Union. It is difficult to discern the Soviets' reason for doing this. It must be to facilitate the transportation of Soviet troops or of goods and matériel plundered by the Soviet Army.

OCTOBER 17.   At 1:00 P.M. the Chinese delegates again met with Malinovsky for a second talk that lasted about three hours. Both sides had to speak through an interpreter; that is why it took rather a long time. First, Chairman Hsiung brought up the following points concerning the transportation of our troops and our taking over the administration in various provinces and cities:

1. We intend to transport to the Northeast by sea two armies of soldiers who will land at Dairen approximately in early November. We intend to send two more armies into the Northeast by overland transportation, through Shan-hai-kuan. We hope that after the landing of the troops transported by sea the Soviets will assist their advance. We also

hope that the Soviets soon will repair and restore the railroad from Shan-hai-kuan to Mukden.

2. The Chinese intend to first airlift a number of military police to various large cities in the Northeast so that they can maintain local order following the evacuation of Soviet troops. Moreover, our headquarters will send personnel to various places to reorganize into a number of security maintenance teams those troops that have gone over to us. We hope the Soviets will give us accommodations and assistance.

3. We hope the Soviets will communicate their specific opinions concerning our taking over the administration of various provinces and cities. Furthermore, we hope that the Soviets also will assist us in having the personnel of our headquarters first inspect the major cities, as a necessary preparation for our taking over.

4. We hope to first take over industries managed by the Manchurian puppet government and Japan, as well as industries jointly operated by Chinese and Japanese. Then too, we hope the Soviets will give us their opinions regarding the resumption of business by the Bank of China and the Commercial Bank and our taking over the Manchurian puppet regime's Central Bank and printing press.

Malinovsky answered as follows:

1. The Soviets reiterated their procedures for evacuating their troops. Malinovsky said that last time he stated that between November 15 and November 20 the Soviets will withdraw their troops northward to a line from To-lun and Noh-erh through Chih-feng, Mukden, and T'ung-hua. From November 20 to November 25 these troops will be withdrawn to a line through Ch'ang-ch'un. Malinovsky hoped that the vanguard of the Chinese forces will reach that line on the same day. Part of the Soviet troops will be transported to Port Arthur and on the twenty-fifth will withdraw further north to a line through K'o-erh-ch'in-yu-i-ch'ien-ch'i, Harbin, and Lin-k'ou. On December 30, at the latest, they will withdraw into the Soviet Union. Malinovsky hoped that, in order to prevent the two armies from encountering one another, Chinese troops will take over the defense only after Soviet troops have withdrawn. Beginning on November 10, each day he will notify us how the evacuation of Soviet troops is proceeding.

2. With respect to places for the landing and assembling of Chinese troops, our delegates told Malinovsky that, in keeping with Soviet procedures for the evacuation of their troops, as stated by the Soviets, in order to reach various places and take over their defense our troops must land there before the Soviets withdraw. As for landing places, besides

Dairen, there also are Hu-lu-tao, Ying-k'ou, and Antung. Malinovsky replied that our troops could land at Hu-lu-tao and Ying-k'ou in early November. But the Soviet Army does not have strong armed forces in those two places, and, since it belongs to the eastern war zone, Antung is not under his jurisdiction. Our troops also can reach Ch'eng-te by an overland route. As for the date when our troops will arrive in Mukden, Harbin, and other places, it can vary by a number of days, which will be no problem.

3. Concerning the extent to which the Soviets can assist us in transporting troops:

a. We are permitted to airlift a small number of troops into the Northeast, but this must be done when Soviet troops withdraw. If we only intend to airlift a small number of military police, this may be done four or five days before the withdrawal of Soviet troops.

b. The Soviets can assist in the early repair and restoration of the railroads between Shan-hai-kuan and Mukden and from Ch'eng-te to Peiping.

c. The Chinese may send personnel to take over railroads other than the Chinese–Ch'ang-ch'un Railroad.

d. The Soviets guarantee that irregular troops will not be allowed along the lines of communication. If there are any, the Soviets will order them to surrender their weapons.

4. The Soviets do not object to our taking over administrative power in the Northeast. Our various provincial governors and mayors may assume their posts on an individual basis. But the Soviets hope that our officials in various places will enter into close contact with the Soviet Army. As for our reorganizing into security maintenance teams those troops that have gone over to us, he must seek instructions from Moscow before responding.

5. All factories operated by the Japanese should be regarded as war booty belonging to the Soviet Army. Even factories formerly operated jointly by Chinese and Japanese also should be regarded as enemy assets, since the Chinese involved cooperated with the enemy. In the future, the Fu-shun coal mines should be operated by the Chinese–Ch'ang-ch'un Railroad, since the mines supply that railroad with coal.

6. With respect to our hope that the Bank of China and the Commercial Bank can resume business and that we can take over the Manchurian puppet regime's Central Bank as well as its printing bureau, Malinovsky hoped that we would inform the Soviet Army commander about any detailed plans.

7. Electrical communications and the postal service in the North-

east have collapsed. At the present, they are limited to military use. Malinovsky hoped that we soon would send persons to restore them.

8. From now on, military matters will be discussed by the vice-chief of staff of our headquarters and the vice-chief of staff of the Soviet Army command. Economic matters will be discussed by a special person to be assigned by the Soviet Army general headquarters. (Major General Pavlovsky is vice-chief of staff of the Soviet Army.)

9. The Soviet vice-chairman of the board of directors of the Chinese–Ch'ang-ch'un Railroad already has arrived at the bureau. The Chinese chairman of the board of directors can fix a date to meet with him.

My Analysis of the Second Talk with Malinovsky

The Soviets are unwilling to see a large number of our troops transported into the Northeast. That is why they constantly try to obstruct us. They even hinted they could not assist us in landing our troops at Ying-k'ou and Hu-lu-tao. It already is very clear that they will not allow us to possess a strong military force in the Northeast.

Under the pretext of taking their war booty, the Soviets intend to plunder the industry of the Northeast and thus succeed to the special influence in the economy of Manchuria formerly enjoyed by Japan.

The Soviet statement that we can transport our troops to Ch'eng-te overland and that they are willing to assist us in repairing and restoring the railroad from Ch'eng-te to Peiping seems to indicate that so far the Soviet Union has no designs on Jehol and Inner Mongolia.

The Soviet statement guaranteeing that they will not allow irregular troops along the lines of communication implies that they cannot guarantee that there will be no irregular troops outside the lines of communication. Moreover, their hope that Chinese troops will not take over defense of various places in the Northeast until Soviet troops have withdrawn further implies that they are unwilling to assist the advance of our troops.

Note 1: After this talk, Special Envoy Chiang told me that during the discussion of the Sino-Soviet friendship treaty, on orders from President Chiang, T.V. Soong told Stalin that all of the industry of Manchukuo should be owned by China. Stalin answered that among the various enterprises in Manchuria those belonging to special company organizations should be regarded as war booty and owned by the Soviets. Those that had belonged to private Japanese individuals could be handed back to China to compensate for the wartime losses of the Chinese people. Soong did not engage in further discussion with Stalin but merely placed Stalin's words in the record of the conference. This is the situation: When talking about enterprises belonging to company organizations, Stalin meant special companies and auxiliary special companies of Manchukuo. The Manchukuo government, as well as legal entities, invested in both these kinds of companies. Other companies had private investment. Enterprises other than those having Japanese private capital all were special companies and auxiliary special companies.

The special company (in theory): For a given enterprise, the government issued a special company decree, which placed it under the jurisdiction of the government. The government appointed the trustees and supervisors.

The special company (in actual practice): When the government considered that a given enterprise was deeply involved with either military objectives or with the people's livelihood, it conferred on that enterprise the right to exercise a monopoly or some kind of control. On behalf of the government the enterprise applied controls and implemented an economic plan. With the exception of the three kinds of companies associated with the Manchurian Heavy Industry Company; namely, aircraft, motor vehicles, and light metals, in principle the Manchukuo government invested in all the rest. Employees of the companies had the status of public servants and could not behave independently.

The auxiliary special company (in theory): The government did not issue a special decree for the enterprise. Trustees and supervisors had to have the approval of the government.

The auxiliary special company (in actual practice): The company could not independently operate any enterprise deeply involved with industry or the people's livelihood. If the government felt there was a need for the company to exercise control over the development of industry and the people's livelihood, it could endow the company with a kind of right and obligation.

The two kinds of companies described above include special finance organizations, heavy industry, industries meeting military needs, communications and postal enterprises, land reclamation and cultivation enterprises, enterprises dealing with the improvement of special agricultural products, films and books, etc., covering almost every field and generally known as national policy companies. They had capital of 7,067,302,000 yuan. The ordinary companies had 3,535,653,000 yuan. [The figures are those of the end of June 1945.] The ratio was 67:33.

The South Manchuria railway was a special company belonging to the communications industry. It had capital of 1,650,000,000 yuan, which is included in the aforementioned figures.

Note 2: This is the situation: On August 18 our foreign ministry negotiated with the Soviets, requesting that Outer Mongolian troops cease their advance. On August 22 the acting Soviet chargé d'affaires notified the Chinese Foreign Ministry that the Soviet government had responded with the following message:

We have no intention of advancing toward Peiping or Kalgan. If our troops have taken several cities and locations outside of Manchuria that was because we simply cannot tolerate Japanese troops remaining to our rear and, therefore, we have to take them prisoner. As soon as Generalissimo Chiang's army arrives in these zones and locations they promptly will be handed over to Generalissimo Chiang's troops.

Today the Hsing-nung Cooperative sent over one million yuan in bank notes issued by the Manchurian Central Bank with instructions that they be used by the Northeast Headquarters. This money was left over from sums issued by the Japanese to meet the expenses of disbanding personnel. Yuan Sung-jui, chairman of the Maintenance Commission of the Kirin Railroad Bureau; Sun Yu-tan, vice-chairman of the commission; and Sun Ch'i-ying, head of the electrical section of the Bureau of Railroads came to report on the condition of the Kirin Railroad. The bureau operates over one thousand kilometers (of railroad) and spends over two million yuan a month. Now that their income has diminished, they hope that the headquarters will come to their aid. Each day there is less rolling stock, and the Soviets are utterly indifferent.

Wu Ying, chairman of the Hsing-nung Cooperative, and his son, Wu Tse-ling, supervisor of the Tokyo Chih-pu Electric Company, also came to see me.

OCTOBER 18.   There is no way to solve the problem of cash needed by the headquarters because we have neither bank notes of the Manchurian Central Bank nor Soviet permission to print new bank notes. Nor is it convenient to borrow from the Soviets notes being used by the Red Army. Therefore, I have asked Ma Tzu-yuan to return to Harbin to negotiate with the Soviet army. He is to tell them that the Bank of China was founded by me personally and that most of its shares are public issues [literally, *shang-ku*, commercial]. In addition, we have to keep the market in Harbin functioning. Consequently, we have asked the Soviets to allow the Central Bank of Harbin to resume business as soon as possible.

Chinese staff members of Manchurian organizations brought me two million yuan in bank notes issued by the Manchurian Central Bank, with the aim of relieving the critical situation of the headquarters. This is quite helpful.

When I think about the Chinese employed by various government organizations in Manchuria whom I have met, I find that most of them have not been properly trained. This shows that the real power in these organizations still was in the hands of the Japanese and that my countrymen were there merely to provide a facade.

OCTOBER 19.   I received a letter from Generalissimo Chiang, dated October 16th and addressed to Chairman Hsiung and me.

+   *Handwritten letter from President Chiang Kai-shek*   +

eleven o'clock, October 16, 1945

Dear T'ien [Hsiung Shih-hui] and Kung-ch'uan [Chang Kia-ngau]:
Your letter has been read in full appreciation. Concerning the shipping of troops, sea and overland transportation are to proceed at the same time. Sea transportation must not stop because of Soviet obstruction of landing at Dairen. But my desire is that besides landing at Dairen there is no need to seek other places of landing, for example at Ying-k'ou. We are determined that the troops transported by sea land only at the harbor of Dairen. There must be no wavering on this point. Meanwhile the railroad from Mukden to Peiping must be speedily repaired. If rail transportation could be restored by the end of the month then the overland transportation of our troops to Mukden before the twentieth of next month should be no problem. Arrangements have already been made to give priority to overland transportation. I ask you, gentlemen, on the one hand to continue negotiating for a landing at Dairen while at the same time giving the utmost attention to overland transportation and the speedy restoration of the Pei-Ning Railroad. As for Soviet apprehensions about certain events and persons hindering cooperation between our two countries, we must give special attention to this and do our utmost to avoid such a situation; generally, we must not allow room for the slightest misunderstanding. For the rest of my message, read my letter to Ching-kuo.

Chung-cheng

On the same day Chairman Hsiung went to talk with Marshal Malinovsky for the third time. He told Malinovsky that the central government is determined to land at Dairen. Malinovsky said that he would communicate that message to Moscow while at the same time he suggested that it would be best for Chairman Hsiung to return to Chungking in order to acquaint his government with Soviet opinion so as to bring about an early solution to the problem of sending Chinese troops to Manchuria. He implied that we need not insist on landing at Dairen.

OCTOBER 20.   Tung Yen-p'ing, vice-chief of staff of the Northeast Headquarters, talked with Soviet major general Pavlovsky and raised the following three issues: landing at Dairen, the establishment of an air traffic control station at Dairen, and the dispatch of Wang Chia-min, the person charged with taking over that city, to go and inspect the situation.

Chairman Hsiung will leave for Chungking tomorrow. I wrote a letter to the generalissimo reporting on problems concerning economics. It went as follows:

This is the situation: When I discussed taking over factories with the Soviets, Marshal Malinovsky suggested that Japanese-run industry be taken as war booty by the Soviets. I then asked him about the Fu-shun coal mines. He replied that their management could be merged with that of the Ch'ang-ch'un Railroad. His tone implied that, as a matter of course, all factories in the Northeast would go to the Soviets as war booty. Even if in the future the Soviet Union should consent to run industry jointly with us, that still would involve almost all industry so that we will have lost our economic autonomy. Industry and mines in the Northeast were divided into two categories: (1) enterprises affiliated with Manchurian railroads and (2) enterprises belonging to companies having special permits from the government of Manchukuo. Of course, the Manchurian railroads were Japanese assets. As for enterprises belonging to companies with special permits from the government of Manchukuo, in some cases their shareholders were all Japanese while, in others, they were in part Japanese. As a result, if the Soviets regard Japanese assets as war booty then almost all important industries will fall into their hands. Ching-kuo recalls that during the Moscow conference you, Revered President, sent a wire alerting him to this situation. Stalin replied that he could agree to turning over to China, as compensation for its wartime losses, whatever had been private property of the Japanese; however, whatever had belonged to companies and organizations in the Northeast must be regarded as war booty. Afterwards, our side merely included Stalin's words in the minutes of the conference and did not discuss them. Now, according to Stalin, almost all of the industry and mines in the Northeast belonged to companies and organizations. The only distinction recognized by the Soviets is the one between Japanese-owned companies and those having special permits from the government of Manchukuo. At the same time, Soviet troops already have dismantled and shipped away machinery in various factories and power plants.

I propose that the government immediately ask the Ministry of Foreign Affairs to raise with the Soviets the following points: (1) A prosperous Manchuria will benefit the economies of both China and the Soviet Union, as well as the Ch'ang-ch'un Railroad, which will be jointly operated by the Chinese and the Soviets. Therefore, the industrial and mining enterprises already existing in the Northeast must not be demolished or reduced in number. (2) All enemy assets in Manchuria should be used to pay debts owed to the people. If there is a surplus it should be used to compensate China for its losses during eight years of war. Consequently, all enemy assets should be confiscated by the Chinese government. This is the situation: the Central Bank of Manchukuo issued bank notes amounting to about 130 billion yuan. In addition, it issued notes backed by government bonds, postal savings accounts, and private savings in the amount of 20 or 30 billion yuan. Therefore, the central government will owe a debt of between 150 and 160 billion yuan to the people of the Northeast. But, even if they are kept intact, the present value of all the industries and mines in the Northeast is only 100 billion yuan.

(3) If the Chinese government must pay for the expenses of Soviet troops because the Soviet Union has sent them to help us recover Manchuria, we would be unwise to compensate them with shares in industries and mines because once joint management begins we will not be free to develop these industries and mines and, in the future, would be unable to attract foreign technology and capital. (4) Among the enterprises affiliated with the Manchurian railroads, the most important are the Fu-shun coal mines. Now that the central government has guaranteed a supply of coal for the railroads, the coal production of the Fu-shun mines cannot be allocated exclusively to the Ch'ang-ch'un Railroad. The same condition is true with respect to other coal mines. (5) We should ask the Soviet government to order its troops at the front to immediately stop dismantling machinery. (6) Whatever the Soviet Union claims as war booty should be restricted to machinery already dismantled. Other assets should not be regarded as war booty.

Because of constraints imposed by the existing situation, militarily and politically we are in a disadvantageous position in the Northeast. If, in addition, we achieve nothing economically, then indeed our presence will be purely nominal. These are my humble opinions. Whether or not they are appropriate must be decided by Your Excellency.

OCTOBER 21.   This afternoon Major General Pavlovsky, vice-chief of staff of the Soviet Army, responded to the various points: landing at Dairen, setting up an air traffic control station there, sending persons to inspect major cities as well as the section of the railroad between Mukden and Yü, reorganizing troops that had gone over, establishing air traffic control stations at Fengtien, Ch'ang-ch'un, and Dairen, landing at Antung, Ying-k'ou, and Hu-lu-tao and borrowing uniforms to be used by the reorganized troops. Pavlovsky replied as follows: (1) The Sino-Soviet treaty designates Dairen as a free commercial port. Permitting our troops to land there would be a violation of the treaty. (2) In the same vein, consent cannot be given to setting up an air traffic control station at Dairen. (3) Accommodations can be provided for persons sent to inspect Fengtien and Kirin. Soviet Army officers can be dispatched to accompany persons sent to inspect the Fengtien–Shanhai-kuan section of the railroad, but no safeguards can be given with respect to their security above Chin-chou. The Soviets cannot permit our sending military personnel to Dairen. (4) The Soviets cannot consent to the reorganization of troops that have gone over to us or countenance our borrowing uniforms. (5) Landing at Ying-k'ou and Hu-lu-tao is permissible. Landing at

Antung is permissible during the first half of November and may begin before Soviet troops withdraw. (6) Air traffic control stations can be set up in Fengtien, Ch'ang-ch'un, and Harbin two or three days before Soviet troops withdraw.

*Despairing of the Negotiations for
Landing at Dairen and What This Signifies*

For a long time before we arrived in Ch'ang-ch'un the Soviets had resolutely rejected our (proposal) to land at Dairen. On October 1, in response to a communication from the military affairs commission, the Ministry of Foreign Affairs informed the Soviet government that the troops of our Thirteenth Army had decided to board American ships at Kowloon around the tenth of October in order to reach Dairen by sea and land there. At the same time we wired Ambassador Fu, asking him to inform the Soviet Foreign Ministry of our plans. Afterward, Ambassador Fu's telegram of October 5 informed us that Soviet vice–foreign minister Lo had asked him what, after all, was the destination of our troops sailing from Kowloon to Dairen and what was their objective after landing. On October 6 the Soviet ambassador saw Vice-Minister Kan. He told him that, according to the Sino-Soviet treaty, Dairen was a commercial rather than a military port and that whoever sent troops to Dairen violates the treaty. This is why the Soviet government resolutely opposes such a move. On October 8 Ambassador Fu wired saying that the various details related to him by Soviet vice–foreign minister Lo on the evening of the sixth were identical to those given by Ambassador Petrov.

The series of events described above indicates that Soviet opposition to the landing of our troops at Dairen already was clear and resolute. I wonder whether Chairman Hsiung still thinks there is hope of retrieving the situation by entering into direct diplomatic talks with Malinovsky. That is why he still raised this issue at the conference. Now, with respect to the questions raised by Vice–Foreign Minister Lo—"What after all is the destination of your troops landing in the Northeast and what is their objective?"—they seemed to imply a reluctance on the part of the Soviets to have us use military force to take over the Northeast or even establish and develop our military strength there. Their intention was all too clear. Why hadn't our foreign affairs officials given this their attention?

This morning, Wang Ching-shan, chief of the merchants' guild of Ch'ang-ch'un, came to report that he has been in charge of selling coffee from Salvador in the Northeast and also has been the honorary consul for that nation. He was arrested yesterday but immediately released. Chu Lien-kuei, chairman of the Power Control Commission of Harbin, came to report that only a small number of Chinese remained on the staff of the power bureau of that city. The rest all had been replaced by Soviets. Sun Chiu-ssu, general supervisor of the railroad police for the Ch'ang-ch'un Railroad, came to report that he had been able to get his job because he was recommended by the mayor of Ch'ang-ch'un.

I visited the Continental Science Academy, now renamed the Northeast Science Academy. The Chinese staff of the academy really were doing their best to protect the equipment there.

OCTOBER 22.   Special Envoy Chiang Ching-kuo came to discuss whether we should immediately reply to yesterday's rejection by the Soviet army's vice-chief of staff of our proposal to land our troops at Dairen. We decided that Vice-Chief of Staff Tung should send a written answer, phrased generally along these lines: In the friendship treaty the Soviet Union guaranteed China entire sovereignty over the Northeast and recognized it as an indivisible part of China. Therefore Chinese troops certainly have the right to land. At present, this issue is being negotiated by the Chinese and Soviet governments. We also protest Soviet rejection of our proposal that our government send representatives to inspect conditions in Dairen. In addition Vice-Chief of Staff Tung was to inform the government of the Soviet refusal to allow us to build an airfield at Dairen.

Hsing Kuang-jui, the head of the Liaoning local security maintenance committee, came to report on conditions in Mukden. He said that the size of the Eighth Route Army in the vicinity of Mukden already was about 100,000 and that they were supported from the rear by the Soviet Red Army, which was devastating local areas and was hated by the people.

Cheng Chin-jung, one of the directors of the Manchurian power company, came again to ask when the takeover could begin. Wen Chung-hsi of the printing bureau came to report on conditions at the bureau.

OCTOBER 23.   Shih Shu-lin and Ho Fang-kai, associate research fellows of the Continental Science Academy, came to report that there remained on the staff of the science academy eight Japanese having doctoral degrees as well as scores of Japanese research fellows.

The Bank of China sent Tai Chih-ch'ien and the Bank of Communications, Chuang Ch'uan here to discuss and plan measures for resuming business after the takeover of both banks.

OCTOBER 24.   Today, Soviet troops searched the Nationalist party branch headquarters of Kirin province in Ch'ang-ch'un, as well as the office of the special envoy of the party branch headquarters. The Soviets also summoned the entire staff of the party branch headquarters for interrogation, including two major figures. All documents of the party branch headquarters were taken away. The alleged reason was that the *Restoration Daily*, published by the party branch headquarters, had printed a report that because of his health Stalin had been forced to abstain from politics and that all his administrative duties were being handled by Molotov. Actually, the Soviets had been jealous of the Nationalist party branch for more than a mere day; today's problems were only the immediate cause.

The Northeast headquarters proposed sending people to Jehol to buy sheets of leather to be used for uniforms. This was rejected by the Soviet Army command. The Soviets said that recently there had been disorderly conditions along the routes into Jehol and urged that they not go.

Yang Te-jung and Chu Mo-ti, the persons sent by the Ministry of Finance to take over in the Northeast, came to see me.

Ma Tzu-yuan is back from Harbin and reports that the Soviet Army has permitted the Bank of China to resume business. So, now, the headquarters can negotiate with the bank for funds and will be less restrained in its activities. Ma's boldness in performing his duties was evident while he was manager of the Heiho branch and assistant manager of the Harbin branch of the Bank of China. However, he was apt to be wayward when conducting business, and this explains why he was unable to hold his posts for long. Nevertheless, in extraordinary times his merits were an asset.

OCTOBER 25.   The party branch personnel detained by the Soviets have been released yesterday. They were told that the incident resulted from the printing and distribution of propaganda without first obtaining the approval of the Soviet High Command. This was a violation of regulations, and, hereafter, the party branch must end all its activities. The Soviet Army command told the secretary of the headquarters, Yang Tso-jen, that for security reasons the headquarters must cancel its plans to send people to make investigations at various places and to examine the Feng-shan Railroad. There is no way of telling whether there has been a change of attitude because of yesterday's incident or whether their intention is to facilitate Eighth Route Army activity.

Chiang Wen-tao of the Public Sales Bureau brought two million yuan on behalf of the Kirin security maintenance committee to express their gratitude to the headquarters. Yang Ts'e, vice-chief of the Harbin Railroad Bureau, came to report that the Soviets intend to change the Harbin Railroad Bureau into the general railroad bureau.

OCTOBER 26.   The political commissar of the Soviet Army command invited Special Envoy Chiang over for a talk. Chiang was told that ever since the Northeast Headquarters came to Ch'ang-ch'un, anti-Soviet movements have been proliferating everywhere in Manchuria and that in Harbin there had even appeared flyers urging "Fight on to Moscow." In the vicinity of Mukden three or four hundred people gathered to shoot at and kill Soviet workers, and anti-Soviet organizations had been found in various other places. Therefore, Marshal Malinovsky was obliged to go to these places to begin eradicating bad elements. This was why the persons who the headquarters planned to send to inspect different places could not be allowed to go. Special Envoy Chiang asked him whether the headquarters was suspected of having directed such anti-Soviet movements. He replied that there was no evidence of this but that the establishment of the headquarters and the outbreak of anti-Soviet activity were so coincidental as to provoke speculation. It's difficult to say if such talk is the result of merely yesterday's incident or whether the headquarters really is suspected of anti-Soviet activity and the central government, of still having a hostile attitude toward the Soviet Union. Or is their intention to create a pro-Soviet regime in opposition to the headquarters?

Today Chairman Hsiung returned to Ch'ang-ch'un. I learned that there had been no progress whatsoever in the Chungking Foreign Ministry's discussions with the Soviet ambassador about our landing at Dairen. As a result, the government had decided to spend no more time discussing the issue, since that only would delay the takeover of the Northeast. Instead, it would first send troops to land at Ying-k'ou and Hu-lu-tao. Hsiung brought me back a letter of reply from the generalissimo. The text is as follows:

+ *Handwritten letter from President Chiang Kai-shek* +

October 25, 1945

Dear Kung-ch'uan:

Your letter of the twenty-first has been received and read. I have referred to the Foreign Ministry the issues discussed in your letter, requesting that they make a serious study of them before deciding on the procedure for negotiation. By any reasonable standards the opposite party should not go to extremes. Yet, with regard to the problem of Manchuria, right now we can only do whatever is possible, and wait for the circumstances to change; what do you think? We can only try our best; there is no need to get worried or lose hope about this. I have asked T'ien-i [Hsiung] to personally relate to you the rest of my message. The task of first importance is still to enable government troops to speedily enter Manchuria; therefore every effort must be made to restore the Pei-Ning Railroad.

Chung-cheng

This evening Vice-Chief of Staff Tung invited Major General Pavlovsky for a talk at the official residence of Chairman Hsiung. Tung told Pavlovsky that we had decided that, pending a settlement with respect to our landing at Dairen, our army would first land at Ying-k'ou and Hu-lu-tao and that we are borrowing American transports for the shipment. In order to determine the state of facilities at both ports, we have decided to borrow American reconnaissance planes to carry out reconnaissance from the air, beginning October 27. The Soviet ambassador in Chungking already had been notified of this by our Foreign Ministry. Major General Pavlovsky replied that he would immediately report to Marshal Malinovsky and that he would notify us as soon as he had instructions.

OCTOBER 27.   Today at 4:00 P.M. I had my first talk with [M.I.] Sladkovsky, economic counselor of the Soviet Army command. Both of us adopted a probing attitude. He is head of the Far Eastern Division of the Soviet Foreign Ministry and in 1935 had been in Nanking and Shanghai. He is an exceedingly shrewd and capable man. Generally, our talk went as follows:

I first told him that I had come here for the purpose of promoting Chinese and Soviet economic cooperation in Manchuria. He then asked what our future economic policy in the Northeast was. I replied that our objective was to provide both China and the Soviet Union with surplus products from the Northeast in order to meet their needs. Similarly, commodities needed in the Northeast would be provided by China and the Soviet Union, with the result that the Northeast would become a good market, to be shared by both countries. This is why I intended, as a first step, to enter into a bartering agreement with the Soviet Union, promoting mutually advantageous exchanges. He then asked about our policy concerning industry in the Northeast. I replied that under Japan, for military reasons, heavy industry in the Northeast had been developed at an accelerated pace but from now on should only be maintained in its present condition. We must give greater attention to developing light industry in order to raise the living standards of the people. I also said that we would consider buying machinery that we needed from the Soviet Union.

After this he asked me how we were going to deal with the industries built in the Northeast by the Japanese. I answered that the industry built by Japan should be used to compensate China for its losses during its war of resistance against Japan. I also stated that what I meant by industry built by Japan was that which the Japanese had invested in. As for industry resulting from investment by the government of Manchukuo, this should be used to meet debts owed to the people by that government. He parried by saying that if we did these things the Soviet Union would not share in profits that could compensate it for its own wartime losses. I responded that in the Sino-Soviet agreement there was no provision with respect to this point. Moreover, during China's eight-year war against Japan, China's people had suffered incalculable losses and deserved compensation. He reacted by saying that the wartime losses of the Soviet Union equalled the total losses of all other Allied nations put together.

At this point I asked him whether the machinery dismantled and removed from the Northeast by the Soviets would be regarded as partial compensation for Soviet losses. He said that this was a very complicated matter and actually should have been settled between the two governments; however, it had only been brought up today and then only incidentally. At the same time he thought we ought to know that the greater part of industry in the Northeast had already been demolished by the enemy. I responded that this was a matter of great importance and should be settled by the governments concerned. Then I remarked that I did not know which types of industry the Soviets wished to cooperatively manage with us in the Northeast. That was why, regrettably, I had not mentioned the question of industry. But, as long as we were discussing the topic of cooperation, our side was most willing to gratify the expectations of the Soviets, although we hoped that the Soviets would try to make allowances when we found ourselves unable to do certain things.

He then asked whether we could allow Soviet specialists to participate in the operation of industry in the Northeast and whether we had a sufficient number of Chinese specialists. I told him that we would be most willing to borrow technical personnel from the Soviet Union, and I asked in what fields the Soviets were ready to provide us with talent. He replied that they were ready to supply us with talent in the fields of metallurgy, electrical engineering, and architecture. I remarked that I feared the Soviet Union would be short of technical personnel, owing to its urgent need for postwar reconstruction and the exploitation of Siberia. Nevertheless, I still hoped that we could obtain first-rate specialists to assist us in the Northeast. He said that he would tell this to the Soviet Ministry of Industry. I then asked if he had other opinions to offer. He said that the Soviets had a genuine need for grain from the Northeast. For example, there was a demand for soybeans in the province of Ussuri. As for commodities needed in the Northeast, the Soviets could provide them. He said that, in summary, if we set aside the question of how compensation was to be handled, there was no doubt that with respect to industry the Soviet Union would carry out its obligation to assist us. He added that he would like to discuss further and more specifically the questions dealt with above.

Finally, I told him that since both sides were willing to cooperate with one another I hoped that the Soviets would keep us frankly informed concerning their opinions. As for the questions of compensation, we were not being demanding of the Soviets; the fact was that China had no foundation whatsoever for industry and that the gap between its industrial situation and that of the Soviets was as great as the distance between heaven and earth. Therefore, we wished to save as much as possible and place it under our ownership.

Today a wire from Generalissimo Chiang arrived requesting that all party activities in the Northeast cease and that party personnel submit themselves to the direction of the headquarters.

OCTOBER 28.   Today, Special Envoy Chiang Ching-kuo called on the political commissar of the Soviet Army. He told the commissar that the headquarters was dedicated to promoting friendly relations between China and the Soviet Union and that the various anti-Soviet propaganda and other activities that the Soviets told us about must have been provoked by traitors and the Japanese. Chiang also said that we were most willing to join the Soviets in combined efforts to eliminate such propaganda and activities and requested that the Soviets keep us posted on news concerning them. He also took the opportunity to tell the commissar that Generalissimo Chiang had ordered that party activities in the Northeast be directed and supervised by the headquarters and that whoever disobeyed the policy and engaged in anti-Soviet activities was to be placed in custody and sent to the central government. Moreover, whichever party branch disobeyed central policy was to cease its activities. The tone of the commissar's response to these words still indicated no sign of trust. He hinted that the Northeast Headquarters was indirectly connected with anti-Soviet activities.

I heard that both yesterday and today, when transports of the central government carrying our soldiers arrived at Hu-lu-tao, bandit troops on the shore fired at them. Our troops tried to land but failed, and the transport had to return to await further orders.

OCTOBER 29.   Today at 1:00 P.M. I went with Chairman Hsiung to talk with Malinovsky for the fourth time. First, Chairman Hsiung stated that he had returned from Chungking and that Generalissimo Chiang sent his regards. Malinovsky expressed his thanks. Then Malinovsky gave a reply to the various issues that Chairman Hsiung had raised, stating, at the same time, that he could only give explicit answers to questions falling within the scope of his own power. His answers to the points raised by Chairman Hsiung were as follows:

1. With respect to our landing at Dairen: Instructions from the Soviet government had been received that did not approve of Chinese troops landing at that place. Because, according to the Sino-Soviet

treaty, the Soviet Union considered Dairen a totally commercial free port that should not be used for military purposes. It followed from this that neither Chinese nor Soviet troops should be permitted to pass through or land there. Recently, an American warship was discovered sailing along the route to Dairen and entered the port. Personnel from the warship were going ashore there; the captain's name was *Hsi-t'o-erh*. The Soviets were exceedingly alarmed by this, which they considered an obstruction to friendly relations between China and the Soviet Union, since no warship belonging to any nation had been expected to appear either in the harbor or along the route.

2. With respect to our landing at Ying-k'ou and Hu-lu-tao, long before, the Soviets had stated that they were not opposed to this. As for the point raised by the Chinese side concerning security for our troops landing at Hu-lu-tao, last time the Soviets had explicitly stated that while there were still a small number of Soviet troops in Chin-chou, there were no Soviet troops in Hu-lu-tao. The Soviets were willing to let Chinese troops land at Hu-lu-tao but could not guarantee a safe landing. We heard that south of Chin-chou Chinese government troops had clashed with local troops; we also heard that these local troops were the Eighth Route Army and that they were not inconsiderable in number. The Soviets were in no position to manipulate the Eighth Route Army, since long before, the Soviet Union had stated that it would not intervene in China's internal affairs. As for Chinese troops landing at Ying-k'ou, we hoped that on November 10, in the city of Ying-k'ou [sentence incomplete]. It was reported that today Chinese troops might be landing at Hu-lu-tao and Ying-k'ou. We anticipate no problems in the landing process. As for China's intention to send persons to Ying-k'ou and Hu-lu-tao to look after the troops who land there, Malinovsky planned to inform Moscow of this on this very day and ask for instructions.

3. With respect to China's request to station its troops in designated areas south of Chin-chou, Chinese troops would be permitted to station themselves in any area south of Chin-chou. Soviet troops in the city of Chin-chou would be entirely evacuated on November 10; the presence of Chinese troops in the city of Chin-chou before this date was undesirable. The Soviets did not object to sending troops from Chin-chou to Hu-lu-tao in order to enable Chinese troops to land safely, but the number of Soviet troops is too small to really guarantee the safety of the Chinese troops.

4. Concerning China's desire that the Soviets provide it with railroad locomotives and rolling stock at Ying-k'ou and Chin-chou, we cannot give an answer today. We hope that China will send as many locomotives and as much rolling stock as possible into Manchuria from Tientsin.

5. With respect to China's desire to reorganize local security troops, the Soviets are unwilling to have this take place before the withdrawal of Soviet troops.

6. Concerning the point raised by China about its intention to airlift the vanguard of its troops into Ch'ang-ch'un and Fengtien, the Soviet government does not really object to this; it only requests that these troops land three days before the withdrawal of Soviet troops. As for the groundwork, all of it could be taken charge of by personnel of the air traffic control station for Soviet air transportation.

7. With respect to China's request that Soviet and Outer Mongolian troops withdraw from Chahar and Jehol, Soviet troops north of Kalgan already have decided to withdraw northward by way of Chahar; Mongolian troops will evacuate at the same time.

8. Concerning your questions about the Port Arthur Commission, who should be the candidate for mayor of Port Arthur, and the drawing of a boundary line—since the military port of Port Arthur does not belong under my jurisdiction you are asked to negotiate these points with Moscow. Naturally, the boundary line would be drawn in accord with the treaty.

9. With respect to your questions about sending administrative personnel to take over in various places, this is the situation: Moscow already has been informed about the list of northeastern administrative organizations and their personnel sent by the Northeast Headquarters, but no reply has yet been received. We dare trust there will be no obstruction to this.

10. You favored us with information about actions of the Nationalist party. This is the situation: The Nationalist party has many organizations in Ch'ang-ch'un. Some are said to be genuine Kuomintang organizations while others are said to be false, but in the final analysis there is no way to distinguish which ones are genuine and which are not. The Soviet Army has raised only one condition and this is that anti-Soviet activities and propaganda are not permitted; however, contrary to our expectations, such activities and propaganda still continue. From the weapons and various documents discovered during the recent search of Kuomintang party branches, we now know that these activities are part of a plan. Over two hundred Soviets have been sacrificed in these incidents. Recently, every night there have been assaults on Red Army men. Consequently, we have been forced to adopt severe measures. If these incidents occur again we will handle them in an even more severe manner. There have been no Japanese among the anti-Soviet elements apprehended. Instead, these people were former officials of Manchukuo and disbanded soldiers. In addition, railroads have been recently torn apart

and trains demolished. There must be a central organization that instigated and directed these incidents, and we cannot avoid suspecting that this organization has utilized the prestige and power of the Northeast Headquarters to expand its influence. In addition, gun powder has recently been found concealed in sacks of grain. For this reason, the Soviet Army, exercising its authority under martial law and in accord with the regulations contained in Article 1 of the military agreement with China, has ordered local commanders to deal with this severely. But, contrary to our expectations, anti-Soviet activities in Ch'ang-ch'un have become still more intense. Recently, the central figure in a Sino-Soviet friendship society, who was not a member of any party, was killed in a branch police bureau. Therefore, we have decided to remove and replace both the mayor of Chang-ch'un and the chief of its public security bureau. I have had to force myself to tolerate this unpleasant situation for the sake of future Sino-Soviet friendship.

After this, Chairman Hsiung reiterated his hopes concerning the points on which he had not received a satisfactory answer. But still there was no result.

Chairman Hsiung stated that we hoped for the following:

1. With respect to the landing of Chinese troops at Hu-lu-tao and Ying-k'ou, that the Soviets would let their troops stationed there know this in the form of an order

2. Because the railroad was blocked at Chin-chou, that the Soviets would provide railroad rolling stock at Ying-k'ou

3. That the Soviets would consent to our directly transporting our troops by rail from Ying-k'ou to Ch'ang-ch'un and that they would extend the deadline for their arrival

4. That the Soviet Army command would dispatch persons to accompany personnel of the Northeast Headquarters to Ying-k'ou

5. That the Soviets would agree to our reorganizing local troops and using them exclusively to maintain local order

6. That the Soviets would resolve the problem of irregular troops in various places

7. That the provincial governor of Kirin and the mayor of Ch'ang-ch'un could immediately assume their duties

Marshal Malinovsky gave the following answer:

1. We had, long before this, notified Soviet troops in Hu-lu-tao.

2. We will make an effort to provide rolling stock at Ying-k'ou, but

we cannot guarantee success. We have no intention of moving the locomotives and rolling stock in storage at Chin-chou northward; these can be turned over for use by Chinese troops.

3. The Soviets do not want Chinese troops transported into the Northeast by rail until the evacuation of Soviet troops has been accomplished and still hope that such troops can be airlifted. As for an extension of the deadline, we shall ask for instructions on this.

4. With respect to our dispatching persons to accompany personnel of the Northeast Headquarters to Ying-k'ou, we shall ask for instructions from Moscow.

5. Concerning the reorganization of local troops, I shall ask for instructions from my government. But, personally, I do not approve of such action, since reorganization will involve only former Manchurian puppet troops and these elements are truly unreliable.

6. With respect to irregular troops who have approached Soviet lines, the Soviet Army either has disarmed them or ordered them to move elsewhere. For example, when irregular troops were discovered in Jehol, they were ordered to move southward.

7. With respect to the provincial governor of Kirin and the mayor of Ch'ang-ch'un assuming their duties, personally I have no objection. If he wishes to do so, the provincial governor of Kirin can go right ahead and assume his duties. As for the mayor of Ch'ang-ch'un, let's give him time to consider.

While answering the first question, Malinovsky reiterated his complaint that an American warship had appeared in the port of Dairen and that its captain, *Hsi-t'o-erh*, had gone ashore to make an inspection. Chairman Hsiung replied that this concerned the question of our landing at Dairen and that, pending a resolution of that question, what had happened there should be put aside until later.

My Analysis of the Fourth Talk with Malinovsky

Malinovsky reiterated over and over that an American warship had sailed into the port of Dairen and that its captain had gone ashore there. This reveals the extent of his dissatisfaction with our relying on American forces to send our troops into the Northeast and even more, the reluctance of the Soviet Union to see American influence penetrate into the Northeast.

Malinovsky's suspicion that the northeastern party branch headquarters are anti-Soviet and the extension of this suspicion to the Northeast Headquarters shows that the Soviet government still is doubtful of our government arriving at a friendly relationship with the Soviets. Therefore, the Soviet government still is unwilling to see our troops move swiftly and without hindrance into the Northeast. Its refusal to help us land our troops at Hu-lu-tao, its failure to specifically promise to provide us with the rolling stock we need at Ying-k'ou, and its advising us to continue airlifting our soldiers are intended to postpone the arrival of our troops in the Northeast. All this is very clear.

Malinovsky's putting off his response concerning the mayor of Ch'ang-ch'un assuming his duties seems to indicate his hesitancy to have us take over administrative power.

Today the Soviets dismissed Chao Wan-pin, chief of the public security bureau of the city of Ch'ang-ch'un, from his post and replaced him with the procommunist Chang Ching-ho. This reveals even more clearly the Soviets' reluctance to see our headquarters immediately take over administrative power in the Northeast.

Today, Tu Yü-ming, commander of northeastern security, flew to Ch'ang-ch'un to confer with Chairman Hsiung about plans for landing our troops.

Chu Hsiu-fu, manager of the Fengtien branch of the Bank of China, came to tell me that, because all Chinese banks in Fengtien had ceased to function, the Soviets had designated Chairman Ch'en of the merchants' guild as the person responsible for establishing a Northeastern Industrial Bank. There is no capital but business already has begun.

In response to a request from the local Soviet command, the Commercial Bank is scheduled to start business today. So too is the Bank of Communications.

I wrote a letter to inform Generalissimo Chiang about my conversation with the Soviet economic counselor.

OCTOBER 30.   According to a wire from Chungking to the Northeast Headquarters, the United States has notified Chungking that the Soviet embassy has sent amphibious boats to Hu-lu-tao.

The Bank of China and I have come to a decision about sending persons with cash to Ying-k'ou and Hu-lu-tao to aid in landing our troops there. Tu Yü-ming and I also came to a decision concerning the amount of such aid.

The following arrived in Ch'ang-ch'un yesterday: Kao Hsi-ping, provincial governor of Antung; Hsü Chen, provincial governor of Liaoning; Cheng Tao-ju, provincial governor of Kirin; and Kuan Chi-yü, provincial governor of Sung-chiang. Today they came to see me.

OCTOBER 31.   The Northeast Headquarters has received a wire from Chungking saying that the Soviet ambassador has informed our Foreign Ministry that the Soviets can guarantee a safe landing at Hu-lu-tao and Ying-k'ou. I also received news that an American warship was on the way to Hu-lu-tao to inspect. It appears that the landing of our troops is imminent.

Today is Generalissimo Chiang's 59th birthday. At noon all of the personnel of the headquarters gathered to dine and to wish him a long life. At 6:00 P.M. there began a recreational program. I heard that in the streets Japanese were seen putting up posters saying "Congratulations and Long Live China, Head of the East Asian Alliance."

Today, at 1:00 P.M. Vice-Chief of Staff Tung met with Major General Pavlovsky, vice-chief of staff of the Soviet Army, who said that as late as an hour ago there had been no news of our troops landing at Ying-k'ou. The platoon of Soviet soldiers sent to Hu-lu-tao for liaison work had arrived there on the twenty-ninth.

From Ch'ang-ch'un to Chungking

NOVEMBER 1–30, 1945

Chang Kia-ngau continues to receive reports of Soviet plundering of Manchuria's industrial enterprises, of Chinese communist Eighth Route Army troop activity in South Manchuria, and the Republic of China (ROC) government's difficulties in reviving the deteriorating Manchurian economy. Chang Ching-kuo informs Chang Kia-ngau that Chinese communist troops were in Ying-k'ou but that Soviet troops, too few to resist, began to withdraw to the north. Chang Kia-ngau interprets this development as a Soviet decision to allow Chinese communist forces to locate at Hu-lu-tao and Ying-k'ou to prevent Nationalist troops from landing in southern Manchuria.

Another meeting with Malinovsky confirms Chang Kia-ngau's worst fears. According to Malinovsky, ROC troops will be allowed to be airlifted into Manchuria as long as they are not assisted by U.S. air force personnel. Chang Kia-ngau also surmises that Chinese Communist forces are already fomenting anti-Soviet activities to undermine Sino-Soviet relations.

Chang Kia-ngau begins working with Soviet officials to restore the Ch'ang-ch'un railway line; to that end a bureau of railroad management under a Sino-Soviet board of directors will be established in Harbin.

On November 7 the Soviets host the Chinese delegation, and on November 9 the Chinese delegation reciprocates.

On November 11 Chiang Kai-shek recalls Chiang Ching-kuo to Chungking to prepare for Chiang Ching-kuo's trip to Moscow to break the impasse in Sino-Soviet negotiations in Ch'ang-ch'un.

*Chang Kia-ngau then learns from Takasaki Tatsunosuke, a Japanese offi-
cial and former general manager of the Manchurian Heavy Industry Company (the conglomerate coordinating Japan's main industries in Manchuria),
that Sladkovsky, then a colonel in the Red Army, had coerced Takasaki into
preparing an affidavit transferring the Manchurian Heavy Industry Company to the Soviet Union. Sladkovsky's high-handed behavior convinces
Chang that the Soviet Union wants to establish the strongest possible property
claims to Manchuria's economic enterprises.*

*On November 15 Chang Kia-ngau learns that the Chinese delegation will
withdraw to Peiping to pressure the Soviets to negotiate the transfer of
Manchuria to the ROC government. After informing the Chinese of this
pending evacuation, Chang Kia-ngau confers with Sladkovsky about the
disposition of Japanese assets. Sladkovsky tells Chang that the Soviets want
to establish joint management with the Chinese over Japanese enterprises in
Manchuria. Both Chang and Sladkovsky agree to consult with their governments about drawing up a list of Japanese enterprises that the Chinese and
the Soviets could agree to manage jointly. Although disagreements still exist
between Sladkovsky and Chang, Chang hopes that there is some basis for
genuine cooperation between the two nations.*

*The Nationalist evacuation from Ch'ang-ch'un is postponed while high-
level diplomatic talks take place between the ROC and the Soviet Union. The
negotiations at Ch'ang-ch'un turn to the question of when Nationalist troops
can be airlifted into the city.*

*On November 20 Sladkovsky and Chang again discuss possible economic
cooperation between their two countries and which former Japanese enterprises should be jointly managed and how. On November 23 the Soviets
grant the ROC government permission to airlift troops into Mukden and
Ch'ang-ch'un. Chang Kia-ngau bids farewell to Malinovsky and Sladkovsky,
whereupon the two Soviet officials reassure Chang that ROC troops should
immediately be airlifted into Ch'ang-ch'un. Chang then wires Chungking of
this new information.*

*On November 24 Chang Kia-ngau flies to Peiping; he arrives in Chung-
king on November 25 and immediately consults with top ROC leaders. The
Nationalist government has already decided to airlift troops into Ch'ang-
ch'un and Mukden because the Soviets are now withdrawing their troops
from southern Manchuria.*

*On November 28 Chang Kia-ngau participates in a high-level meeting to
discuss the recovery of Manchuria. The president of the Executive Yuan, T.
V. Soong, and Foreign Minister Wang Hsüeh-t'ing take the position that the
ROC should not agree to any economic negotiations with the Soviets until the
political takeover of Manchuria has been solved. Chang Kia-ngau recognizes
that if the ROC government adopts this position it will be impossible to come*

to terms with Malinovsky, who expects to conclude an agreement on the Sino-Soviet joint management of former Japanese enterprises before the Red Army pulls out of Manchuria.

Chang Kia-ngau realizes that he cannot change the views of Soong and Wang and that Soviet duplicity has made it difficult for ROC government leaders to trust the Soviets. Yet Chang believes that an economic agreement with the Soviets is still possible and would hasten the recovery of Manchuria. He yields to the majority view, however, and with his colleagues' help begins to formulate a reply to Sladkovsky. He proposes that any discussions of economic cooperation before the Soviets withdraw from Manchuria will only create "unfortunate misunderstanding," that the ROC government will discuss economic cooperation with the Soviets only after the ROC recovers Manchuria, and that the ROC government will make every endeavor to cooperate with the Soviets.

+ + + + + +

NOVEMBER 1.   I invited Tung Yü-shu, chairman of the board of directors of the Northeastern Electric Communications and Telephone Company, and Tung Min-shu, head of the Postal Control Bureau, to come see me. I told them that the persons sent by our government to take over the two bureaus had arrived and that these persons were to be welcomed by them and enabled to assume their duties. Formalities attending the takeover could not be avoided. The purpose of our taking this step at that time was to take over economic organizations from personnel of the Manchurian puppet regime. They agreed and left.

Tou Ching-lin, head of the Ch'i-ch'i-ha-erh Railroad Bureau, came to see me. He told me that the task of changing the gauge of the rails of the track north of Harbin by the Russians began on September 3 and was completed on October 9. On October 12 a train from Moscow arrived in Ch'i-ch'i-ha-erh. A representative of the communications commission of the Soviet government came to Ch'i-ch'i-ha-erh to deliver a lecture to personnel of the Railroad Bureau. He first asked whether the staff of the Railroad Bureau understood the spirit of the Sino-Soviet agreement. He then said that if within 30 years China could manage the railroads in Manchuria by itself, control could be returned to the Chinese.

Today, the four persons versed in Russian whom I had searched for and engaged in Peiping arrived in Ch'ang-ch'un.

NOVEMBER 2.   I learned that six of the machines in the Feng-man power plant at Kirin still are awaiting shipment to the Soviet Union and that Eighth Route Army men already have gone there to cause trouble. I am deeply worried that one day our power supply may stop. I also received news that the Eighth Route Army had sent persons to try to take over the Fengtien Electric Communications and Telephone Bureau but that they were expelled by the Soviet Army.

Ch'en Ti-ch'iu, the special envoy sent by our Ministry of Communications to take over enterprises having to do with communications, came to see me, accompanied by his colleagues. I told him that for the time being the railroads could not be taken over and that all we could do was make an investigation to determine what additional materials were needed. We might be able to first take over the postal organizations. All personnel presently employed by the postal system, from the general bureau in Ch'ang-ch'un to the branch bureaus, should be retained and conditions not changed. We might also be able to take over the Electric Communications and Telephone Bureau. There too everything should remain unchanged. This is why yesterday I personally talked with the people formerly in charge of the two bureaus. With respect to civil aviation, at present taking that over is even more out of the question. I personally asked special envoy Ch'en to first send persons to Chin-chou and Ying-k'ou to make arrangements for taking over the railroads and to assist in the transportation of our troops.

NOVEMBER 3.   Wu Wang-sun, head of the Economics Bureau of the Ch'ang-ch'un municipal government, came to see me. He said that he was willing to find ways to ship more coal to the headquarters so that its fuel would not run short. He also told me that he had issued orders for several small factories to resume production. They will be placed under the control of the Economics Bureau and financially assisted by the bureau. This man is a graduate of the Harbin Industrial University. Until recently, when he assumed his duties at the bureau, he had been engaged in business of his own. He has enjoyed the trust of the Soviet Army. I commended and consoled him. I told him that in the future there must, as a matter of course, be cooperation between China and the Soviet Union. Therefore, whoever had helped the Soviets in the Northeast during the period it was occupied by the Soviet Army still would be relied on and not discriminated against.

Chi Pin, formerly one of the directors of the Hsing-yeh Bank, is now in charge of the Hsing-nung Cooperative. Accompanied by Ching Tzu-kang, he came to see me and told me how the cooperative was organized. He said that there are well over one hundred prefectures in the Northeast, that there is one cooperative in each prefecture, and that under each cooperative there are branch cooperatives and business offices totaling over seven thousand. Their funds come from the government and their yearly need is ten billion yuan. During the planting season the cooperative sends persons to supervise the peasants and to instruct them in the type of seeds and number of *mu*

[one-sixth of an acre] to be planted. At harvest time the agricultural organization in each village does the purchasing. The peasants turn over their produce to units organized by grain merchants. In accord with the official standard of prices, for each ton of grain the peasants are given a ration of fifteen
square yards of cloth. The peasants then sell the cloth for from 60 to 70 times
the price they were paid for their grain to make up for losses suffered
because of the official price. Ordinary rations of daily necessities are one or
one-and-a-half catties of bean oil, one or one-and-a-half catties of lamp oil,
two boxes of matches, one or two catties of salt, one catty of cotton, and one
bundle of cotton yarn. The Hsing-nung Cooperative has received loans of
more than seven billion yuan. The Hsing-nung Bank has loaned the cooperative over three billion yuan. The savings that the peasants have deposited in
the cooperative amount to more than ten billion yuan. Such deposits comprise 80 percent of what the peasants have obtained from the harvest. This
time the Soviet Army's transactions in grain were entrusted to grain merchants. For each ton of grain they received three yuan from the Soviets. The
merchants received a commission of 60 cents as well as a transaction fee of 40
cents, altogether totaling one yuan. Recently, cotton has dropped in price
from 50 yuan to 30 yuan, and there has been an extraordinary shortage of
hemp sacks.

NOVEMBER 4.   This afternoon Special Envoy Chiang Ching-kuo went to
see the political commissar of the Soviet Army command. The political commissar told Special Envoy Chiang that a large number of Eighth Route Army
men were discovered in Ying-k'ou and that since the Soviet troops stationed
in Ying-k'ou were small in number, resistance was impossible so the Soviet
troops had already begun to withdraw. He also stated that because organizations promoting anti-Soviet movements continued to be discovered in various places, the Nationalist headquarters could not be allowed to reorganize
former puppet troops who had gone over to our side. From this talk it is very
clear that the Soviets deliberately are allowing Eighth Route Army men in
Hu-lu-tao and Ying-k'ou to obstruct the efforts of government troops to land
there.

NOVEMBER 5.   At one o'clock this afternoon Chairman Hsiung, Special
Envoy Chiang, and I met with Marshal Malinovsky for the fifth time.
Malinovsky remarked that the Eighth Route Army men found in Ying-k'ou
were from China Proper and had entered Ying-k'ou by way of Chin-chou.
Since there were quite a large number of them and they had fought in the
war against Japan, the Soviet Army was in no position to make them hand
over their weapons. The Eighth Route Army had forced the small number of

Soviet troops stationed in Ying-k'ou to leave and had even forced the small number of Soviet troops in Hu-lu-tao to leave. For if the Soviet army had chosen to act against the Eighth Route Army, this would have necessitated its transferring troops back to Ying-k'ou and Hu-lu-tao, thus delaying the deadline for troop withdrawal, something the Soviets did not want to do. Chairman Hsiung asked what attitude the Soviets would adopt if government troops and the Eighth Route Army came into conflict. Marshal Malinovsky said the Soviets would not interfere. Then we began discussing the question of our administrative personnel going into the various provinces to take over. Malinovsky answered that our administrative personnel could go into the various provinces to take over but were only permitted to use local police forces and must not reorganize troops, since that might leave room for pro-Japanese elements. He added that we also could take over the various local postal and telegraph organizations but not yet the general organization in Ch'ang-ch'un. Neither could we take over the railroads, since they still were under the jurisdiction of the Soviet Army's united military transportation organization. After this we discussed the question of airlifting government troops. Malinovsky stated that we were free to airlift government troops into the Northeast and that he would not oppose this even if we borrowed U.S. planes to transport them. However, American air personnel must not do the groundwork.

My Analysis of the Fifth Talk with Malinovsky

From the beginning the Soviets had agreed that our government troops could land at Ying-k'ou and Hu-lu-tao. Marshal Malinovsky already said this in our first and second talks. On October 21 the vice-chief of staff of the Soviet Army likewise said this to our Vice-Chief of Staff Tung. The Soviets did not respond affirmatively to our request that the Soviet Army assist our government troops as they landed at these two places and traveled by rail from Ying-k'ou to Mukden. Although I dare not draw from this the conclusion that their attitude was totally false, I wonder how things developed into the present situation. The Soviets have openly admitted the presence of the Eighth Route Army in Hu-lu-tao and Ying-k'ou. Moreover, they acknowledge that the Eighth Route Army are Chinese troops who fought the Japanese, so that the Soviets were in no position to stop them from being there. This has amounted to making it impossible for government troops to land at both places. In my opinion, the process has evolved in this way:

1. The Soviets are unwilling to have us rely on the United States to transport our troops. In other words, they are unwilling to have the

United States acquire a foothold in the Northeast. The landing at Dairen of personnel from an American warship to inspect conditions there aroused resentment on the part of the Soviets. On October 29 during the fourth talk, Malinovsky's tone and countenance were stern when he mentioned the landing of personnel from this American warship. On October 29 Vice-Chief of Staff Tung notified the Soviets that we had decided to borrow American transports to send our troops to Hu-lu-tao and Ying-k'ou. This also must have caused dissatisfaction among the Soviets. Therefore, postwar antagonism between the United States and the Soviet Union and the fact that we must rely on the United States may be an important factor obstructing the entry of our troops into the Northeast.

2. Although I dare not say that the actions of personnel belonging to party branch headquarters in the Northeast were always free of indiscretions, nevertheless, the central government issued no instructions hostile to the Soviets. Possibly, the Eighth Route Army secretly had its underground personnel concoct anti-Soviet activities for the purpose of undermining Sino-Soviet relations. For a long time the Soviets have been suspicious of the Nationalist party, and, naturally, it was easy to enhance that suspicion.

NOVEMBER 6.   Generalissimo Chiang sent a wire saying that there must be no wavering on our landing at Ying-k'ou and requesting that the Soviets assume responsibility.

Today at 12 M. Kargan, the Soviet vice-chairman of the board of directors of the Ch'ang-ch'un Railroad, came to see me. He told me that he had received a wire from his government requesting that he decide on a list of Soviets to be appointed supervisors of the railroad. I discussed and made up such a list with him.

On November 9 I shall take up my post at the Railroad Bureau. As soon as the agenda is agreed upon by both China and the Soviet Union, I shall call a meeting of the board of directors. Kargan said that, according to the Sino-Soviet agreement, the way in which the railroad police is to be organized should be decided through discussions between the two governments. At present for the sake of expediency he has formed a temporary police organization and has placed in charge of it Sun Chiu-ssu, formerly vice-chief of the public security bureau of the municipal government of Ch'ang-ch'un. Six hundred Chinese policemen have been engaged and are carrying out their duties along the tracks in the vicinity of Ch'ang-ch'un. Railroad police also are in the process of being organized in other regions. Since this organization is temporary, I did not argue with him. He also stated that as soon as a permanent organization has been decided on, the chairman of the board of directors shall be in charge. I then stated that the present railroad police must take responsibility if, after the evacuation of the Soviet Army and before the arrival of our troops, irregular troops dismantle railroad tracks and demolish bridges. My idea was to place the responsibility for such destruction on the Soviets in order to prevent them from delaying the deadline for the evacuation of their troops under the pretext that there were security problems along the railroads or that Soviet troops must be sent to protect the railroads. Kargan suddenly referred to zones under railroad protection along both sides of the railroads, saying that our discussion of railroad police made him think of this question. I replied that the special zones demarcated on both sides of the railroads had been created by tsarist Russia and Japan. Their aim was to use loans to perhaps jointly manage the railroads with China so as to expand their spheres of influence, but this no longer was relevant to the twentieth century; in Article 9 of the Sino-Soviet agreement, concerning railroad police, there are no regulations governing this issue. Kargan then said that he wanted the board of directors placed in Ch'ang-ch'un, and the Railroad Bureau in Harbin. The reason for this is that, in addition to being a commercial center, Harbin already has housing for the Railroad Bureau as well as all of the needed equipment. Kargan also told me that, in accordance with the Sino-Soviet agreement, the head of the Railroad Bureau is to be chosen from among Soviet personnel and that Kargan had already chosen Zhuravliev, head of the Railroad Bureau for the section of the Trans-Siberian Railroad between Vladivostock and Ussurisk, for this post.

This afternoon the various provincial governors came to ask for funds. They said they must have funds before they could take up their posts. Stating that I had come to the Northeast without a cent in my pockets, I gently advised the provincial governors of the importance of their economizing to the best of their ability during this transitional period.

NOVEMBER 7.   Today is the anniversary of the Soviet Union's October Revolution. Together with Chairman Hsiung Shih-hui, Special Envoy Chiang Ching-kuo and Vice-Chief of Staff Tung Yen-p'ing, I went to the general headquarters of the Soviet Army to express our congratulations.

At 5:00 P.M. we went over to Marshal Malinovsky's reception where Malinovsky gave a speech. The general tone was, "The Soviet Union was the first nation to renounce extraterritorial rights. Recently, it also has entered into the Sino-Soviet agreement. All of this symbolizes a love of peace and righteousness on the part of the Soviet Union."

Chairman Hsiung responded with another speech, which generally ran as follows:

The Soviet Union was not only the first nation to renounce its extraterritorial rights but it also was the first nation to assist China in fighting a war of resistance. Add to these the Sino-Soviet agreement, and it goes without saying that the Chinese government and the Chinese people are grateful. Furthermore, the present mission of Marshal Malinovsky in the Northeast has great historical significance.

After dinner songs and dances were performed by the Frontline Red Army Fighters' Song, Dance, and Drama Ensemble. Before the performance began there was a fifteen-minute break, and Marshal Malinovsky suddenly came to talk with me. He said,

Hereafter, the work of the first stage will be Your Excellency's. Your Excellency always has enjoyed high prestige within economic circles, is rich in experience, and has long been renowned. I also know that Your Excellency is a thinker and will be able to resolve all problems. I hope that Your Excellency will not be swayed by the gold dollar (i.e., the American dollar).

I replied, "The people and the land form the economic resources of every nation. The gold dollar actually is not an important factor. I will first make use of the manpower and material resources of both China and the Soviet Union and resort to the gold dollar only when these two things are not enough." Malinovsky then said, "Stress the spiritual." I said,

Because of their products China and the Soviet Union naturally must enter into trade with the nations of the world. Therefore, it would be difficult for our two nations to completely ignore the gold dollar. I hope that the Soviets will go as far as they can in frankly telling us their opinions so as not to leave room for any estrangement.

Malinovsky answered, "Of course. Fortunately, by relying on Your Excellency's wisdom every problem can be settled." I said: "I am deeply grateful and I hope the marshal continues to trust me." Malinovsky answered: "I will trust Your Excellency forever."

This conversation merited a good deal of retrospection on my part. I did not know what economic policies were involved; still less did I know why, from the tone of his remarks, Malinovsky attached so much importance to my work.

At noon today I invited for lunch the following persons: Liu Che, a director of the Chinese–Ch'ang-ch'un Railroad, Wang Wen-po, assistant head of the board of the railroad, Wan I, another director (Liu Tse-jung, the foreign affairs special envoy stationed in Sinkiang, was preoccupied with important duties there, so Wan I was appointed to replace him), and Wang Shu-jen, a member of the Economic Commission.

NOVEMBER 9.   At 5 P.M. Chairman Hsiung gave a reception for Marshal Malinovsky, the Soviet air force marshal, the chief of staff, and Red Army officers, 30 in all. Other guests also numbered 30. First, Chairman Hsiung gave a speech. Marshal Malinovsky replied with another speech. After that I stood up to deliver my speech, the general idea of which was as follows:

> It is nearly three hundred years since China and the Soviet Union established diplomatic relations. There are three reasons why they have been unable to develop an intimate relationship: (1) communications were difficult, (2) aside from trade along the border, there were no economic relations, and (3) thinking of the leaders of the two nations differed. Today, with airplanes for communications, the two nations are very close. In addition, there is our expansive Northeast to serve as a field for experimentation in economic cooperation. Furthermore, the wise leaders of the two nations do not really differ from one another in the realm of thought and spirit. I dare trust that economic cooperation surely will succeed; from this economic cooperation we can go a step further and form all kinds of relationships between our two nations. However, the attainment of this goal requires three major conditions: (1) fairness, (2) both must benefit, and (3) no subterfuge. I surely will abide by these three great principles, and I dare trust that Marshal Malinovsky also will assume the role of matchmaker for cooperation between our two nations. Recently, Marshal Malinovsky told me that the Soviets have decided to first hand back to us the telegraph organizations as well as the printing press. This is like giving a dowry to a bride. The bride now wishes the two nations a friendship that lasts 100 years.

Tomorrow, Chairman Hsiung returns to Chungking to report. I wrote a letter to Generalissimo Chiang to report on the recent situation here. This morning I began work at the Ch'ang-ch'un Railroad Bureau.

NOVEMBER 10.   Today, Chairman Hsiung flew to Chungking, planning to return to Ch'ang-ch'un in four or five days. Meanwhile, Vice-Chief of Staff Tung negotiated with Major General Pavlovsky about all arrangements for airlifting our troops to Ch'ang-ch'un. It has been decided that starting from November 17 the troops will first land in Mukden; beginning on the twentieth they will land in Ch'ang-ch'un. The Soviets will assume responsibility for ground service and military protection at both the Mukden and Ch'ang-ch'un airports. The Soviets also will demarcate areas in both places for the stationing of airlifted troops. The last day when the Soviets will provide service and protection will be November 20 in Mukden and November 23 in Ch'ang-ch'un. After these dates our side is to take charge.

In the morning I worked in the office of the board of directors of the Ch'ang-ch'un Railroad Bureau. I prepared a speech to give this afternoon at the meeting to set up the board of directors. At four o'clock in the afternoon there was a joint meeting of the directors and supervisors. I first delivered my speech. Then Kargan, vice-head of the board of directors, gave a speech in reply. After that Levashoff, head of the board of supervisors, made a speech, and Mo Te-hui, vice-head of the board of supervisors, gave a speech in reply. Besides these people, there were the following at the meeting: directors Malie, Efstiznef, Kozlov, Liu Che, and Wan I; supervisors Trubi-hin, Lifanoff, Kao Lun-chin, and Chiu Wei-ying. When the meeting was over we had cocktails and photos were taken. Then we parted.

NOVEMBER 11.   Special Envoy Chiang Ching-kuo showed me a letter to him from Generalissimo Chiang, who plans to ask him to take a trip to Moscow. I am all for this. I feel that we must arrive at a spiritual understanding with the Soviets; in comparison, all negotiations are nonessential. Even if our airlifted troops arrive, obstructions still may occur. Moreover, even if we may have a small number of troops in Mukden and Ch'ang-ch'un, what about the other places? It would be better to reach a thorough understanding with Soviet leaders concerning the future of the Northeast. I informed Generalissimo Chiang of this in a letter. It happens that Wang Ming-te, vice-chairman of the Aviation Commission who has been here to make arrangements for the airlift, is finished with his task and about to go back to Chungking. I asked him to take the letter.

I got a report saying that the Bank of China in Fengtien is under surveillance by the Eighth Route Army and that the Bank of China in Harbin had opened but is now closed.

The general headquarters of the Soviet Army has removed Ts'ao Chao-yuan, the mayor of Ch'ang-ch'un, from his post and has replaced him with Soviet communist party member Liu Chü-ying. It also dismissed Wu Shu-hsün, head of the security maintenance brigade of the public security bureau, and replaced him with Ho Kuei-fan, a member of the communist party.

NOVEMBER 12.   In the morning I went to the board of directors of the Ch'ang-ch'un Railroad Bureau. The Soviet vice-chairman of the board of directors invited me there to discuss the question of delaying the date of withdrawal by Red Army train maintenance personnel of the northern section because operating trains along the northern section always has been the responsibility of the Red Army train maintenance team. Now, the Soviet Army soon must leave and since Chinese personnel and workers had not yet been recruited, he asked that the date of evacuation be postponed for three months. He said that as soon as Chinese personnel and workers had been recruited, Soviet personnel would leave. He hoped that the Chinese government would propose this to the Soviet government. I surmised that the Soviets already had reached a decision about this matter; however, for the sake of maintaining a facade of respect for China's sovereignty, they want us to advance this proposal. Since this matter is merely a factual thing, I promised to do so. I immediately wired both the Ministry of Foreign Affairs and the Ministry of Communications and showed the telegram to the Soviet vice-chairman of the board of directors. He immediately wired Moscow.

According to reports, more than two thousand Red Army men have arrived from Mukden. The security maintenance brigade of the municipal government is also enlisting members. The Northeast Headquarters has received news that a large number of armed bandit troops are lying in ambush around the Ch'ang-ch'un airport. The people are in a state of anxiety. They think that the Soviets are hatching other plots to obstruct the airlifting of our troops to Ch'ang-ch'un and will even allow armed antigovernment bandit troops to imprison central government takeover personnel.

NOVEMBER 13.   Today the Soviets came to tell me they are preparing to transfer the Electrical Communications and Telephone Company to us. It happened that this morning I got a wire from Chairman Hsiung, advising a postponement of such a takeover. I had to fabricate and give to the Soviets an excuse for postponing it. But the Soviets still requested that we begin taking over tomorrow. I and Ching-kuo have the same view: we think that the Soviets have one overall plan for the Northeast and that these small issues really do not affect their general plan.

Today I received a document having to do with the methods used by the Soviets to compel the persons in charge of the Manchurian Heavy Industry Company and the electric company to voluntarily hand these enterprises over to the Soviet Union, the reason being that the above enterprises both had aided the enemy during the war.

The following list is a report on the course of negotiations, as related by Takasaki Tatsunosuke, general manager of the Heavy Industrial Company. The negotiations were between him and Sladkovsky, representative of the Soviet Far Eastern Trading Company (i.e., economic adviser to the Soviet Army command).

1. On October 24, 1945, Colonel Sladkovsky asked Takasaki, general manager of the Manchurian Industrial Co., to have the various enterprises belonging to the Manchurian company handed over to the Soviet Union.

2. Takasaki gave the following oral response:

Since the various enterprises belonging to the Manchurian Industrial Company now also are considered part of the postwar settlement [literally *chieh-kuo*, meaning result, but obviously having another meaning in this context], naturally they must be taken over by the Soviet Union or China. But as for requesting that they be handed over at a time when Manchukuo no longer exists, this truly is beyond the power of the general manager of the Manchurian Industrial Company. However, if the Allied nations issue orders for such a takeover, naturally I will be obliged to obey. I shall list those enterprises making up the Manchurian company and am prepared to render an accurate account of such enterprises to facilitate handing them over. I can also comply with the desires of the parties involved in such a takeover by instructing employed personnel to give an account of their businesses. Through appropriate measures I also can ask the various companies belonging to the Industrial Company to give an account of their operations.

3. Colonel Sladkovsky requested a written version of this oral response. General Manager Takasaki replied as follows: "Since the request for handing over the Manchurian Industrial Company comes from the Soviet Union then naturally the Soviet Union should first issue a written order to us before we, in the position of a defeated nation, can issue a document acknowledging its request."

4. Colonel Sladkovsky rejected this, saying,

Actually, the Soviet Union can proceed with the takeover by relying on its real strength; there is no need to resort to the formality of issuing a written order and requesting a document of acknowledgement. For you to submit to us a written request to hand over the Manchurian Industrial Company legitimizes our taking over. Therefore, that is the way things should be done.

5. Takasaki then confronted him with this question: "If we hand over the Manchurian Industrial Company to the Soviet Union then in the future China is bound to disagree and how shall we handle that?" Colonel Sladkovsky answered: "The Soviet Union will take the responsibility for solving problems having to do with China." Sladkovsky never ceased requesting that Takasaki unilaterally submit a written request.

6. As a result, on the twenty-sixth of the same month Takasaki wrote and submitted the following draft:

Most of the companies making up the Manchurian Industrial Company were run for military purposes so, in my opinion, should be taken over by the Soviet Army as the representative of the armies of the Allied nations. If things are conducted in this manner, it is my hope that the companies involved will be speedily restored to their normal condition, that their staff members will be given back their jobs, and that the daily life of these staff members will be stabilized.

7. Colonel Sladkovsky thought that the above was inappropriately worded. Therefore, he proposed the following revision:

The various companies belonging to the Manchurian Industrial Company have been used to meet the needs of the Japanese Kwantung Army. In other words, they were run for military purposes. Consequently, on principle, we regard them as a Soviet military objective. In accord with conditions agreed upon between the Soviet Army and the Kwantung Army, we ought to make up a detailed list of these companies and hand these companies over as property belonging to the Soviet Army command. When the Companies making up the Manchurian Industrial Company resume business, I will make up a complete list of all technical personnel, staff members, and workers for your reference in case of need. I beg that you guarantee them a livelihood.

8. After examining the foregoing revision by the Soviets, the general manager of the Manchurian Industrial Company observed that the company knew absolutely nothing about the alleged agreement between the Soviet Army and the Kwantung Army. Therefore he hoped that the Soviets would delete this point. "We also hope that the Soviets will change 'the opposite party to whom we hand over' to 'the Soviet Army as the representative of the Allied nations in Manchuria.' "

9. Colonel Sladkovsky said:

There is no need to insert the word "representative." Actually, among the armies of the Allied nations, the Soviet Army is the only one now in Manchuria. Therefore, handing over Manchurian industry to the Soviet Army is tantamount to handing it over to the Allied nations. There is no need for revising the terminology.

10. As a result of various diplomatic talks, on the twenty-eighth and twenty-ninth of the same month the following version was decided on:

The various companies under the jurisdiction of the Manchurian Industrial Company have provided for the needs of the Kwantung Army. We, the business executives of these companies, now transfer to the Soviet Union our rights to the entire assets, including buildings for manufacturing enterprises, buildings for business operations, residences, and various other buildings. We enclose a register of the names of these companies and an inventory of the buildings for enterprises that should be handed over to the Soviet Union. It is our hope that when the enterprises listed in the register mentioned above resume operation, all specialists, technicians, clerks, and workers who have been employed in these enterprises will be given jobs, irrespective of their nationality and that, in addition, their lives, property, and livelihood will be guaranteed. October 29, 1945. Jointly signed by the general manager of the Manchurian Industrial Company and representatives of the various companies. To: Red Army command of the Soviet Army.

11. On October 28 the representatives of the various companies in Ch'ang-ch'un signed the document mentioned above and affixed their seals to it. As for representatives in other places, they did the same thing separately in Liaoning, Fu-shun, An-shan, Dairen, Fu-hsin, and Harbin between the thirty-first of the same month and November 6.

12. Later, on November 9 General Manager Takasaki submitted the following document:

Owing to the great kindness of Your Excellency and Your Excellency's advisers, between October 30 and November 6 I had the opportunity to inspect various companies related to the Manchurian Industrial Company and to meet with the highest-ranking cadres, with whom I had been out of contact for eight months. I have thus come to understand the actual conditions in these companies. For this I am deeply grateful. With respect to the document of October 29, cadres of the various companies all have acknowledged and signed it. As they signed their names they also expressed the hopes that I summarize and submit to you:

a. Please speedily decide on a policy for operating the various companies and give an early reply with respect to the concerns of the representatives of the various companies.

b. In order to help us prepare a catalog of assets, please list separately and indicate clearly that portion already removed by the various companies, that portion still to be removed in the future, and that portion that should be retained.

c. As you decide on a policy for operating the enterprises, it also is our hope that you will decide which staff members are to be kept on and which are to be dismissed. In addition, we hope that until you reach this decision you can guarantee a minimal living for the people currently employed in these companies and also will allow them to continue living in their present residences until they can obtain new ones.

d. There is a great danger that during the period when these companies are not functioning mobs will cause damage to them. We hope that you will try to maintain order.

e. We hope that as you take over the various companies, in addition to exercising the right to claim debts owed to them, you also will give ample consideration to the debts owed by them. We especially have in mind debts owed to staff members of the companies, such as the deposits of such staff members as well as their departure bonuses. We hope you will continue to pay these.

November 9, 1945, Takasaki Tatsunosuke, General Manager of the Manchurian Industrial Company. To: The command of the Soviet Red Army.

13. The establishment of the northeastern Sino-Soviet Industrial Commune is being arranged in the office of Colonel Sladkovsky in the Ta-hsing Building. The general manager and several staff members of the Manchurian Industrial Company are assisting.

The following is the document of acknowledgment signed by the person in charge of the electrical company:

Before the war ended the Manchurian Electrical Company also worked to meet the needs of the Kwantung Army. Now, as business executive of the company, I transfer to the Union of Soviet Socialist Republics the right to its entire assets. The assets of the company include its buildings for manufacturing, its building for business operations, its residences, its warehouses, and various other structures. On behalf of the staff, I hope that when the enterprise begins, the specialists, technicians, skilled workers, clerks, and other workers of the company—i.e., whoever worked for it—will be given jobs as well as guarantees concerning their lives, property, and livelihood, irrespective of their nationality. October 30, 1945. Hirajima Toshio, chairman of the board of directors, Manchurian Electrical Company.

After reading the above documents I have come to appreciate how concerned the Soviets are with the industry and mines of Manchuria and how much they desire to have a share in these. This is an important reason for their efforts to make impossible the penetration of American influence into Manchuria and for obstructing the dispatch of our troops into the Northeast. First, the Soviets schemed to snatch from the Japanese as war booty the industries and mines of Manchuria. Meanwhile, fearing that scheme might not succeed, they dismantled important machinery and transferred it into their possession. It is all too clear that there is no way to resolve the problem of the takeover without solving the economic problem. Now I can discern the significance of Marshal Malinovsky's statement on November 7 that "Hereafter, work of the first stage will be Your Excellency's."

I learned from a report that the Soviets have given their Far Eastern Trading Company one million yuan in their army bank notes for the compulsory purchase of the buildings of the Ta-hsing Company, which will then be used to conduct business.

According to a report from the Japanese, American planes bombed the Northeast three times, beginning in June 1944. The coke oven of the An-shan Iron Works was damaged in these bombings and production reduced by more than half. Various factories in Mukden and T'ieh-hsi also were bombed and damaged.

NOVEMBER 14.   In the morning, Mr. Mo Liu-ts'un came to talk. He thinks the situation in the Northeast is gloomy and foreboding, almost like conditions before the Mukden Incident. He thinks that we must first speedily announce that we will transport no more troops here in order to relieve Soviet worries; only then can we look for a turnaround in the economic and political situation. Therefore, I asked him why he shouldn't visit Chungking, since it seemed to me that he has discerned the heart of the problem.

In the afternoon, I discussed with Kargan, the Soviet vice-chairman of the board of directors of the Ch'ang-ch'un Railroad, the question of the Committee for the Drafting of Regulations and the Assessment Committee. His idea is that we still should stick to the original plan when deciding upon regulations. First, we should read one another's drafts and then, when discussion has made things clear, go to Chungking for a conference. As for the assessment, we can first hold a meeting in Ch'ang-ch'un and leave the decision for a meeting in Chungking. Next we can send the draft separately to the two governments for their approval. Then we discussed the employment of personnel. Kargan desired that we first discuss and decide on an outline for the organization of the board of directors and next, arrange for the personnel of the board of directors. After this, we could discuss the organization of the bureau and its personnel. I told him we could proceed in this manner. When I brought up a candidate for the vice-chief of the bureau, he wished to consider Yang Ts'e. I said that Yang already is advanced in age and that we needed for this post an energetic person able to implement my proposals. He said he was not opposed. We also discussed the question of the railroad police. He felt that the Chinese government should assume the responsibility of providing funds for the railroad police. He also said that the board of directors of the Railroad Bureau intends to set up a police inspectors' division and create the post of general inspector. I replied that I could approve. I also agreed to having a Soviet person assume the general inspectorship, but I proposed adding the post of vice-general inspector, which would be held by a Chinese. The reason why I agreed to having a Soviet person assume the general inspectorship is that we had the right to decide the candidacy for the chief of the Railroad Bureau. I am seeking a balance between the rights of both sides. Kargan also wants a crime investigating section set up in the Railroad Bureau. I answered that I had no objection. Finally, he said the directors should be assigned separate duties so that they could deal with various matters. I indicated that I agreed.

At 6:00 P.M. Sladkovsky, economic counselor to the Soviet Army command, invited me for a talk. First he brought up the issue of various Soviet commercial organizations, such as the Far Eastern Bank, the Far Eastern Transportation Company, the Grain Export Company, the International Travel Service, and the International Bookstore, intending to register with the Chinese government. I said that I could assist. Then he raised the question of the Grain Export Company's planning to operate three airplanes of its own for communication between various locations in the Northeast, with the aim of conducting business. I asked that I be given time for consideration before replying. Finally, he mentioned briefly that with respect to industry he intended to regard confiscated enemy property as Soviet war booty and to cooperate with us concerning the property.

NOVEMBER 15.   In the afternoon, accompanied by Economic Counselor Sladkovsky, Yemchenko, representative of the Soviet National Bank, and Yelinez, deputy manager of the Far Eastern Bank, came to see me. Yemchenko stated that the general office of the Far Eastern Bank, originally located in Harbin, temporarily had ceased to function because of Japanese interference. Yesterday, shareholders of the bank held a provisional meeting in Harbin where it was decided to resume business. In the future, the bank's board of directors and its general office will move to Ch'ang-ch'un. The bank in Harbin will become a branch office. If warranted by the expansion of business, a branch office also may be set up in Mukden and Dairen. Yemchenko said that the chief business of the bank is to serve the Ch'ang-ch'un Railroad as well as to develop Sino-Soviet trade. He also said that the site of the bank would be that of the former Cheng-chin Bank, and that tomorrow or the day after he will have the bank's tablet hung out. Last, he stated that the nature of the bank is purely commercial and will serve commercial needs.

I first told him that to set up a bank he must register it with the Chinese government, in accord with Chinese law, and that I wanted to have the bank's regulations and procedures for resuming business sent to me so that I could forward these to our Finance Ministry. Representative Yemchenko said that as far back as 1927 the bank had established branch offices within China's boundaries and that it had registered with and obtained the approval of our Finance Ministry. He added that this approval had not been withdrawn, that the Japanese had compelled the bank's branch offices within Manchuria's boundaries to cease functioning, and that he expected the Chinese government not to raise obstacles to the bank's resuming business. I replied that I would report these details to the Finance Ministry though I still hoped that he would send me details about when the bank was going to resume business, about the location of the general office after it had moved from Harbin to Ch'ang-ch'un, and about the location of the branch offices that were going to be set up so that I could pass on this information to Chungking. He promised to do this, adding that he hoped this would not hinder the starting of business. I told him there was no cause to worry, and that I would do my best to help. I then asked Sladkovsky whether he had things to discuss.

He said that he was very delighted that Soviet and Chinese bankers meet and engage in such a pleasant discussion and that he intends to inquire whether today he could be given an answer to the question he raised yesterday concerning the Grain Export Company's request to operate air transportation of its own. I told him that I already have wired the Ministry of Communications and that as soon as a reply arrives I will give him an answer.

At 4:30 P.M. Chiang Ching-kuo invited me to the office of the foreign affairs special envoy. He told me that he had just received by airplane a handwritten statement from Chairman Hsiung T'ien-i [Shih-hui], which read as follows:

1. The headquarters is under orders to move to Shan-hai-kuan. Except for those who are to remain as members of the military delegation, all of its personnel will be flown back to Peiping and then will move on to Shan-hai-kuan.

2. There will remain in Ch'ang-ch'un a military delegation to keep in contact with the general headquarters of the Soviet Army. It will stay or move with that headquarters.

3. Vice-Chief of Staff Tung Yen-p'ing will head the military delegation. Hu Shih-chieh will be a member. The rest of the personnel will be decided by Vice-Chief of Staff Tung, in conjunction with Messrs. Chang Kia-ngau and Chiang Ching-kuo.

At ten o'clock on the same night Vice-Chief of Staff Tung invited Major General Pavlovsky for a talk and notifed him about the date of withdrawal.

Chiang Ching-kuo produced and showed me another handwritten letter from Generalissimo Chiang. The gist of this was,

The Northeast Headquarters has decided to withdraw. Let's see what the Soviet reaction is after a day or two. If there still is hope of retrieving the situation, we then can indicate that we really do not wish to establish our military power in the Northeast; neither do we wish to provoke anyone. To create local political organizations we can use popular elections. In econom-

ics we can cooperate with the Soviets. The Foreign Affairs Ministry already
has formally notified the Soviet ambassador about the date of withdrawal of
the headquarters.

In my opinion, Generalissimo Chiang is withdrawing the headquarters
as a stratagem to counter Soviet efforts to obstruct our takeover and secretly
assist the Eighth Route Army. In addition he also wants to find out what the
Soviets' real attitude is. At the same time, we are preparing to give the
Soviets a military, political, and economic palliative to dispel their suspicion
of the National government. If in this context our foreign affairs authorities
can be flexible in applying this stratagem, there well may occur a change in
the situation, but we will have to wait and see how things develop in the
future. Chairman Hsiung was in Chungking participating in this decision to
withdraw. A part of the reason for this decision must have been the panic
among the personnel of the headquarters caused by Soviet replacement of
the mayor of Ch'ang-ch'un and the head of its public security bureau, as well
as by the rumor that antigovernment troops had gathered in Ch'ang-ch'un. I
always thought that the Soviets have in their minds a design for the Northeast and that their allowing the Eighth Route Army men in Ch'ang-ch'un or
Mukden openly to flaunt their power is only a transitional measure. They
never will go to the extent of allowing antigovernment troops to imprison
central government personnel and incur for themselves the shameful responsibility of destroying the Sino-Soviet agreement. Nor do I believe they ever
will change their original plan because of the withdrawal of our headquarters. If, in keeping with Generalissimo Chiang's instructions, we had been
candid and explained our situation to the Soviets, this might have been more
effective than withdrawing our headquarters. Generalissimo Chiang has instructed us concerning three points. Militarily and economically, there are
two points in these instructions. I also have mentioned this point in my letter
[the word *hsin* (letter) is missing in the original text] to Generalissimo Chiang
of November 11.

When Vice-Chief of Staff Tung notified Major General Pavlovsky about
the withdrawal of the headquarters, Pavlovsky's reaction was exceedingly
calm. He also informed us about the number of remaining enemy prisoners-
of-war as well as that, following their arrival in Ch'ang-ch'un, our airlifted
troops are to enter the metropolitan district of the city after November 24.

NOVEMBER 16.   At 10:00 A.M. I gathered together all the takeover
personnel of the Northeast Headquarters and announced to them the order
for evacuation. The gist of my talk was, "On orders from the Generalissimo,
our headquarters will temporarily withdraw to Peiping and await further
instructions."

Knowing that all of the takeover personnel would be infuriated by this information, I went ahead and gave them an account of the course of events, urging them to be calm in order not to cause incidents that might irreparably worsen Sino-Soviet relations.

We came to the Northeast with the aim of repossessing the territory of our homeland, acting on the basis of the Sino-Soviet Treaty of Friendship and Alliance as well as the trust between Allied nations. But the fact remains that for fourteen years the Northeast has been a subjugated area; local order has not been restored and it is impossible to prevent bad elements from taking advantage of this opportunity to cause trouble. This has caused our government to feel that, in order to safeguard the establishment of administrative organizations, it must stabilize the social order by bringing into the Northeast a number of troops. Initially, we felt that the easiest way to transport our troops into the Northeast was to land them at Dairen. But Marshal Malinovsky stressed the point that Dairen is a free port so Chinese troops must not land there. Repeated negotiations have produced no results. Chairman Hsiung proposed that the question of our troops landing at Dairen temporarily be shelved and that Chinese troops first land at Ying-k'ou and Hu-lu-tao. However, on October 27 and 28, when our troop transports arrived at Hu-lu-tao, they were fired upon from the shore by armed forces of unknown background. This obstructed the landing of the transports, which were obliged to sail back. On the fifth of this month Marshal Malinovsky suddenly notified us that certain armed troops from Mukden had arrived in Ying-k'ou and were constructing defense works. For this reason the Soviets could not be responsible for the safety of Chinese troops landing at Ying-k'ou. Now imagine if we had gone ahead and carried out our original plans, this certainly would have resulted in large-scale combat. Our compatriots in the Northeast have suffered deeply for fourteen years. We cannot bear to see a war of any kind recur in the Northeast or any incident that would add to the suffering of the people. Today, inspired by a spirit of great wisdom, humaneness, and bravery, our generalissimo and our government have decided to yield to reality. In the interests of the safety of our compatriots in the Northeast, as well as the preservation of friendly relations among Allied nations, they have decided to move the headquarters to Shan-hai-kuan. The rest of the takeover personnel are to be withdrawn to Peiping. Today, we leave the Northeast, but we have obtained much valuable knowledge. We have been like parents coming here to visit children parted from us for fourteen years. Even though we must leave after only one look, nevertheless, already we have expressed our feelings of concern and longing, comparable to those between blood relations, which have lasted for fourteen years. To sum up, we need not regret departing but should leave as pleasantly as we came. Finally, I hope that when you arrive in Peiping or even Chungking you will behave with forbearance, like statesmen, and that none of you will say a word about the matter of our taking over sovereignty in the Northeast.

In the morning I sent Secretary Keng to see the Soviet economic counselor and tell him that we are ready to comply with the request that their grain company operate its own air transports. This was to show that our friendship for the Soviet Union is not affected by the withdrawal of the headquarters. At 8:00 P.M. the economic counselor came to press for a response concerning the issue of economic cooperation. It seems that the Soviets, having learned about the withdrawal of our headquarters, are anxious to settle the question of economic cooperation so that they can decide on the attitude and steps they should take with respect to our takeover. The conversation went as follows:

SLADKOVSKY: You have favored me by sending a person to tell me that the issue of the Soviet grain company operating three airplanes has been fully settled. I am very grateful for this. But I want to know whether Your Excellency has formal proposals concerning the question of industrial cooperation.

I: I already have informed my government about our previous conversation as well as about my personal opinions, asking it to try to find a channel for complete cooperation between us concerning this question.

SLADKOVSKY: On what conditions is cooperation to be based?

I: I have asked my government to formulate a plan of action concerning this that will serve as a basis for negotiations. But I don't know whether Your Excellency has a plan of action.

SLADKOVSKY: I have received instructions that the most important thing with respect to industrial cooperation is to seek for methods of creating a reasonable organization.

I: Please tell me your general ideas.

SLADKOVSKY: We Soviets want Chinese participation in the many kinds of factories that formerly belonged to the Japanese and to which we now have assigned Soviet managers. We want China to take part in the management of these factories in accord with the principle of both China and the Soviet Union having an equal share.

I: Last time I discussed classifying the industries here into two types: one, those belonging to the South Manchuria Railway, the other, those belonging to the Heavy Industry Company. The latter were organized in accord with the law of the Manchurian puppet government and include scores of units. Which type are those indicated by Your Excellency or do they also include industries other than the two types mentioned above?

SLADKOVSKY: Since they are involved with the Ch'ang-ch'un Railroad, the industries operated by the Manchurian railroads are another matter. Negotiations concerning them should take place at another time. What I intend to discuss today concerns the various factories other than those industries belonging to the Manchurian railroads.

I: Please specify whether, in the final analysis, Your Excellency is indicating those (factories) belonging to the Heavy Industry Company or whether various light industrial factories also are included.

SLADKOVSKY: I am indicating the industries that formerly belonged to the Japanese. Of all the industrial capital in the Northeast, the Japanese owned approximately 70 percent and Manchurians, 30 percent. Now we Soviets are willing to jointly manage the above industries with China, on the principle that both nations enjoy an equal share.

I: The Heavy Industry Company includes scores of units. I have made an investigation: Japanese investment made up only one-third of total capital in the Northeast, while Manchurian investment comprised two-third. Under these circumstances, shouldn't the Manchurian share belong to China?

SLADKOVSKY: The intelligence I have obtained differs slightly from Your Excellency's description. The various enterprises run by the Heavy Industry Company made up more than 80 percent of the total industry of Manchuria. Aside from this, 10 percent belonged to the Manchurian railroads, while the other 10 percent belonged to other sources of investment. As for the enterprises belonging to the Heavy Industry Company, over 70 percent of these belonged to Japanese, while Manchurian investment accounted for less than 30 percent.

I: The Japanese are exceedingly shrewd people. They invested sparingly, while obtaining the capital for industrial investment in the form of loans from the Central Bank and the Hsing-yeh Bank. If we count the loans and bonds issued by the Heavy Industry Company, this will prove that my statement is well-grounded and that Manchurian investment made up 70 percent of the capital of the Heavy Industry Company, while Japanese investment comprised merely 30 percent.

SLADKOVSKY: During our previous talk Your Excellency made the point that there existed the possibility of China and the Soviet Union jointly managing industries.

I: I wish first to understand the scope of such joint management. I maintain that light industry should be turned over to the people to manage. We can consign their management to private individuals. On the one hand, this will give private persons a chance to operate enterprises, while, on the other, funds obtained can be consigned to meet the debts of these enterprises to the banks. This is my personal opinion. I do not know Your Excellency's views.

SLADKOVSKY: But how are we going to handle other enterprises, excepting light industry?

I: My personal opinion is that since the Chinese government is willing to jointly manage heavy industry with the Soviets, we first should transfer to private management the more than 260 light industrial units formerly run by the Japanese because the people, who have suffered deeply from the disasters of war, should be given an opportunity to restore their private economy.

SLADKOVSKY: Then, what about heavy industry?

I: Discussion has to wait until my government has sent instructions. But if Your Excellency can inform me in relative detail about measures contemplated I will include them in my report to my government. It is likely that in this way we can more easily find a channel for settling the question.

SLADKOVSKY: I already have expressed my opinions; namely, organize a company and operate it on the principle of each having an equal share.

I: During our previous talk I inquired about which types of industry the Soviets would want to take part in. The Soviets are to play the major role in those that they want to take part in, while the Chinese are to play such a role in the rest of the industries, thus running the industries separately.

SLADKOVSKY: This is a matter of detail. The issue now is how we should settle the question of the various factories to which the Soviets already have assigned Soviet managers.

I: If the manager of a factory already is Soviet, even if someone from our side joins its managerial staff, his position merely will be that of a common shareholder. What cooperation to speak of is there?

SLADKOVSKY: It is precisely for this reason that I wish to discuss with Your Excellency ways of jointly and cooperatively managing, based on new principles and new managerial methods.

I: What Your Excellency considers to be detail, I regard as principle. Because if all the factories are operated by the Soviets, then Chinese technical specialists will not have a chance to develop their technology. That is why I maintain that in factories where Chinese investment comprises the greatest share, the Chinese play the major role and the Soviets, a minor role. In the opposite situation, the Soviets should play the major role, and the Chinese, the minor role. The aim of this is to give the Chinese the opportunity to develop freely their technology. The nature of Soviet industry is different from China's, since Soviet industry is concentrated in the hands of the state. In China private enterprises are able to develop freely. Here in the Northeast there are many factories whose capital originally was Chinese but which the Japanese either confiscated or else purchased through compulsion. Reasonably, they now should be returned to the people.

SLADKOVSKY: Your Excellency considers this a principle, but I still regard it as a detail.

I: Why don't we combine principle and detail in our discussion?

SLADKOVSKY: The question that Your Excellency has brought up is one that I find very interesting: that the Chinese play the major role in running certain enterprises and that the Soviets play the major role in operating others.

I: May I request that Your Excellency furnish a list of enterprises that the Soviets intend should be jointly managed?

SLADKOVSKY: At present I do not yet have such a list. But right now we wish to formulate a speedy plan of action that will settle the question, since a number of factories already have Soviet managers assigned to them.

I: Please forgive me for not being able to give you a general answer before I have at hand a specific plan of action.

SLADKOVSKY: I shall make a detailed report the next time we converse.

I: There exists another option. That is to make a list of the enterprises that originally were here in Manchuria and designate exactly which enterprises should be jointly managed.

SLADKOVSKY: But I still desire to settle exactly how to operate the factories that already have Soviet managers assigned to them.

I: It is only appropriate that everything be settled at the same time. It would be unsuitable to do this rashly now. I still hope for a settlement based on an overall plan of action.

SLADKOVSKY: In my opinion, until a general settlement is reached it would be best to keep in their respective factories the Soviet managers already assigned.

I: I shall consider this and make a serious study of it. We will wait until I receive a reply from my government and settle everything together.

SLADKOVSKY: When we meet next time we can take turns reading the lists of the enterprises.

I: My objective in coming here in the first place was to seek genuine cooperation between China and the Soviet Union. I shall try my best to do whatever I can to contribute to this cause.

SLADKOVSKY: The various opinions Your Excellency has raised indeed can serve as the basis for genuine economic cooperation betweeen the two nations.

I: But the political environment could hinder the development of economic cooperation.

SLADKOVSKY: That's true. But my jurisdiction extends only to economic matters, so the topic of our discussion must be limited to the same.

I: Your Excellency might convey this message to the authorities in charge.

SLADKOVSKY: Does Your Excellency mean that politics and economics are closely related?

I: Yes.

SLADKOVSKY: Is it Your Excellency's idea that political and economic problems must be settled at the same time?

I: That is exactly my idea. Let me try to give an example. If I only report on the economic situation and ignore political problems, my government certainly will blame me for the incompleteness of my observations.

SLADKOVSKY: I shall follow your wishes and convey the message to my government.

I: Please also convey the following message. As the delegate of my government, I several times have engaged in discussions with Marshal Malinovsky. Whenever Marshal Malinovsky has been unwilling to do something, I have suggested to my government that we not press him to do it. That is, that we not act in opposition to the desires of the Soviets. This should prove how very sincere I am with respect to Sino-Soviet cooperation.

SLADKOVSKY: When we meet next time we shall take turns reading one another's lists of enterprises.

I: Very good.

SLADKOVSKY: (as he was leaving) In Your Excellency's opinion is there hope for successful economic cooperation?

I: The withdrawal of the headquarters at this time fully indicates a friendly and compliant attitude on our part and affords the best opportunity for a change in the atmosphere. I hope that on my behalf Your Excellency will ask Marshal Malinovsky to make good use of the opportunity.

SLADKOVSKY: Your Excellency's ideas are very clear.

Today, in a discussion with Major General Pavlovsky, Vice-Chief of Staff Tung brought up the following point: During its occupation of the Northeast the Soviet Army has opened the following air routes:

1. From Chih-t'ai to Vladivostok via Ch'i-ch'i-ha-erh, Harbin, and Mu-tan-chiang

2. From Khabaraovsk to Dairen via Chia-mu-ssu, Harbin, Ch'ang-ch'un, and Mukden

He requested that these two air routes be turned into civil air routes.

My Analysis of Today's Discussion
with Economic Counselor Sladkovsky

The fact that Counselor Sladkovsky has revealed to me Soviet hopes indicates that because we are withdrawing our headquarters, the other side is anxious to settle the economic question so it can take a step further and resolve the issue of our takeover. This demonstrates fully that the economic question is the key factor.

I urged the Soviets to designate the industries in which they want to cooperate and then we could jointly manage a small number of factories, with the Soviets playing the major role, thus limiting the number of factories under joint management. But Sladkovsky insisted that all factories to which Soviet managers had been assigned be jointly managed. His idea was that all factories belonging to the Heavy Industry Company be under joint management.

Sladkovsky's remark that the opinions I raised indeed could serve as a basis for genuine cooperation between the two nations seems to indicate that there still is room for negotiation.

NOVEMBER 17.   Recently, the Northeast Headquarters has been a scene "haunted by the sound of the wind and the cry of the cranes." A report says that, following the murder of a policeman from the public security bureau of Ch'ang-ch'un, posters accusing the Nationalist party of having directed this appeared all along the streets. There also have been slogans demanding the expulsion of the headquarters. In addition, on the sixteenth the Soviets dismissed the policemen originally assigned to defend the head-quarters and replaced them with armed police. Running water for the head-quarters also has been cut off, and the telephone lines have been discon-nected. The feeling is that a great catastrophe is about to occur. Fearing that they will become fish in a pond, takeover personnel from the central govern-ment all yearn for an early departure.

Today, withdrawal of the headquarters began. More than one hundred and sixty people left Ch'ang-ch'un by airplane. The scene was a little disor-derly. At twelve o'clock Major General Pavlovsky invited Vice-Chief of Staff Tung to visit him and gave him the following notice:

On orders from Marshal Malinovsky I am notifying Your Excellency of the following decision and I request that Your Excellency report it to your government: "In accord with orders from Moscow, until they receive other orders Soviet troops will postpone their evacuation and strengthen the defense of cities in several places so as to enable the Chinese government to establish its political power in the Northeast and lay down a firm foundation for its political authority. Our purpose is to help the Chinese government implement the treaty of Sino-Soviet friendship and alliance, signed on August 14, 1945."

Late tonight, Major General Pavlovsky came to see Vice-Chief of Staff Tung. He was accompanied by Lieutenant General Karlov, the garrison commander. They indicated that the Soviets are determined to eradicate all mob action, to strictly protect various central government organizations as well as the residences of their personnel, and to ban all propaganda disadvantageous to the central government. They also expressed the hope that we will take over the municipal government and public security bureau of Ch'ang-ch'un.

My Analysis of the Two Statements Mentioned Above

The first notice was meant to indicate that the Soviets were not violating the Sino-Soviet friendship treaty and thus counteract adverse reactions internationally.

The second notice was a reply to the question with which Vice-Chief of Staff Tung had confronted Major General Pavlovsky, concerning all recent conduct of the public security bureau. This indicated that they were not secretly assisting the Eighth Route Army.

NOVEMBER 18. Today there was a profusion of requests to be sent home from personnel who have not been evacuated.

In addition, my colleagues actually confronted me with questions because today I changed the order of the list of personnel to be evacuated, giving priority to a number of army men. It is rather regrettable that public servants should be so uneasy.

I received from Chungking a wire requesting that the evacuation be postponed. I gathered that the government had conducted negotiations with the Soviet ambassador and that conditions had changed. But since I know well the thoughts and feelings of my colleagues, I wired Chungking, asking that every day three planes be sent in order to reassure them. Today three planes arrived.

Chiang Ching-kuo wired that the government is engaged in diplomatic talks with the Soviet ambassador.

NOVEMBER 19. Today Major General Karlov [Karlov appeared earlier as a lieutenant general; the contradiction is in the text], the Soviet district commander, summoned newspaper reporters to announce policies for propaganda. He stated that it is not permissible to oppose the Nationalist government, Generalissimo Chiang, friendly relations between China and the Soviet Union and the Allied nations of Great Britain and the United States, or to worsen relations between the Nationalists and the Communists. Newspaper reporters are only permitted to explain the spirit of the Sino-Soviet friendship treaty and the meaning of the liberation of the Northeast by the Soviets. Moreover, all posters in the streets denouncing the central government will be torn down and replaced by posters supporting the united government and international cooperation. The above is merely a gesture to show that the Soviets are fulfilling their promise. But the new posters are hard to explain. Did the persons responsible for them have an understanding with the Soviet Union at a time when General Marshall is in Chungking discussing cooperation between the Nationalists and the Communists? Or did the Communists act unilaterally?

In the evening Major General Pavlovsky reminded me that formerly we had notified the Soviets that our airlifted troops would arrive in Mukden on the seventeenth and in Ch'ang-ch'un on the twenty-second. They wished to know whether we still were going to do this. I gathered that the Soviets are anxious to know whether we want to discontinue negotiations. Vice-Chief of Staff Tung replied that he would wire Chungking for instructions. Soon there came a reply saying that our government is in the midst of discussions with the Soviet government concerning our takeover of the Northeast and will temporarily suspend the airlifting of Chinese troops to the Northeast until a settlement results from the discussions between the two governments.

Today, a small problem arose. When Chang Ch'ing-ho, head of the public security bureau of Ch'ang-ch'un, was dismissed from his post and replaced by Yü T'ien-fang, Sun Chiu-ssu, chief of the general contingent of the Ch'ang-ch'un Railroad's railroad police, immediately questioned the Soviet chairman of the board of directors of the Ch'ang-ch'un Railroad. He replied that the Soviets knew nothing about this. Therefore, I asked Vice-Chief of Staff Tung to confront the Soviet vice-chief of staff with this question.

NOVEMBER 20.   Last time, when the Soviet economic counselor asked me about industrial cooperation, I told him that I had not yet received any instructions from my government. However, several days have passed, and it would be inappropriate to delay further. Therefore, at 6:00 P.M. I called on him to indicate that the withdrawal of the headquarters does not mean that we will discontinue the discussions. Our conversation ran as follows:

I: With respect to the issue of economic cooperation discussed last time, I have received a reply from my government. The reply is that the Chinese government is very willing to enter into close economic cooperation with the Soviets, but the topic we are discussing includes the question of wartime compensation. Since this issue has become central to the discussions, it should be negotiated and settled by the the governments of the two nations. For this reason we request that Your Excellency's side notify your ambassador in China concerning Soviet opinions, for discussion with the enemy government.

SLADKOVSKY: I shall convey the message as you request. But with respect to economic cooperation, has the Chinese side agreed to it and acknowledged it in principle? Moreover, does *economic cooperation* denote the industrial cooperation we discussed last time?

I: According to my humble interpretation, *economic cooperation* in the instructions seems to have a broad connotation. Particularly related to this are the questions of wartime compensation and the questions of every kind of cooperation.

SLADKOVSKY: How is the problem of factory management to be settled at this time?

I: Since it is related to all other problems, naturally it should be settled along with the rest.

SLADKOVSKY: I also know that this issue can be settled by the central government. But at present there are urgent problems awaiting speedy settlement. Because many factories have been damaged, no one is taking care of them, and there is an urgent need to find ways to protect them.

I: Let me wire Chungking again and ask for specific measures.

SLADKOVSKY: Is it possible for me to make contact with Soviet personnel remaining in the factories, so that they can try to protect the assets and maintain normal order in them?

I: Does Your Excellency mean that, pending a settlement by the two governments, Your Excellency will find ways to care for and maintain the factories?

SLADKOVSKY: Pending a settlement by the governments of the two nations, I shall order the small number of Soviet personnel remaining in the factories to try to maintain all the assets of the factories.

I: Let me pass on to my government the point raised by Your Excellency. Are there other questions beside this?

SLADKOVSKY: The several talks I previously had with Your Excellency all were in the nature of private conversations. Now, may I pass on to Your Excellency the official opinion of the Soviet government concerning industrial cooperation, which is as follows: The Soviets consider it necessary that we organize a limited corporation, to be jointly operated by the Chinese and the Soviets, for the purpose of managing the various enterprises formerly belonging to the Manchurian Heavy Industry Development Company and the Manchurian Electrical Company. The two companies mentioned above were originally established to meet the needs of the Japanese Kwantung Army. As war booty of the Red Army, they should be regarded as property of the Soviet Union. However, out of consideration for friendly relations with China, the Soviet government is willing to have the enterprises belonging to the two companies jointly managed by both Chinese and Soviet representatives, in keeping with the principle of equal ownership. The assets should be equally divided between the two sides. In other words, the Soviets should own 50 percent and the Chinese, 50 percent. To manage these enterprises we shall organize a company jointly operated by the Chinese and the Soviets, under the following conditions:

1. The company shall be organized on the principle of equality. The two sides will each contribute half of the capital of the company. As long as the company exists, this ratio will not be changed.

2. A number of Soviet economic organizations will participate in this company. For example, the Khabaraovsk Coal Company, the Far Eastern Power Company, and the Far Eastern Bank. We expect the Chinese also to have actual persons and legal entities participate [in the company].

3. Fifty percent of the assets of the two aforementioned companies—those formerly belonging to the Japanese—will be contributed by the Soviets in the form of shares in those companies. The shares contributed by the Chinese should equal the amount contributed by the Soviets from whatever is left over from funds belonging to the Japanese and other sources.

4. The Soviets participating in this company will provide suitable specialists, as well as technical assistance, in order to restore and develop the various enterprises belonging to the company.

5. The land surface being used by the enterprises belonging to the two aforementioned companies, along with all of their underground rights, both should be transferred to the newly organized company.

6. The Chinese and Soviet participants will join in managing the affairs of the company. Higher-level cadres of the company from both sides will enjoy equal voting rights. The Chinese representative will be the general director of the company; the Soviet representative will be the company's assistant general director.

7. The executive duties of the company will be performed by a general manager designated by the Soviets and an assistant general manager designated by the Chinese.

I: I immediately shall submit this document to my government. I presume that the Soviets also are negotiating this matter with my government through the Soviet ambassador to China. I hope that we can achieve a settlement in principle on this matter in Chungking. Moreover, do the measures for cooperation proposed by the Soviets apply merely to enter-prises belonging to these two companies? What are your opinions con-cerning other companies, such as the various enterprises belonging to the Manchurian railroads?

SLADKOVSKY: At present we are concerned only with the enterprises belong-ing to the two aforementioned companies.

I: It would be best if the question of the enterprises belonging to the South Manchurian Railway is discussed and settled at the same time by the central government.

SLADKOVSKY: I shall give this point my attention. Is Your Excellency going to leave?

I: Until now, I have had no intention of leaving. As long as the environment here does not interfere, I shall try to stay and work.

SLADKOVSKY: The environment can be overcome by fruitful work.

I: In a favorable environment I will do my best to achieve the basis for cooperation between us.

I wired my government about the Soviet government's opinion concern-ing industrial cooperation, as presented by Economic Counselor Sladkovsky. This is my message:

> To Special Envoy Chiang Ching-kuo:
> Forward this to T'ien-i and also submit it to His Excellency the presi-dent. I have mailed to T'ien-i, for him to forward to you, the record of my previous talk with the Soviet economic counselor. Today, I met him for another talk to give him a reply. I told him that the Chinese government is very willing to enter into close economic cooperation with the Soviets; however, since the matters brought up by the Soviets include the question of their taking confiscated enemy assets in Manchuria as war booty, my government's opinion is that the issue should be discussed by the two governments. I asked that the Soviet ambassador negotiate directly with the central government. At this point, the economic counselor stated that what he previously had discussed were all his personal opinions and that today he had received official orders from Moscow. I immediately told him that I would pass this on to my government, but that, since this is a big issue, would the Soviet ambassador please negotiate directly with my govern-ment? He promised to do as requested. I now expressly am wiring this message. I shall send the rest in a letter.

NOVEMBER 21.   To prepare for presenting my opinions to my govern-ment, I made a study of the enterprises belonging to the Manchurian Heavy Industry and the Manchurian Electric companies.

Vice-Chief of Staff Tung met with Major General Pavlovsky. Tung told the Soviets about our decision to suspend temporarily airlifting our troops. He also brought up the question of the chief of the railroad police contingent of the Ch'ang-ch'un Railroad. The Soviets promised to restore Sun Chiu-ssu to his post at once. From now on I shall have the absolute right to decide on candidates for this post.

NOVEMBER 22.   I received from Chairman Hsiung T'ien-i a wire saying,

On November 17 the Soviet ambassador to China submitted an official communication to our Foreign Ministry. Its chief points are,

1. Chinese government troops can land without hindrance in Ch'ang-ch'un and Mukden. The Soviet Army will give them the assistance needed.

2. The Soviet Army strictly adheres to the Sino-Soviet treaty. With respect to the communist party in Manchuria, in the past the Soviet Army has not given it any assistance, and this continues to be the case at present. It stopped communist party activities within the northeastern region because a central Chinese regime has not been established.

3. If the Chinese government desires the Soviet Army to postpone its evacuation, it can postpone it for one or two months.

On the nineteenth of the same month our Foreign Ministry replied to the official communication of the Soviet ambassador. The chief points in our reply are,

1. The Soviet Army must assume responsibility for disarming various armed troops in the municipal districts of Ch'ang-ch'un and Mukden, as well as in the airports around those cities, who have not been recognized by the Chinese government. It also must allow the ground personnel of Chinese transport planes to first go to Ch'ang-ch'un and Mukden to direct the landing and taking off of planes.

2. If the central government needs to use the Pei-Ning Railroad and various ports, the Soviet Army must accommodate us as far as possible.

3. The Soviet Army must give moral and material assistance to our takeover personnel. It also must help such personnel travel to various places to arrange for the organization of railroad police corps.

If the Soviets agree to the above, then the date for evacuation of the Soviet Army can be postponed for one month.

Today, at 2:00 P.M. Vice-Chief of Staff Tung led members of the military delegation: Mi Hsin-min, Ch'iu Nan, and others—eight in all—to visit Marshal Malinovsky. This was their first official visit. In accord with orders from the central government, Tung has taken up the position of head of the delegation following the withdrawal of the headquarters.

Malinovsky said that he already had given orders to dismiss the head of the public security bureau and replace him. He hoped our side would recommend a successor but this does not mean the Chinese will take over the public security bureau of Ch'ang-ch'un. It only means that the Chinese will assist the Soviets in looking for a candidate, with the aim of having the public security bureau exercise protective duties with respect to the Chinese delegation and Chinese citizens. He also expressed the hope that the headquarters will return to Ch'ang-ch'un soon. Pending the arrival of Chinese government troops and the firm establishment of the central government's administrative foundation in the Northeast, the Soviet Army will temporarily postpone its evacuation.

Chairman Hsiung T'ien-i wired that tomorrow is the deadline for the withdrawal of the headquarters and hoped I will leave Ch'ang-ch'un tomorrow. I wired back telling him that I will leave Ch'ang-ch'un as soon as all of the personnel to be evacuated have left. I also wired to urge Wang Chi, assistant chairman of the board of directors of the Ch'ang-ch'un Railroad, and Wan I, a director, to come to Ch'ang-ch'un at an early date so that after my departure there will be persons to look after matters concerning the Ch'ang-ch'un Railroad.

NOVEMBER 23.   In the afternoon I called on Marshal Malinovsky to say goodbye. Economic Counselor Sladkovsky also was there. The conversation went as follows:

I: Since I assumed the post of the chairman of the board of directors of the Ch'ang-ch'un Railroad, work has started in every way. I intend in a few days to go to Chungking and especially have come to say goodbye. At the same time I intend to express to Your Excellency some of my personal opinions.

MALINOVSKY: Is Your Excellency leaving here permanently?

I: It is only a short visit to report to Chungking. In the interests of the railroad and from an economic angle, I am very anxious for an improvement in the political environment. At present, there seems to be a layer of fog between China and the Soviet Union. I hope it can be eliminated.

MALINOVSKY: In my opinion, there is no layer of fog. The Soviets are adhering absolutely to the Sino-Soviet treaty.

I: I wish to ask a personal question. In their last notice the Soviets stated that they temporarily would postpone the evacuation of their troops to help our central government establish its political power. What is the significance of this?

MALINOVSKY: Because your government troops have not arrived south of
Mukden, the Eighteenth Group Army [Eighth Route Army] is there. If
a place evacuated by Soviet troops is not taken over and defended by
government troops, then the Eighteenth Group Army is bound to take
advantage of the opportunity and enter. Therefore, for the time being
the Soviet Army must not withdraw. Once your government troops
arrive and are considered sufficient to maintain order, Soviet troops will
begin to withdraw. Why are the Chinese able to send more than twenty
planes to Ch'ang-ch'un to evacuate the personnel of their headquarters
but still do not transport their troops here?

I: Please allow me to speak frankly. The Eighth Route Army is at Shan-hai-
kuan. We cannot land at Ying-k'ou. Only a small number of our troops
can be airlifted to Ch'ang-ch'un and Mukden. Moreover, since there are
illegal troops in those places, I'm afraid the landing of our troops will
provoke clashes.

MALINOVSKY: There must not be clashes.

I: Furthermore, in Mukden there exists a local government and, at the same
time, there are troops issuing their own bank notes by making use of the
Northeastern Industrial Bank.

MALINOVSKY: At present, there are only Soviet troops in Mukden. As for the
issuance of bank notes, that is true. Furthermore, these illegal bank
notes are being circulated at a ratio of ten to one. I already have ordered
their circulation stopped.

I: Our provincial governors haven't the least bit of military power. Therefore, even though Your Excellency, the marshal, repeatedly has urged
that they go and take over, how do they dare do so?

MALINOVSKY: It is precisely for this reason that the Soviet Army has decided
temporarily to stay here.

I: I am not versed in military affairs. But suppose we could transport 50,000
troops here. With the assistance of the Soviet Army these should be
sufficient to take over various places.

MALINOVSKY: (no reply)

I: I have had several talks with the economic counselor. Recently he told me
he had received instructions from Moscow concerning conditions for
industrial cooperation. I already have reported this to Chungking by
wire. This time, when I return to Chungking, I naturally will learn my
government's opinion.

MALINOVSKY: In the former Japanese industries here, Japanese investment
comprised more than half of their total capitalization. But the Soviet
government is willing to cooperate with China on the principle of each
country having an equal share. In other words, the capital owned by the

Soviets is not to exceed 50 percent. This will demonstrate fully the friendly spirit of the Soviets.

I: I sincerely hope for an early settlement of political problems so that economic work can begin.

MALINOVSKY: When does Your Excellency intend to return to Ch'ang-ch'un?

I: I shall return before long. I only hope that when I arrive in Chungking the political conditions already have improved.

MALINOVSKY: Certainly, they could improve soon.

I: We first must give attention to the early restoration of communication along the railroad between Shan-hai-kuan and Mukden. This is very important from an economic standpoint. It would be best to make the Eighth Route Army withdraw from the rail line.

MALINOVSKY: Indeed, this point is very important.

My Analysis of My Talk with Marshal Malinovsky Today

Malinovsky has banned the issuing of bank notes by the communist army in Mukden. He also said the political situation in the Northeast certainly could improve. He then remarked that while our side had airplanes to evacuate our headquarters personnel, we have not yet transported our troops here. It is very clear that he does not want the airlifting of our troops hindered. Furthermore, he hopes the headquarters will return to Ch'ang-ch'un and continue negotiations.

I tried sounding him out by stating that our side might transport 50,000 troops to the Northeast. He did not answer, which seems to indicate that he acquiesced because he is extremely outspoken and if he does not approve of something he usually rejects it immediately.

I went a step further and proposed that the Eighth Route Army withdraw from the rail line all the way from Yü-kuan to Mukden. He neither agreed nor disagreed. This also seemed to indicate that he would not help the Eighth Route Army to occupy the railroad for long.

On the basis of this conversation, I wired T'ien-i and Ching-kuo to urge that our troops be airlifted here soon.

The Soviets have ordered that Ts'ao Chao-yuan, the original mayor of Ch'ang-ch'un, be restored to his post.

NOVEMBER 24.   In the morning I packed and wrote a letter to Marshal Malinovsky thanking him for his sincere gestures in yesterday's talk. I also stated that I hoped the clouds soon would disperse. At 1:00 P.M. I left Ch'ang-ch'un on an army plane. At 5:00 P.M. I arrived in Peiping. I stayed at a hostel on Nan-ch'ang street, which Special Envoy Shih Chih-jen had arranged for me.

In the evening, Mr. Li Te-lin came and we had a long conversation. He remarked that the influence of the communist party in the north is growing day by day, that its influence is felt all around Peiping, and that for the time being efforts to open the Peiping-Hankow Railroad have not been successful. If we cannot lay hold of the Northeast, problems are bound to occur in northern China that will affect the whole situation.

NOVEMBER 25.   At 9:30 A.M. I left Peiping by plane and at 5:00 P.M. arrived in Chungking. T'ien-i and Ching-kuo came to the airport. Together, we went to Ling Yuan to pay our respects to Generalissimo Chiang. I told him that there is a change in the situation, that there should be no problem sending 50,000 government troops to the Northeast, and that it would be best to decide soon on a plan for economic cooperation so that we could anticipate taking over the provinces and cities of the Northeast without hindrance.

Later, I met with T'ien-i and Ching-kuo and learned that on November 20 the Soviet ambassador replied to the official communnication from our Foreign Ministry of November 19. The gist is as follows:

1. The Soviet government has instructed its Air Force command to take measures necessary to guarantee an unhindered landing of Chinese troops in Ch'ang-ch'un and Mukden. The Chinese side can send ground personnel to the airports in Ch'ang-ch'un and Mukden to look after matters. The Soviet government does not object at all to airplanes transporting Chinese troops back and forth.

2. Troops not belonging to the Chinese government never have entered Ch'ang-ch'un. In the past there have been no obstructions to the landing of Chinese troops in Ch'ang-ch'un; such obstructions do not exist now.

3. With respect to individual questions that still may need to be discussed, the Soviet government considers it best for Marshal Malinovsky and Chinese representatives to continue deciding these at the local level.

NOVEMBER 26.   At noon I had lunch and a discussion with Generalissimo Chiang at his official residence. We decided that we must occupy Chin-chou and that our troops now advancing from Shan-hai-kuan must temporarily stop at Chin-chou. We formulated the following points, which the Foreign Ministry will send in reply to the Soviet ambassador:

1. We are preparing to airlift troops to Ch'ang-ch'un and Mukden.

2. Since the Soviet government now declares that Soviet troops already have evacuated areas south of Mukden, our army is sending troops into that area. These troops will be able to reach the area of Chinchou within several days.

3. With respect to other questions that have not been settled, as well as the question of postponing for one month the withdrawal of Soviet troops, we will accept the Soviet proposal and immediately dispatch delegates to Ch'ang-ch'un to settle questions right there.

After lunch I went to the Ministry of Foreign Affairs and, together with Minister of Foreign Affairs Wang Hsüeh-t'ing, drafted a reply.

NOVEMBER 27.   In the morning I conferred with Ch'ien I-li of the Resources Commission about the question of Sino-Soviet industrial cooperation. In the afternoon Ministers Yü Ch'iao-feng and Wang Shih-chieh came to discuss issues relating to the Northeast. In the evening Minister Ho Ching-Chih came to see me. We drafted both primary and secondary measures for industrial cooperation in the Northeast.

NOVEMBER 28.   At 11:00 A.M. Generalissimo Chiang invited T.V. Soong, president of the Executive Yuan, and Wang Hsüeh-t'ing, minister of Foreign Affairs, along with T'ien-i and Ching-kuo, to discuss the question of industrial cooperation in the Northeast. President Soong said that there are only two ways of settling the problem of the Northeast. One is to wait calmly for a change in the general situation. The other is to sacrifice our own interests for the general good. But he also said it is not within the bounds of the Sino-Soviet treaty for the Soviets to regard Japanese investment in the Northeast as their war booty and as their share of investment in cooperatively operated enterprises. Under no circumstances can we agree to this. Foreign Minister Wang observed that discussing economic cooperation before accomplishing our takeover would be tantamount to voluntarily submitting to Soviet pressure and was bound to arouse resentment among the people. He said that therefore the political problem must be settled before taking up the issue of economic cooperation. Nothing resulted from the conference. At 4:00 P.M. I went to the Ministry of Foreign Affairs to continue the discussion with Minister Wang. We decided to first bring up primary measures: namely, principles for discussion with respect to cooperation. Moreover, we decided to make the following statement to the Soviets:

More than one nation is involved in the handling of enemy assets, since the issue hinges on compensation. Furthermore, after receiving on October 1 of this year our memorandum addressed to the respective Allied nations, Molotov admitted that the question of compensation should be discussed in the future by the Allied Control Council for Japan. Therefore, it would not be suitable for China and the Soviet Union to settle it by themselves. As for specific measures for industrial and economic cooperation, these could be discussed after political problems were settled.

In the evening I saw President Soong of the Executive Yuan. He repeated his previously stated view that certainly at present Sino-Soviet economic cooperation cannot be discussed. Therefore, the opinion of Messrs. Soong and Wang is directly opposed to Malinovsky's expectations. Indeed, the views of Soong and Wang are correct, both from a legal angle and from the point of view of reason. But Marshal Malinovsky is anxious to settle the economic question before Soviet troops withdraw. Actually, I think it would have been all right to discuss both simultaneously. But Messrs. Soong and Wang are deeply worried that even after obtaining the right of economic cooperation the Soviets will not allow us to accomplish the takeover without hindrance, so that our government will have assumed too great a responsibility. Moreover, the various obstructions created by the Soviets have made it impossible for us to trust them. However, based on impressions I received from my contacts, while I dare not say that a settlement of the economic question will result in our takeover being unhindered, I believe such a settlement will solve the greater part of the problem. But today, since responsible officials of the government have such views, I only can act in accord with them. The principles for discussing economic cooperation that I have formulated in reply to the Soviets consist of the following three points:

1. If we discuss problems of this kind before the Soviets have withdrawn their troops and before the Chinese government has accomplished its takeover of the Northeast, this will create in the outside world an unfortunate misunderstanding.

2. After the Chinese government has accomplished its takeover of administrative power in the Northeast, it will enter into detailed discussions with the Soviets about measures for economic cooperation.

3. Within limits permitted by the Plan for Early Stage Economic Reconstruction, passed and promulgated by the Chinese government in the month [the author left a blank here] of this year, the Chinese government will try its best to cooperate with the Soviets.

Note 1: On September 18, 1945, the Chinese government delivered to the foreign ministers of both the United States and the Soviet Union a memorandum listing its expectations with respect to reparations from Japan. The following proposals were made:

1. Everything on Chinese soil belonging to the Japanese empire and to Japanese citizens should be regarded as conceded to China, including the unqualified right to the industries, deeds, interest on capital, and various assets, including buildings, power plants, various factories, flour mills, textile mills, dock yards, ships, shipyards, machinery, mines, telephone and wireless equipment and material, railroad rolling stock and repair shops, etc. Japanese citizens affected by this should be compensated by the Japanese government.

2. In any parts of China or Taiwan, where troops of the Allied nations are stationed and which the Allied nations have agreed to return to China, all necessary and urgent measures must be taken to prevent the enemy from demolition, destruction, concealment, movement, transference, and other such activities.

3. When various assets within Japan are divided up among the Allied nations as partial compensation for their losses, China should be given a good percentage of them, together with priority for the delivery of these goods. These assets include light and heavy industry, machinery, mining equipment, rolling stock, all raw materials for and products of shipbuilding and other things. This is to compensate for the prolonged sacrifices and losses sustained by the Chinese nation and its people.

Letters exchanged between Foreign Minister Wang and the Soviet foreign minister [these letters are reproduced in English in the diary]:

September/18/1945—Letter to V.M. Molotov
    With reference to our conversation on September 15, I have the honor to enclose herewith for your consideration a memorandum on the views and proposals of the Chinese government regarding Japanese reparations. I should be grateful if you could give an indication of your opinion relating thereto, as my government regards this question as one of urgency and importance.

October/1/1945—Molotov's reply
    I hereby acknowledge receipt of your letter of September 18 and of the memorandum annexed to it on the question of reparations from Japan. I fully realize China's interest in the hastening of the settlement of the question of reparations from Japan. I deemed it necessary to say on my part that the consideration of this question should be one of the tasks of the Allied Control Council for Japan. The Soviet government in the memorandum of

September 24 of this year, which is already known to you, has expressed its view about the necessity of creating it without delay. With the aid of the Allied control council, the governments of the four powers could most successfully define their agreed action on the question of reparations from Japan, including the working out and putting into force of concrete measures concerning the forms and order of reparation payments referred to in your memorandum.

Note 2: In the Principles for Economic Reconstruction of the First Stage, passed at the 148th meeting of the standing committee of the Highest National Defense Commission, the following four articles concern foreign capital:

1. In enterprises having joint Chinese and foreign investment, no fixed limitation should be placed on the percentage of total foreign investment. In both public and private organizations, only the chairman of the board of trustees must be a native Chinese; the general manager does not have to be.

2. State enterprises may negotiate for foreign loans or foreign investment through the government organizations in charge, provided that they have the sanction of the government and thus are in accord with the general plan for reconstruction. Private enterprises may also negotiate by themselves but must submit their plans to the organization in charge for its approval and to be recorded.

3. Foreign enterprises in China that have direct investment from foreigners and are run by foreigners should be operated in accord with Chinese law. As for special enterprises whose operation requires special permission, they first must apply for our government's approval before such special permission can be given.

4. The government retains the right to manage alone or operate jointly with private or foreign capital any enterprise beyond the fiscal resources of private capital or that the government feels merits special attention. These include large-scale shale rock mines or petroleum mines, iron and steel works, and navigation enterprises, etc.

NOVEMBER 29.   I called on Messrs. K'ung Jung-chih and Lung Chi-chou.

NOVEMBER 30.   In the afternoon I saw Tung Pi-wu, a representative of the Chinese Communist Party in Chungking. I told him that Marshal Malinovsky considered it necessary to open the railroad between Yü and Mukden. I also told him that Soviet troops are waiting for our government troops to arrive and then will withdraw northward from Chin-chou. I asked

Tung to persuade the Eighth Route Army to back away from the rail line between Mukden and Chin-chou. He promised to transmit the message to Yen-an. I feel that since the Soviets tacitly are allowing us to open the Mukden-Yü Railroad, upon learning of this, the Eighth Route Army naturally will change its attitude and not obstruct the advance of our troops. As a result, government troops soon will be able to arrive and assist in our takeover. The deadline for the withdrawal of Soviet troops is very near. I must try my best to do whatever can gain time.

Tso Shun-sheng came for a visit. He remarked that recently the Communists have been starting wars everywhere, that they intend to grab political power in North China, and do not seem very enthusiastic about a united government. I thought this very unwise from the communist standpoint.

In the evening I invited to dinner all the members of the Economic Commission.

Back to Ch'ang-ch'un

DECEMBER 1–31, 1945

Chang Kia-ngau and other high-level Republic of China (ROC) officials draft a proposal to Soviet officials in Manchuria that negotiations begin over the use of former Japanese properties in Manchuria. The ROC government proposes that the Soviet Union provide financial and technical expertise and concur with China on which former Japanese industries shall be operated in tandem. Chiang Kai-shek approves the proposal, but T. V. Soong and Wang Hsüeh-t'ing insist on one major change: the negotiations on economic cooperation must not begin until the ROC government has recovered Manchuria without further hindrance.

On December 2 Chang Kia-ngau flies to Peiping, confers with top officials there, and then flies to Ch'ang-chun on December 4. The next day he confers with Malinovsky. The Soviets appear eager to help the ROC government airlift troops into Ch'ang-ch'un and Mukden and disclose that Soviet troops will be out of Manchuria by February 1, 1946. But Malinovsky's promise is contingent on a quick resolution for economic cooperation between the two nations. Chang Kia-ngau then presents the ROC plan. Malinovsky responds that he hopes discussions will take place before Manchuria reverts to the ROC government.

Chang Kia-ngau confides to his diary that the Soviets will find reasons to delay their withdrawal until the Chinese side agrees with the Soviets. Chang now worries that Sino-Soviet negotiations are likely to end in failure.

On December 7 Chang Kia-ngau resumes economic cooperation negotiations with Sladkovsky. Chang repeats his government's position. Sladkovsky insists that the major Japanese-owned and -operated industries are Soviet war booty but that the Soviet Union will invite China to jointly manage those industries already under Soviet Army control. Negotiations between Chang and Sladkovsky become stalemated over the war booty issue and over whether the industries in question actually produced weapons and matériel to be used against the Soviet Union.

Sladkovsky argues that negotiations on economic cooperation not be postponed until Soviet troops are withdrawn from Manchuria, and he presses the ROC government to agree in principle to economic cooperation. Chang promises to consult with his government, and both men agree to draw up lists of the candidate industries.

Chang meets with Sladkovsky to discuss the industries that might be jointly managed by the two countries. They exchange lists and continue to discuss how the various industries might be conducted.

On December 14 Chang Kia-ngau sends a progress report on the current negotiations to Chungking along with a cost-benefit evaluation of the types of industries that the ROC government might consider for joint economic management.

On December 18 Chang Kia-ngau flies to Peiping and then to Nanking to meet with President Chiang Kai-shek. In Nanking Chang participates in high-level discussions on how to speed up the recovery of Manchuria. After considerable discussion the ROC leadership agrees that ROC troops will be airlifted into the four main cities of Manchuria and that the Ministry of Economics should send a team to Ch'ang-ch'un to study the kinds of enterprises that will be jointly managed with the Soviet Union. The ROC will also pay the Soviet Union a sum, not to exceed ten billion yuan of national currency, for a capital share in those enterprises that both countries finally agree to jointly manage. Those enterprises, however, will not be controlled by any single, large company, as was the case for Japanese enterprises in Manchukuo.

On December 21 Chang Kia-ngau returns to Ch'ang-ch'un and confers with city officials on how to establish local governance in Manchuria. On December 24 Chang and Sladkovsky meet again. Chang presents the new ROC government position on joint economic cooperation. Sladkovsky does not see why a Chinese team must visit Manchuria because he and Chang Kia-ngau have already drawn up their respective lists. Chang presents the new ROC proposal for ten billion yuan as compensation to the Soviet Union for its casualties in Manchuria and for its capital investment in the jointly managed economic enterprises. Chang emphasizes there should be no more discussion of war booty. The two men then discuss how each enterprise would *be separately managed by both countries rather than placed under a large conglomerate.*

On December 27 Chang flies to Mukden and then travels by train to Harbin for more meetings with Soviet officials on transferring local government economic enterprises to the ROC government.

+ + + + + + +

DECEMBER 1.　　In the morning I went to Ch'ien I-li's to discuss adding to the outline for the discussion of Sino-Soviet economic cooperation. On the whole, we planned to promise the following:

1. Concerning commercial cooperation, the two sides will enter into a bartering agreement.
2. Concerning technical cooperation, we will try our best to appoint and employ Soviet technical specialists.
3. Concerning financial cooperation, in keeping with the principles for economic reconstruction issued by the central government, we welcome Soviet investment in the Northeast.
4. Concerning industrial cooperation, the Chinese and Soviets can meet together to designate the types of industry to be operated jointly and then discuss cooperation.

At eleven o'clock I went to see Generalissimo Chiang to report on the outline we had formulated. He gave his approval. At twelve o'clock, together with Ch'ien I-li, I went to see President T. V. Soong of the Executive Yuan. He was of the opinion that the fourth point should be changed in this way: the Chinese and Soviets can propose the types of industry to be operated jointly and discuss them. Then we went to see Foreign Minister Wang Hsüeh-t'ing. He said we should add this to the fourth point: that the question of enemy assets must be discussed by the two governments and approved by the Allied nations. Furthermore, he suggested that we add one more point: that negotiations for economic cooperation can take place only after our takeover has been accomplished without hindrance. I immediately added the three aforementioned points to the outline. This is the result of several days' deliberation.

This morning I visited Finance Minister Yü Hung-chün. He told me he was negotiating with the Soviets measures for recalling army bank notes issued by the Soviet Army. The Soviets stated that they had issued 28 billion yuan worth of army bank notes. They hoped we would recall the bank notes within two months after the withdrawal of Soviet troops. Minister Yü feels we should recall them in six months. For this reason, at 4:00 P.M. I called on the Soviet ambassador, who still insisted we recall the bank notes within two months. Over the phone Minister Yü and I decided to act in accord with the Soviet view.

DECEMBER 2.   At 8:30 A.M. I arrived at the airport. At 9:30 A.M. the plane took off. At 4:30 P.M. I arrived in Peiping. Again I stayed at the Hostel for Special Envoys of the Ministry of Communications.

DECEMBER 3.   In the morning Hsiung Che-min, the mayor of Peiping, came for a visit. At eleven o'clock I summoned the personnel of the headquarters and the various provincial governors of the Northeast for a conference. I reported all that transpired during my discussions in Chungking. In the afternoon I invited the responsible persons of the Central Bank, the Bank of China, and the Bank of Communications to discuss how we could prevent the national currency from affecting prices in the Northeast when used by government troops after they arrive there. I urged that the banks speedily send persons there to take care of the matter.

In the afternoon Tai Yü-nung came for a visit. In the evening I went to Mr. Li Te-lin's for a long talk. He remarked that the government is too timid in its negotiations with the Soviets. This illustrates how outsiders, unfamiliar with the real situation, are prone to criticize.

DECEMBER 4.   At 8:00 A.M. I went to Tai Yü-nung's to have breakfast. I had invited Special Envoys Ch'en Ti-ch'iu and Shih Chih-jen to go with me. We discussed the question of railroad police along the various northeastern railroads because Tai has 25,000 men in his Loyal and Patriotic Army who he hopes to reorganize into railroad police.

At 10:00 I arrived at the airport. At 11:00 the plane took off. Traveling with me was Special Envoy Chiang Ching-kuo. At 3:30 P.M. I arrived in Ch'ang-ch'un. The Soviets sent their garrison commander and the commander of their National Defense Army to meet us. All along the way we were protected by police.

DECEMBER 5.   At 1:00 P.M., together with Ching-kuo and Vice-Chief of Staff Tung Yen-p'ing, I visited Marshal Malinovsky. We talked for two-and-a-half hours. First, Ching-kuo told him the following:

1. Our troops soon will be airlifted to Ch'ang-ch'un.
2. Our administrative personnel for various provinces and cities plan to take along, when they go to assume their posts, a small number of military and regular police. This is in order to meet the need for

maintaining local order. We hope that as our administrative personnel take up their posts the Soviets will dispatch liaison officials to accompany them.

3. We hope the Soviets will disarm illegal troops in the area.

4. After our administrative personnel for provinces and cities in the Northeast assume their posts, any regime not recognized by the central government shall be disavowed, and if there is resistance the Soviet Army will help us deal with it.

Meanwhile I remarked that we are transporting one division of troops to Ch'ang-ch'un while two divisions are being sent to Mukden by rail. Marshal Malinovsky replied as follows:

1. The Soviets are willing to assume the responsibility for guaranteeing the safety of our airlifted troops as they arrive in Ch'ang-ch'un. Moreover, the Soviets do not object to our transporting two divisions of our army to Mukden.

2. The Soviets are making increased efforts to have armed troops not recognized by our government surrender their weapons.

3. He will seek from Moscow instructions concerning the organization of a security maintenance corps and the dispatch of liaison officials.

I took this opportunity to tell him that while in Chungking I talked with Tung Pi-wu and expressed the hope that he would indirectly advise the Eighth Route Army from Yen-an to back away from the Pei-Ning Railroad line and not disturb or hinder the northward advance of our troops. I hoped the Soviets also would give the same advice. Malinovsky replied:

The Soviets have no way of doing this, since there are no Soviet troops south of Mukden. But if your troops advance toward Mukden, you can from time to time inform us about how far they have advanced so that before your troops reach Mukden the Soviet Army command can send persons to establish liaison.

Judging from the tone of Malinovsky's remarks, the Soviets are not raising any problem concerning the transportation of our troops to Mukden by rail. Therefore, the Chinese Communists also shouldn't hinder us. Sending our troops northward without hindrance would be the happiest event, because the arrival of our troops in Mukden and Ch'ang-ch'un will symbolize our takeover.

I told him that we intend first to take over the various cities that are stations along the Ch'ang-ch'un Railroad, such as Dairen, Mukden, Ch'ang-ch'un, and Harbin. Malinovsky replied:

> The mayors of the various cities can go right ahead and assume their posts. The new mayor of Ch'ang-ch'un especially can go right ahead and assume his duties, since the current mayor is very anxious to leave. But I earnestly hope we soon can settle the economic question. I hope Your Excellency speedily will discuss this issue with the Soviet economic counselor.

His words implied that the question of economic cooperation is inseparable from our taking over administrative organizations. I strongly suspect that the takeover of the various provinces will not be accomplished until the economic question has been resolved. I then explained our plan for settling the economic question, as follows:

> Before September 18, 1945, our foreign minister sent to your ambassador to China an official communication stating that all industrial assets in the Northeast formerly belonging to Japan be used to compensate China for its wartime losses. However, after we take over the Northeast and Soviet troops withdraw, we will discuss the following measures for cooperation with the Soviets:
>
> 1. After we have taken over the nine northeastern provinces, China and the Soviet Union can enter into a barter agreement, which will be valid for one or two years.
> 2. We are prepared to employ Soviet technical personnel.
> 3. If industries and mines in the Northeast need funds for development, the Soviets may invest in and manage them, in accord with the decrees of our country.
> 4. With respect to enterprises in the Northeast, the Soviets may propose specifically those they are interested in and these will be discussed.
>
> An incidental note: In order to avoid misunderstanding among Chinese citizens the aforementioned points must be discussed only after we have accomplished our takeover of the Northeast and the Soviets have withdrawn their troops. We ask for Soviet understanding.

Malinovsky replied: "I still hope we first begin discussion of the economic question."

Major General Pavlovsky expressed the following opinion concerning the date for the withdrawal of Soviet troops:

> After the Soviet Army received orders to strengthen city fortifications in several places, large numbers of Soviet troops continually arrived in the

Northeast. If, as has been decided, Soviet troops are to complete their withdrawal by January 3, 1946, the Soviet Army immediately must begin withdrawing. Meanwhile, the Chinese also must complete their takeover before January 3. Otherwise, the Soviet Army must keep a part of its troops here to assist the Chinese government in its takeover.

I replied, "I will report to my government procedures that the Soviets consider appropriate." Malinovsky said, "In the final analysis our aim is to assist the Chinese government in establishing its political power in the Northeast." I replied, "I immediately will ask my government for instructions."

Together with Ching-kuo, I sent to Generalissimo Chiang and Chairman Hsiung a wire reporting in detail our conversation. We also asked Chairman Hsiung to forward the report to President Soong of the Executive Yuan and Foreign Minister Wang and again request that they press the mayors of the various cities in the Northeast to come to Ch'ang-ch'un immediately. In his wire to the generalissimo, the mayor of Fengtien recommended that Tung Wen-chi be put in charge of arranging lodging and supplies for the troops. He hopes Tung's name will be publicly announced immediately. He also proposed that beginning December 10 we start airlifting our troops to Chinchou. As soon as the troops gain a firm foothold, they will begin their northward advance. The deadline for the withdrawal of Soviet troops has been extended to February 1.

My Thoughts and Feelings Concerning Today's Talk with Marshal Malinovsky

There exist two major discrepancies between our central government and the Soviets: (1) The Soviets insist that we first settle the question of economic cooperation before we discuss our taking over the Northeast. They can allow us to first take over Dairen, Mukden, Ch'ang-ch'un, and Harbin, since these cities lie along the Ch'ang-ch'un Railroad. But it seems that we still have to wait before taking over the various provinces. Officials of our central government, like President Soong and Minister Wang, insist that we first take over and then discuss the economic question. (2) Because of the imminence of the deadline for the withdrawal of their troops, the Soviets try to gain time whenever they can. For example, on November 15 we notified the Soviets about our decision to withdraw our headquarters. Precisely on the seventeenth the Soviets notified us that Soviet troops will postpone their withdrawal to assist us in establishing political power in the Northeast. The Soviets' notice served two purposes. One was to demonstrate their spirit of adhering to the Sino-Soviet treaty. The other was to afford ample time for discussing the economic question. I find their sharp-witted diplomacy admirable. On the other hand, we are slow to act and our methods are inflexible. We only know how to adhere to principles but do not know how to adapt our methods in order to implement our principles. This is particularly true of President Soong. He feels that we can accomplish nothing in our negotiations with the Soviets and that this will result in our efforts being in vain. Minister Wang is discreet and careful. He always bases his ideas on legality and reason. After contacting a wide range of people in Chungking, I am deeply worried that Sino-Soviet negotiations may end in failure.

DECEMBER 6.   In the morning I worked in the office of the board of directors of the Ch'ang-ch'un Railroad. In the evening I had supper at Ching-kuo's. After supper the Soviet vice-chairman of the board of directors of the Ch'ang-ch'un Railroad invited us to listen to music.

Today I received from Wang Shih-hsien a wire that Tung Pi-wu had asked him to forward. Tung, in response to his own wire, received a reply from Yen-an that the Eighth Route Army can withdraw from along the Pei-Ning rail line and that Yen-an hopes our troops will avoid battle by not pursuing or attacking the Communists. Consequently, since the Eighth Route Army has arranged to withdraw, we can expect even less hindrance to the northward advance of our troops. I did not first reach an understanding with Generalissimo Chiang before communicating with Tung. However, I was pressed for time because of the imminence of the deadline for the withdrawal of Soviet troops. It could not be helped.

DECEMBER 7.   In the morning I went to the office of the board of directors of the Ch'ang-ch'un Railroad to study the outline for the organization of the Railroad Bureau. The Soviet vice-chairman of the board of directors came to talk. He said he hoped we could soon decide on the outline for the organization of the Railroad Bureau. Then we could discuss such issues as resolving the problem of the railroad police, dormitories for staff members, etc.

The Soviet economic counselor requested that I immediately grant him time for a meeting. As a result, at 5:00 P.M. I called on him. The conversation went as follows (those present were, on the Soviet side, Economic Counselor Sladkovsky and his assistant, Lomochaichev, and on ours, two Russian-language secretaries, Mi Hsin-min and Keng K'uang):

I: I had planned to call on Your Excellency. Since Your Excellency invited me, I expressly have come for a talk. On behalf of Your Excellency, I already have communicated with our Ministry of Economics concerning the Soviet intention to set up in the Northeast branch companies of their Grain Export Company, the Far Eastern Overseas Transportation Company, the Soviet Travel Service, and the International Bookstore. But these various organizations should formally apply for registration with our Ministry of Economics. I shall send personnel to assist with the entire registration procedure.

SLADKOVSKY: Who does Your Excellency intend to send to assist us?

I: I shall ask Secretary Keng to come at some other time and communicate with Your Excellency about this.

SLADKOVSKY: Very good.

I: When I was in Chungking I made a detailed report to my government about the plan for economic cooperation that the Soviets have brought up. But at that time the atmosphere was unfavorable. There were two reasons for this: (1) We had encountered problems in our efforts to take over administrative organizations in the Northeast. (2) It was rumored that the Soviets had seized the industries and mines of the Northeast. Therefore, when I discussed the issue with my government it observed that, although economic cooperation is possible in principle, a specific discussion should take place after the Soviets withdraw their troops. I raised this point during my talk with Marshal Malinovsky. At that time, Your Excellency also was present. I presume Your Excellency already has heard it. I always have believed that economic cooperation should be based on voluntary action by both sides and must serve the interests of both sides. Otherwise, I'm afraid there will be no solid and lasting foundation for cooperation. Consequently, we must see to it that public opinion on both sides regards Sino-Soviet economic cooperation as fair and that the world's people do not consider such cooperation damaging to China's interests and respectability. The plan that your nation proposed last time has made the Chinese government and informed Chinese opinion feel that if the Soviets follow the example of the Japanese Heavy Industry Company by concentrating all heavy industries in one organization, they will be continuing to engage in the outdated tricks of Japanese imperialists. Therefore, it is my personal opinion that we should try our best to avoid creating among the general public the feeling that what is being done in the Northeast is fundamentally no different from Japanese imperialism.

SLADKOVSKY: Please give an example.

I: The Chinese public never has been able to understand why the Soviets still must continue the former Japanese method of concentrating heavy industry in one place.

SLADKOVSKY: I am startled to hear Your Excellency mention in the same breath the plan proposed by the Soviets and the methods of the Japanese imperialists. Your Excellency ought to know that the industries formerly operated by the Japanese were not aimed at China but functioned solely as instruments of hostility toward the Soviets, being entirely set up and operated for military purposes.

I: But the coal mines are an industry absolutely essential in peacetime. Neither are the machine industry, the fertilizer industry, nor the power plants related to military needs.

SLADKOVSKY: I would like to dwell on Your Excellency's opinion about the parallel between the Japanese and the Soviets. If I report Your Excellency's remarks to my government, then not only the Soviet government but also the Soviet public will regard them as an insult of unsurpassed dimension.

I: Your Excellency considers my remarks an insult. How can I explain? I only can feel regret. But I honestly am telling Your Excellency about the reaction of Chinese public opinion. This demonstrates my sincere desire to bring about an understanding between our two sides.

SLADKOVSKY: I quite disapprove of Your Excellency's view concerning the parallel between Japan and the Soviets. The Japanese had complete control of the industries they operated. So-called Manchurian investment was merely a facade. How can this be placed on the same plane with the plan for economic cooperation proposed by the Soviets? Public opinion in China is extensive and complex; certainly, the arguments are not uniform. But I believe that all the Chinese people know that Japanese industries in the Northeast were entirely related to military needs and that, instead of being aimed at China, these military industries were targeted on the Soviet Union.

I: My original intention was candidly to tell Your Excellency about Chinese views and public opinion. I also mentioned these Chinese arguments when I last talked with Marshal Malinovsky.

SLADKOVSKY: From Your Excellency's talk with Marshal Malinovsky and the various talks with me, I understand that in principle the Chinese government approves of economic cooperation. Now I would like to know the details.

I: I outlined four measures for Marshal Malinovsky.

SLADKOVSKY: Today, I wish to know the details.

I: Since Your Excellency was present last time when I discussed these measures with Marshal Malinovsky, I expected Your Excellency to have a complete knowledge of them. I earnestly hope that Your Excellency will consider the reaction of the Chinese people, as well as their state of mind. As for the four measures, let me re-enumerate them:

1. Soviet engineers assigned by the Soviet Union to the various factories formerly under the jurisdiction of the Heavy Industry Company can stay on in these factories. Moreover, when necessary, the Soviet Union may assign more.

2. In the barter agreement to be entered into in the future not only can we provide the Soviets with agricultural products but, excepting what we need for ourselves, we also can furnish the Soviets with surplus products from our mines and industries.

3. If in the future, when we set up new industries, we wish to cooperate with foreign capital, we also can try our best to negotiate with the Soviet Union.

4. We request that if the Soviet Union is particularly interested in certain types of industry among our present industrial and mining enterprises, the Soviets should provide us with a list so that we can report to our government and ask our government to consider this interest.

SLADKOVSKY: Does Your Excellency mean that, pending a bilateral settlement of the question of industrial cooperation, China has no intention of participating in the various industries now under Soviet control?

I: Pending the withdrawal of Soviet troops, Soviet personnel can stay in the factories to maintain them on our behalf.

SLADKOVSKY: The Soviets proposed their plan on the basic assumption that these industries comprised Soviet war booty. But out of consideration for its friendship with China, the Soviet government has offered joint management to the Chinese government. The intention is to invite China to join in managing the industries already under Soviet control.

I: While I was in Chungking our economic specialists advanced the opinion that coal mines and power plants absolutely were not industries meeting military needs. Moreover, the so-called war booty question involves the issue of reparations, and the issue of reparations is not just a matter for discussion between our two governments but must be brought up for joint discussion among a number of governments. Aside from this, the desires of our people also must not be ignored. The Chinese people hope that in the future they can operate their own heavy industries. They will be greatly disappointed if, after having the Soviets assist them in regaining their lost lands, they still do not have the chance to operate their own heavy industries. Your Excellency should not regard this as empty talk. Your Excellency ought to know that the irrepressible power of tens of millions of people in the Northeast will be a force far stronger than the productive power of machinery and equipment in the factories. The Soviet plan merely attaches importance to immediate reality, but I have in mind the far-reaching prospects of such cooperation. That is why I wish to see the two sides find common ground for starting this cooperation.

SLADKOVSKY: I cannot approve of Your Excellency's views:

1. Your economic specialists say that coal mines and power plants were not related to military needs. I have evidence showing that these industries were created to meet military needs.

2. I also cannot accept your contention that war booty must be discussed jointly by various nations. Your Excellency should know that since the war booty is in the hands of the Red Army, China has only two options. One is to try to cooperate and continue joint management; the other is to do nothing and let everything deteriorate. Your Excellency should know that once industry has been restored, resulting in jobs for the common people, resentment naturally will disappear. I do not wish to engage in a political debate, since I am not empowered to do so, but I feel that Your Excellency's remarks are somewhat lacking in coherence because, on the one hand, China asks the Soviets to send liaison personnel to assist in taking over political organizations, while, on the other, it refuses to participate in factories already in Soviet hands. Actually, economic cooperation can help to further consolidate Chinese political organizations. Therefore, a settlement of the economic question also will result in settling political problems. I wish frankly to tell Your Excellency that I cannot fully understand the Chinese viewpoint.

LOMOCHAICHEV: Please allow me to express an opinion. War booty and reparations are two separate questions. War booty connotes all assets that either now or in the future will be of use in fighting battles. It should belong to the side that seizes and possesses it.

I: In our opinion war booty merely denotes movable property.

LOMOCHAICHEV: It is not limited to movable property. The recent war in Europe established a precedent for this.

SLADKOVSKY: The former Japanese factory manager already has signed an affidavit testifying that these types of factories were designed to meet military needs.

I: For example, take the coal mines. Some were developed before the war and others, only recently. How can we regard all of them as industries meeting Japanese military needs?

SLADKOVSKY: Everyone knows that during the last two or three years all industries in the Northeast were managed for military purposes. In the case of the coal mines, only coal dust was given to the people to use; all the rest went to meet military needs.

I: Part of the coal was exported abroad and part went to meet the needs of the railroads.

SLADKOVSKY: The Fu-shun Coal Mine was not listed among the organizations belonging to the Heavy Industry Company. Moreover, in the Northeast rail transportation was almost entirely military.

I: Originally, China developed the Pen-hsi-hu Coal Mine, but the Japanese seized it.

SLADKOVSKY: The current magnitude of the Pen-hsi-hu Coal Mine's operations cannot be compared to before. Now, the mine has equipment totally installed by the Japanese.

I: I think that the question of war booty must be negotiated and settled between our two governments. As for myself, I have two requests:

1. Please give me the affidavits. I shall use them as reference material.

2. Please make an inventory listing the industries and mines that the Soviets are most interested in, so that I can submit it to my government for consideration. The inventory can serve as the revised version of your original proposal.

I, myself, am eager to enter into sincere cooperation with the Soviet Union. That is why, in my opinion, I already have taken into consideration Soviet interests. At the same time I hope Your Excellency also will take into consideration the desires of the Chinese people. When first I came to the Northeast, the people here came to tell me the Soviet Army had dismantled and removed the machinery in the factories. At that time, I advised them not to openly accuse the Soviets because the Soviets might have had other reasons for their actions or be doing it out of hatred for the Japanese. We had no way of telling.

SLADKOVSKY: I fully trust Your Excellency's sincerity. That is why the Soviets also based their previous proposal on the spirit of friendship.

I: Your Excellency must bear in mind the difference in temperament between our two nations. The Chinese people attach a great deal of importance to land. Therefore, they deeply cherish their mineral products. Furthermore, at present China does not yet have heavy industry, while the Soviet Union already possesses a gigantic industrial complex. Will Your Excellency please reconsider this?

SLADKOVSKY: Fundamentally, we must consider the desires of both sides before we can settle this issue. But, actually, the Chinese should realize that China must rely on Soviet help before it can restore the heavy industry of the Northeast. While fighting against Japan and its allies, the Soviet Union suffered enormous losses, which it must be compensated for. If you observe the situation from this viewpoint, Your Excellency can understand even better the goodwill in this action of the Soviets. Soviet willingness to hand over to China half of what the Soviets have acquired really is based on a spirit of friendship toward China.

I: The people of any nation would like to have the opportunity to manage their own industry independently. I urge Your Excellency to consider this point.

SLADKOVSKY: Summarizing the various points discussed above, I understand that, for the time being, the Chinese have no intention of entering into joint management of industries already in Soviet hands.

I: The question of war booty still constitutes the basic problem. Until this issue is settled, we cannot enter into a discussion of whether to take part. However, pending the withdrawal of Soviet troops, we can allow your engineers to stay on in the factories, to take care of matters on our behalf. This would mean that half the problem has been solved.

SLADKOVSKY: But what about after Soviet troops withdraw?

I: This is exactly the point I would like to discuss.

SLADKOVSKY: I never have been able to understand Your Excellency's point of view.

I: Your Excellency fails to understand my viewpoint because Your Excellency holds different views concerning the basic issue.

SLADKOVSKY: So the Soviets should manage the factories by themselves.

I: The aim of my talk today is to try to make Your Excellency understand the basis for the viewpoint I have stated.

SLADKOVSKY: The Soviets have proposed a specific plan and, therefore, we need a specific response from your country.

I: Since the Soviets and Chinese have different views about the definition of war booty, for the time being we cannot give a specific reply.

SLADKOVSKY: I understand that until the question has been settled, we must allow the present state of affairs to continue. To summarize, we regard these industries as war booty, belonging to the Soviet Union. In other words, they are possessions of the Soviet Union. As for our proposal for joint management, we have made this entirely out of the spirit of friendship.

I: Somehow it sounds unsavory to link the issues of war booty and economic cooperation.

SLADKOVSKY: After we reach an agreement we can stop using the term *war booty* and, instead, can regard the enterprises as objectives for cooperation.

I: It would be best if the Soviets can modify their tactics. This might enable the two sides to move closer.

SLADKOVSKY: Let me repeat that since the Soviets have proposed a specific plan, the Chinese must furnish a specific reply. During Your Excellency's talk with Marshal Malinovsky, Your Excellency said that specific negotiations must wait until after Soviet troops have withdrawn. I feel there is no basis for this statement.

I: I do not wish my people to gain the impression that the agreement for economic cooperation was entered into under Soviet military pressure.

SLADKOVSKY: The important thing now is that we first arrive at a specific conclusion. The announcement can take place after the withdrawal of Soviet troops.

I: I do not object to continuing, for the time being, to exchange opinions, but I hope Your Excellency soon will give me the data promised so that I can have it on hand for reference.

SLADKOVSKY: First, I would like to know whether the Chinese government has approved in principle of the economic cooperation proposed by the Soviets. We can discuss and settle upon the formulation of an agreement before Soviet troops withdraw. As for announcing that agreement, we can postpone that so as to not let the outside world know about it.

I: I shall transmit Your Excellency's ideas to my government.

SLADKOVSKY: In a few days I shall send Your Excellency a list of the factories concerned with military needs.

I: Incidentally, I have a few other remarks to make. It seems there is no need to include in the list the motor vehicle and aircraft industries in the Northeast, which are of an exceedingly small scale, because these industries will be of little importance to the Soviets, but their exclusion will have a favorable psychological impact on the Chinese people.

SLADKOVSKY: I shall carefully consider this point.

I: My personal opinion is that we can let the Chinese operate some of the factories by themselves while turning over others to joint management by the Chinese and the Soviets. As for the question of war booty, if temporarily we do not get involved in it, this might lead to better relations between the two sides. These are my earnest thoughts, reflecting a sincere desire to bring about cooperation between our two countries.

SLADKOVSKY: During our previous exchange of opinions, the two sides were very close. In your talks with me Your Excellency also repeatedly expressed approval of cooperation between our two countries. It so happens that the opinion concerning this issue expressed by the Soviet government coincides with the views we discussed. That is why the Soviets have formally proposed a plan to act upon. We urge the Chinese to speedily give us a specific reply, so that we may settle the question quickly and without hindrance.

I: I shall transmit your message to my government. But at the same time I also request that Your Excellency consider the opinions I have expressed. Did Your Excellency discover, from the inventory of northeastern industries that I sent you last time, that, actually, the Manchurian puppet government constituted the entire source of capital for companies operated by the Japanese?

SLADKOVSKY: Legally speaking, this was not entirely the case. So-called Manchurian puppet capital was merely camouflage. Most of the industries here were created by the Mitsui and Yasuda system and the like. In addition, the Japanese moved the entire machine-building industry to Tokyo.

I: Would Your Excellency please make a careful study of the inventory I sent you so that you will know the true picture. It is the result of working three weeks, day and night, on my part.

SLADKOVSKY: In a few days I shall be able to send Your Excellency the affidavits I have. To facilitate the compiling of these documents, I intend to regard the company rather than the factory as the basic unit.

I: I still want to add another point. I think the power industry should be given to the various municipal governments to operate.

SLADKOVSKY: To be sure, the several power plants in the Northeast were established to meet civilian needs. But neither the Kirin nor the Yalu River hydroelectric power plants are local in nature.

I: As soon as it is sent to me I shall forward Your Excellency's materials to my government. If, pending a reply from my government, we have opinions to exchange, we can do so at any time.

SLADKOVSKY: I still have a small question concerning which I would like to hear Your Excellency's views. In various provinces and cities in your country, such as Shanghai, Hankow, Tientsin, Canton, and other places, there are quite a number of enterprises operated by foreigners. Are they still being run by foreigners? Your Excellency said the Chinese dislike the fact that the Soviets have proposed a plan for joint management. But then why are foreigners allowed to manage enterprises in various provinces and cities?

I: Now, in compliance with Chinese law, foreigners must register with our government the enterprises they formerly set up in the foreign concessions. In order to establish new enterprises they first must obtain permission from our government. As for mining and power enterprises, we have other decrees and they must operate in conformity with those decrees. Although there are also enterprises run by foreigners outside the concessions, these are now very small in number. As for the Chinese and the Soviets jointly operating enterprises, from the beginning I have not objected to this in principle.

My Analysis of Today's Talk

Economic Counselor Sladkovsky discussed in the same breath the economic question and the question of our taking over the administration of various provinces and cities of the Northeast. He also clearly stated that there is no need for us to request that the Soviets send liaison personnel to help our takeover personnel enter the various provinces. He is of the opinion that when the economic question is settled, the political problem also will have been settled. But I doubt whether, after settling the economic question, we will be able to entirely take over the administration of the nine northeastern provinces.

DECEMBER 8.   I received from Generalissimo Chiang a wire responding to my wire of December 5 reporting on my talk with Marshal Malinovsky. Its message was as follows:

> [illegible character] to Ch'ang-ch'un.
> Special Envoy Chiang will forward this to Chairman Chang. I have received the wire of Wei Hai, submitted by Chairman Hsiung. (1) The airlifting of troops can begin as soon as preparations have been completed. In a few days ground personnel for the airport and personnel to construct camps for the troops will fly to Ch'ang-ch'un to make preparations. (2) Wait for railroad communication to be restored before deciding on a date for our troops to advance from Chin-chou. As these troops advance toward Mukden, first dispatch personnel to establish firm contact with the Soviet Army. (3) If the date for the withdrawal of Soviet troops is too near, I can have the Foreign Ministry arrange with the Soviet ambassador for expedient measures. That is, the date on which Soviet troops finally will complete withdrawal can be moved to February 1. But there is no need to specify the date on which Soviet troops will begin their withdrawal. This has been agreed upon by both sides. We can verbally express approval but wait until the end of the month to exchange documents. At present, it is not necessary to announce this to the outside world because both sides previously have agreed upon January 3 as the deadline, and it would not be suitable to change the deadline so soon after it was announced. (4) I already have ordered personnel for various provinces and cities in the Northeast to prepare to fly to Ch'ang-ch'un and await orders. Tung Wen-chi can become mayor of Mukden. (5) With respect to the question of economic cooperation, continue to proceed according to the policies in my instructions. (6) While in the Northeast and, particularly, in front of the Soviets don't ever again mention Tung Pi-wu or matters related to the communist party.—Chung-cheng

Today I dispatched to Generalissimo Chiang a wire reporting in detail my talk yesterday with the Soviet economic counselor. I requested that the central government speedily decide whether we should make economic concessions to obtain, in exchange, an unhindered political position in the Northeast. I also asked which types of industry and mining enterprises we are ready to give in on and manage cooperatively with the Soviets. In addition, I asked the generalissimo to send to Ch'ang-ch'un Messrs. Weng Yung-ni and Ch'ien I-li, the chairman and vice-chairman of the Resources Commission, to handle settlement of the economic issue.

Since in his wire Generalissimo Chiang stated "Don't mention again Tung Pi-wu and matters related to the communist party," I expressly wired Chairman Hsiung to explain. The message was as follows:

The other day, when I talked with Malinovsky, my chief aim was to sound him out about the Soviet attitude toward the advance of our troops from Chin-chou. At first, I got nowhere. Then Ao [Chang Kia-ngau] stated that I had had a private talk with Tung Pi-wu and this gradually elicited a reply from him. The future is full of nettles; sometimes a little twisting and turning cannot be avoided.

Today, I went to inspect (matters) at the State Council of Manchukuo. I plan to station a number of garrison troops there following the arrival of our troops in Ch'ang-ch'un. Inside the State Council building almost all furniture and documents have been completely destroyed or abandoned.

DECEMBER 9.   At 1:00 P.M., together with Special Envoy Chiang and Vice-Chief of Staff Tung, I went to call on Marshal Malinovsky. I told him that we had received from our government instructions that contain the following points:

1. Our country agrees to postpone until February 1, 1946, the date when Soviet troops will complete their withdrawal from the Northeast. Our Foreign Ministry will exchange documents about this with the Soviet ambassador in China.

2. We intend to start airlifting our troops between the twelfth and fifteenth of this month.

3. As soon as it has been confirmed we will notify the Soviets of the date when our troops from Chin-chou will enter Mukden.

4. We intend first to take over the following four cities: Dairen, Mukden, Ch'ang-ch'un, and Harbin. The various provincial governors are awaiting orders to go to their posts.

Marshal Malinovsky replied as follows:

1. He will immediately report to the Soviet government our agreement to postpone to February 1, 1946, the date when Soviet troops will complete their withdrawal from the Northeast.

2. China can airlift its troops to Ch'ang-ch'un at any time.

3. He already has ordered Soviet troops stationed in Mukden to communicate at will with Chinese troops advancing from Chin-chou.

4. The Chinese first can take over the three cities of Ch'ang-ch'un, Mukden, and Harbin. The city of Dairen is under the jurisdiction of the commander of another army zone. Malinovsky immediately will ask Moscow for instructions concerning whether that commander can negotiate with the Chinese about this issue.

I then told Malinovsky that with, regard to the economic question, I already had reported to my government my recent talks with the Soviet economic counselor concerning differences in the point of view of the two sides with regard to their basic understanding of the questions of war booty and reparations. In other words, the Chinese felt that movable property might be considered war booty but that immovable property should not. Actual objects might be regarded as war booty but property rights should not. Furthermore, the problem of reparations could not be settled between our two countries, China and the Soviet Union. At the same time, I intend to continue my discussions with the Soviet economic counselor in the hope of finding common ground where both sides can agree.

Malinovsky replied:

In the past, the Northeast was a base for anti-Soviet activities. In requesting economic cooperation with China, the Soviet Union merely seeks to obtain security for itself. I certainly will bear in mind the public opinion of your country. We do not wish to occupy your land. Even with regard to mines, we only want the machinery and equipment on the surface of the land; we do not seek possession of resources underground. Moreover, we can let your country independently operate a number of industries and mines. We still hope that this question can be resolved through speedy and simple measures. We do not object to a third nation managing enterprises in the Northeast for the purpose of peaceful economic development. The Soviet Union must be on the alert against possible attempts to damage the friendship between China and the Soviet Union. Furthermore, if your country wishes to retain and employ surrendered Japanese troops, the Soviets will not object.

Marshal Malinovsky's remarks were exceedingly candid and straightforward. Deep in my heart I felt extremely delighted. From this talk I could discern between 80 and 90 percent of the Soviet attitude.

Li Tse-fen, alternate name, Yü Fu, commander of the Fifth Division, came to visit.

DECEMBER 10.   I invited Hasegawa Chōji, assistant general director of the Manchukuo Central Bank, and Mori, one of its directors, to come and see me. I appointed them chief liquidators for the Central Bank. Aside from this, I appointed one or two persons from each division of the bank to be assistant liquidators.

DECEMBER 11.   At 5:00 P.M. Sladkovsky, economic counselor of the Soviet Army general headquarters, together with his assistant, Lomochaichev, came to see me. Mi Hsin-min and Keng K'uang served as interpreters for our side. The talk went as follows:

I: Is the material available that Your Excellency promised to give me when we last talked?

SLADKOVSKY: Today, I can tell Your Excellency about this material. The Soviets propose that, in addition to the various enterprises belonging to the Manchurian Heavy Industry Company and the Manchurian Electric Company, there be added to the joint stock corporations to be cooperatvely operated by the Chinese and the Soviets other industries formerly under the management of the Kwantung Army, such as the Dairen shipyard, built in 1943–1944; the Ssu-p'ing coal refinery; and the Chin-chou oil refinery. Furthermore, there are the cement factories in Pen-chi, Dairen, Harbin, and Fu-shun. Naturally, any buildings and property belonging to these various aforementioned enterprises also should be turned over to the newly organized [jointly managed] companies. But the Soviets are willing to relinquish their right to participate in other enterprises operated by the Japanese, as well as by the Manchurian puppet government. Although these enterprises also served the Kwantung Army, the Soviets will hand them over to the Chinese government. On the other hand, naturally we do not include in the list of enterprises to be relinquished those operated by Russians in various places in the Northeast, meaning those that, instead of being owned by the Soviet state, are privately run by individual Russians. These include the brewery in Harbin and the flour mill in Ch'ang-ch'un. Their number is small and their scale, not large. I feel these should be incorporated into the newly organized, jointly managed companies. After the two sides meet together to carry out a study, Chinese and Soviet specialists can prepare an inventory of the various enterprises belonging to the Manchurian Heavy Industry Company and the Manchurian Electric Company. But already we have preliminary statistics. When we compare the output of industries and mines belonging to jointly run enterprises to that of all similar industries and mines, the output of coal mines belonging to jointly run companies comprises 18 percent of total coal output. The output of jointly run machine-building industries comprises 33 percent of total output. The output of jointly run mines producing metallic ores comprises 81 percent of total production. The output of jointly run cement factories comprises 37 percent of total output. And the output of jointly run electric industries comprises 89 percent of total output.

I: Please tell me how many coal mines will belong to the company.

SLADKOVSKY: They are the coal mines of Fu-hsin, Ho-kang, Mi-shan, Hsi-an, Pei-P'iao, Pen-ch'i, Hsi-chien, Ho-kang, Ying-ch'eng-tzu, Chi-hsi, Ma-shan, Cha-lai-noh-erh, Mu-lin, Hui-ch'un, and Lao-hei-shan. There are two or three other coal mines whose names we at present do not yet know. I hope that our two sides will send specialists to confirm this.

I: How many factories in the machine-building industry will belong to the company?

SLADKOVSKY: This has not yet been decided.

I: The Fu-shun coal mines are not listed in the inventory. Does this mean they also do not belong to the Ch'ang-ch'un Railroad?

SLADKOVSKY: The question of enterprises belonging to the Ch'ang-ch'un Railroad does not fall within my jurisdiction.

I: What about the nonferrous metal industries?

SLADKOVSKY: All of the nonferrous metal industries that belonged to the Heavy Industry Company will join the company.

I: It would be best if Your Excellency made a detailed inventory, written in the Chinese language, to show me, listing the names of coal mines and various other mines as well as factories belonging to the nonferrous metal industry, along with various other industries and mines.

SLADKOVSKY: If we consider the value of their factories rather than their output, we expect 94 percent of the enterprises in the ferrous metal industry to join the company.

I: Aside from factories directly under its jurisdiction, the electric company also has affiliated enterprises, such as the Electric-Chemical Works of Kirin Province. The electric company contributes to the capital of these enterprises. Will they also join the intended cooperatively managed company?

SLADKOVSKY: Enterprises in the city of Kirin will not join.

I: I would like to have a precise and accurate inventory of these enterprises.

SLADKOVSKY: I will be able to have the inventory sent to you by tomorrow afternoon.

I: When I talked with Marshal Malinovsky I expressed the following personal opinions. Formerly, the Japanese placed under the jurisdiction of the Heavy Industry Company, which they operated in the Northeast, all enterprises having to do with heavy industry. Actually, this kind of organization was no longer a company as such but was tantamount to a governmental organization in disguise. I also said to Marshal Malinovsky that the Chinese must be given the opportunity to independently operate a number of heavy industries. This is why I wish to have an inventory listing all of the industries and mines that interest the Soviets, so that we may know what they are. There is among the Chinese people a pervasive feeling that these enterprises of the Japanese were a pretext for seizing possession of the entire resources of Manchuria. Consequently, the Chinese people have no sympathy for this.

SLADKOVSKY: Your Excellency's views indeed are correct. Truly, the Japanese established the Heavy Industry Company with the intention of controlling all industries in Manchuria. They not only wanted to control enterprises directly under the jurisdiction of the company but also aimed to control enterprises run by other companies. Therefore that company was tantamount to a governmental organization. But the company we now wish to organize will not adopt the entire plan of the Heavy Industry Company. Furthermore, (1) This company will not be run by the Soviets alone but will be jointly managed by China and the Soviet Union. (2) We will let a Chinese assume the chairmanship of the board of trustees of this jointly managed company. (3) The Soviets have no intention of controlling all the industries in the Northeast, for the jointly managed company is a purely commercial organization. Therefore, it seems inappropriate to liken the measures for joint management proposed by us to Japanese behavior in former days.

I: I told Marshal Malinovsky that from a Chinese point of view, while China and the Soviet Union might operate industries jointly, the principle of equality in the final analysis is not the same as the Chinese operating these industries by themselves. Now, the Chinese are very anxious to have the opportunity to independently manage their own heavy industries. For example, they want to run by themselves an iron and steel works. Their desire is reasonable and well-founded; we should pay attention to it.

SLADKOVSKY: Your Excellency has said that the food industry, the textile industry, and everything belonging to the realm of light industry should be kept in the hands of the Chinese. The Soviet Union has respected the wishes of the Chinese by not adding these kinds of industries to the list of jointly managed enterprises. A large number of these industries were formerly owned by Mitsui and Mitsubishi, and the greater part or even all of their products went to meet the needs of the Japanese army. Nevertheless, the Soviets are willing to relinquish all of it. Even those industries that we intend to have jointly managed are not all inclusive but merely comprise a number of enterprises in those industries. That percentage I have mentioned previously.

I: As for the iron and steel industries, if we add the An-shan and Pen-ch'i industries, this would be tantamount to including every iron and steel plant in the Northeast. Moreover, the Tung-pien-tao Development Company includes a wide range of enterprises. If we include the company, that would be tantamount to adding all the mines and enterprises owned by Tung-pien-tao. Again, the Manchurian Mining Company is an administrative organization. Whoever wished to acquire a certificate to open mines had to obtain its permission. Actually, it was tantamount to a mining ministry.

SLADKOVSKY: Personally, I am of the opinion that the company we now intend to organize will not be the same as the ones under Japanese jurisdiction. Its power should not extend beyond the enterprises under its management.

I: But if the Soviets add to the list the aforementioned organizations, then how am I to conclude there is a difference?

SLADKOVSKY: After making a careful study, Your Excellency naturally will come to acknowledge that there is a difference. I am wondering, after all, what specific proposals the Chinese have to make.

I: Since I must wait for Your Excellency to send me the detailed inventory, I have not yet reported to my government on the various points in our previous talk. But my personal opinion is that we might as well consider placing a number of enterprises under joint Sino-Soviet management. For example, suppose there are four coal mines. Perhaps we could, after consideration, choose two of these to be placed under Sino-Soviet management, letting the Chinese run the other two by themselves. Again, suppose there are two iron and steel works. In this case, the Chinese and the Soviets can jointly operate one while the Chinese operate the other by themselves. Here is another example. There are hydroelectric power plants on both the Yalu River and the Sungari River. We might jointly operate the plant on the Yalu River and let the Chinese operate the plant on the Sungari River. I deeply hope through such measures to find a path to a compromise between our two sides.

SLADKOVSKY: I already have stated in explicit detail and have discussed with Your Excellency the Soviet point of view. But Your Excellency always has discussed principles, without ever giving a specific answer. I request that Your Excellency forthwith provide me with specific measures.

I: I very much wish to consider Your Excellency's opinions. In our various talks I have tried to discern Your Excellency's intentions and inclinations by having Your Excellency first express specific opinions.

SLADKOVSKY: Your Excellency's position is more advantageous than mine. I already am under orders from my government while Your Excellency is not. My actions are constrained by the orders of my government, while Your Excellency is freer to act. Therefore, I hope Your Excellency will bring up specific measures, so that I can report them to my government.

I: I already have wired my government, asking for speedy instructions. I also very much hope that my government can give me a specific answer. But I still hope that Soviets will openly state their opinions so that the views of our two sides can coincide at least 60 or 70 percent. In this way, once a formal answer has been proposed we immediately can reach an agreement.

SLADKOVSKY: Please understand the position I'm in. Until now I only have been able to report to my government Your Excellency's personal views. This really has been embarrassing to me, since the Soviets clearly have expressed their opinions. The Chinese now must express specific opinions so that I can submit a precise report to my government.

I: Tomorrow, as soon as I receive the inventory, I shall report to my government.

SLADKOVSKY: Tomorrow afternoon I shall have the inventory delivered to Your Excellency. I think that the Soviet proposal already takes into consideration the opinions Your Excellency expressed the first time we talked: (1) we have put only the two companies on the list of enterprises to be jointly managed by the Chinese and the Soviets, and (2) the list excludes entirely light industry.

I: I never have approved of comprehensively including the two big companies. Moreover, I repeatedly have expressed the opinion that a number of enterprises should be set aside for the Chinese to operate by themselves.

SLADKOVSKY: Already, a very large number of enterprises are not included.

I: Heavy industry has relatively weighty significance. The Chinese wish to operate a number by themselves.

SLADKOVSKY: Even in the realm of heavy industry, a large number of factories once run by the South Manchuria Railway, like the Special Steel-Making Company, are not included in the list. These can be given to the Chinese to run by themselves.

I: From the vantage point of our long-range interests. I hope Your Excellency will consider leaving room for fulfilling the wishes of the Chinese people.

SLADKOVSKY: The jointly managed companies have been set up for the purpose of developing the economic resources of the Northeast, promoting the welfare of the Chinese people.

I: It is only human for the Chinese to want to run a number of heavy industries. During my first talk with Your Excellency, I directly indicated that including all heavy industries in one organization would not conform with the desires of my government and people.

SLADKOVSKY: I only can reiterate once again that all industries in the Northeast are war booty of the Soviet Army. Already, our not placing all of them on the list is an indication of a very great concession on the part of the Soviets. Your Excellency should know that, in operating their industries in the Northeast, the Japanese were not aiming at China but at the Soviet Union. Now the Soviets merely wish to allocate to themselves a part of this entire industrial complex, and even that part will be jointly managed by the two sides.

I: To be sure, as Your Excellency says, the aim of all Japanese institutions was to oppose the Soviet Union, but 40 million Chinese people in the Northeast have shed blood and sweat to construct the industry there and we must acknowledge their contribution.

SLADKOVSKY: I also acknowledge this; that is why the Red Army cherishes good feelings toward the Chinese. But, actually, the Japanese operated their industries to prepare for a war against the Soviets. Therefore, the Soviet Union has an unqualified right to regard these industries as war booty. Instead of desiring to totally own these industries, the Soviet Union merely seeks joint management.

I: I am deeply grateful for the friendly feelings of the Soviet Union. In the eyes of ordinary Chinese people, the willingness of the Chinese government to place the Ch'ang-ch'un Railroad under joint Sino-Soviet management is also a friendly gesture toward the Soviet Union. However, jointly operating industries and mines is a relatively large matter that merits a considerable amount of time and discussion on both sides.

SLADKOVSKY: Indeed, settling this question will require a considerable amount of time.

I: For that matter, my hair has turned almost entirely white.

SLADKOVSKY: But after we achieve a settlement Your Excellency will be rejuvenated.

I: Handling of this issue is an exceedingly large responsibility. I must take into consideration the aims of my government, as well as popular opinion among my people. I must not only keep in mind the present but also the judgment of later generations.

SLADKOVSKY: When in the future joint management has been achieved, its results will leave with the Chinese Government and people the impression that we are not making a mistake by now opting for joint management.

I: Even though in the future we might obtain good results, right now we should avoid any step that could cause public resentment. We should give consideration to this irrespective of whether or not there is reason for this resentment.

DECEMBER 12.   In the morning Chiang Ching-kuo came to say that today he is leaving for Peiping because Generalissimo Chiang will arrive there today.

The Soviet vice-chairman of the board of directors of the Ch'ang-ch'un Railroad came to see me. During our long conversation the question of the Fu-shun Coal Mine came up. I said the mine should belong to the Chinese government. He said he first would like to make a study of its history. I told him that in the future the coal produced by this mine certainly should first satisfy the needs of the railroad.

In the afternoon, accompanied by Yen Te-shun, his chief secretary, the mayor of Ch'ang-ch'un, T'sao Chao-yuan, came to see me. In the evening I invited for supper Li Tse-fen, commander of the Fifth Division of the National Army, and Ch'iu Hsing-hsiang, assistant commander of the division and chairman of its political department. We discussed the issue of regulations for army pay.

DECEMBER 13.   The Soviet economic counselor sent me the inventory of enterprises to be jointly managed. It comprises the following items:

1. Coal mines: nine
2. Power plants: steam power plants in various places, fourteen. Excluded are the Feng-man Hydroelectric Power Plant, along with its various transmission lines and transformers, as well as the Yalu River Hydroelectric Power Plant.
3. Iron and steel industry: steel- and iron-making factories, three, ore-selecting factories, two
4. Iron mines, three
5. Brick factories, two
6. Nonferrous metal and light metal industries, nineteen
7. Machine-building factories, six
8. Chemical engineering plants, eight, inclusive of oil refineries, two, and stratified-rock oil factories, two
9. Salt flat, one

10. Cement factories, four
11. Civilian airports, eight
    Total: industries and mines, 73 units; civilian airports, eight units

Besides the above, there is an inventory of the enterprises the Soviets will hand back to the Chinese government. It comprises the following:

1. Power plants, 17
2. Coal mines, 26
3. Iron and steel factory, 1
4. Machine-building factories, 23
5. Generator-building factories, 11
6. Other [machinery?] building factories, 6
7. Cement factories, 7
8. Oil refineries and coal refineries, 1 of each
9. Textile factories, 12
10. Food industries, 41
    Total: 147 units

In addition, the Soviets also sent a memorandum. Its main points are

1. Assessed value of enterprises: those to be placed under joint Sino-Soviet management are worth 38 billion yuan, and those to be handed back to China are worth 22 billion yuan.
2. The following jointly managed companies will be organized:

a. The Northern Coal Mine Company
b. The Southern Coal Mine Company
c. The Iron and Steel Company
d. The Nonferrous Metal Company
e. The Machine-building Company
f. The Hydroelectric Power Plant Company
g. The Combustion Power Plant Company
h. The Chemical Industry Company
i. The Cement Industry Company
j. The Civil Aviation Company
k. The Sungari River Steamship Company

3. In the case of the Iron and Steel Company, the Nonferrous Metal Company, the Hydroelectric Power Plant Company, the Civil Aviation

Company, and the Northern Coal Mine Company, Soviet shares will comprise 51 percent; the rest will comprise 49 percent.

In companies where the Soviets own 51 percent of the shares, the chairman of the board of trustees and the general manager will be chosen from among Soviet representatives; the vice-chairman of the board of trustees and the vice-general manager will be chosen from among Chinese representatives.

4. The following Soviet organizations will join the various joint stock corporations: the Khabaraovsk Coal Company, the Ural Metal Company, the General Bureau of Coke, the Far Eastern Power Company, the Far Eastern Bank, the General Bureau of Locomotives, the General Bureau of the Machine-building Industry, the General Bureau of Rail Transportation, the General Bureau of Lead Mines, the General Bureau of the Cement Industry, the General Bureau of Civil Aviation, the Steamship Company of the Lower Reaches of the Hei-lung chiang River, and the Far Eastern Transportation Company.

Affixed: the inventory and the memorandum.

MEMORANDUM

1. All Japanese enterprises in the three northeastern provinces formerly serving the Japanese Kwantung Army will be regarded as war booty of the Red Army and will belong to the Soviet Union.

2. A number of Japanese enterprises in the three northeastern provinces, listed in Inventory No. 1 and having an approximate value of 22 billion yuan, will be given to China and will belong to China exclusively.

3. Japanese enterprises in the three northeastern provinces, listed in Inventory No. 1 and having an approximate value of 38 billion yuan, will belong to the organization of the various joint stock companies managed jointly by the Chinese and the Soviets. The Soviet Union will give to China half of the sum total of capital for the respective enterprises, to be used as shares that China will invest in the various companies managed jointly by the Chinese and the Soviets.

4. There will be organized the following joint stock corporations, to be managed jointly by China and the Soviet Union:

a. The Northern Coal Mine Company
b. The Southern Coal Mine Company
c. The Iron and Steel Company
d. The Nonferrous Metal Company
e. The Machine-building Company

f. The Hydroelectric Power Plant Company

g. The [Combustion ?] Power Plant Company

h. The Chemical Industry Company

i. The Cement Industry Company

j. The Civil Aviation Company

k. The Sungari River Steamship Company

5. Within the Iron and Steel Company, the Nonferrous Metal Company, the Hydroelectric Power Plant Company, the Civil Aviation Company, and the Northern Coal Mine Company, Soviet organizations will have 51 percent of the shares; Chinese legal entities and actual persons will have 49 percent.

Within the Combustion Power Plant Company, the Machine-building Company, the Chemical Industry Company, the Cement Industry Company, the Sungari River Steamship Company, and the Southern Coal Mine Company, Chinese legal entities and actual persons will have 51 percent of the shares while Soviet organizations will have 49 percent.

The above-mentioned proportion of capital must be maintained throughout the duration of the existence of the respective companies. Liquidation can take place only after agreed upon by the Chinese and Soviet governments.

6. Regarding the right to develop underground resources in the area: rights formerly belonging to the Japanese Manchurian Heavy Industry Company, the Japanese Manchurian Electric Company, and other Japanese companies and enterprises that will be incorporated into the various joint stock companies under joint Sino-Soviet management will be transferred to the ownership of the various joint stock corporations listed under Article 4.

7. The following Soviet organizations will join the various limited corporations [the Russian names in the following list are in the original text]: the Khabaraovsk Coal Company (*Khaborovugol*), the Ural Metal Company (*Uralmet*), the General Bureau of Coke (*Glavkoks*), the Far Eastern Power Company (*Dalenergo*), the Far Eastern Bank (*Dalbank*), the General Bureau of Locomotives (*Glavparovoz*), the General Bureau of the Machine-building Industry (*Gummach*), the General Bureau of Rail Transportation (*Guyt* or *Guigt*), the General Bureau of Lead Mines (*Glartsinkosvinets*), the General Bureau of Civil Aviation (Civil Aeronautical Administration) [here the name is in English], the Steamship Company of the Lower Reaches of the Hei-lung chiang River [no Russian name is given for this company], and the Far Eastern Transportation Company (*Daloneshtrans*), etc.

8. Within the various joint stock corporations where the Soviets own 51 percent of the shares, the chairman of the board of trustees will be chosen from among Soviet representatives. The vice-chairman of the board of trustees will be chosen from among Chinese representatives. The executive duties and rights of the various respective companies will be exercised by a general manager, to be designated and assigned by the Soviets, and an assistant general manager, to be designated and assigned by the Chinese. In the various joint stock companies where the Chinese own 51 percent of the shares, the chairman of the board of trustees will be chosen from among Chinese representatives and the vice-chairman of the board of trustees, from among Soviet representatives. The executive duties and rights of these companies will be exercised by a general manager to be designated and assigned by the Chinese and an assistant general manager to be designated and assigned by the Soviets.

[The following continues the narration from where it was interrupted by the inventories and the memorandum.] Wang Wen-wei, special envoy of the Central Bank, arrived in Ch'ang-ch'un. He brought five million yuan of the circulating currency for Manchuria that has been printed, as well as twelve persons on the staff of the bank. Kan Yü-p'ei of the Sino-Soviet Friendship Society of the Northeast came to see me.

DECEMBER 14. I invited Yagi, a director of the Manchurian Iron-making Company, and spent the whole day talking with him. I asked him about the details, as well as the importance, of the various industrial and mining enterprises that the Soviets wish to manage jointly. Then I deliberated on his opinions and immediately prepared a report to send to the central government for its information. The report concerns the two following points: (1) In the final analysis, the extent to which industries the Soviets designate as set up for military purposes actually provided for those needs and (2) what percentage of total mineral production came from the mining enterprises that the Soviets want managed jointly? I affix here the entire report:

Agreements and Differences in Soviet
and Chinese Definitions of Military Terms
(My Own Opinions Sent to Chungking)

The Soviets maintain that the various industries included in the Heavy Industry Company were entirely set up to meet the needs of the Kwantung Army and should be Soviet war booty. If we carefully study ways in which each of the products of the various industries and mines were used, this viewpoint is not likely to be accepted by the Chinese people. My reasons for saying this are as follows:

Of the various heavy industrial enterprises, only four kinds were operated entirely for the needs of the Kwantung Army:

1. The aircraft factories: These factories really fulfilled a military purpose, but their production was small. In 1942 they produced only 186 airplanes and 784 engines. In 1944 they produced only 425 airplanes and 420 engines.

2. The motor vehicle industry: After the completion of the motor vehicle factories, only 50 percent of their products served military needs. Twenty percent served the Manchurian railroads, and 30 percent went to meet civilian needs. Only during the most recent year did they serve entirely the needs of the Kwantung Army. Figures for their production: in 1943 they assembled 2,820 motor vehicles, partially manufactured 375, and repaired 15,000.

3. The gunpowder industry: The greater part of the industry really served military needs. In 1943, it produced 9,219 tons of nitric acid explosives and 9,552 kilograms of fuse. In 1944, it produced 10,280 tons of nitric acid explosives and 12,808 kilograms of fuse. But its products also included radar tubes manufactured for industrial use. In 1943 it produced 32,237 kilograms of such tubes.

4. The man-made petroleum industry: The two factories both were under the jurisdiction of the Kwantung Army. The Ssu-p'ing Coal Oil Refinery was experimental and had not yet begun production. The Chinhsi Oil Refinery also had not yet begun production.

Although part of the steel, iron, coal, and charcoal produced served military needs, the quantity was small. For example, the military used the following percentages of the products of the Manchurian iron-making industry: cast iron, only about 3 percent; steel plates, only about 16 percent, and steel pieces, only about 10 percent, including exports to Japan. [See the following table.]

Type	Year	Output	For Military Use	For Export to Japan	For Internal Use or for Export to Korea
Cast Iron	1942	1,340,808[1] kilowatts	24,644 (1.8%)	723,555	587,609
	1943	1,710,267	56,602 (3.2%)	657,273	996,392
	1944	1,159,400	36,000 (3.1%)	587,252	536,148

Steel Pieces	1942	737,955		76,200 (including military use) 10.2%	
	1943	843,035		14,300 (including military use) 1.6%	
	1944	439,000			
Steel Plates	1942	457,833	74,700 (16%)		379,533
	1943	485,673	79,800 (16.2%)	4,000	384,893
	1944	282,000	22,000 (7.8%)	11,000	371,100
Coal	1942	24,168,670[1] kilowatt	2,541,594 (10.4%)	643,193	940,809
	1943	25,320,425	2,726,439 (10.8%)	576,767	1,363,612
	1944	25,626,704	2,712,527 (10.8%)	589,612	1,567,865

TRANSLATOR'S NOTE: Kilowatt is the unit of measurement given here, although the character is unclear, as is whether it actually means kilowatt. But the watt radical is clearly legible, and Chinese dictionaries do not list a more suitable term under this radical. The translator conjectures that, in a great hurry and temporarily at a loss for the proper term, the author used whatever word came into his mind at the moment. He probably meant tons.

If we consider the total production of the Northeast, only 10 percent of the coal and charcoal served military needs. In the Heavy Industry Company the output of coal mines comprised 70 percent of the entire production. Therefore, only about 7 percent of the total production of coal mines of the Heavy Industry Company served military needs.

In 1944 the output of aluminum of the Manchurian Light Metal Company was 8,441 tons, of which 1,025 tons met military needs, comprising only about 12 percent of total output. In 1942, the output of manganese was only 55 tons. In 1943, it was 241 tons and, in 1944, 402 tons. The figures were very small. Even if all of these served military needs, the amount would have been miniscule.

Copper, lead, and zinc were the three products of Manchurian mines that were related to the military. In 1944, copper output was 2,076,137 tons. Of this a total of 62,462 tons went for military and paramilitary needs, only about 4.9 percent of total output. In 1944 lead output was 5,432,324 tons. A total of 787,059 tons went for military and paramilitary needs, amounting to only about 14.4 percent of total output. In 1944 zinc output was 50,000 tons. A total of 98,366 tons went to meet military and paramilitary needs. This amounted to only about 19 percent of total output. The insufficiency was met by imports.

In 1943 the total output of cement was 1,503,240 tons, of which 700,631 tons went to meet military needs, accounting for 46 percent of total output. In 1944 total output was 1,132,550 tons; of this, 421,361 tons went to meet military needs, or about 37 percent. The output of the four factories listed by the Soviets comprised 39 percent of total production. Therefore, the amount that went to meet military needs was no more than 14.4 percent of total output.

Perhaps the Soviets feel that the greater part of the products of industries and mines in the Northeast was exported to Japan and so went to meet Japanese military needs. Indeed, there is a basis for this, but if the products of industries and mines in the Northeast are to be regarded as war booty because they met Japanese military needs, then how to deal with these should be subject to a joint decision by the United Nations.

If the Soviets maintain that all products of industries and mines in the Northeast indirectly met Japanese military needs, then, in this age of total warfare, everything in the world is related to the military. Even grain or the people's labor can be considered war booty.

DECEMBER 15.   After his trip to Peiping to see Generalissimo Chiang, Chiang Ching-kuo came back to Ch'ang-ch'un He told me that he had obtained the gist of the generalissimo's instructions:

1. We cannot acknowledge the Soviet Union's request for war booty. But the Chinese government can allow the Soviets to have a portion of Japanese investment in Manchuria as compensation for losses suffered by the Soviets during the war.

2. We can negotiate with the Soviets about organizing jointly the operation of Sino-Soviet industrial and mining enterprises.

3. We must retrieve control of as many as possible of the kinds of enterprises that the Soviets want jointly operated.

In the morning I invited the following persons to discuss the question of issuing the circulating currency: Ke Tsu-lan, manager of the Bank of China in Ch'ang-ch'un; Li Mo-lin, manager of the Yi-fa-ho Bank; assistant manager Yü Liu-li of the Central Bank in Harbin; T'ien I-min, manager of the Bank of China; Ho Chih-an, chairman of the board of trustees of the Bank of Harbin, as well as chairman of the Bankers' Professional Association; and Chu Hsiu-fu, manager of the Bank of China in Fengtien. All agreed that (1) the use of the national currency will be prohibited in the Northeast, (2) the ratio between the circulating currency and the national currency may at any time be jointly discussed by the various banks; the rate of exchange with China Proper also may at any time be discussed and determined. With respect to the exchange and remittance of circulating currency into China Proper, for the time being transactions involving large sums cannot be carried out.

In the evening Ching-kuo and I acted as cohosts at a banquet for the following persons: the Soviet vice-chairman of the board of directors of the Ch'ang-ch'un Railroad, the chief of staff of the Soviet Army, the Soviet commander of the Ch'ang-ch'un garrison, and others. During the dinner Special Envoy Chiang formally notified the Soviets that Madame Chiang Kai-shek soon would arrive in Ch'ang-ch'un to extend consolations to the common people as well as to Soviet troops.

DECEMBER 16.   Chao Chün-mai, mayor of Ch'ang-ch'un who had arrived from Peiping, came for a talk. In the evening I had supper at Ching-kuo's residence and a casual conversation with him.

DECEMBER 17.   At 12:00 P.M. I called on Marshal Malinovsky to say goodbye. I told him that I intended to go to Peiping and from there to Nanking. With respect to the economic question, Malinovsky said that although the Soviets regard all industrial and mining enterprises in the Northeast as their war booty, they are willing to hand back a number to China. Moreover, they even have promised to exempt a number of heavy industries, which we wish to operate ourselves, and give them to us. [From Malinovsky's point of view] this demonstrates that the Soviets already have been very lenient. As for the question of our taking over Dairen, he was not yet able to give us a reply, since he had not yet received instructions.

At one o'clock I boarded the airplane. It was unable to start because its engine was frozen. So I had to return. The flight was postponed until tomorrow. In the evening I drafted an analytical report concerning the industries and mines the Soviets propose to have operated jointly. I will take it to Chungking to use in discussion.

DECEMBER 18.   At 9:00 A.M., together with Ching-kuo, I left for Peiping by army plane. I had received from Generalissimo Chiang a wire saying that he hoped I would arrive in Peiping before ten o'clock. But, because the plane stopped briefly in Chin-chou, it already was 3:00 P.M. when we arrived in Peiping. Generalissimo Chiang already had flown to Nanking before three o'clock. I shall have to fly to Nanking to see him.

During the stop in Chin-chou I took the opportunity to discuss the following issues with my superior, Tu Yü-ming: issuing the circulating currency, recall of the national currency bearing the seal of his army command, and the amount of circulating currency needed for army pay each month. After arriving in Peiping I exchanged opinion with Chairman Hsiung T'ien-i on various issues.

Today, Vice-Chief of Staff Tung Yen-p'ing saw Soviet major general Trotsynko. Tung told him that, in order to maintain liaison with the Soviet

Army, the northeastern security maintenance command intends to dispatch a team of liaison personnel to each of the following sections of the railroad: between Hsin-min and Mukden; between Yi-hsien, Fu-hsin, and T'ung-ao, and between Chih-feng, To-lun, Noh-erh, and Lin-hsi. Tung also gave him the names of our liaison personnel. Trotsynko replied that he will give us an answer after making a study. He also said that since November Soviet troops have withdrawn from Chin-chou to Hsin-min. He can guarantee that the railroad between Hsin-min and Mukden will be handed over intact. He added that at any time our troops may enter areas south of the line extending from Fu-shun, Mukden, Hsin-min, Chang-wu, and Chih-feng through To-lun and that in Liao-yang, Hai-ch'eng, An-shan, etc., there remain only a small number of Soviet troops to watch property. He said that we need have absolutely no apprehensions about Soviet troops hindering our troops from entering. When I asked him about the Antung region, he replied that this belongs to the eastern battle zone and is not under the jurisdiction of his army command, and so on. This indicates that Soviet troops in South Manchuria and the southern parts of Jehol already have withdrawn northward. That is an accomplished fact.

DECEMBER 19.   At 10:30 my plane took off from Peiping. There was a brief lunch stop in Süchow. At 3:00 P.M. I arrived in Nanking and was lodged at the Determination Society. At 8:00 I went to Generalissimo Chiang's official residence for supper where I met Foreign Minister Wang Hsüeh-t'ing and Chiang Ching-kuo. After dinner we had a long conversation and did not part until 11:30. The following issues were decided upon:

1. This year we will first take over the four cities of Ch'ang-ch'un, Mukden, Harbin, and Dairen. Early next month we will take over the various provincial governments.

2. Beginning from the twenty-fifth, we will first airlift one regiment of troops to Mukden. We will continue to airlift our troops, using ten planes a day, and will complete the airlift on the tenth of next month.

3. With respect to the economic question, the Ministry of Economics will send personnel to Ch'ang-ch'un to make a study of the types of enterprises to be operated jointly and to discuss the issue with the Soviets.

4. With respect to the war booty question, we will give the Soviets a payment to compensate for expenses incurred by them as a result of postponing the date for withdrawing their troops. The sum will not exceed ten billion yuan of national currency. (By national currency we mean the circulating currency in the Northeast.)

5. Instead of being concentrated in one company, the enterprises to be operated jointly will be divided into a number of units. Electric enterprises will not be incorporated into jointly managed companies.

6. As soon as the Soviets have completed withdrawal of their troops, the two sides will send representatives to discuss the economic question. We will adopt the procedure of open negotiations.

After we adjourned, Foreign Minister Wang Hsüeh-t'ing accompanied me to the Determination Society. We talked some more.

DECEMBER 20.   After breakfasting I arrived at the airport where I received a phone call from Generalissimo Chiang, who desired to have another talk before I left. I immediately rushed to his official residence, and we talked for twenty minutes. Generalissimo Chiang reiterated the various points discussed and decided upon last night and asked me to tell the Soviets the following:

1. We will give the Soviets compensation of about ten billion yuan in national currency because of their postponing the withdrawal of their troops.

2. With respect to the types of enterprises to be operated jointly by the Chinese and the Soviets, our Ministry of Economics will consider this and send personnel to Ch'ang-ch'un to discuss the question with the Soviets.

3. We can approve of setting up a joint management company, but it must be divided into a number of units. We will not establish one single company, like the Heavy Industry Company of Manchurian puppet times. And we will not incorporate electric enterprises into jointly managed companies.

At 9:30 my plane took off. At 1:00 I arrived in Peiping. After a brief rest I went to Chairman Hsiung T'ien-i's. I also invited the various provincial chairmen of the Northeast. I reported what had transpired during the discussions in Nanking and the various points of Generalissimo Chiang's instructions. Then I invited Sun Yueh-chi of the Resources Commission to come and gave him the same information.

DECEMBER 21.   At 8:00 A.M. my plane took off from Peiping. At 1:00 I arrived in Ch'ang-ch'un. I immediately talked with Vice-Chief of Staff Tung Yen-p'ing, Division Commander Li, and Chao Chün-mai, mayor of Ch'ang-ch'un. Mayor Chao arrived in Ch'ang-ch'un only yesterday. He has decided to assume his post and take over the municipal government tomorrow. In the afternoon I saw Ts'ao Chao-yuan, the former mayor of Ch'ang-ch'un appointed by the Soviets, and asked him to give an account of his administration. I somewhat consoled him.

Today, the Soviets notified us that they already had designated and dispatched three liaison teams: (1) the Chih-feng team, (2) the Chang-wu team, and (3) the Hsin-min team. They also indicated the locations where these teams will meet with our liaison personnel.

DECEMBER 22.   At 10:00 A.M. the Ch'ang-ch'un branch of the Central Bank officially began business. I was in charge of the key and unlocked the front door, after which the opening ceremony was held. There, to express their congratulations, were the Soviet economic counselor and his colleagues: the manager of the Far Eastern Bank, Soviet directors and supervisors of the Ch'ang-ch'un Railroad, and representatives of the Soviet garrison command. On our side, there were bankers and officials of our various organizations in Ch'ang-ch'un. At twelve o'clock Mayor Chao took over the Ch'ang-ch'un municipal government. He begins work at his office this very day. Former Mayor Ts'ao instead becomes a counselor to the municipal government. In the afternoon Messrs. Mo Te-hui and Wang Chia-chen arrived in Ch'ang-ch'un from Peiping.

In the evening Mayor Chao came to discuss future administrative measures.

Today I sent to T.V. Soong, president of the Executive Yuan, a wire telling him what had transpired during my talk with Generalissimo Chiang in Nanking. I also told him that I intend to organize a Hsing-yeh Company to restore medium and small industries.

I sent to Finance Minister Yü Hung-chün a wire telling him that I intend to allow the military currency issued by the Soviets to continue to be used legally, at a value equal to that of the circulating currency issued by us. I also reported on what happened when the Ch'ang-ch'un branch of the Central Bank started business.

I received from Chiang Ching-kuo a wire stating that he holds me in high esteem. He sounded very sincere. Consequently, I sent in reply a wire in which I praised him for his calm and resolute character. This is an impression I received from observations during several months of working with him. I know that he genuinely possesses these virtues. I was not being excessive in my praise.

DECEMBER 23.   I took a walk and rested for the entire day, pondering the questions of the future.

DECEMBER 24. At 4:00 P.M. I went to see Soviet economic counselor Sladkovsky and told him I already have received instructions from the central government. The following is a record of our conversation:

I: During my recent trip to Nanking I recounted to Generalissimo Chiang, as well as to other officials in charge, your inventory and what had transpired during our conversations. Now, my government has decided to ask its Ministry of Economics to consider and send persons to Ch'ang-ch'un to discuss these issues.

SLADKOVSKY: Why does your government still wish to send persons to hold separate discussions?

I: Last time, Your Excellency mentioned that we could have specialists discuss the types of enterprises to be incorporated into jointly managed companies.

SLADKOVSKY: This was an idea I had before the Soviets compiled and gave you the inventory of types of enterprises. Now, since the inventory has been compiled and delivered, naturally, there is no more need to send specialists to discuss the issue.

I: I recall that Marshal Malinovsky proposed that we enter into further discussions concerning the types of enterprises China wants to set aside to operate independently. Your Excellency also made such a statement. That is why my government made this decision.

SLADKOVSKY: Since this is the case, I will not insist on a different opinion. Please tell me who will be sent and when they can come. I presume this will not delay the issue.

I: It should not take too long. Now, I intend to inform Your Excellency about the several principles for cooperation, as instructed by my government:

1. If your country raises the question of war booty, this is bound to create many misunderstandings among the Chinese people. Even if, in the future, such cooperation succeeds, the Chinese people will think that the Soviets got their share because of war booty, which will give the Chinese people a lasting unfavorable impression of the Soviets. For this reason, the Chinese government proposes, instead, to compensate the Soviet Army with a sum for military expenses. Nominally, it is a payment for the Soviet Army's postponing the date of withdrawing its troops. We intend to fix the figure at ten billion yuan in northeastern circulating currency. In the future, after deciding on the types of enterprises to be operated jointly, the Soviets can use these ten billion yuan as capital. For their part the Soviets will not again raise the question of war booty. At the time that they withdraw

their troops, the Soviets first will transfer to the Chinese government control of all enterprises, such as industries and mines, which the Soviets propose be jointly operated. We are proposing this solely out of a desire to create in the minds of the Chinese people love and respect for the Soviet Union.

2. We want enterprises that will be operated jointly divided into a number of units. We do not want to have all these enterprises merged into one big company. This is because the Chinese people regard all of the following companies as, by nature, instruments of a kind of economic invasion: the East India Company in the days of British rule in India, the South Manchuria Railway when the Japanese controlled Manchuria, and the Heavy Industry Company of Manchurian puppet times. We fear the Chinese people will hold the same views if now, following the withdrawal of Soviet troops, China and the Soviet Union set up a single company. This is why we wish to set up a number of units. In the future, when the time is favorable, we can set up a liaison office overseeing the various companies that can obtain results comparable to having one company. But our current proposal will persuade the Chinese people that the Soviet Union is willing to conduct multifaceted economic cooperation with China and that this does not suggest it is attempting an economic invasion of China.

3. China always has regarded electric enterprises as a type of public utility that should be managed by the Chinese government or by a municipal government. Now, the Chinese government already has decided that, except for electric enterprises already under joint Sino-foreign management in the concessions, no new electric enterprises can be under joint Sino-foreign management. Even with regard to electric enterprises already under joint Sino-foreign management in the concessions, we will not extend permission to do business beyond the expiration of their licenses. Therefore, we hope that electric enterprises will not be incorporated into jointly operated companies.

4. Even before the Soviets withdraw their troops, as soon as persons sent by our Ministry of Economics arrive, we can begin to discuss, as well as decide on, the types of enterprises to be run cooperatively. At the same time, we can discuss ways of organizing jointly operated companies.

5. After we have made a draft and as soon as the Soviets complete withdrawal of their troops, our two sides will appoint official delegates to discuss this draft. In this way the nations of the world, as well as the Chinese people, will know that no secret conditions [although the term *conditions* is used, obviously the meaning is *concessions*] have been offered by China for the withdrawal of Soviet troops. Conse-

quently, the foundation of our economic cooperation can still be more propitious and stable.

SLADKOVSKY: How will we assess the value of the enterprises that in the future will be managed cooperatively? On the basis of their original value or according to the actual value of such property in its present condition?

I: In my humble opinion, according to the former, original price, deducting depreciation and current losses.

SLADKOVSKY: Suppose an enterprise has been almost entirely destroyed. How do we assess its value?

I: Suppose an enterprise worth one million yuan has been damaged to an extent that it is worth only 50,000 yuan. We then must invest capital of 950,000 yuan before it can be restored to its original condition. China and the Soviet Union should meet this expense by each providing half.

SLADKOVSKY: If the Soviets are unwilling to provide capital for restoring an enterprise, can they indicate this unwillingness in advance?

I: Since the companies are under joint Sino-Soviet management, there must be bilateral agreement on everything. There is no need to decide in advance.

SLADKOVSKY: It would be best to decide in advance.

I: We could have the specialists discuss this.

SLADKOVSKY: I will transmit to my government the various points advanced by the Chinese. But doesn't the dispatching of persons to discuss the economic question unnecessarily complicate procedures? Furthermore, will something in the nature of a conference take shape?

I: After we have decided upon the draft, there should be no problems in open discussions.

SLADKOVSKY: Right now, in various factories, damage is being done every day. It would be best for Your Excellency's side to speedily send persons to the factories to take charge and temporarily set aside the question of whether or not you officially will take over. This will add to the favorable impression your people will receive.

I: I shall consider this.

SLADKOVSKY: With respect to power enterprises, most power went to meet industrial needs and was not totally for municipal consumption. I still ask you to consider this.

I: The electric enterprises included (1) large hydroelectric power plants, (2) municipal power plants, and (3) power plants affiliated with coal mines. They were by nature very complex. We can let the specialists take their time discussing this issue.

SLADKOVSKY: Very good.

1: I intend within a few days to take a trip to Mukden and Harbin. If by the time I return to Ch'ang-ch'un Your Excellency has received from your government a wire in reply to your message, we can further discuss this matter.

In the morning I went to the Central Bank. I also went to the office of the board of directors of the Ch'ang-ch'un Railroad. There I deliberated with the Soviet vice-chairman of the board of directors and decided to recommend Wang Chu-t'ing to be vice-head of the Railroad Bureau. Tonight, Tung Chieh-chen, mayor of Mukden, went to Mukden to prepare to assume his post. The Soviet Army command sent a liaison officer to accompany him.

DECEMBER 25.   In the morning, I went to the office of the board of directors of the Chinese–Ch'ang-ch'un Railroad Bureau. There I explicitly stated to the Soviet vice-chairman of the board of directors that our Economic Commission should take over the Fu-shun Coal Mines and that we will send Chang Hsing-fu there to take charge. He expressed his approval.

I told the Soviet Army command I will fly to Mukden tomorrow.

In the evening I invited for supper the various major figures of the Northeast Headquarters.

DECEMBER 26.   Because of bad weather today the plane trip was canceled.

In the evening, together with Ch'en Ti-ch'iu, special envoy of the Ministry of Communications, I made a study of the draft regulations for the Chinese–Ch'ang-ch'un Railroad Bureau.

DECEMBER 27.   In the morning I saw Zhuravliev, head of the Chinese–Ch'ang-ch'un Railroad Bureau.

At 12:00 I left for Mukden by plane and arrived there about 1:00. Lieutenant General Kovtun-Stankevich, Soviet garrison commander, came to meet me. I immediately went to the municipal government, where several hours before there already had been a ceremony inaugurating Mayor Tung. After a brief stay I went to the Central Bank, which also begins business today. The president of the bank is Han Li-ju. Then I called on the Soviet garrison commander to express my consolations. In the evening Mayor Tung gave a feast for the garrison commander and his assistant, representatives of the Far Eastern Trading Company, and others. Lieutenant General Kovtun-Stankevich made a speech stating that he is willing to help Mayor Tung establish independent and autonomous administrative power.

DECEMBER 28.   In the morning I saw the current heads of Mukden's general contingent of public security and police bureau.

At 11:00 at the Central Bank I saw local representatives of various circles. Then I had lunch at the Bank of China. Immediately afterward I went to the airport. Because of the bad weather the plane could not take off. Instead, at seven o'clock in the evening I took a special train for Harbin.

DECEMBER 29.   At 8:00 A.M. the train passed through Ch'ang-ch'un. Because of a need to change the locomotive, the train did not start again until twelve o'clock. At 5:00 P.M. I arrived in Harbin. In the evening I was invited to a banquet given by the head of the Chinese–Ch'ang-ch'un Railroad Bureau. Present were various Soviet bureau chiefs. After dinner a film was shown.

DECEMBER 30.   I went on a round of sightseeing in the metropolitan district of Harbin. Sixteen years have passed since I went abroad in May 1929 to make a study of foreign banks. On that trip at Harbin I boarded a train of the Trans-Siberian Railroad in order to reach Europe via the Soviet Union. When I passed through Harbin then, I learned that outside the metropolitan district there were frequent robberies and such. Apparently, today there is no more of this.

I received visitors from among the local gentry.

DECEMBER 31.   In the morning I went to the office of the Chinese–Ch'ang-ch'un Railroad Bureau. The Soviet head of the bureau accompanied me on a visit to its various bureaus and sections. In the afternoon, together with Vice-Chief of Staff Tung, I called upon Major General Karchakov, garrison commander at Harbin. Previously Karchakov served as military attaché in the Soviet embassy in China. He is a composed, refined person. He expressed a willingness to cooperate fully with the newly appointed mayor. I also discussed with him the issue of changing the head of the police bureau of the municipal government. He said he was willing to assist me in this. I paid a visit to the consumers' cooperative set up by the Soviets. Ma Ying-lin, current head of the Bureau of Industry and Commerce of Pin-chiang province, came to see me. Ma was a student at Peking University and is a very outspoken person. I promised to give him work in the future and consoled him somewhat.

At eleven o'clock in the evening I attended a party held by the Soviet Army at the Railroad Club. Attending the party were Soviet civil and military officials, as well as local Soviet emigrants and their families. There were about two thousand people. Sitting opposite me was Major General Maksimov, garrison commander of northern Manchuria. In his position as a host he repeatedly raised his glass to me in various toasts, forcing me to drink. After dinner, dancing began. I was unable to stand. When the dancing was over, the host dragged me over to sit down beside him and raised various questions. I tried my best to avoid answering. When I returned to my residence it already was about 3:00.

In Manchuria

JANUARY 1–31, 1946

Chinese officials in Harbin begin taking over banks and other local government organs from Soviet troops. Chang Kia-ngau learns from Foreign Minister Wang Hsüeh-t'ing that international negotiations between the United
States and the USSR have produced several diplomatic moves that Wang
believes will constrain the Soviet Union in its negotiations with China. He
also reports to Chang that a truce between the Chinese Communists and
Nationalists will soon occur.

 Back in Ch'ang-ch'un, Chang Kia-ngau again confers with Malinovsky.
Chang reports that local governance in Mukden and Harbin is being transferred to Republic of China (ROC) control and wonders why Dairen cannot
be included. Malinovsky replies that he is still awaiting instructions from
Moscow about Dairen's status. Discussion then shifts to how to deal with the
irregular military units that are causing disturbances in certain parts of
Manchuria. Malinovsky also wonders why Soviet commercial agents cannot
acquire former Japanese properties such as real estate. Chang explains that
new ROC government laws are being drawn up to deal with the issue of
former Japanese property in China.

 Nationalist troops begin to be airlifted into Ch'ang-ch'un, but Chang
Kia-ngau worries that the ROC troops entering southern Manchuria are not
moving northward rapidly enough to occupy the major cities along the
Ch'ang-ch'un railway line. On January 10 Chang Kia-ngau learns from

President Chiang Kai-shek about the discussions under way in Chungking to resolve the Sino-Soviet economic cooperation deadlock. Government officials are studying which types of enterprises should be selected for joint management between China and the Soviet Union. Chang Kia-ngau is informed by his staff about the severe shortage of coal, which might prevent the Nationalist military from using Manchuria's main railway lines.

On January 11 the Nationalists and Communists agree to a truce in China that is not supposed to limit the ROC government's efforts to recover Manchuria. Chang Kia-ngau receives instructions from Chungking that the ROC government is still drafting new laws but that the Soviets will be allowed to rent former Japanese properties.

On January 15 Nationalist troops enter Mukden. Chang Kia-ngau writes to President Chiang and Minister of Economics Weng Wen-hao to urge that the ROC government concede more to the Soviets on economic cooperation. Chang argues that unless concessions are made, the Soviets will impose great difficulties on the ROC government in its efforts to recover Manchuria. Chang Kia-ngau fears that the Soviets will not help the Nationalists in their takeover on the grounds that the Soviets do not want any conflict with Chinese communist troops. Chang regrets that the ROC government did not send a team of economic experts to Ch'ang-ch'un last December to negotiate with the Soviets night and day to resolve the economic cooperation issue. Had both sides agreed to some terms, the Chinese communist troops would not have penetrated into southern Manchuria in such large numbers and the Soviet attitude toward the ROC government would not have hardened.

Chiang Ching-kuo returns from the USSR and tells Chang Kia-ngau that Stalin said that Sino-Soviet economic cooperation to manage former Japanese enterprises should be discussed before Soviet troops leave Manchuria. Chang and Sun Yueh-chi then consider what further economic concessions the Chinese might offer to facilitate a speedy settlement with the Soviets so that Nationalist forces could rapidly recover Manchuria. Chang and Sun communicate their views to both Minister Weng and President Chiang Kai-shek and list the various industries for which Sino-Soviet cooperation might be readily agreed on.

On January 21 Chang Kia-ngau confers with Major General Trotsynko and learns that armed irregular troops are making their appearance in many areas where Soviet forces must deal with them. Therefore, the Nationalist troops will have to delay their arrival in Ch'ang-ch'un for several more weeks. He informs Chang that Soviet troops evacuated Ying-k'ou on January 13.

President Chiang wires Chang Kia-ngau that the ROC government cannot agree to all former Japanese assets being Red Army war booty and that Chang Kia-ngau should only discuss selecting enterprises for Sino-Soviet management. President Chiang is adamant that the former South Manchuria

Railway and the Fu-shun Coal Mine, as well as their affiliated enterprises, will not be jointly managed with the Soviets. He also identifies enterprises that can be considered for joint management.

Chiang Kia-ngau then informs the Soviets of these new ROC terms for Sino-Soviet management and of ways in which former Japanese properties can be used by Soviet commercial agents.

On January 26 Chang and Sladkovsky meet to discuss Chang Kia-ngau's recent proposals. Sladkovsky complains that many enterprises now held by the Soviet Army are not on the ROC list for Sino-Soviet joint management and demands that both sides quickly reach an agreement. Chang defends his proposals. Both men are still far from an agreement.

On January 28 Chang learns of the murder of engineer Chang Hsing-fu and his party by communist Eighth Route Army soldiers. Chang also learns there will be another delay in Soviet troop withdrawal from Manchuria. Chang then meets with Sladkovsky, but there is still no progress.

On January 31 Foreign Minister Wang wires Chang Kia-ngau to ask Vice-Chief of Staff Tung Yen-p'ing whether the Soviet Army will withdraw on January 31, as they had promised, and to report back to Wang. Chang learns from a Chinese communist local newspaper of communist plans to push ahead with elections of new officials for the provincial and subprovincial governments in Manchuria. Chang confides to his diary that the Soviets are transferring the cities along the Ch'ang-ch'un railway line to the Nationalists but are allowing the Chinese communist forces to occupy the hinterlands. Chang speculates that the Soviets have allowed this in order to give military aid to the Chinese Communists without difficulty. He worries that no one in the ROC government seems to be aware of this new development.

+ + + + + + +

NEW YEAR'S DAY, 1946. Today, Yang Cho-an, mayor of Harbin, was formally sworn into office at the municipal government. Upon getting up in the morning, I vomited but made an effort and attended to supervise the swearing in. I urged the new mayor to get rid of bad bureaucratic habits, transform trends, implement Sino-Soviet friendship, and prepare to establish a foundation for popular election of the mayor.

Today, too, the Harbin branch of the Central Bank opened. I presided over the opening ceremony.

The citizenry were overjoyed by the accession to office of a mayor appointed by the central government and the opening of the Central Bank. When I recalled how for fifteen years the land had been subjugated, I could imagine the mixed feelings of joy and sadness in their innermost hearts.

In the afternoon, together with Vice-Chief of Staff Tung, I called upon

Major General Maksimov, garrison commander of northern Manchuria. He immediately treated us to wine and dinner. He had invited Mayor Yang; Major General Karchakov, commander of the district; and the Soviet head of the Railroad Bureau. In addition, he had invited Li Chao-lin, formerly vice-provincial governor of Chahar province. Li is a member of the communist party and took part in resistance work against Japan in northern Manchuria. After entering Manchuria, the Soviet Army appointed him vice-governor of the province. Recently, he has been persuaded to resign the post. Now, he is head of the Sino-Soviet Friendship Society.

During dinner I told Major General Maksimov that the various provincial governors we have assigned to northern Manchuria will be assuming their posts one by one. He replied that he will do his best to help them. Then he asked whether our governor for Hsingan province will assume his post at the same time, implying that there are independence movements near Hailar. Upon learning this I felt that perhaps in provinces adjacent to the Soviet Union the Soviets were promoting noncentral forces. From this I infer that there still will be problems in our taking over.

Foreign Minister Wang Hsüeh-t'ing's wire of the twenty-eighth, which Chairman Hsiung received and forwarded to me from Ch'ang-ch'un, says,

> The deadlock between the United States and the Soviet Union was broken at the conference of the three ministers in Moscow. From now on it will be awkward for the Soviets to act independently and without constraint. The general international situation has improved, the Nationalists and the Communists have resumed talks, and opinion on both sides gradually is moving toward a truce. It seems that we can hope for a compromise on other issues.

I can see from this wire that Foreign Minister Wang never has come to understand that the Soviets have a regional strategy for the Northeast that will not be altered by any change in the international situation.

I wired Chairman Hsiung about the question of the northeastern Hsing-yeh Company:

> I personally informed the president about the matter of the northeastern Hsing-yeh Company to gain his approval. After returning to Ch'ang-ch'un, I wired President Soong of the Executive Yuan to inform him; as of today I have received no reply. Since you are near him, could you personally urge him to reply so that I can proceed?

My reason for organizing the Hsing-yeh Company is to turn over to private companies [literally "people's companies"] the light industries handed back to us by the Soviets so that they can raise the capital and manage them. This will ease the burden on the state treasury. Moreover, it will induce local people of means in the Northeast to invest, thus dispelling the suspicion that only people from China Proper are profiting from such management.

JANUARY 2.   At 8:00 A.M. I took a train to Ch'ang-ch'un, arriving at about 1:00. In the afternoon the following persons came to see me: Wang Wen-po, assistant chairman of the board of directors of the Chinese–Ch'ang-ch'un Railroad; Wang Shu-jen, member of the Economic Commission; Mo Liu-ts'un, assistant chairman of the board of supervisors of the Chinese–Ch'ang-ch'un Railroad; Kao Lun-ching and Ch'iu Wei-ying, supervisors of the Chinese–Ch'ang-ch'un Railroad; Liu Han-tung, governor of Liao-peh province; and Mayor Chao of Ch'ang-ch'un.

JANUARY 3.   At 3:00 P.M. I called upon Marshal Malinovsky to wish him a Happy New Year and also to thank him for the hospitality of Soviet commanders in both Mukden and Harbin. I told him about the date on which Madame Chiang will arrive in Ch'ang-ch'un to console Soviet troops, as well as the date on which the security maintenance corps will reach Ch'ang-ch'un. He remarked that everywhere large numbers of bandits have appeared and that while exterminating these bandits the Soviet army had incurred heavy casualties. He also said that the Soviets have long awaited the arrival of our government troops and asked why they are so slow in coming. Finally, he brought up the question of the Soviets purchasing housing in the Northeast. For a detailed account of this, read the following. What merits attention is his remark that everywhere there are bandits. Obviously, communist troops already have begun operating everywhere in the Northeast.

Record of a Discussion That, Together with Chief of Delegation Tung, I Had with Marshal Malinovsky

Time: 3:00 P.M. January 3, 1946.
Place: General headquarters of the Soviet Army.
Additional participants: On our side: Ch'iu Nan and Hsü P'ei-yao. On the Soviet side: Major General Trotsynko.

MALINOVSKY: Did Your Excellency have a pleasant trip to Mukden and Harbin?
I: I thank the marshal for accommodating me with an airplane. But because of an ailment, after returning from Mukden to Ch'ang-ch'un, I took the train to Harbin.
MALINOVSKY: It must have been a nice opportunity to inspect the railroad.

I: When I went to Harbin, I originally planned to return on December 29 of last year. But because the Soviet garrison commander wanted us to take over the duties of the municipal government on New Year's Day, I postponed my return until yesterday. While I was in Mukden I saw Lieutenant General Kovtun-Stankevich, garrison commander at Mukden. While in Harbin I saw Major General Karchakov, the garrison commander, and Major General Maksimov, garrison commander of northern Manchuria. We got along very amiably. Furthermore, at your Army Club in Harbin we spent New Year's Eve of 1945 together in a very happy mood. That night, inadvertently, I drank until intoxicated.

MALINOVSKY: That all sounds very good.

I: Already, we have taken over the municipal governments of both Mukden and Harbin. Everything went well, and the garrison commanders told me they would join forces with the municipal governments in maintaining local order. In a day or two, one by one, our provincial governors will be able to reach their posts and assume their duties. Then the work here will be concluded.

MALINOVSKY: That's very good. I hope such favorable conditions will exist not only in the cities but also in the provinces.

I: In my opinion, if the question of Dairen can be resolved soon, our task will be completed. I imagine that it would not take very long to be resolved.

MALINOVSKY: I have not given this matter attention because Dairen does not belong to the region under my jurisdiction. But I already have informed the responsible authorities in Dairen.

I: This is the only question between us that is unsettled. If it can be resolved, then I can bring my trip to a close.

MALINOVSKY: Perhaps at this very moment they are requesting from Moscow instructions concerning this matter. The time in Moscow is diametrically the opposite of here. While we work here, people in Moscow are still asleep. For example, in Moscow it now is merely nine o'clock in the morning.

I: Today, let me take the opportunity to notify the marshal of two things: (1) Around the fifteenth of this month Madame Chiang will come to Ch'ang-ch'un to console our allies, the troops of the Soviet Union. Matters having to do with procedures for her reception and measures for her protection by the police after she arrives in Ch'ang-ch'un will be discussed by Vice-Chief of Staff Tung and Major General Trotsynko, chief of staff of your army. (2) With respect to the airlifting of Chinese troops, we now plan first to airlift to Ch'ang-ch'un three regiments of the Second General Contingent of the security maintenance corps and, as appropriate, assign them to serve various municipal governments.

TUNG: The total number will be about four thousand men. In separate groups they will accompany the various provincial governors to different places. About one or two hundred men will go to each place.

MALINOVSKY: Recently, in various places groups of bandits have caused great disorder. Generally, there are in each group as many as four or five hundred men. In addition, all of them act in the name of troops belonging to the central government. Therefore, it is very difficult to deal with them.

I: In Harbin I heard about similar situations. Unavoidably, there are in various places people who, taking advantage of opportunities, will use subterfuge to seize a certain amount of military power, with the aim of extorting status from the government in the future. All of these people are nothing but opportunists.

MALINOVSKY: A coal mine north of Harbin actually has been flooded by bandits. In several places, Soviet troops already have been compelled to fight the bandits. During these bandit extermination activities Soviet troops have suffered very large casualties, sometimes amounting to as many as two hundred men.

I: From the marshal's point of view, what would be the best way of exterminating these bandits?

MALINOVSKY: I really have not thought about ways of exterminating them. Only, the Soviet troops were forced to fight when the bandits caused too much disorder. Because of this condition I earnestly hope that when Soviet troops begin to evacuate the many factories in various places, especially Mukden, now guarded by them, your army immediately will take over their defense. This will prevent traitors from taking advantage and harming both Chinese and Soviet interests. I already have asked Major General Trotsynko to discuss with Vice-Chief of Staff Tung of your army detailed measures for effectively taking over the defense and protection of the factories. Last time I sent a letter to Chairman Hsiung of your Northeast Headquarters about installing special electric wire along the Ch'ang-ch'un Railroad in order to facilitate communications between my country and the military port of Port Arthur. Now more than one month has passed and I have not received an answer. I wonder what, after all, the situation is.

I: Because this question is closely related to the Ch'ang-ch'un Railroad, my government has made it my concern. Regrettably, of late I have been so preoccupied with other matters that I have not dealt with it sooner. Now I have submitted to Bureau Head Ju of the Ch'ang-ch'un Railroad Bureau a request that he ask the person responsible for electrical installations to supply me with data having to do with this question. As soon as I have received the data I will make a study of it and as speedily as I can report to my government my opinion, based on this study.

MALINOVSKY: I hope Your Excellency will deal with this question as speedily as possible. Because our army will withdraw soon, I fear that from now on we may not have an opportunity to discuss the question personally.

I: I will deal with it as soon as I can.

MALINOVSKY: In places like Mukden, Ch'ang-ch'un, and Harbin, our commercial organizations have been purchasing housing for their own business needs. Their transactions with property owners were completed, and they made payment in full. But when, as required by customs, they tried to register with the local government, all of them were rejected because they did not have the approval of the central government. From our point of view, all property owners have the right to dispose of housing in their possession. The approval of the central government does not seem necessary. Formerly, small countries such as Holland were able to purchase housing freely in your country. Is it possible that you regard the Soviet Union as less important than these small countries? I am puzzled by this.

I: Today I have come to wish the marshal a Happy New Year. As for the issue of how to deal with housing, originally I had intended to put this off until a later date and then bring it up for discussion with the economic counselor of your army. Since the marshal has now asked about this, let me take the opportunity to give you a brief account. Following the Japanese surrender, our central government issued a decree stating that enemy and puppet assets will be confiscated by our government. Owing to this decree, the local governments have not dared to rashly register housing purchased by your side. Your country also is a party to the United Nations declaration of 1942, published in London, wherein it was agreed that no enemy assets should be disposed of arbitrarily. There were two measures: (1) The unrestricted purchase and sale of enemy property are prohibited. This is to make it impossible to sell enemy property for the purpose of preventing its confiscation. (2) The disposal of all enemy property should be delayed until after the enemy's surrender, when it should be handled by the governments of the nations concerned. Before going to Mukden and Harbin I heard about the dispute concerning housing. Special Envoy Chiang was not in Ch'ang-ch'un. Therefore, acting on his behalf, I sent a wire to the Ministry of Foreign Affairs asking for instructions. In my opinion, right now there are two facts: (1) The Soviets need the aforementioned housing. (2) The purchase and sale of enemy housing are prohibited. We should try to find a way to deal with the two issues separately and not let them interfere with one another. Can we wait until the economic counselor of your army and I have made a careful study? I trust that certainly we will not treat the Soviet Union any worse than other countries but rather treat it even better than other countries. Please rest assured of this.

MALINOVSKY: That's excellent.

I: My original intention in coming here was to wish the marshal a Happy New Year. As for other matters, let's wait until I discuss them with the economic counselor of your army. Vice-Chief of Staff Tung also has several military questions he intends to discuss with Major General Trotsynko.

MALINOVSKY: For a very long time we have awaited the Chinese troops. I wonder why they are so long in coming.

I: This largely is because it takes time to prepare equipment to protect them from the cold. And because of transportation difficulties.

MALINOVSKY: Currently, newspapers in various countries are indulging in speculations based on the assumption that the Soviet Army is preventing Chinese troops from entering the Northeast. They really have no idea of how anxiously we await the Chinese troops.

I: Fortunately, now there has been set a date for our taking over the defense of the Northeast. From what I hear, everywhere in China there has been a very favorable reaction to our taking over the cities.

MALINOVSKY: At present, our task amounts to one word: "wait," in the hope that soon we can return to our country.

I: We feel the same way. It has been eight years since I was in my native place. I also hope to go back soon for a look.

MALINOVSKY: Although away from home, still you are in your own country, while we are in a foreign land. I hear that Mr. Chiang Ching-kuo is currently in Moscow. Is this true?

I: Yes, it is.

MALINOVSKY: Will he still come here?

I: Yes. It would be appropriate for Mr. Chiang to be here, since he is versed in Russian, while I am not familiar with that language.

MALINOVSKY: In a year or so you will know it well.

I: I regret that I have not been able to learn a new foreign language, but I am very willing to become acquainted with more Soviet friends.

JANUARY 4.　　　I received from Chairman Hsiung the following wire:

The airlifting of troops will begin, instead, on the fifteenth. Every day we will dispatch ten airplanes and airlift men of the Second General Contingent of the northeastern security maintenance corps with the aim of assigning separate groups to protect our various provincial governments. Plans for sending troops should be decided upon in conjunction with Soviet plans for withdrawal of their troops. I hope you will discuss with the Soviets and together decide upon a date for the withdrawal of Soviet troops outside of Mukden and then wire me.

In the morning I went to the office of the board of directors of the Chinese–Ch'ang-ch'un Railroad to discuss an outline for organizing railroad police, as well as regulations governing the payment of railroad personnel. I asked the Soviet vice-chairman of the board of directors when, after all, the Chinese–Ch'ang-ch'un Railroad will begin operating; he replied that it will begin when Soviet troops complete their withdrawal.

Temporarily, the site of the Manchurian Daily News Agency has been given to the Sino-Soviet Friendship Society for its use.

The following persons came to see me: Chang Chiung, newly appointed head of the police bureau of the city of Ch'ang-ch'un; Tou Han-hsiang, manager of the Dairen branch of the Bank of China; Li Mo-lin, manager of the Yi-fa-ho Bank; and Ch'en Kung-liang, special envoy of the Finance Ministry.

Today the Fourth General Contingent of the northeastern security maintenance corps was set up.

JANUARY 5.   Today, 223 officers and soldiers of the Second General Contingent of the security maintenance corps were airlifted into Ch'ang-ch'un.

Today, I sent a wire to Chairman Hsiung stating that I hope that, in accord with the original proposal, the Fifth Division still will be sent to Ch'ang-ch'un. My wire ran as follows:

> I was deeply disappointed to learn that no longer will the Fifth Division be sent to Ch'ang-ch'un. I presume this is because, after entering Mukden in a few days, the troops can be sent north by rail. Last time, in a wire to you I stated that if already there are central government troops in Ch'ang-ch'un and Mukden, sending government troops by rail between Ch'ang-ch'un and Mukden will make it easier to present our case to the Soviets. If we rely strictly on sending our troops from south to north and unexpected complications occur along the railroad when Soviet troops already have withdrawn northward from Ch'ang-ch'un, the situation will be inconceivable. I urge you to reconsider. As soon as we have completed airlifting the security maintenance corps, let's continue to transport the Fifth Division. This matter is crucial; I dare not remain silent.

I discussed with officials of the Central Bank the exchange rate for the circulating currency of the Northeast. We decided that the exchange rate between the Northeast and Peiping should be one yuan of circulating currency to eleven yuan of national currency. Exchange rates with other places in China Proper will increase in proportion to distance. An office where money can be exchanged will be set up in Shan-hai-kuan to serve travelers going in and out of Manchuria.

Today, the Soviets notified us that we also can take over the city of Dairen, that Port Arthur shall be used jointly by China and the Soviet Union, and that there will be a Sino-Soviet military commission set up to deal with matters of joint use. The Soviets also notified us that they are in the process of choosing and appointing Soviet members of the military commission.

I went to examine the metropolitan area of Ch'ang-ch'un. The houses that the Soviets want to purchase include one large building and three movie theaters. The former was intended to serve as an office and the latter, as theaters. In addition, there are another house and many residences. They did not seem very important.

JANUARY 6.   Because following the arrival of our troops in Mukden there will be an increase in military transportation and owing to the rail needs of withdrawing Soviet troops, the railroads will need more coal. Last year on December 25, after I discussed this matter with the Soviet vice-chairman of the board of directors of the Ch'ang-ch'un Railroad, it was decided that we will take over the Fu-shun coal mines formerly belonging to the South Manchuria Railway. Consequently, I asked Chang Hsing-fu, special envoy of the Ministry of Economics for the takeover of industries and mines, to assume charge of the takeover by going to Fu-shun via Mukden. Vice-Chief of Staff Tung will assign two men to accompany Chang.

I received from Foreign Minister Wang a wire saying, "We can rent to the Soviets the houses they want to purchase and might as well ask for a low rent."

Today is Sunday. In a moment of leisure I took a stroll to the K'ang-te Palace. Only after arriving there did I realize that, following two raids by the Red Army and the Communists, nothing was left. Even all the light bulbs had been removed. I had heard that there was a library in the palace. When I asked the porter, he led me there. Upon entering, I saw that the floor was littered with crates for books and paintings, as well as split strips of wood. When I lifted one or two wooden strips I saw that underneath were several books. Browsing through them, I found that they all were Ming Dynasty editions. I took these books back with me. Then I asked the person in charge of general affairs to continue searching among the wooden strips and piles of dust the next day.

The looters had taken away scrolls of paintings and calligraphy after tearing off the cylindrical pieces of wood [these pieces of wood are fixed at the bottom of scrolls bearing Chinese paintings or calligraphy so that the scroll can be hung or rolled up].

JANUARY 7.   Today Vice-Chief of Staff Tung had a discussion with Major General Trotsynko and told him that tomorrow personnel of the two provincial governments of Sung-chiang and Nunkiang intend to take up their respective posts. He asked Trotsynko to notify the Soviet Army in those localities and send Soviet liaison officials to accompany our personnel there. Trotsynko replied that he will do so. Tung also notified Trotsynko that starting today the Central Bank in Ch'ang-ch'un will communicate with Chungking by means of its own private radio station. Trotsynko said he had no objections but before replying will ask for instructions from his superiors.

Major General Trotsynko pointed out that the railroad is short of fuel; therefore, although the Soviet Army is preparing to begin its withdrawal on January 15, it is questionable whether it can carry out its plan. Trotsynko assured Tung that before February 1, surely, Soviet troops in Jehol and around Kalgan will be able to withdraw into Outer Mongolia. In that case there will be no problem concerning the withdrawal of Soviet troops from Jehol.

The Foreign Ministry of the central government employs ordinary, everyday procedures to deal with negotiations here. Where our military organizations are concerned, there is a lack of preparation and liaison work. There remain only 22 days until the deadline for the withdrawal of Soviet troops. Yet, there are no arrangements for anything. Suddenly I feel that I cannot fulfill my task. Consequently, I have written to Chang Yueh-chün to try to relieve me. Meanwhile, I also have written a letter to President Chiang stating my difficulties and hinting that I hardly am equal to my duties.

Wang Wen-po, vice-chairman of the board of directors of the Chinese–Ch'ang-ch'un Railroad, came to say that he intends to take a trip back to Chungking and seek a post with the United Nations so that he can go abroad.

P'eng Chi-ch'un, governor of Nunkiang province, as well as Liu Po-k'un and Liang Chung-ch'uan, members of the provincial government, came to see me.

JANUARY 8.   Today takeover personnel for the two provinces of Liao-peh and Sung-chiang, respectively, arrived in Ssu-p'ing and Harbin. The provincial government of Sung-chiang is quartered in Harbin.

I invited Li Mo-lin, Ch'ih Shih-fu, and Ma Tzu-yuan to discuss the list of names for the preparatory committee of the northeastern Hsing-yeh Company, which we plan to set up, and solicited their opinions concerning the exchange rate for northeastern circulating currency. They all considered appropriate a ratio of thirteen yuan of national currency to one yuan of circulating currency.

I wrote a letter to Minister Yü of the Finance Ministry discussing two drafts: regulations setting up a trust company to be in charge of housing and measures to control exchange rates for the northeastern circulating currency.

Concerning the Soviets' request that they assume control of special wires for telegraph and telephone communication between the Soviet Union and the military port of Port Arthur, I wrote a letter to Minister Yü Ch'iao-feng of the Ministry of Communications asking him to deal with this matter.

In the evening I hosted a feast for all directors and supervisors of the Chinese–Ch'ang-ch'un Railroad Bureau.

JANUARY 9.   Today, I read in the January 6 issue of the Chungking *Ta-kung Pao* General Wedemeyer's remarks at a press conference following his arrival in China. Wedemeyer said that, with American assistance, General Tu Yü-ming's troops will be sent to the Northeast. He also said that he intends soon to take a trip to the Northeast. These remarks will further provoke the Soviets and make them apprehensive about American influence penetrating the Northeast. General Wedemeyer did not know that when we met for the first time, Marshal Malinovsky had already hinted at his angry feelings over an American warship sailing into Dairen harbor in October of last year to inspect, and its captain going ashore, or that Marshal Malinovsky explicitly stated to me that he was unwilling to see American political influence infiltrate the Northeast by means of the American dollar. After today's further expression of American intentions to foster China's military strength in the Northeast, Soviet suspicion and jealousy are bound to increase further.

Today I sent a person to inform the Soviet economic counselor that, with respect to the question of the Soviets purchasing land, I already have wired Chungking, asking whether the articles of the commercial treaty apply to the purchase of housing and land. Then, in a few days the Ministry of Economics will send Sun Yueh-chi here. Sun has been delighted by this.

Today, two planes for the airlift collided in the skies over Ch'ang-ch'un, one crashing into the tail of the other, and fell into the suburbs. Thirty-six persons were killed and eleven injured.

Wang Ning-hua, head of the Finance Bureau of Kirin, came to see me. He told me that because of an illness Governor Cheng Tao-ju cannot come immediately. In his capacity as deputy governor, Wang will go and take over.

I received from Chairman Hsiung a wire saying that he already had wired the central authorities asking them to make a decision concerning the question of whether we should continue to send the Fifth Division to Ch'ang-ch'un. Incidentally, at the same time the Soviet garrison commander of Ch'ang-ch'un personally told Mayor Chao that we should first take over the outskirts of Ch'ang-ch'un and for that we must have a number of troops. This tallies with my own thoughts expressed in my previous wire to the central government. Consequently, in response, I sent Chairman Hsiung a wire in which I told him about this Soviet opinion.

JANUARY 10.   President Chiang sent a wire to me. This is the message in general: "Respecting the economic question, Minister Wong [Wong Wenhao] already has written his opinions. Generally, they agree with mine. We are waiting for the approval of President Soong of the Executive Yuan." The wire runs as follows:

> Minister Wong already has wired Sun Yueh-chi, special envoy of the Ministry of Economics, ordering him to come to Chungking for a personal talk before going to the Northeast. He also has been ordered to hurry to Ch'ang-ch'un before the fifteenth. Previously, Minister Wong formulated and submitted principles governing economic cooperation in the Northeast. In general, I share your attitude. Moreover, Wong already has formulated a general outline of the types of enterprises to be placed under joint management. I already have asked him to discuss this with President Soong of the Executive Yuan, decide on it, and speedily implement it. I should be able to send the plan with Sun. With respect to the problem of housing, I already have ordered the Foreign Ministry speedily to decide on measures for settling it and report to me.

Major General Trotsynko, the Soviet chief of staff, told Vice-Chief of Staff Tung that, owing to a shortage of vehicles for transportation, Soviet troops in Mukden will not be able to begin withdrawing until the fifteenth of this month. If the railroad can allocate ten trains a day, they will need fifteen days to complete their withdrawal. At present, the problem of fuel poses the greatest difficulty. The Soviets already are stockpiling coal in Mukden, Ch'ang-ch'un, and Harbin. Harbin, which is a rail junction, particularly needs a large amount of coal. Right now a Soviet director of the Chinese–Ch'ang-ch'un Railroad is investigating the fuel supply situation. As yet we have had no reply. Therefore, Trotsynko has no way of estimating the date when Soviet troops will complete their withdrawal from Ch'ang-ch'un and Harbin. At present, the output of the Fu-shun mines is very small. In addition, the availability of locomotives has been a problem. Trotsynko hopes Chairman Chang [Chang Kia-ngau] will order the various other railroads to temporarily halt passenger service so as to save locomotives and fuel that can be transferred to the Chinese–Ch'ang-ch'un Railroad for use in transporting Soviet troops and so on.

Major General Trotsynko also told Tung that Soviet troops along the line of Chia-pu-ssu, To-lun, and Ch'ih-feng will be able to begin withdrawing on the twenty-third of this month and that within eight days will have withdrawn from China.

JANUARY 11.   I saw the Soviet chairman of the board of directors of the Ch'ang-ch'un Railroad and asked him about the coal supply situation. He said that throughout its entire length the Chinese–Ch'ang-ch'un Railroad needs fifteen thousand tons of coal each day. He hopes that the two mines of Fu-shun and Hsi-an can provide four thousand tons daily. Even this will not cover half the amount needed. He also said that the rail line north of Harbin originally used coal produced by the Mu-leng mine, but the mine recently has been occupied by bandits and badly damaged. The coal of the Cha-lai-noh-erh mine is of poor quality. Now fuel for the railroad has to be supplemented with wooden logs. And so on. I concluded from this that the supply of fuel is indeed a problem. The blame must be placed on the Soviet Army, which has allowed bandits to run rampant. And now they are using the situation as an excuse for delaying the withdrawal of their troops.

I drafted a notice governing the confiscation of immovable property formerly belonging to the enemy.

In the evening I hosted a feast for Wang Ning-hua, deputy governor of Kirin province, as well as Shang Ch'uan-tao, Hu T'i-chien, and Wu Chih-kung, members of the provincial government.

Today, Major General Trotsynko wrote a letter to Vice-Chief of Staff Tung saying that in the area of K'o-erh-ch'in-yu-i-ch'ien-ch'i and Tao-an plague has been discovered. He requested that we send troops there to assist in eradicating the disease. I wonder if he has other motives.

Today, the Nationalists and the Communists bilaterally reached an agreement and decided to issue orders for a truce, as well as an end to activities obstructing communications. To implement the orders for a truce, there will be set up here a military mediation headquarters to be organized by Nationalist, communist, and American representatives. There is a supplementary statement: "The truce will not affect implementation of the National government's plan for reorganizing troops south of the Yangtze River or its sending its troops into the nine northeastern provinces for the purpose of restoring its sovereignty or its transferring its troops within the nine northeastern provinces."

JANUARY 12.   General Leonov, Soviet communications commander, came to see me. He said that, in a letter to Chairman Hsiung, Marshal Malinovsky specifically stated the Soviet Army's intention to use the telegraph and telephone wires of the Ch'ang-ch'un Railroad for transmitting messages [between Port Arthur and the Soviet Union]. He hopes that we speedily settle this issue. I replied that, in fact, we would accommodate them but that this should be done in such a way that there will be no hint of any violation of national sovereignty. I will give instructions to the board of directors of the Ch'ang-ch'un Railroad that the board issue an order to the head of the Railroad Bureau granting the Soviets priority in the use of several through wires. We also will enjoy the same right. I intend to leave the final decision until after a careful study and discussion of this question.

Tu Yü-ming, our superior, wired the Northeast Headquarters saying that about four or five hundred armed irregulars had attacked Ying-k'ou; during the fierce battle a truck drove out from the direction of the armed irregulars. After the defeated bandits retreated, it was discovered that aboard the truck were Soviet Army men and that one Soviet soldier had been killed and another wounded. This indicates that armed irregular troops supported by the Soviets in various places will constantly obstruct our takeover. At locations that they do not consider important, the Soviets do not actively assist the armed irregular troops but instead allow them to remain elusive. Ying-k'ou is a place the Soviets feel they can let us take over. But in my opinion these armed irregular troops scattered in the countryside will create a situation in which, while we occupy the cities, they will occupy the countryside.

JANUARY 13.   General Leonov, Soviet communications commander, came to discuss and decide upon the issue of the Soviet Army using the telegraph and telephone wires of the Ch'ang-ch'un Railroad to communicate between Port Arthur and the Soviet Union. Technically speaking, the chairman of the board of directors of the Chinese–Ch'ang-ch'un Railroad will issue instructions to the head of the Railroad Bureau generally indicating that the wire to be used is a through wire but that the Soviets will install equipment along the line for amplifying stations and transmission stations. At present, while Chinese personnel of the Railroad Bureau still are unfamiliar with the operation of such equipment, we can have Soviet personnel of the Railroad Bureau supervise their operation. The Chinese government has the same priority in the use of the wires, etc. Commander Leonov also requested that all along the rail line communications be kept strictly secret. I replied that I can issue over a wide area orders that things be carried out in accord with his request.

As for the question of Soviet intentions to purchase housing and land in the metropolitan districts of Mukden, Ch'ang-ch'un, and Harbin, the primary opinions of the Foreign Ministry are the following:

> We have decided to confiscate, as partial indemnification to China, all public and private property within our national borders that formerly belonged to Japan. The third section of the fourth article of Measures for Dealing with Enemy and Puppet Assets in Recovered Regions, promulgated on November 23, 1945, by the Executive Yuan, stipulates that the central government will reclaim the right to all assets formerly belonging to

Japanese emigrants or already purchased with the capital of the Japanese or their puppets.

Since we are restricted by the above decree, we have not considered it appropriate to register the request of the Soviets [wire of January 3]. But then I made a study of the measures for dealing with enemy and puppet assets; in it there are no stipulations concerning requests by Allied nations to use or purchase enemy or puppet property. Meanwhile, the Soviets have asked why, since people of all nations are allowed to purchase property in China, the Soviets alone are being discriminated against. Consequently, I wired the Foreign Ministry to inquire whether or not we could tell the Soviets that if they need to purchase enemy or puppet property they should wait until after we have taken over that property. Then they could discuss the matter with the municipal government and make the purchase. Or they first could rent the property until we grant them the priority to purchase it [wire of January 4]. Subsequently, I received in reply a wire saying "The Executive Yuan and departments belonging to it cannot alter the law. Still, it would be best to resolve this question by renting or loaning the property" [wire of January 8]. In accord with the message from the Foreign Ministry, I explained matters to the Soviets and they replied as follows:

In accord with the twelfth article of the Sino-Soviet commercial treaty signed on June 16, 1939, which stipulates that Soviet state-run economic organizations and the Soviet people, with respect to both their persons and property, should enjoy the same favorable treatment as the people of any third nation, as well as equivalent legal entities, and in accord with an appendix to that treaty that defines any third nation as applying to nations that since 1928 have entered into treaties with China on the principle of equality, we now state that since Britain and the United States are able to purchase immovable property in China, the Soviet Union, in accord with the above treaty and following the example of Britain and the United States, also be able to enjoy this right. Now, the Soviets are willing first to hand back to Chinese governmental organizations enemy property purchased by the Soviets and then to repurchase it from the Chinese. But, because the Soviets already have made payments to the Japanese and there is no way to recall these, they only can make a very low payment to the Chinese.

I wired this reply to the Foreign Ministry [wire of January 9]. Today, I received from the Foreign Ministry, in reply, a wire:

Although the twelfth article of the Sino-Soviet commercial treaty stresses stipulations of most-favored nation treatment with respect to both persons and property, still, in the new treaty between China and Britain the article on the purchase of immovable property is on the condition that Britain will permit Chinese to enjoy the same rights in its territory. Soviet law, however, prohibits aliens from purchasing movable property in Soviet territory. Consequently, it would be difficult for us to grant the Soviets this right, for if other nations follow their example and make the same requests, our government will be unable to refuse. Moreover, even if the British should wish to purchase enemy property within our borders, we could not accommodate them. Now, since the Soviets are willing first to hand back to us the enemy housing they purchased, we can be lenient and loan or rent to them instead of selling it. Furthermore, the Legislative Yuan is formulating new laws having to do with the question of the purchase by aliens of immovable property. Presumably, it will not discriminate against the Soviet government and people purchasing property in China. Right now restrictions imposed by current laws and treaties prevent the Foreign Ministry from dealing with this issue in other ways. We presume the Soviets can understand this. [Wire of January 11]

JANUARY 14.   In the morning I discussed with the Soviet vice-chairman of the board of directors of the Chinese–Ch'ang-ch'un Railroad Bureau the wording of the order implementing the Soviet request to use through telegraph and telephone wires. He raised an objection to the phrase "priority in using," saying that since communication between the Soviet Union and Port Arthur is to be via a through wire, only the Soviets can use this wire. There is no need to insert the phrase "priority in using," which merely would cause misunderstanding on the part of those executing the order. He insisted on changing the wording to "designating several wires to be used for the above purpose." Then in the afternoon General Leonov came to tell me that already they have adopted the revision proposed by the Soviet vice-chairman of the board of directors. But I intend to alter "If we have no Chinese familiar with the equipment" to "When we have no Chinese familiar with the equipment we can employ Soviet personnel."

At 5:00 P.M. I went to see the Soviet economic counselor. I told him that with respect to the issue of the Soviets purchasing housing and land, I already had received from the Foreign Ministry a wire in reply to my own. I also gave him the general gist of the message. Greatly dissatisfied by the message, he insisted that the twelfth article of the Sino-Soviet commercial treaty clearly defined most-favored nation treatment as applying to the purchase of property and that there must be no other interpretation. They can only remit to the Chinese government, as payment for purchase, the sum still not paid in full to the Japanese. Then he said he had received orders from Moscow urging him to continue discussing the question of joint operation of heavy industries by China and the Soviet Union. Furthermore, he reiterated that the Soviet Union will hand back to the Chinese government industries and mines worth over 22 billion yuan, while only placing under joint Sino-Soviet management industries and mines worth 38 billion yuan and that among the latter are enterprises in which China will have 51 percent of the shares and will appoint a Chinese general manager, while there are other enterprises in which the Soviet Union will have 51 percent of the shares and a Soviet general manager. He concluded by asking why our side still remains irresolute. I inferred from his tone that he is very anxious and that there is a possibility of concessions, but he asked that the Fu-shun coal mines be added to the enterprises under joint management and also proposed that China and the Soviet Union manage jointly the aviation company as well as the Sungari River Steamship Company.

JANUARY 15.   I received from President Chiang a handwritten order (dispatched January 10) and forwarded to me by Chairman Hsiung. In it are listed the following items:

Representatives of our government and Chinese communist representatives already have discussed and decided upon measures for ending clashes and restoring communications, which we now make public. At the same time, we issue the following orders:

1. All fighting must stop immediately.

2. Except for stipulations in the appendix to item five, which follows, all troop movements must stop within China's borders. But troop movements necessary for the following purposes are exempted: for repatriation, for taking over defense, for logistical purposes, and for administrative and local security.

3. Activities that damage or obstruct any lines of communication must stop. All objects obstructing such lines of communication should be dismantled and removed at once.

4. For the purpose of implementing the truce agreement, there immediately should be set up in Peiping an Executive Headquarters for Military Mediation. The executive headquarters will be made up of three members: one representing the National government of China, a second representing the communist party of China, and a third, the United States. All necessary instructions and orders should be agreed upon unanimously by the three members and then promulgated in the name of the president of the National government of the Republic of China through the Executive Headquarters for Military Mediation.

5. Appendix:

a. The second point of this order will not affect continuing the implementation of the National government's plan to reorganize its troops south of the Yangtze River.

b. The second point of this order will not affect the National government's sending troops into the nine northeastern provinces to
restore China's sovereignty there or transferring these troops
within the nine northeastern provinces.

c. The lines of communication mentioned in the third point of this
order will include postal communications.

d. Each day the National government should notify the Executive
Headquarters for Military Mediation concerning troop movements carried out under the above stipulations.

6. Beginning this same day and ending at 12:00 P.M., January 15 of
this year, the above-listed orders must be fully implemented, without
fail, in various places. We hope these orders will be carried out dis-
creetly, soberly, and with respect. They must not be disobeyed. This is
imperative.

Already, the orders for the truce have appeared in the papers. All over
the country the response is good. The common people all think that from
now on they can have peace. These are my apprehensions: In the Northeast,
already the armed irregular force sustained by the Soviets has pervaded the
entire nine provinces. At any time soldiers of the Eighth Route Army from
Chefoo who are infiltrating the area around Ying-k'ou and Antung, as well as
others infiltrating northern Manchuria from Inner Mongolia, could merge
with the armed irregular forces being sustained by the Soviets. Moreover, at
any time the Chinese Communist Party could proclaim the Eighth Route
Army to be Chinese communist troops. Furthermore, I noticed that after
orders for the truce were issued, in publicized remarks made at a press
conference in Chungking, Chou En-lai stated, "Except for other stipulations
in our public notices, once the truce begins Chinese communist troops will
remain where they are, to await a settlement by the Political Consultative
Conference." I presume from this that if the Chinese Communist Party
announces that all noncentral government armed forces in the Northeast are
Chinese communist troops, then they could demand that these troops remain where they are. The result would be that before central government
troops arrive, Chinese communist armed forces already will have gained a
foothold in the Northeast and then can demand legitimacy there.

Today, I received from Chairman Hsiung a wire of the fourteenth, sent
from Ch'in-huang-tao. In the wire he said that the government already is
prepared to send by rail to Ch'ang-ch'un, at any time, one division of troops.
He requested that I discuss with the Soviets a date for taking over the
defense of Ch'ang-ch'un. He said it would be best for these troops to reach

Ch'ang-ch'un before Soviet troops withdraw and asked that we prepare rolling stock. He said that we definitely will take over Mukden on the fifteenth and, right after that, Liao-yang, An-shan, T'ieh-ling, Fu-shun, and various other places. He also said that on the fourteenth four thousand bandits attacked Ying-k'ou and captured Pan-shan.

I likewise had a wire from my superior, Tu Yü-ming, telling me that seven thousand men of the armed irregular forces attacked Ying-k'ou and that five thousand men attacked and occupied Pan-shan. These men also damaged the railroad station of Sha-la, near Fu-hsin, as well as the railroad east of Kou-pang-tzu. Moreover, nearly ten thousand men of the armed, irregular forces entered An-shan and forced the An-shan Power Plant to stop supplying power to regions west of Chin-chou. I have some doubts about the actual number of men in the armed irregular forces. But, undoubtedly, already Chinese communist military strength gradually has grown, and open attacks such as these indirectly amount to a show of force for the Soviet Union, which, apparently, the Soviets appreciate. If we can settle the question of economic cooperation soon, incidents like these should not occur along the Southern Manchuria railroad corridor.

I sent Keng K'uang and Mi Hsin-min to see the Soviet economic counselor to tell him the proposal he made yesterday to have the Fu-shun coal mines jointly managed places me in a difficult position. I asked that he seriously reconsider.

I dispatched to the head of the Chinese–Ch'ang-ch'un Railroad Bureau the orders of the chairman of the board of directors concerning the Soviet Army command's request for telegraph and telephone wires to be used in communicating between the Soviet Union and Port Arthur. At the same time, I wrote Marshal Malinovsky a letter notifying him. I enclosed a copy of the orders.

Today, in the afternoon, over two thousand government troops entered the city of Mukden. As their train approached the Mukden station, it was fired upon by Soviet soldiers and three men were killed.

In the evening, I hosted a banquet for Han Chün-chieh, the governor of Heilungkiang province, and the following members of the Heilungkiang provincial government: Chu Han-sheng, chief secretary; Liu Shih-fan, head of the civil affairs bureau; Wu Yueh-ch'ao, head of the finance bureau; Liu Shao-hsing, mayor of Hei-he; Tung Jung-shu, head of the Police Bureau; and Li Chih-shan, head of the security maintenance bureau as well as Wu Han-t'ao, the governor of Hekiang province, and the following members of the Hekiang provincial government: Fu-Po-p'ing, chief secretary; Chu Pu-t'ang, head of the finance bureau; Yang Ta-ch'ien, head of the education bureau; Li Te-jun, head of the construction bureau; and Li Lung-fei, chief of the police bureau.

JANUARY 16.   Today, Sun Yueh-chi, representative from the Ministry of
Economics, arrived in Ch'ang-ch'un. He brought me the central government's instructions about principles for dealing with the Soviets on the question of economic cooperation. Accompanying them were the opinions of Minister Wong Yung-ni [alternative name for Wong Wen-hao], signed by him and
submitted to President Chiang. Generally, Wong approves of the following
points: to merge the three mines of Pen-hsi-hu, Hui-chun, and Cha-lai-noh-
erh into one jointly managed Sino-Soviet coal mine company; to turn the Pen-
hsi-hu Iron Works into a jointly managed Sino-Soviet iron and steel company;
and to merge the motor vehicle manufacturing and repair plants of Mukden,
Antung, and Harbin, along with the Chin-chou Heavy Mechanism Manufacturing Factory, into a Sino-Soviet manufacturing company.

Since there is too wide a gap between the central government's instructions and the Soviet proposal, this very night I wrote a letter to President
Chiang and Minister Wong stating emphatically that at present in the Northeast, crises lurk in every corner and our general situation there is in imminent peril. I pleaded that they further relax the terms offered by our side. I
did not finish the letter until 2:30. It is only half a month until the date when
the Soviets are to withdraw their troops, and this kind of procrastination on
our part only will give the Soviets an opportunity to make all kinds of
preparations disadvantageous to our side. These will further add to the
difficulties of our taking over.

Today, there were several kinds of occurrences indicating a change in
the Soviet attitude: (1) When our side asked the Soviets to send troops to
assist our security maintenance corps in its takeover of the Chiu-t'ai mining
zone, which is under the jurisdiction of Kirin province, the Soviets replied
that they could not comply because President Chiang and the Chinese Communist Party have already ordered the two sides to end their clashes and that
the Soviet Army's stance is not to take part in China's civil war. They declared that the Soviets have no connection at all with the Chinese Communist Party and that, so long as the Chinese Communists do not attack the
Soviet Army, the Soviets will not interfere. Since in former statements the
Soviets have never used the term *the Chinese Communist Party*, its open use
today means that the so-called armed irregular force has already become an
accepted fact. In other words, the Soviet side will refuse to assist us in our
takeover, under the pretext of not wanting to clash with communist troops.
(2) About five thousand men of the general contingent of our security maintenance police, organized in Kirin province, have been disarmed by personnel
sent by the Soviet garrison commander. They were returning to the metropolitan district of Ch'ang-ch'un after having been organized in the area of Ta-
t'ung and Hsiao-shuang-ch'eng, both under the jurisdiction of Ch'ang-ch'un
prefecture. The reason given for disarming them was that they had not first

notified the Soviet side about this organizing activity. The men of the contingent were sent to a detention center for prisoners of war. This indicates that, pending the withdrawal of Soviet troops, we first must notify the Soviets concerning any armed activity on our side. The Soviets stated their reason for disarming the men of the contingent as follows: When interrogated, the men of the contingent replied that they were policemen. Subsequently, the Soviets inquired at the police bureau and were told that nothing was known there concerning the matter. Therefore, the contingent was disarmed. All these are signs of unfriendliness.

To sum up, in December of last year, when the Soviets proposed their plan for economic cooperation, the central government should have immediately dispatched a team to Ch'ang-ch'un, including representatives of concerned ministries and commissions, to negotiate with the Soviets, night and day, right here, and speedily settled the issue. Then the armed Chinese communist irregulars would not have grown so rapidly and the Soviet Union would have been somewhat hesitant about cultivating the Chinese Communists. Furthermore, there would not have taken place a worsening of the Soviet attitude, such as we have today.

JANUARY 17.   In the morning, I invited Yagi, the Japanese, to come for a talk. I solicited his opinion about restoring light industry in the Northeast. At 5:30 P.M. I accompanied Sun Yueh-chi on a visit to the Soviet economic counselor. There was only commonplace conversation.

JANUARY 18.   Ching-kuo came to talk. Recently, he was in the Soviet Union and on behalf of President Chiang saw Stalin twice. They talked for about six hours. The gist of their talk is as follows:

1. With respect to the economic question in the Northeast, Stalin said that the term *war booty* must not be discarded but that the jointly managed enterprises could be divided into a number of companies. He said that everything will be discussed before the withdrawal of Soviet troops from the Northeast and subsequently published.

2. With respect to the question of the Chinese Communist Party, he said that the Nationalist party should be able to coexist with the communist party because without the communist party the Nationalist party will tend to become more corrupt each day. The future will witness how the two parties compete and, eventually, one party will win out.

3. With respect to the question of the Open Door policy, he said that this is an instrument of imperialist invasion. Therefore, while opening its doors, China also should be prepared to close its doors.

4. With respect to the question of Sino-Soviet relations, he said that while on the surface China is friendly to the Soviet Union, secretly, it actually is hostile to the Soviet Union. He remarked that if this continues the relationship cannot last.

Ching-kuo brought with him the following handwritten letter from President Chiang.

+ *Handwritten letter from President Chiang Kai-shek* +

January 16, 1946

Dear Kung-ch'uan: [Chang Kia-ngau]
My son Ching having returned, you will be able to learn at firsthand all that has happened in the Soviet Union; I shall not go into it here. With respect to the principles underlying economic cooperation, for the time being we can only reduce their scope; we ought not make them too broad. I have no alternative. However, you have to bear these difficulties alone and naturally you suffer. This suffering I constantly share with you and you are always in my thoughts. Please do not be overwrought. It is enough if our sovereignty and legality are not adversely affected in such a way as to give others a precedent.

With seasonal greetings,
Chung-cheng

Those in the central government assisting President Chiang in making decisions on questions having to do with the Northeast are T.V. Soong, president of the Executive Yuan; Wang Hsüeh-t'ing [Wang Shih-chieh], minister of foreign affairs; and Wong Yung-ni [Wong Wen-hao], minister of economics. Because they played an important role in the signing of the Sino-Soviet friendship treaty, Soong and Wang fear being attacked again. Soong has adopted an attitude of great indifference and Wang, one of extreme discretion, while Wong, pivoting between the attitudes of Soong and Wang, merely contributes by choosing the industrial and mining enterprises to be jointly managed. As a result, President Chiang is restricted by sovereignty as well as theories of legality and reason. That is why he instructed me that "we only can reduce their scope; we ought not to make them too broad."

JANUARY 19.   At noon, I had lunch with Ching-kuo. We talked about the danger that may result from our procrastination and irresolution concerning the economic question in the Northeast and the unlikelihood that terms offered by our side will meet with Soviet approval. In the evening Sun Yueh-chi and I deliberated on the extent to which we can make concessions. As a first step we will allow the following:

1. Coal mines: Besides Pen-hsi-hu, Hui-chún, and Cha-lai-noh-erh, we will add to the list of mines to be jointly operated three mines of the Mi-shan coal mines: Yuan-shan, Ma-shan, and Chi-hsi.

2. Power: The Soviets did not list in their inventory the Yalu River Hydroelectric Power Plant. Apparently, their intention is to hold on to it for themselves. I intend to propose that this power plant be placed under the joint management of China, the Soviet Union, and Korea. At the Sungari River Hydroelectric Power Plant, six of the eight generators have been dismantled by the Soviets. These must be replaced. I intend using loans to purchase generators from the Soviet Union. Moreover, I intend, when appropriate, to employ Soviet technicians.

3. We will add to the list of nonferrous metal industries to be jointly managed the Antung Aluminum-making Factory.

4. We will add to the list of chemical industries to be jointly managed the Pen-hsi-hu Charcoal Refinery and the two cement factories of Pen-hsi-hu and Harbin.

Measures for secondary concessions:

1. We will further add to the list of coal mines to be jointly managed, the following: the two mines of Ti-tao and Ch'eng-tzu-he of the Mi-shan coal mines, the two mines of Niu-hsin-t'ai and T'ien-shih-fu under the jurisdiction of Hsi-chien near Pen-hsi-hu, and the mine of Hsi-an.

2. We will further add to the list of power plants to be jointly managed the Pen-hsi-hu Steam Power Plant.

3. We will further add to the list of enterprises to be jointly managed the Pen-hsi-hu Special Steel Factory.

As for civil aviation and the Sungari River Steamship Company, these are involved with communications so we will not discuss them with the Soviets.

Sun Yueh-chi and I together wrote a letter to Minister Wong about the above opinions for him to forward and submit to President Chiang. The original text is as follows:

To His Excellency Vice-President Wong of the Executive Yuan, to be forwarded and submitted to His Excellency President Chiang:

Concerning the question of joint management with the Soviets of industries and mines in the Northeast, after much deliberation, Ao and Sun Yueh-chi [here the letter writer refers to himself in the third person] have concluded that if we conduct negotiations now they are more likely to succeed because at the moment, with the date for withdrawal of their troops approaching, the Soviets are anxious to settle the economic question. Conversely, after withdrawing their troops, acting on the pretext that the industries and mines of the Northeast are their war booty, they might send troops to protect and take over the various enterprises that in the inventory were earmarked for joint management. We fear that by that time negotiations will have become more difficult. It is all right with us if, as suggested in the instructions brought by Yueh-chi, the central government decides never to make further concessions. But if this is not to be the case then we might as well take advantage of this moment, when the Soviets are hoping for a settlement, by assuming the initiative in making concessions as an indication of both our sincerity and resoluteness. In this way we can achieve a solution in one breath while, paradoxically, reducing the amount of our loss, instead of repeating our past experience in diplomatic negotiations when by procrastinating we accentuated our losses. During a discussion with Ching-kuo, he also approved of this idea. Now, for the time being, we have formulated the following preliminary measures:

A. In the realm of coal mines, we will add (1) from the Mi-shan coal mines, the three mines of Yuan-shan, Ma-shan, and Chi-hsi, (2) the coal mine of Cha-lai-noh-erh, (3) the coal mine of Hui-ch'un, and (4) the coal mine of Pen-hsi-hu.

B. Power: (1) The Soviets have not listed the Yalu River Hydroelectric Power Plant in either the inventory they will hand back to us or the inventory to be jointly managed. This cannot be an oversight but, rather, seems to indicate their intention of holding on to it for themselves. We intend to propose that this power plant be managed jointly by the three nations of China, the Soviet Union, and Korea. (2) At the Sungari River Hydroelectric Power Plant, six of the eight generators already have been dismantled by the Soviets. These must be replaced. We intend to purchase generators from the Soviet Union with loans that we will repay in full within ten years. During this period we will employ Soviet technicians when appropriate. This will mean that, while the Soviets are involved, it will not be jointly managed.

C. Iron and steel: We intend to manage jointly with the Soviets the Pen-hsi-hu Iron and Steel Works, including the Miao-erh-kou Iron Mine and Ore Selection Workshop.

D. Nonferrous metal industry: We will manage jointly with the Soviets only the Antung Aluminum-making Factory.

E. Machine building: In addition to the Dairen Locomotive Factory and the An-shan Machine Factory in the original inventory, we will manage jointly with the Soviets the four other factories.

F. Chemical industry: We will manage jointly only the Pen-hsi-hu Charcoal Refinery.

G. Cement factories: We intend to manage jointly the two factories in Pen-hsi-hu and Harbin.

With respect to civil aviation and the Sungari River navigation enterprise, since these two are involved with communications, we consider it inconvenient to discuss them.

If the Soviets do not approve of these concessions, we should offer the following secondary concessions:

A. Coal mines: We will add the two mines of Ti-tao and Ch'eng-tzu-he of the Mi-shan mines, the two mines of Niu-hsin-t'ai and T'ien-shih-fu belonging to Hsi-chien near Pen-hsi-hu, and the mine of Hsi-an.

B. Power: We will add to the plants to be jointly managed the Pen-hsi-hu Steam Power Plant.

C. We will add to those enterprises to be jointly managed the Pen-hsi-hu Special Steel Factory. These secondary concessions will be as far as we will go. The Soviets can accept them or not. We still wait for Your Excellency's decision on whether this is appropriate and we pray that you will speedily transmit to us your instructions.

> Respectfully in your employment,
> Chang Kia-ngau
> Sun Yueh-chi

I discussed with the Soviet vice-chairman of the board of directors of the Chinese–Ch'ang-ch'un Railroad Bureau the draft of regulations for the board of directors of the Chinese–Ch'ang-ch'un Railroad.

JANUARY 20.   I exchanged opinions with the technical personnel sent by the Ministry of Economics and the Resources Commission.

I invited Ching-kuo to my residence and we had supper together. We discussed procedures for the reception for Madame Chiang Kai-shek when she arrives in Ch'ang-ch'un.

I received from Foreign Minister Wang a wire that there has been a change of mind regarding the issue of the Soviets purchasing housing. The Soviets can purchase housing but not land. Therefore I immediately began formulating a plan and asked Wan I, a director of the Chinese–Ch'ang-ch'un Railroad, to assist in drafting it.

JANUARY 21.   Today, Vice-Chief of Staff Tung Yen-p'ing met with Soviet major general Trotsynko, who told Tung that already on January 15 the Soviet Army began to withdraw but that he dared not say when they will complete their withdrawal because communications are very difficult. Then he said that, with respect to our taking over Fu-shun, he hopes we will station powerful, well-equipped troops there because in that region there is a large number of armed irregular troops and bandits. He also said that, pending the actual consolidation of our defenses, Soviet troops temporarily will not withdraw. He said that, with respect to our taking over the two provinces of Hekiang and Heilungkiang, there is in Chia-mu-ssu and Pei-an a large number of armed irregular troops, all calling themselves government troops. Right now the Soviets are trying to wipe out these troops, and Trotsynko hopes we will wait a week to ten days before taking over. I told him that, concerning our taking over Dairen, our personnel intend to go there to take over on January 27 and 28; I will go along with them. Major General Trotsynko replied that he will immediately notify the Soviet authorities in charge and, in accord with our agreement, will send liaison officials to accompany us there.

As for our pressing him about what has become of Chang Hsing-fu, Major General Trotsynko replied that Chang and his group arrived in Fu-shun on the eleventh of this month and then, on the same day, took a train to return to Mukden. He said that three days ago Mayor Tung, of the city of Mukden, reported the matter to Lieutenant General Karlov, Soviet garrison commander of Mukden; after receiving Lieutenant General Karlov's report, the Soviet Army headquarters immediately sent a lieutenant general, together with a powerful force, to make a search for Chang and his party. He said the results have not yet been reported.

Major General Trotsynko also told Tung that Soviet troops in Ch'ih-feng have decided to begin withdrawing on the twenty-third of this month and that Soviet troops evacuated Ying-k'ou on January 13.

I received from President Chiang a wire of the twenty-first:

With respect to the new plan that the Soviets have proposed concerning enterprises in the Northeast to be jointly managed, my opinions are as follows:

1. We cannot acknowledge the point, raised in the Soviet memorandum, that all assets of Japanese enterprises in the Northeast are war booty of the Red Army and therefore belong to the Soviet Union. We shouldn't discuss this. Instead, merely discuss with them enterprises to be jointly managed and specific measures.

2. The following enterprises absolutely will not be listed among those to be jointly managed: enterprises affiliated with the former South Manchuria Railway and the Fu-shun Coal Mine. Previously, when the agreement was being discussed and signed in Moscow, it was stated clearly that these enterprises should be recovered by China.

3. All enterprises west of the former South Manchuria Railway line

should not be placed under joint management. Therefore, naturally, the Pei-p'iao Coal Mine, which is far away in Jehol, will not be jointly managed.

4. Since Northeastern Aviation and the Sungari River Steamship Company are not industrial or mining enterprises, they should not be listed in the plan for joint management.

5. Owing to legal reasons as well as precedent, in the various industrial and mining types of jointly managed companies, shares held by our country are not under 50 percent. [This is how the sentence appears in the original text. The translator assumes the author actually meant "should not be under 50 percent." See the following sentence.] (Without exception, our stocks should comprise 51 percent.) In all of these companies the chairman of the board of trustees and the general manager should be Chinese. These are important expectations of our country. If the Soviet Union can honor these requests, negotiations will stand a better chance of success and it also will be easier to develop the enterprises in question. You should explain this explicitly to the Soviet representatives.

6. As for which specific enterprises should be jointly managed, give attention to the following important points: (a) The An-shan Iron and Steel Works should be managed by China. (b) At this point, we will not discuss the products of nonferrous metal mines. (c) Sawdust factories and a number of chemical fertilizer factories should be managed by China.

7. Articles 2 and 6 through 9 of the Outline of Measures for Joint Management of Industries and Mines by China and the Soviet Union, which I last time called to your attention, ought still to be brought up by the opposite side.

8. In all enterprises to be taken over by us, we should request from the Soviets substantive assistance to enable us to take over without hindrance and prevent them from being occupied by irregular organizations or armed forces.

9. The results of these negotiations must not be formalized as agreements until after we complete our takeover of the Northeast.

I received a handwritten copy of a wire from Foreign Minister Wang to Special Envoy Chiang Ching-kuo, dated the twentieth of this month:

(I) have read your wire of the twentieth.

1. With respect to the issue of economic cooperation in the Northeast, the president already has considered carefully the Soviet memorandum and has sent a viable plan to Chairman Chang. Presumably, this can lead to an agreement.

2. Yesterday, the Soviet ambassador personally told the president that the Soviet government regards as invalid the point made in the announcement of the Economic Commission of the Northeast Headquarters to the effect that enemy assets in the several northeastern provinces

will be returned to the Chinese government. The issue has to do with Soviet investment in the Northeast and involves Japanese enterprises, once serving the Kwantung Army but now war booty of the Soviet Army. He then said that on account of the currently friendly relations between China and the Soviet Union the Soviet government already has proposed that we organize a Sino-Soviet joint stock company to manage the Japanese enterprises that once served the Kwantung Army. The Soviets also will concede to us half of the value of these enterprises and, furthermore, will hand over to our government the majority of Japanese enterprises. He hopes that we speedily will deal with this issue and so forth.

3. In dealing with the question of economic cooperation, we should negotiate on the actual items. Concerning the war booty question, we must not stubbornly adhere to a theoretical position (in other words, enterprises in Manchuria formerly operated by the Japanese should not be regarded as compensation to China). Otherwise, we will lose our position if, at a future date, this issue is brought up before the Far Eastern Commission or another international organization.

I urge you to give this attention and please transmit to Chairman Chang.

We can see from this wire that the attitude of the Foreign Ministry still is one of rigid insistence on principle, legality, and reason, while oblivious to the peculiar situation of Sino-Soviet relations in the Northeast and the imminent peril to our situation in the nation at large.

JANUARY 22.   At 2:30 P.M. Madame Chiang arrived in Ch'ang-ch'un. Her aim is to enhance Sino-Soviet friendship by consoling Soviet officers and soldiers, as well as comforting our compatriots in the Northeast after fourteen years of subjugation. Before her arrival the Soviets notified us that Marshal Malinovsky had left for Chita to vote in the elections because today happens to be election day for the Soviet Union. He feared that he would not be able to rush back in time. Instead, he will have General Leonov, supervisor general of the Communications Corps, meet her plane on his behalf. Hearing this, I realized that it implied rather an unfriendly attitude on the part of the Soviet Union. Otherwise, why can't he rush back in time?

After arriving at the airport, Madame Chiang, accompanied by General Leonov, inspected the honor guard. Then, escorted by the garrison commander of Ch'ang-ch'un, she was driven to her temporary residence. The same evening Mayor Chao hosted a welcoming banquet for her at her residence.

Today, the economic counselor of the Soviet Army command sent me a letter stating clearly the names of Soviet participants in enterprises to be jointly managed by China and the Soviet Union. The letter is as follows:

Letter from Sladkovsky, economic counselor of the army command of the Soviet Union, January 22, 1946
To Chairman Chang of the Economic Commission:
    Please find listed below the complete names of Soviet participants in the various joint stock companies to be jointly managed by China and the Soviet Union.

1. The Khabarovsk Coal Mine Complex
2. The Power Control Bureau for the Far Eastern Region
3. The Far Eastern Bank
4. The General Bureau of Locomotives
5. The General Control of the Coke Industry
6. The General Control Bureau for the Lime Industry
7. The General Control Bureau for the Steel-tempering Machinery Construction Industry
8. The General Control Bureau for the Man-Made Liquid Fuel Industry
9. The General Control Bureau for Civil Aviation
10. The South Heilungkiang Navigation Company
11. The Far Eastern Transportation Company
12. The General Control Bureau for the Iron and Steel Industry in the Urals
13. The General Control Bureau for Lead Mines

I received from Wong Yung-ni, the vice-president of the Executive Yuan, a wire of the twenty-first. He still desires that negotiations continue under my charge. The wire is as follows:

I respectfully have read all your letters. After repeated personal discussions with His Excellency the president, I still request that you continue negotiations with the Soviets. With regard to the plan for joint management proposed by the Soviets, in a special wire His Excellency the president will send you his instructions. I respectfully first am sending you this wire of reply.

JANUARY 23.   In the morning I took Madame Chiang sightseeing on the streets of Ch'ang-ch'un. At 3:00 P.M. at the Central Bank, along with Special Envoy Chiang and Vice-Chief of Staff Tung, I hosted a tea party welcoming her. Major General Trotsynko, chief of staff of the Soviet Army, attended on behalf of Marshal Malinovsky and expressed his apologies, saying he was sorry that Marshal Malinovsky had not been able to rush back in time. I delivered a welcoming speech and then announced a list of names of Soviet commanders to receive medals awarded by us. Madame conferred the decorations and delivered a speech to which Major General Trotsynko replied with a speech.

In the evening, at Madame's residence, I hosted a banquet welcoming her.

I received from President Chiang a handwritten letter dated January 20. The letter goes as follows:

+   *Handwritten letter from President Chiang Kai-shek*   +

ten o'clock, January 20, 1946

Dear Kung-ch'uan:*

Your letter of the seventeenth has been respectfully read. The Ch'ang-ch'un negotiations have now to depend on your achieving a diplomatic breakthrough. Fortunately (your position) is unofficial, so that you do not have formal responsibility. It would have been even more inconvenient if the Ministry of Economics had officially sent people to take charge of this matter. For the rest of my message, please read my letter to Ching-kuo. Please proceed according to this principle. As for the concrete measures, tomorrow as soon as I receive the Economic Ministry's plan of action, I will have it sent to you. But I would expect it not to go beyond the scope of this principle, which is to be our utmost limit.

Chung-Cheng

JANUARY 24.   In the morning, Madame visited barracks and the hospital of the Soviet Army. At 12:00 the citizenry of Ch'ang-ch'un held a mass assembly to welcome her. At 2:30 there was a tea party at which she expressed her consolations to popular representatives from various circles and broadcast a speech. At 7:00 P.M. the Soviet Army headquarters hosted a banquet for her. Madame delivered a speech in which she said, among other things, "China is a genuine friend of the Soviet Union. Certainly, in the future we will be able to achieve intimate cooperation, both economically and culturally." After the banquet, we saw a film.

I took out time to study the question of foreigners purchasing land in the Northeast. In accord with the principle in the wire from the Foreign Ministry, that the Soviets may purchase housing but not land, I formulated the following expedient measures:

---

*[As distinct from the other four letters, the form of address here has the word *hsien-sheng* attached to Chang Kia-ngau's name, a term more or less analogous to the expression "the honorable." Whereas the term denotes respect just as *hsiung* does, it suggests a far greater measure of formality and seriousness than *hsiung*, which carries a sense of casualness.]

1. As a special gesture of friendship, the central government specially grants to the Soviets the right to purchase a designated number of houses in the Northeast (the land on which the housing is located only can be rented). This right may be exercised only once. It must not become a precedent or be regarded as an agreed-upon right and benefit. With respect to the future purchase of property in China by foreigners, we will deal with this in accord with the explicit regulations of Chinese law, when we have such regulations.

2. In order to prevent disputes we will ask the Soviets to designate specifically and clearly the housing they intend to purchase as well as the area and location of the land they wish to rent with the housing. Then we will dispatch personnel to jointly inquire into the matter with the Soviets. If, indeed, there is no likelihood of complications with property rights, the housing and land will become public property. Then we and the Soviets will discuss and formulate contracts.

3. The duration of rental of the land will be fixed at 10 years. If, when duration expires, the Soviets need to continue renting, duration may be extended through agreement by both sides. But such an extension may not exceed 30 years.

4. Upon expiration of the period of rental, the housing shall be handed back to China without compensation to the Soviets. If, however, prior to the expiration of the period of rental, the housing undergoes destruction and rebuilding is necessary, approval of the renter shall be obtained. Then, when the period of rental expires, the housing still shall be handed back to China without compensation.

5. Use of the land is restricted to the land's surface. Excavating and exploring are forbidden. Also forbidden are the installation of radio stations and military establishments.

6. The Soviets must fulfill obligations imposed by Chinese law.

7. Housing must not be transferred, sold, mortgaged, or rented.

8. The price of housing and the rent should be discussed and determined when deeds are being formulated.

9. On the Chinese side, a deputy designated by the municipal government will be in charge of formulating the deeds.

I submitted to the Foreign Ministry these principles, appending a summary of explanatory notes.

JANUARY 25. At 9:00 A.M. Madame left Ch'ang-ch'un by plane. Special Envoy Chiang and Vice-Chief of Staff Tung left with her for Chin-chou. On the Soviet side, seeing her off on behalf of Marshal Malinovsky was General Leonov. He also stated that because of weather conditions Marshal Malinovsky had not been able to rush back in time; if she could have stayed two more hours the Marshal would have been able to arrive and say good-bye.

Along with Yueh-chi, I made final decisions about principles and contents for the plan of economic cooperation, to be delivered to the Soviets. At 5:30 P.M. I called on the Soviet economic counselor and personally delivered the plan to him. At the same time, I handed to him the Memorandum for the Rental of Land and Purchase of Housing, affixing to this the Principles and Measures for the Formulation of Rental Deeds.

Today, the chief of staff of the Soviet Army command personally told Yang Shu-jen, secretary of the Northeast Headquarters, that while on their way back to Mukden from Fu-shun, Chang Hsing-fu and the six other persons in his group were kidnapped by the Eighth Route Army; seven persons were killed. He feared Mr. Chang also was among those killed. I was extraordinarily stunned to hear this. Mr. Chang is a famous engineer. If, unfortunately, in spite of my making all kinds of arrangements for his safety prior to his departure for Fu-shun, he has met with disaster, this is because of my sending him there. How can I escape the reproach of my conscience? Throughout the night I found it hard to sleep.

Today, I went to the office of the board of directors of the Chinese–Ch'ang-ch'un Railroad to exchange with the Soviet vice-chairman of the board of directors opinions concerning the draft for the organization of the board of directors of the railroad.

JANUARY 26.   At 5 P.M. I called on the economic counselor of the Soviet Army command to exchange opinions concerning our plan for economic cooperation. Our conversation went as follows [The following is a record in clear script, apparently by one of Chang Kia-ngau's secretaries, with minor corrections in the author's own handwriting.]:

Record of a Talk with Economic Counselor Sladkovsky of the Army Command of the Soviet Union (January 26)

I: I presume Your Excellency has read the measures as well as the contents of the plan for economic cooperation that I sent you yesterday. What are Your Excellency's thoughts and feelings?

SLADKOVSKY: Because of the shortness of time, I still have not communicated with Moscow. Therefore, what I shall express today are completely my personal opinions:

1. The government of the Soviet Union regards as its war booty all industrial and mining enterprises in the Northeast formerly belonging to the enemy and used to aid the Kwantung Army. But, having

taken into full account the friendship between China and the Soviet Union, the Soviet government is willing to hand back to China a number of these industries and mines and to place a number of others under joint Sino-Soviet management. However, a great number of the enterprises earmarked by the Soviet Union for joint management have not been listed by China among types of enterprises to be jointly managed. The Soviet Union must consider that all enterprises not listed are ones that the Chinese are unwilling to manage jointly with the Soviets. Therefore, the Soviets must regard all omitted enterprises as belonging to the Soviets.

2. I wonder how to understand the term *having to do with national resources*, which has been raised by your side, since in all the enterprises concerned there is nothing not related to national resources.

3. Your side has raised the point that steam power plants will become either enterprises affiliated with factories or public utilities. Does this mean that, in the future, enterprises affiliated with factories will be placed under the control of factories?

4. With respect to hydroelectric power plants, your side has remarked that in areas adjacent to dams, fields have been flooded and the people have suffered losses. Does this mean that after compensation is given to people who suffered such losses, thus wiping out these losses, we will be able to jointly manage the hydroelectric plants?

5. Your side states that at present it is not appropriate to discuss joint management of the Civil Aviation Company and the Sungari River Steamship Company. Does this mean that in the future your Ministry of Communications will be in charge of discussing this question?

In addition to the aforementioned points, I must respectfully inform Your Excellency about my general thought and feelings concerning the plan proposed by your side. They are as follows:

The Soviets won the victory over Japan. For more than ten years the various industrial and mining enterprises managed by the Japanese were targeted completely on the Soviet Union. Today, by defeating the enemy the Soviet Union has acquired these as war booty. Yet the Soviets proposed to hand back to China a portion of this war booty while operating jointly with China another part of it, according to the principle of equality. But I deeply regret that today the Chinese obliterate and ignore this fundamental Soviet spirit.

I deeply fear that, in view of this situation, we will be unable to arrive at an accord. For example, most of the coal in the mines that the Chinese propose should be managed jointly contains lime. Output is small and their equipment, inadequate. Their estimated total output comprises only 10.5 percent of coal output in the Northeast. If the Soviets accept this proposal, in the future the jointly managed companies will be totally without a commercial foundation, comparable to planting radishes in the desert, and it is bound to totally disrupt the spirit of cooperation between China and the Soviet Union. It would be all right if, to begin with, these enterprises existed for the purpose of scientific experimentation; from a commercial viewpoint, it will not do at all.

Next, the plan proposed by your side has omitted the An-shan Iron Mine, which is tantamount to refusing to manage jointly with the Soviet Union the iron and steel enterprises of the Northeast. Furthermore, your side has omitted the electric enterprises and has not listed the very important Feng-man Hydroelectric Power Plant. In the future, how are we going to coordinate the supply of power needed by various important industries in the Northeast?

Again, your side has omitted the various nonferrous metal mines. I would like to ask where various factories are going to obtain needed resources? As for your side's suggestion that it is not appropriate to discuss the aviation company, does this mean that your side permanently will refuse to discuss it? There also are many relatively minor points that, if in the future discussed with specialists, will be shown to have many unreasonable aspects. For example, the Chinese only offer two cement factories. How can it be worthwhile to organize this number into a company? Then, concerning the organization of jointly managed enterprises, the Chinese propose that this be divided into two types. In one, the Chinese must own 51 percent of the shares, and the chairman of the board of trustees and the general manager, both be Chinese. Doesn't this contradict the principle of equal employment for both sides?

Last night, when I studied China's proposal, I felt that the enterprises that China proposes be jointly managed will not provide each company with an adequate foundation for development. I really dare not report all this to my government; I hope the Chinese government will reconsider and revise its proposals.

To sum up, we have dragged out these discussions long enough. Further procrastination is bound to affect all military and political issues. In the interest of both countries, we really must speedily arrive at a solution. I am very willing to discuss this with Your Excellency but urge that we first have a basis for reaching an agreement. Only then can our discussions be fruitful. In all frankness, I must respectfully tell Your Excellency that, as in all negotiations, eventually we cannot avoid bringing up the bitter truth.

I: I now will answer simply the various points raised by Your Excellency:

1. The Chinese cannot agree on the question of war booty as set forth by the Soviet Union. But because we do not wish to let a dispute over this point obstruct discussion, we propose temporarily not discussing this question but, instead, discussing first the enterprises to be jointly managed.

2. We mean by "having to do with national resources," the products of mines.

3. Regarding steam power plants, if these are power plants affiliated with industries and mines, they can be placed under the control of the industries and mines concerned.

4. As for hydroelectric power plants, we feel that losses suffered by the people in areas adjacent to dams, owing to the flooding of their fields, cannot be determined merely in terms of money. This is because the people think their losses should be compensated for by the splendor of the enterprises. Besides, water and land are involved in generating hydroelectric power. As for the Chinese people's concept of land, many times I respectfully have told Your Excellency about it.

5. The Chinese have not yet given consideration to the Civil Aviation Company and the Sungari River Steamship Company because the Soviets never have brought up this issue. Therefore, at present we cannot discuss it. This does not mean that we refuse to discuss it or that we permanently will not discuss it.

6. Actually, China has omitted the nonferrous metal mines because their output is small and China is very much in need of such mineral products. But if in the future the jointly managed industries need these mineral products, China still can provide them.

7. In companies related to national resources, China should hold 51 percent of the shares. This is stipulated by China's Mineral Product Act and largely is the case in China Proper where we jointly manage mines with the British and the Americans.

8. Actually, the plan China proposes is the result of painful effort. It also indicates our very great sincerity. Although Your Excellency is not totally satisfied, still I know that already my government has made the greatest effort.

Just now, Your Excellency said you fear that if we procrastinate further in this matter, it will affect the general political and military situation. I also am in severe agony. Now, since Your Excellency has mentioned this point, I likewise would like to bring up mine, which is that, since we have insufficient armed force, our efforts to take over political power in the various provinces of the Northeast are constantly being

obstructed by the Eighth Route Army. However, we fear that if we
employ sufficient force, this will provoke the suspicion of Soviet troops
in those localities. Therefore, at present our takeover of administrative
power in various places is more apparent than real. I hope Your Excellency will mention this to your military superiors. With respect to Your
Excellency's question about why certain types of mineral product industries are not listed, this concerns technology; let me invite Special Envoy Sun Yueh-chi to discuss it with Your Excellency tomorrow. (We
adjourned.)

Sladkovsky, as he stood up, added: Actually, the reason the Soviets
wish to enter into intimate economic cooperation with us is because the
Soviets do not want a third nation to enter the Northeast. It does not
mean that the Soviets want to monopolize the advantages.

I: The Chinese intend to reconstruct the Northeast by relying on their own
efforts. If the Soviets can hand the Northeast back to us so that we can
accomplish our takeover without hindrance and freely reconstruct it, I
dare to guarantee that within a year we can restore its economy without
relying on external forces. Your Excellency, please rest assured of this.

Today, at the office of the board of directors of the Chinese–Ch'ang-
ch'un Railroad, I continued to discuss the draft of the organization of the
board of directors and of the railroad bureau. I invited for a talk colleagues
from the finance bureau of the Economic Commission.

JANUARY 27.   At 5 P.M. I invited the Soviet economic counselor and
Sun Yueh-chi to have a long talk. By his tone, the Soviet economic counselor
indicated an extraordinary interest in the iron mine of the An-shan Steel
Works and the He-kang Iron Mine. Apparently, he will not abandon this
matter.

JANUARY 28.   I received from Mayor Tung of Mukden a report saying
that at 8 P.M. on January 16, after reaching the railroad station of Li-shih-chai
on their way back to Mukden from Fu-shun, Chang Hsing-fu and the group
of people with him were dragged off the train by armed irregulars from that
region and ferociously stabbed to death. It has been concluded that all are
dead. Clearly, this incident indicates that the Soviets are unwilling to have
us take over the Fu-shun coal mines before the question of economic cooperation has been settled. To fall in with the purposes of the Soviets and, at the
same time, flaunt their strength, the armed irregulars have committed this
atrocity. Immediately, I drafted a letter in the name of the head of our
military delegation, Vice-Chief of Staff Tung, demanding an explanation
from the Soviet Army command:

This is the situation. Previously, Chang Hsing-fu, deputy head of the Bureau of Industry and Mines of the Economic Commission and special envoy of the Ministry of Economics for the Takeover of Industries and Mines, accompanied by five engineers, went to the Fu-shun coal mines to take control. On January 7, together with Mari, the Soviet assistant vice-chairman of the board of directors of the Chinese–Ch'ang-ch'un Railroad, the party left Ch'ang-ch'un for Mukden. After they arrived in Mukden, Mr. Mari went by himself to Fu-shun. Two days later, Mr. Chang Kia-ngau asked Mr. Kalgin, Soviet vice-chairman of the board of directors of the Chinese–Ch'ang-ch'un Railroad, whether Mr. Chang couldn't proceed to Fu-shun. Mr. Kalgin replied that certainly Mr. Chang could proceed, but he feared that Mr. Chang dared not go. Later, Tung Wen-chi, the mayor of Mukden, reported by telephone that at 3:00 P.M. on the fourteenth, accompanied by seven engineers, two contingent chiefs of the railroad police, and seven policemen, Mr. Chang departed. Prior to this, Mr. Mari told Mr. Chang that he could go to Fu-shun and that they had already established liaison with Soviet troops there. After Chang and his group arrived in Fu-shun, the Soviets drove them to the Coal Mine Club, their temporary lodging place. But the guns that the policemen brought along were taken away by the local public security bureau.

Immediately, Soviet soldiers replaced the posted Chinese sentries. In the course of time, the Soviet soldiers guarding the gate of the Coal Mine Club were temporarily withdrawn. At 8:00 P.M. on the sixteenth, Soviet Army officers, accompanied by local police, announced to Chang Hsing-fu that we could not take over this region and advised him immediately and speedily to return to Mukden. At 8:40 P.M. on the same evening, Chang and his group were led to the railroad station. After waiting nearly an hour in the waiting room of the station, Chang and his party boarded the special train that had brought them from Ch'ang-ch'un to Mukden, but the soldiers dispatched by the Soviets were in another coach. When the train reached the station at Li-shih-chai, 25 kilometers from Fu-shun, Eighth Route Army soldiers boarded it, dragged Chang and the seven other men off, stripped them of their clothing, and ferociously bayonetted them to death. [Here ends the report made by Tung Wen-chi.]

Concerning this incident, Chang Kia-ngau, chairman of the board of directors of the Chinese–Ch'ang-ch'un Railroad, personally asked Kalgin, the Soviet vice-chairman of the board of directors, to make an official inquiry to your army command. I personally also have raised the issue with your army's chief of staff. Furthermore, your chief of staff personally told Yang, a member of our military delegation, about this incident, saying that while on their way back to Mukden from Fu-shun, Chang Hsing-fu and his group were kidnapped and killed by the Eighth Route Army, that only one person escaped, and that already one corpse has been found. In addition to the above, now we have been told on the telephone by Mayor Tung about the aforementioned series of events. Upon hearing this I am extraordinarily

shocked. The background of this case is as follows: Formerly, the Fu-shun
Coal Mine provided for the Chinese–Ch'ang-ch'un Railroad, but recently
the mine has not been able to supply the railroad with enough coal. Kalgin,
the Soviet vice-chairman of the board of directors of the Chinese–Ch'ang-
ch'un Railroad, repeatedly indicated to Chang Kia-ngau, the chairman of
the board of directors of the railroad, that personnel should be sent to Fu-
shun to straighten out matters. So it was decided that the Soviets would
send Mari, the Soviet assistant vice-chairman of the board of directors, and
the Chinese Chang Hsing-fu to inspect and readjust matters in Fu-shun.
The expectation was that there might be at Fu-shun ample coal for the
Chinese–Ch'ang-ch'un Railroad, which in turn would facilitate both Soviet
military transportation and ordinary commercial transportation.

Furthermore, Mr. Chang was a Chinese specialist on mining and one of
the few persons in China talented in that field. Because he was an important
person in the central government, Mr. Chang was selected to go to the
Northeast and preside over the takeover of industries and mines. Today,
with his death, not only has the Chinese government lost a specialist on
industry and mining, but, moreover, this will affect the feelings of people at
large as well as public opinion throughout our nation. It really is a cause for
deep regret that such an unfortunate incident should occur now, since the
site of this incident, the station of Li-shih-chai, happens to be within your
army's defense zone, and Chang and his group were being escorted by your
army. I request that your army command send persons to determine the
truth about what happened and send me a detailed reply, so that I can
report to my government. I would be very grateful.

To: His Excellency, Major General Trotsynko
From: Tung Yen-p'ing, head of the Military Delegation, National Government, Republic of China, January 00, 1946 [Two zeros were given in place
of the actual date.]

Kan Yü-p'ei, the person in charge of the Sino-Soviet Friendship Society,
came to tell me that he has learned from Soviets who frequent the society
that because of inadequate fuel supplies for the Chinese–Ch'ang-ch'un Railroad, the date for the withdrawal of Soviet troops still may have to be
postponed. Meanwhile, since the number of Chinese troops arriving is
small, as soon as Soviet troops withdraw, our government troops and administrative takeover personnel may find themselves threatened. In addition,
there still are a number of questions unsettled and so forth. This shows that
the crux of postponing the date for the withdrawal of Soviet troops is the still
unsettled status of a number of questions.

At 5 P.M. I called upon the Soviet economic counselor. I requested that
he revise the original Soviet proposal and make the greatest concessions.
Our side also will reconsider and make final concessions. I took this step
because the date for the withdrawal of Soviet troops already has arrived, and

I had to cut the Gordian knot. Sladkovsky's remarking during our conversation that threats to the Soviet Union from Manchuria be eliminated through economic cooperation reflects the basic policy that in the future the Soviets will pursue toward the Northeast and Sinkiang. We must give this our attention. The record of our talk is appended as follows: [The following record was copied in clear script, with a few minor corrections in the author's handwriting.]

Record of My Talk with Economic Counselor Sladkovsky of the Soviet Army Command (January 28)

I: Today, I have come to see Your Excellency with the aim of having an informal exchange of opinions in which I can express to Your Excellency my personal thoughts and feelings. The spirit of the Chinese proposal is to not disappoint the Chinese people. Because, with the restoration of the Northeast, the Chinese people presume that China's sovereign rights can be restored. If China and the Soviet Union jointly manage all important industrial and mining enterprises in the Northeast, the Chinese people will feel that, although that region has been restored to them, still nothing has been obtained. Next, in China's technical circles it is hoped that after the restoration the Chinese may also manage by themselves a number of heavy industries there. There will be dissatisfaction if we jointly manage all enterprises there. Consequently, a number of heavy industries must be handed over to the Chinese to manage by themselves. My idea is that if the Soviets truly wish to enter into economic cooperation with the Chinese we may as well follow several kinds of procedures. There is no need jointly to manage everything. For example, a certain kind of enterprise can employ Soviet technical personnel; another type can use loans to purchase Soviet machinery. Another type of enterprise can supply the Soviets with products. Although the methods vary, Soviet desires will be fulfilled. The chief thing is that, no matter what the international question, popular opinion within one's own country must be taken into consideration. Today, I also want to ask why the Yalu River Hydroelectric Power Plant still has not been earmarked for joint management. Furthermore, in the final analysis, is the Sungari River Steamship Company a company that constructs steamships or one that provides transportation by steamship? Because if it is the latter, being jointly managed will contradict the principle on which China abolished the right of foreigners to engage in internal transportation.

SLADKOVSKY: We did not earmark the Yalu River Hydroelectric Power Plant because it is located in Korea. The Sungari River Steamship Company provides transportation by steamship. The Sungari River intersects with the Heilungkiang, which in turn extends right to the Soviet border; thus, it would appear that the function of this company differs from internal navigation. Next, the opinion expressed by Your Excellency seems to indicate that your viewpoint concerning war booty consistently differs from that of the Soviets. It would seem that the Chinese people regard the Soviet Union as mistaken in insisting that the Soviets participate in the management of various enterprises. Actually, the Soviets are willing to set aside a number of enterprises and let the Chinese participate. Your Excellency has mentioned the thoughts and feelings of your people; thus, I must explain the thoughts and feelings of the Soviet people. Along the Soviet border there is no place where there have been more incidents than on the border with China. For ten years troops and industries in Manchuria have constituted the gravest threat to the Soviet Union, culminating in a war in which the Soviet people suffered unparalleled losses. Therefore, in their hearts and minds the Soviet people feel there can be no peace in the Far East unless the problem of Manchuria is settled. Consequently, so far as the interests of the Soviet Union are concerned, the most important question is how to eliminate the threat from Manchuria. Therefore, we really must enter into economic cooperation in the hope that in the future there no longer will occur unpleasant incidents in Manchuria. Last time, I mentioned that economic cooperation must be built on not only a political but also a commercial foundation. If in a certain type of enterprise each side merely makes political concessions to achieve cooperation while failing to provide a commercial foundation, that type of enterprise will not endure. For example, if in jointly managed companies there is no complex coordination between the An-shan Iron Mine, the Feng-man Hydroelectric Power Plant, important coal mines, and a number of nonferrous metal mines, then the companies will not have a solid foundation and cannot develop. Take for example the Pen-hsi-hu Coal Mine. I do not deny that the mine is a good one. But its output can meet only the needs of the mine itself. Again, take for example your proposal concerning the Mi-shan, Hui-ch'un, and Cha-lai-noh-erh mines. If these three mines are organized into one company, how will that company be able to compete with the He-kang Coal Mine? Consequently, I believe that if we accept the Chinese proposal, this will preclude setting up enterprises having a commercial foundation. Therefore, your proposal is unacceptable.

As for Your Excellency's proposal that one way of cooperating is for China to supply the Soviet Union with products, actually, the Soviets do not wish to monopolize the various products of the Northeast but, instead, are willing to have a number of products meet the needs of China. Therefore, the Soviets really do not welcome this type of procedure.

Certainly, in the interest of the Chinese people, the best policy is to develop light industry and raise the living standard of the people. The heavy industries involved in national defense really cannot benefit the people directly. Now, what the Soviets want to participate in is heavy industry, related to the military. For example, the An-shan Iron Works totally served military production; the Feng-man Hydroelectric Power Plant totally served the needs of expanding military industries. The Soviet Union not only wants no share of light industry in the Northeast but is willing to do its very best to assist in the development of such industry. Take, for example, the food and textile industries. The Soviet Union is prepared to assist them under any conditions. Finally, I would like to tell Your Excellency that the Soviet Union absolutely will not relax its control over industries in Manchuria having to do with the military.

I: In my opinion, there are many ways to eliminate the threat from Manchuria, brought up by Your Excellency. Eliminating this threat does not necessitate our jointly managing every enterprise. As for Your Excellency's point about all jointly managed enterprises being properly coordinated and provided with a commercial foundation, I am not against this. However, there are in Manchuria only a small number of important industrial and mining enterprises; therefore, China must have a number to manage independently. For example, there are only two iron and steel works; China must have one. There are only two large coal mines in northern Manchuria; China also must have one. With respect to nonferrous metal products, if in the future the jointly managed industries have need for these, we indeed can provide them. The Chinese mentality attaches great importance to mineral products from beneath the ground, but we can relax somewhat our control over manufacturing enterprises. Therefore, I deeply hope that Your Excellency will recommend that your government revise its proposal and make the greatest concessions. I also will report to my government Your Excellency's opinions and ask it to make the greatest concessions. If such a spirit can prevail on both sides, perhaps there is hope of reaching a settlement.

SLADKOVSKY: I also very much hope for a quick settlement. I will report to my government Your Excellency's opinions. I hope your Excellency will step up your efforts. (Adjourned)

This morning I invited colleagues from various departments of the Economic Commission to decide together on an operational procedure. President Chiang sent a wire [dated the 28th], asking me to forward to Marshal Malinovsky this message:

> To General Malinovsky and all officers and soldiers of the Soviet Army general headquarters:
> During her recent trip to Ch'ang-ch'un to extend consolation to your army on behalf of Chung-cheng [Chiang Kai-shek], Madame Chiang was given a warm reception by generals, officers, and soldiers of your army. Not only is Madame Chiang very delighted and grateful, but the friendship between the Chinese and Soviet peoples is increasing further and diplomatic relations between the two countries are becoming even more intimate. I particularly am convinced of this and purposely am expressing to you my gratitude. Chung-cheng

JANUARY 29.   Today, Vice-Chief of Staff Tung saw Major General Trotsynko, the Soviet chief of staff, to deliver to him the formal letter to the Soviet Army command pressing for an answer concerning the murder of Chang Hsing-fu. Tung also verbally pressed for such an answer. Major General Trotsynko replied, "The Soviets already have taken steps necessary to arrest the criminals. At present, already two have been arrested. We again will send you a written reply after investigation of the incident has been completed." Then, Trotsynko said he had a statement: "Chang Hsing-fu was an important person in your central government. But you did not notify the Soviet Army general headquarters about the itinerary of his trip." Vice-Chief of Staff Tung retorted by asking how it could be said that the Soviet Army command was not informed about Mr. Chang's movements when he was traveling with the Soviet assistant vice-chairman of the board of directors of the Chinese–Ch'ang-ch'un Railroad and under escort by the Soviet Army. Trotsynko replied argumentatively,

> Mari is a member of the staff of the Chinese–Ch'ang-ch'un Railroad and has nothing to do with the Soviet Army general headquarters. Since Chang was an important person in your central government, it would seem that, as in the case of other important persons involved in your takeover, you should have notified the Soviet Army general headquarters so it could dispatch liaison officials to escort Chang on his trip.

Vice-Chief of Staff Tung then asked Major General Trotsynko whether our personnel taking over Dairen would be safe while traveling there. Major General Trotsynko replied that, according to his assessment, there are no problems concerning safety. But because a very small number of Soviet troops are stationed south of Mukden, he cannot guarantee there absolutely will be no disturbances by armed irregulars. If we consider it too risky to send our personnel there by rail, why not use other means to send them there? He said we can decide this for ourselves. As for the metropolitan area of Dairen, he assumed there would be no problem.

The board of directors of the Chinese–Ch'ang-ch'un Railroad met to discuss the organization of the board of directors of the Railroad Bureau.

Mayor Shen Chün-yi came to see me. He had a rather hesitant attitude about our taking over Dairen.

Today, Major General Trotsynko sent Vice-Chief of Staff Tung a formal document rejecting absolutely an inquiry from our army command in Mukden to the Soviet garrison commander of Fengtien, asking whether our army command can order all clandestine armed forces to assemble at a location designated by our army command so that we can take them over.

JANUARY 30.   I discussed with Kalgin, the vice-chairman of the board of directors of the Chinese–Ch'ang-ch'un Railroad and Ju-la-fu-li-fu, the head of the Railroad Bureau, sending our government troops from Mukden to Ch'ang-ch'un by using coaches of the Pei-Ning Railroad. They expressed approval.

At noon today the board of directors of the Chinese–Ch'ang-ch'un Railroad met to continue their discussion of regulations for the organization of the board of directors and of the Railroad Bureau. We still did not finish our discussion. In the evening I invited Bureau Head Ju for supper.

I received from Special Envoy Chiang Ching-kuo a wire from Chungking: "Please send to Chungking by plane the plan prepared for secondary possibilities for economic cooperation with the Soviets. It is not suitable to transmit by telegraph."

JANUARY 31.   I received from Minister of Foreign Affairs Wang a wire [dated January 30]. Its message is as follows:

> February 1 is the date for the completion of the withdrawal of Soviet troops. Please transmit to Vice-Chief of Staff Tung Yen-p'ing that on February 1 he clearly ascertain from the Soviet Army command the situation surrounding the withdrawal of Soviet troops and inform me about it by wire. Mr. Tung's stance can be one of firm friendship but must be clear. If the Soviets give him indications, you can let me know and I will transmit these to our government. Mr. Tung need not reply directly to the Soviets. I already personally have told President Chiang. In addition, I am expressly wiring you about it.

Today at noon, the board of directors of the Chinese–Ch'ang-ch'un Railroad again met for discussion about the organization of the Railroad Bureau.

The discussion had already ended when the Soviets proposed that in addition there be created the post of assistant bureau head. This provoked a great dispute lasting about two and a half hours. Nothing came of it. We proposed submitting the issue to our government for a decision. The Soviets insisted that we approve creation of the post. I stated that we have not the right to grant such approval. The two sides agreed to discuss the matter further tomorrow.

Tomorrow, the date for the withdrawal of Soviet troops will have arrived, but the Soviet Army still shows no sign of withdrawing northward from Ch'ang-ch'un. There has been no progress at all with respect to our taking over administration in the various provinces. This month has passed quickly. My viewpoint is that since the beginning of the Political Consultative Conference on January 10, Sino-Soviet relations with respect to the Northeast have been encumbered by the relationship between the Nationalists and the Communists. If we had reached a settlement with the Soviets before the tenth, political issues between the Nationalists and the Communists might not have become part of the question. In spite of secret Soviet speculations that the irregular armed forces they have nurtured here inevitably will reflect Soviet political interests, this problem would not have been able to surface. Now the truce agreement is a fact, and the Political Consultative Conference has been convened. Only the Political Consultative Conference can deny the legitimacy in any locality of Chinese communist armed forces. I read in the *Liberation Daily* of January 20 the following item of news. The heading is "In order to resolve the question of the Northeast, people belonging to various circles in Chungking advocate the establishment of united governments of a local nature." [The article reads as follows:]

On the fifth of this month the Society for Political Reconstruction of the Northeast proposed to the Political Consultative Conference that there be established a local organization for democratic politics and a Commission for Northeastern Political Affairs to be organized by persons genuinely representing the people of the Northeast as well as persons from various parties and factions. After the establishment of the Commission for Northeastern Political Affairs, the Northeast Headquarters and organizations affiliated to it will be abolished. Simultaneously, organizations reflecting the popular will are to be established at different levels in various provinces, cities, and prefectures of the Northeast. These will prepare for popular, general elections within a year's time to choose leaders of both the popularly elected organizations and the government at various levels. After the establishment at various levels of the popularly elected organizations and popularly elected governments, the Commission for Northeastern Political Affairs will have completed its task and will be abolished. All economic or financial enterprises and organizations in the Northeast should have as their primary concern the welfare of the people of the Northeast. Industry in the Northeast must be dealt with and the currency regulated in ways that are fair and reasonable.

The opinions stated above should be regarded as the Chinese communist plan for the Northeast. Therefore, the Soviets can well afford to hand over to us the cities along the Chinese–Ch'ang-ch'un Railroad, while letting Chinese communist armed forces occupy the various provinces and regions and contend with us for power. They can then leave without being concerned. I fear that perhaps already during this month the Soviets have been preparing for this chess game. Perhaps the central government presumes that since the truce agreement stipulates that the Northeast is an exception, it can send troops to recover our sovereignty. But it does not know that, owing to secret support from the Soviets, for a long time Chinese communist armed forces there have grown in strength day by day. Moreover, because of the vastness of the areas adjacent to the Soviet Union, the Chinese Communists easily can obtain aid from the Soviets, while for us supply is difficult because we can rely only on the Peiping-Fengtien rail line and one or two small harbors. It is difficult to fortell a military victory. Certainly, the various persons in the central government charged with making policy have not been able to perceive this. I shudder as I view and ponder the future.

From Ch'ang-ch'un to Chungking

February 1–28, 1946

On February 1 Chang Kia-ngau confers with Malinovsky and Sladkovsky in
what will be their last meeting. Sladkovsky and Chang review their previous
negotiations on Sino-Soviet cooperation for Malinovsky. A major obstacle is
that each side has drawn up different lists of Japanese enterprises they want
included under Sino-Soviet management. But the Chinese side also objects to
the continued use of the term war booty, whereas the Soviet side refuses to
withdraw that term from discussions. Chang then asks Malinovsky when the
Soviet armed forces plan to withdraw from Manchuria. Malinovsky replies
that no date has been set to leave Ch'ang-ch'un but that Soviet troops are
withdrawing from southern Manchuria. He urges the Chinese side to include
the He-kang coal mines and the An-shan iron and steel enterprises for Sino-
Soviet management. Malinovsky also wants joint Sino-Soviet management of
the Civil Aviation Company. He then admits for the first time, in the presence of Chang Kia-ngau, that Chinese communist military forces may number as many as 500,000 troops, that they are everywhere in southern Manchuria, but that the Soviet Union has no intention of intervening in Chinese
affairs. Malinovsky finally suggests that the Chinese side should formulate
another plan for Sino-Soviet economic cooperation so that an agreement can
be reached before Soviet troops leave Manchuria. Chang Kia-ngau interprets Malinovsky's remarks as an ultimatum, and he decides to depart for
Chungking the next day, flying first to Peiping and then on to Chungking,
arriving on February 4.

Chang Kia-ngau immediately reports Malinovsky's views to President Chiang Kai-shek. After some discussion, Chang finally suggests to the president that the Republic of China (ROC) government should either terminate discussion with the Soviets on economic cooperation or propose a new plan that would offer some major concessions.

Chang Kia-ngau continues to meet with leading officials as well as with the president. He learns that no more Chinese troops will be sent to Ch'ang-ch'un until an agreement on a Soviet troop withdrawal from Manchuria is reached.

On February 10 Chang Kia-ngau meets with President Chiang, T. V. Soong, Chiang Ching-kuo, and Wong Yung-ni to draw up a new plan for Sino-Soviet economic cooperation. The ROC will add the He-kang coal mines to the list of enterprises to be jointly managed, as well as the An-shan iron and steel enterprises, but will insist that the Soviets return the Fu-shun coal mines.

More rounds of visits with top officials follow for Chang. On February 16 there is a huge public demonstration in Chungking to protest the recent murder of Chang Hsing-fu in Manchuria.

On February 18 Foreign Minister Wang shows Chang Kia-ngau a letter from President Chiang Kai-shek stating that economic cooperation can only be carried out after the Soviets have withdrawn their troops and the ROC government has recovered Manchuria. On February 20 Chang Kia-ngau learns that Chiang Ching-kuo has asked Foreign Minister Wang if the ROC government shouldn't agree to Soviet demands; otherwise it might be impossible to agree on Soviet troop withdrawals from Manchuria.

Chang Kia-ngau confides to his diary his fears that if an economic cooperation agreement is not quickly negotiated with the Soviet Union then the Chinese communist troops will have become so strong in Manchuria that the Nationalists will have to use great force to take over areas outside the major cities. Chang also fears that the more nationalistic members of the ROC government will begin to criticize their leaders for their inability to recover Manchuria. With Chinese communist troops already in Manchuria and secret negotiations with the Soviet Union being leaked, Chang fears that there will be no way to recover Manchuria.

Just as Chang Kia-ngau fears, on February 22 some thirty thousand people demonstrate. They criticize the Soviet Union, demand that Soviet troops be withdrawn from Manchuria, and call on the ROC government to eliminate all puppet governments. At the end of February Chang wires his colleagues in Ch'ang-ch'un explaining why his return to that city has been delayed. The Soviet embassy in Chungking lodges a formal protest with the ROC government over the recent public demonstration. The

ROC leaders now decide that Soviet anger should cool before Chang Kia-ngau returns to Ch'ang-ch'un to resume Sino-Soviet economic cooperation negotiations.

+ + + + + + +

FEBRUARY 1.   Today is the date for the Soviets to withdraw their troops from the Northeast. I am anxious to know Soviet intentions and inclinations; thus, at 1 P.M. I asked Vice-Chief of Staff Tung to call on the Soviet chief of staff, Major General Trotsynko, to ask him about the actual conditions surrounding the withdrawal of Soviet troops. Trotsynko replied,

> With respect to the conditions surrounding the withdrawal of Soviet troops, by now Soviet troops in Jehol already have withdrawn entirely into Outer Mongolia. Beginning January 15, Soviet troops in Mukden also began withdrawing; as of today only 80 trainloads have managed to withdraw. Even these have encountered the greatest difficulties. Because of the need to wait to replenish coal and change locomotives, many trains have had to stop along the way for as long as two or three days. With respect to Soviet troops in the area of Hsin-min and Chang-wu, by now they already have withdrawn entirely.

Then Tung asked whether he could give us the dates when Soviet troops will complete their withdrawal from Mukden and when they will withdraw from Ch'ang-ch'un and Harbin. He replied, "Right now, there still is no way to give you the dates." From this already it is very clear that the Soviets purposely and unilaterally are delaying the date for withdrawal of troops from the Northeast.

At one o'clock I called on the Soviet economic counselor to sound him out. First, I discussed the question of housing. He insisted that the Soviets cannot purchase again whatever housing they already have paid for in full. I then allowed them to pay us a total sum. In the future, the two sides will settle all accounts at the same time. He asked whether there will be obstructions when the Soviets have transactions with municipal governments. I replied that there will be no obstructions. Then we discussed the economic question. He said Marshal Malinovsky would like to talk with me. Immediately, it was arranged for me to see Malinovsky at 4 P.M.

Marshal Malinovsky and I talked for two and a half hours. Today's talk with Marshal Malinovsky was exceedingly important. Soviet views were fully disclosed. Our authorities suspect that even if we reach an agreement on economic cooperation the Soviets still may not withdraw their troops. Judging from Marshal Malinovsky's tone, this really is not the case. On the other hand, the most important point is that the Soviets acknowledge as units of the Eighth Route Army only armed irregular forces south of Fengtien and the area of Jehol. Our talk went as follows:

My Talk with Marshal Malinovsky
(at 4 P.M. February 1, 1946, Economic Counselor Sladkovsky was present.)

MALINOVSKY: I deeply regret that during Madame Chiang's recent trip to Ch'ang-ch'un I was unable personally to pay my respects. I express my deep gratitude for Madame Chiang's visit.

I: I was delighted and grateful that in Ch'ang-ch'un Madame was received on your behalf by the chief of staff of your army. It is too bad that Your Excellency happened to be away so that you were unable to meet with her. This is regrettable.

MALINOVSKY: I hear that Your Excellency intends to take a trip back to Chungking.

I: I intend to go there during the Spring Festival [the Chinese lunar New Year] holidays. There are many questions that I must report on to my government and seek a solution to.

MALINOVSKY: When Your Excellency arrives in Chungking please convey for me to President and Madame Chiang my gratitude for Madame Chiang's visit to Ch'ang-ch'un.

I: I will. Just now, Counselor Sladkovsky mentioned that Your Excellency wanted to talk with me. I have not seen Your Excellency for a long time. I also am very willing to talk.

MALINOVSKY: Before Your Excellency leaves Ch'ang-ch'un, I wish to exchange with Your Excellency opinions about the question of Sino-Soviet economic cooperation. For a long time Your Excellency and Counselor Sladkovsky have engaged in negotiations on this question. The Soviet government has invested me and Counselor Sladkovsky with full power to deal with this matter. Now much time has passed and much discussion has taken place. Yet, there has been no progress at all. Now, let me first ask Counselor Sladkovsky to give us a report on the state of negotiations about this case.

SLADKOVSKY: Negotiations began as early as November of last year. On November 20 the Soviets proposed an inventory. In this inventory there was listed for joint management by China and the Soviet Union the various enterprises formerly affiliated with the Manchurian Heavy Industry Company and the Manchurian Electric Company, as well as a number of factories that formerly served the Kwantung Army and that were purely military in nature. During the negotiations Mr. Chang indicated that the Chinese wish to manage a number of factories by themselves. So I reported his views to my government. In the inventory that it proposed the second time, the Soviet government greatly reduced the total number of enterprises to be managed jointly. I told Mr. Chang that the Soviets regard as war booty all the aforementioned types of enterprises because they belonged to a military industry targeted on the Soviet Union. But there are a large number of factories that, although they met Japanese military needs, the Soviets are still willing to hand back to China. Mr. Chang indicated that the Chinese are unwilling to establish a large company suggestive of having a monopolistic nature. Therefore, the Soviets proposed organizing eleven companies. In the second inventory it proposed, the Soviet government reduced the number of coal mines from 22 to 9, the number of power plants from 54 to 16, the number of machine-building industries from 14 to 6, and the number of iron and steel industries from 3 complexes (Tung-pien-tao, An-shan, and Pen-hsi-hu) to 2 (An-shan and Pen-hsi-hu). But in their answer the Chinese thoroughly eradicated the Soviet position on war booty. Actually, the Chinese have omitted all important enterprises in the Soviet inventory. If we adhere to the Chinese proposal, we definitely will not be able to create companies having a commercial value. I discussed this issue with Mr. Chang many times. Our specialists also discussed it once with Mr. Sun Yueh-chi. Mr. Chang also said in their proposal that, when appropriate, the Chinese still can increase slightly the number of coal mines. The Chinese omitted all power plants, on the grounds that power plants are public utilities. Hydroelectric power plants were not listed on the grounds that in areas adjacent to dams, privately owned fields and land had been flooded. Actually, there is no basis at all for all this. Furthermore, the Chinese allege that the reason why many enterprises are not listed in the inventory is that these were formerly private property. The omission of the very important An-shan Iron Mine is tantamount to refusing to cooperate with us in the iron and steel industry. Where other types of industry are concerned the Chinese also have omitted most factories. Furthermore, the Chinese propose that the organization of companies be changed into two types and that in enterprises having to do with national resources China and the Soviet Union cannot be equal. I must draw a conclusion concerning this proposal: namely, the Chinese proposal cannot be conducive to the success of the negotiations.

I: After discussions started, our side could not agree to the Soviet interpretation of war booty. Our circuitous negotiations caused a delay of a number of days. Then, after I returned to Ch'ang-ch'un from Nanking, I indicated to Counselor Sladkovsky that we must follow another path. But

Counselor Sladkovsky said that the Soviets must stand firm on the war booty issue. Consequently, I proposed to Counselor Sladkovsky that we temporarily set aside the question of war booty, discussing instead the types of enterprises actually to be managed cooperatively. Therefore, our Ministry of Economics made a careful study, resulting in the Chinese delivering to you their counterplan. The general spirit of this plan is as follows:

The Chinese maintain that the Chinese people attach great importance to underground resources, which cannot be regarded as war booty. Therefore, if we place the majority of our mines under joint Sino-Soviet management, our people will conclude that foreigners have been given all rights to our mines. That is why Mr. Sun Yueh-chi indicated that we are willing to place a number of excellent mines under joint Sino-Soviet management, but we wish to manage the rest by ourselves. Mr. Sun already has communicated to Counselor Sladkovsky the details of our proposal. In the future, China still can provide you with products from mines managed by China and can appoint Soviet engineers in these mines. As for the iron and steel industry, the Chinese must manage by themselves one of the two iron works. If in the future we need to replenish machinery in the hydroelectric power plants, we can purchase it from the Soviet Union. We may very well even appoint and employ Soviet engineers in these plants. All in all, the Chinese government must take into consideration popular opinion among its own people and the expectations of its young technicians. Therefore, we want, within the limits possible, to employ various methods of cooperating with the Soviets, but we will not use only one type of method for joint management.

If, after my return to Chungking, I discuss this issue with various circles I must be prepared to deal with not only economic but also political opinions. Therefore, I would like to take advantage of this opportunity to discuss with Your Excellency the political question. Politics and economics are intimately related. At present, the Chinese government has been plunged into a very difficult situation because the general public reproaches our government for spending several months taking over only a few cities. As for taking over provinces, this has been nominal. The reason is that in areas outside the provincial capitals there has been extraordinarily rampant activity by the Eighth Route Army. This has created a situation in which the central government only shoulders obligations under the Sino-Soviet treaty but cannot enjoy the rights it deserves. Therefore, in the opinion of the Chinese public, if now we formulate measures for economic cooperation with the Soviets perhaps we still will have only obligations while others enjoy rights. Now, I've stated this frankly. Then, respecting the question of withdrawal of your troops: by now the date of withdrawal is already here. I wonder what are recent Soviet plans for withdrawing troops.

MALINOVSKY: It seems that before the thirteenth of last month there was no difficulty in your taking over various prefectures.

I: Recently our effort to take over Chiu-t'ai prefecture was frustrated by local armed irregular forces.

MALINOVKSY: I will settle this problem on your behalf. Personally, I do not wish to stay here permanently. I deeply desire to go back to my own country soon. We can temporarily set aside the war booty question and not discuss it. Instead, we wish to speedily settle upon the measures for economic cooperation. Within Chinese territory all goods, whether above or below the ground, sooner or later will belong to China. The Soviets have no intention of taking possession of them. But in order to achieve dynamic economic cooperation, we must have a healthy, reasonable organization. For example, if you omit He-kang from the coal mines and An-shan from the iron works, there will be no need whatsoever to discuss economic cooperation. Nor must hydroelectric power plants be omitted. They must not be regarded as public utilities but instead should be considered the foundation for the major source of power. I understand well the state of mind that causes the Chinese to want an opportunity to run industries by themselves. But joint management does not mean that all the enterprises will belong to the Soviet Union. Products of the jointly managed enterprises still will meet the needs of the Chinese. As for the question of importing and exporting products, we will formulate another agreement. You must know that the Soviets are not willing to let the nine northeastern provinces again become a base for anti-Soviet activities.

This kind of plan for cooperation is merely a precautionary measure for our own safety and really does not imply an ambition for economic aggression in the Northeast. Manchurian industry existed purely to meet military needs. Furthermore, topographically Manchuria is adjacent to the Soviet Union and protrudes a long way into Soviet territory. Therefore, we must rely on economic cooperation to eliminate the threat that Manchuria poses to the Soviet Union. I am deeply aware that China and the Soviet Union will never go to war. But I fear that a foreign power, a wolf in sheep's clothing, may encroach on Manchuria. Furthermore, although Japan has been defeated in the war, there is no guarantee that in several years it will not again become a military factor. Japan's imperial government and people differ from those of defeated Germany, which cannot become again an integrated nation. This is why the Soviets are very anxious to establish an organization for economic cooperation with the Chinese. In this we have not the least ambition. The sooner this question is settled, the sooner an economic foundation can be reinforced and the greater the benefit for China.

With respect to the political question, I well understand what Your Excellency says about the difficult conditions in taking over the various provinces and cities. But the Soviets really are not hindering the transportation of Chinese troops or China's taking over various places. On the contrary, they have given China all kinds of assistance. Moreover, Soviet troops remain here precisely for the purpose of helping the Chinese complete the task. Certainly, three or four thousand of your troops airlifted into Manchuria and your two divisions that have entered Fengtien will not be able to consolidate China's strength in Manchuria because the Eighth Route Army and other armed forces allegedly have 500,000 men. The Chinese should settle this by themselves. If you want the Soviet Union to settle this for you, then I assert that we have no right to interfere in China's internal affairs. The Soviets cannot take the blame for the complicated political situation in the Northeast. Concerning the question of the withdrawal of Soviet troops, at present they are in the process of withdrawing. Troops stationed in Chih-feng, To-lun, etc., as well as those stationed beyond the railroad line, such as Hsin-min and Chang-wu, have already withdrawn entirely. However, in order to maintain our line of communication, we have not been able to withdraw totally from along the railroad line.

In sum, if the Chinese continue to procrastinate on the question of economic cooperation, while engaging in activities that smack of gambling and conniving, then industry will come to a standstill and continue to be destroyed; the social order never will be restored. Therefore, we should seek a sincere and realistic settlement of this question. On the other hand, certainly the counterplan proposed by the Chinese will not settle the question.

I: The Chinese have no intention of conducting negotiations with the Soviets in a way that smacks of gambling. They very much wish to find a path to a settlement on economic cooperation agreeable to both sides. With respect to the political question, since for the time being our troops cannot arrive, we have no way of dealing with armed irregular forces in various places. Even with respect to the takeover of the various provinces, in every province the Soviets should assist us in taking over the various county seats around the provincial capitals.

MALINOVSKY: The Soviet Army has not hindered Chinese troops from entering. Your troops can go right ahead and enter various places by way of Fengtien. Nor have the Soviets placed any restrictions on their number.

I: Formerly, there was no Eighth Route Army here. Therefore, the armed forces in various prefectures should be regarded as armed irregular forces.

MALINOVSKY: According to our intelligence, the regular Eighth Route Army was south of Fengtien, and in Jehol. As for armed forces north of Fengtien, they all were irregular troops. There even were troops who claimed to belong to the central government of China. We hear that such troops all are secretly in liaison with representatives of your central government. There is a man by the name of Kuo Ch'a-sheng (a transliteration), who calls himself commander in chief of the Northeastern Army. Subsequently, the Soviets found out that he was chief of staff to General Tu Yü-ming. These troops often made trouble for the Soviet Army, killing its officers and soldiers. The Chinese should find ways to suppress them.

I: How are we to suppress them?

MALINOVSKY: You can issue orders disbanding them. The Soviets cannot interfere in China's internal affairs. I presume that eventually the Chinese and these troops will find a path to a compromise. Actually, Soviet troops are not large in number, so we cannot send many troops to the various prefectures to assist China in its takeover. To sum up, you cannot entirely fix on the Soviets the blame for your difficulties in taking over. Currently, you should speedily send into the Northeast a large number of troops, and your takeover officials going into outlying prefectures should behave more boldly.

I: On what date do Soviet troops intend to leave Ch'ang-ch'un?

MALINOVSKY: No definite date has yet been set.

I: After my return to Chungking, may I report to my government that Soviet troops beyond the rail line already have withdrawn, that those in other places are in the process of withdrawing, and that only those stationed along the rail line for the purpose of temporarily ensuring communications are postponing their withdrawal? Can I report in this way?

MALINOVSKY: Yes. All in all, we hope that the two sides can speedily settle all questions, so that Soviet troops quickly can withdraw. I also would like to ask why the Chinese have refused to discuss the issue of jointly managing the Civil Aviation Company and the Sungari River Steamship Company.

I: Ours is not a permanent refusal. We cannot immediately discuss this matter because it involves communications and has not yet been studied or discussed by our ministry in charge. Furthermore, our central government's policy with regard to civil aviation is to gradually manage it by ourselves. River navigation involves the right to internal navigation. We must take time to study both these issues.

MALINOVSKY: We can manage the Civil Aviation Company along the lines of the Sino-Soviet Aviation Company in Sinkiang. As for the Sungari River Steamship Company, the Sungari cannot totally be regarded as an internal river of China's because the river intersects with the Ussuri and the lower reaches of the Amur in the Soviet Union.

I: I also would like to ask Your Excellency how far the Soviets are willing to go in making concessions. For example, the Soviets insist that the An-shan Iron Works be added. Does this mean that after we have added An-shan to the cooperatively managed enterprises, the Pen-hsi-hu Iron Works will be handed over to us, to manage by ourselves?

MALINOVKSY (After reflecting a moment): It would be best for us [the Chinese] to formulate another plan representing the central government, just as the Soviet plan represents the Soviet government. Your current plan can be regarded only as a plan of your Ministry of Economics. Let's resume our discussion as soon as your side has proposed a plan representing the views of your central government. (We adjourned and stood up.)

MALINOVSKY: I hope we soon can settle this question, so that before long Soviet troops and I can leave here.

This talk was tantamount to an ultimatum from the Soviets. We cannot procrastinate further or remain irresolute. Therefore, I decided immediately to take a trip back to Chungking.

Today, Vice-Chief of Staff Tung negotiated with the Soviet chief of staff, Major General Trotsynko, concerning the question of taking over Chiu-t'ai. There is a coal mine at Chiu-t'ai that can provide for the needs of Ch'ang-ch'un. Furthermore, it is on an important road leading into Kirin. On January 30, when, together with administrative personnel and five contingents of security maintenance police, the head of Chiu-t'ai prefecture arrived at the rail station, armed irregular forces of the local regime refused to let them get off the train. These troops had surrounded the station. Someone calling himself head of the prefecture under the local regime announced, "We cannot hand over the prefecture before a conclusion has been reached by the Political Consultative Conference." This demonstrates that, as far as the Northeast is concerned, not only has the Political Consultative Conference become a shelter for the Eighth Route Army but other armed irregular forces can demand to exist under the shelter of the Eighth Route Army.

In his talk with Trotsynko, Vice-Chief of Staff Tung called the local regime in Chiu-t'ai a puppet organization and not an organization of the regular communist party. Major General Trotsynko retorted by arguing that this regime cannot be called a puppet organization because when the Soviet Army entered the Northeast there were no legitimate governments existing in the various places, so that in order to maintain local order, the Soviets had to allow the people to organize their own provisional governments. Vice-Chief of Staff Tung replied, "By puppet organizations we mean illegitimate organizations not recognized by our government." Major General Trotsynko again retorted saying, "The provisional organizations of the cities of Mukden, Ch'ang-ch'un, and Harbin all have obeyed the Chinese government and have been handed over without hindrance. According to Soviet interpretation, these organizations should be regarded as provisional regimes organized by the people to maintain local order following the overthrow of Manchukuo." On the basis of this situation, pending the withdrawal of Soviet troops, we must rely on Soviet assistance in taking over various local administrations. Finally, Major General Trotsynko asked to be allowed to obtain from the Soviet commander of the Kirin region a clear answer and then give us a reply concerning our taking over Chiu-t'ai.

Today, in the morning there was a meeting of the board of directors of the Chinese–Ch'ang-ch'un Railroad. Before the meeting I first consulted the Soviet vice-chairman of the board of directors about putting into the minutes, as something on which the two sides failed to agree, the question of creating the additional post of assistant vice-head of the Railroad Bureau. We first will settle all other issues. I obtained his approval. Consequently, during the meeting we passed entirely the regulations for the Railroad Bureau.

FEBRUARY 2.   Today is New Year's Day according to the lunar calendar. One after another, my colleagues came to wish me a Happy New Year. I talked separately with each of them. At 12:00 I went to the airport. At about 1:00, the plane took off. At 2:30, it arrived in Chin-chou. My superior, Tu Yü-ming, came to the airport, and we talked for about half an hour. Then the plane immediately took off, arriving in Peiping at 4:00. I went to my residence for a brief rest. Then I went to Chairman Hsiung's residence for supper. We discussed in detail the various questions and parted only at midnight.

FEBRUARY 3.   In the morning I went visiting in Liu-li-ch'ang, Pei-hai, and other places. There were very few visitors. The scene was different indeed from that of fourteen years ago. I went to the Liu Kuo Hotel in the Legation Quarter. The hotel was occupied entirely by the U.S. Army.

At noon, I invited for lunch Shih Shu-teh, special envoy of the Ministry of Communications in North China. I asked him in detail about railroad conditions in North China and about the transportation situation there. At 5, I again went to Chairman Hsiung's residence for a talk.

FEBRUARY 4.   At 8:30 A.M. my plane took off from Peiping. At 2, I arrived in Chungking. At 5 I went to President Chiang's official residence to report what had transpired during my talk with Marshal Malinovsky before leaving Ch'ang-ch'ung. The president said, "If the Soviets do not withdraw their troops, then we will not advance or discuss the issue of economic cooperation. We will shelve it and see what happens." I told the president that I fear that, in the future, rivalry between the Soviet Union and the United States will become an unalterable fact. Moreover, these two countries will compete with one another in expanding their spheres of influence. In China, the Soviets certainly will utilize the communist party to expand their influence on both sides of the Great Wall. If the Northeast becomes totally red, then North China also will become red, and in the future China will be no more than a field of contention between the United States and the Soviet Union. At present in the Northeast, by utilizing the Eighth Route Army, the Soviets can establish a local regime based on popular election, totally ignoring our central government. Therefore, I requested that the president reconsider our guideline for making a decision: that either we absolutely no longer will discuss economic cooperation with the Soviets or that we again propose a counterplan, making the greatest possible concessions. Meanwhile, we also will raise conditions, which hopefully the Soviets will implement. We will have one more discussion with the Soviets. In order to avoid suggestions that diplomatic negotiations are becoming localized, this talk should be held in Peiping or Chungking. The president said that he will consider the issue and again discuss it with me.

Wong Yung-ni, vice-president of the Executive Yuan, came for a talk. I told him about my talk with the president.

FEBRUARY 5.   At noon, Foreign Minister Wang Hsüeh-t'ing invited me for lunch. We discussed Marshal Malinovsky's remarks, as well as ways of dealing with the Soviets in the future. We decided to ask the Soviets to send to Peiping persons to enter into informal negotiations with us. We will ask Wong Yung-ni personally to take charge.

FEBRUARY 6.   Mr. Mo Liu-ts'un came to ask me about recent developments in our negotiations with the Soviets and decisions of the central government. I gave him the general picture.

For a discussion of ways to disburse army pay in the Northeast, I invited the head of the Bureau of Military Logistics of the Ministry of Military Affairs and the head of the Division of the State Treasury of the Ministry of Finance.

FEBRUARY 7.   President Chiang invited me to supper. Present were Foreign Minister Wang Hsüeh-t'ing, Wong Yung-ni, vice-president of the Executive Yuan; and Special Envoy Chiang Ching-kuo. My brother Chang Chün-mai also was invited to supper. Before and after supper we discussed the plan we will propose to the Soviets. We decided to allow the addition to the list of jointly managed enterprises of the An-shan Iron and Steel Works and the He-kang Coal Mine, as desired by the Soviets. Vice-President Wong of the Executive Yuan will formulate another counterplan. The Civil Aviation Company can be jointly managed in the same way as the China Aviation Company but must not violate the International Aviation Agreement. These will constitute our final concessions. Reason dictates that under such exceedingly urgent circumstances we should use the quickest way of beginning talks with the Soviets. Because as long as we are paying the price of adding An-shan and He-kang, we may as well notify the Soviets as early as possible with the aim of retrieving the situation, however miniscule the possibility. We should not still go through the various procedures of formulating a plan, discussing it, and submitting it for approval and instructions. In my capacity as chairman of the Economic Commission, how can I go beyond the limits of my power and deal with matters under the jurisdiction of other people? In my innermost heart there is only a burning anxiety.

The president personally told me, "Still there is no definite date for the withdrawal of Soviet troops; we temporarily will postpone sending the Fifth Division to Ch'ang-ch'un." Immediately I wired this message to Vice-Chief of Staff Tung. This indicates that suspicion and distrust between the Chinese and the Soviets are growing deeper from day to day. Because they fear being intercepted and plunged into a trap, our troops dare not advance. The Soviets dare not totally withdraw their troops from Mukden, for fear that we will take over the enterprises they wish to operate cooperatively.

FEBRUARY 8.   Today at 10:30 A.M. Chou En-lai and Tung Pi-wu came for a talk. They asked about the state of negotiations between the Chinese and the Soviets. I told them indirectly that there still exists a divergence between the Chinese and Soviet viewpoints. They said that the problem of the Northeast should be settled politically. In other words, all military problems should be settled right there in the Northeast by adding representatives of various parties to the northeastern Political Commission and by organizing within the Northeast Headquarters a small team of participants from the Chinese Communist Party as well as from the National government. Their tone was decidedly different from when we met on November 30 of last year. I presume that they made these proposals because their armed forces in the Northeast are sufficient to resist ours. Furthermore, they have the truce agreement and the Political Consultative Conference to back them up. At 5 P.M. I discussed with Wong Yung-ni, vice-president of the Executive Yuan, our plan for the greatest concessions.

At noon, Lu Tso-fu [one of the greatest industrialists of modern China and founder of the Minsheng Steamship Company] hosted a banquet for the

Canadian ambassador to China. The ambassador remarked that the Nationalist party's survival should be considered on a spiritual basis. It seemed he
was reproving the Nationalist party for the muddled political situation and
for its lack of efficient administration.

FEBRUARY 9.   Summarizing my discussion with Yung-ni yesterday and
taking into consideration opinions of the Foreign Ministry, I discussed with
Foreign Minister Wang and Vice-President Wong of the Executive Yuan the
final plan concerning economic cooperation that we will propose to the
Soviets.

In the afternoon, a representative of the Society for Political Reconstruction of the Northeast came to see me. He proposed that we first settle the
question of the Northeast by political consultation and then achieve a breakthrough with the Soviets through diplomatic channels. I told him about what
had transpired during the Sino-Soviet negotiations and made the point that
in cooperating economically we should not make excessive concessions but
take into consideration the interests of our own people.

I received from Vice-Chief of Staff Tung a report saying that yesterday
the Soviets notified us that on February 12 we can take over the prefecture of
Chiu-t'ai. As for taking over the prefecture of Nung-an, Major General
Trotsynko rejected our request, made on February 1, that he send liaison
officials to accompany our personnel there. The reason was that there were
no Soviet troops stationed in Nung-an. Yesterday, liaison officials suddenly
were sent to discuss matters with us. These officials said they were to listen
to our orders and to await assignment. So far as I can see, taking over these
one or two prefectures really is not of much consequence.

FEBRUARY 10.   At 5 P.M. President Chiang invited me for a talk. Also
present were President T.V. Soong of the Executive Yuan, Foreign Minister
Wang Hsüeh-t'ing, Vice-President Wong Yung-ni of the Executive Yuan,
and Special Envoy Chiang Ching-kuo. We discussed the plan, formulated
yesterday, to be proposed to the Soviets. However, it did not seem advisable
for Vice-President Wong of the Executive Yuan to go to Peiping to hold
discussions with the Soviets. We fear that the Soviet economic counselor will
not be able to make commitments in Peiping and still will need to return to
Ch'ang-ch'un to ask for instructions. This will cause a delay and prevent a
speedy decision. Consequently, we decided, on the one hand, to ask the
Foreign Ministry to notify the Soviet ambassador in Chungking about the
proposed plan, telling him that this constitutes our final concessions, while,
on the other hand, I will take the plan back to Ch'ang-ch'un to discuss it with
the Soviets.

The most important points in this plan are the following: We will add to the list the He-kang Coal Mine, but the Soviets must hand back to China the Fu-shun coal mines. We will add the An-shan iron and steel enterprises (including the Anshan Steel-tempering Plant, the Liao-yang Iron Mine, the An-shan Fire Brick Factory, and the Kobe Mechanism Factory of An-shan). But Chinese stock must comprise 51 percent, and the chairmen of their board of trustees and their general managers must be Chinese. Soviets can be employed to head the steel-tempering plant and the mine field [presumably the author is referring to the Liao-yang Iron Mine]. The Dairen Oil Refinery can be jointly managed but must adhere to all decrees of the Chinese government concerning gasoline. We also can permit joint management of the salt flats on the Liaotung Peninsula, as well as of civil aviation in the nine northeastern provinces, but we will raise separate conditions governing such joint management.

Mrs. Chang Hsing-fu came to see me. I told her about what had happened during the murder of her husband. Really, there were no words with which I could comfort her.

FEBRUARY 11. Simultaneously, Britain, the United States, and the Soviet Union promulgated the Yalta secret agreement. In it, (1) Outer Mongolia [a people's republic] should remain in its present condition. (2) Rights that formerly the Russian empire held in Manchuria and that in 1904 were destroyed by Japan's surprise attack should be restored to the Soviet Union. (3) Dairen should be opened as an international port. The Soviet Union should be guaranteed priority in that harbor. (4) Port Arthur will remain a naval base under rental to the Soviet Union. (5) The Chinese-Eastern Railroad, as well as the South Manchuria Railway, which leads to Dairen, should be managed jointly by a company organized by the Chinese and the Soviets. The Soviet Union should be guaranteed priority. (6) China should retain entire sovereignty over Manchuria.

Without obtaining the consent of our government, Britain, the United States, and the Soviet Union entered into this secret agreement, which has led to the signing, on August 14, 1945, of the Sino-Soviet Treaty of Friendship and Alliance. Undoubtedly, when the Chinese people as a whole read about this agreement, they will be enraged.

FEBRUARY 12. At 11 A.M. I called on T.V. Soong, president of the Executive Yuan. I asked for his opinion concerning the fixed remittance rate of one yuan of northeastern circulating currency to thirteen yuan of national currency. He said that, as for this remittance rate, we can allow remittances to take place freely in the market, at open prices. There is no need for the government to regulate them, and thus the central government can be spared this obligation. I then asked whether we can use enemy property as backing [the text uses the term *preparation*, which makes no sense; thus I have translated the term as *backing*] for issuing bank notes. He said he feared the Soviets will collect the circulating currency and then demand from us control of such property. He is unwilling to make an open commitment. He went on to say that with respect to the Soviet request for economic cooperation, he fears nothing will result from the negotiations. We might as well shelve them; continued negotiations merely will plunge us into a deeper and deeper predicament.

At twelve o'clock I called on Foreign Minister Wang Hsüeh-t'ing. He said,

> The U.S. State Department has addressed a communication to the governments of China and the Soviet Union, stating that current negotiations between China and the Soviet Union concerning economic questions must not obstruct the principles of the open door and of equal opportunity for various nations to have access to China's raw materials and markets. Furthermore, the question of Japanese reparations should be settled by the Reparations Commission. The State Department hopes that both the Chinese and the Soviets will notify the U.S. government about the state of their negotiations.

FEBRUARY 13. In the morning I called on President Sun Che-sheng [Sun Fo, the son of Sun Yat-sen] of the Legislative Yuan. I asked for his opinion concerning our negotiations with the Soviets. He said, "The Soviet government does not trust our National government. That is why they request economic cooperation. If within a year or two the Soviet Union has confidence in our government, then they very well may not make this request." Then I asked him whether we should continue the negotiations on economic cooperation, since political consultation still will take considerable time. He replied, "We may as well continue with the negotiations." He added, "Formerly, the Japanese monopolized the economy of Manchuria. Today we may just as well give to the Soviet Union a number of the enterprises there." His opinions are totally opposed to those of President T.V. Soong of the Executive Yuan.

In the afternoon Tai Li-an, head of the Division of Currency of the Finance Ministry, came to see me. He maintained that in order to implement formally the exchange rate for northeastern circulating currency, the Executive Yuan must issue an order. Furthermore, if we set up a Commission for the Control of Remittances to oversee remittances of circulating currency, that commission must not depart from the system of the Four Associated General Headquarters.

At noon I lunched at Special Envoy Chiang Ching-kuo's. In the afternoon Mo Liu-ts'un came for a visit. I exchanged with both of them opinions concerning our negotiations in the Northeast.

FEBRUARY 14.   At 11:00 A.M. I again called on President T.V. Soong of the Executive Yuan to continue our discussion about the remittance rate of northeastern circulating currency. I told him about the opinion of Division Head Tai of the Division of Currency of the Finance Ministry. Soong held firm to the opinion he expressed the day before yesterday. He said he was very apprehensive about the central government shouldering the responsibility for the northeastern currency system and so is unwilling to get the central government involved by having it announce a remittance rate. I then told him that this is merely a remittance rate and not a rate of exchange with the national currency. He still insisted that if the banks will freely allow remittance at open market prices, the Executive Yuan will not object to a remittance rate of one yuan of circulating currency to thirteen yuan of national currency. Furthermore, with respect to the question of using enemy assets in the Northeast as backing for issuing the northeastern circulating currency, I told him that since northeastern circulating currency actually will be nonconvertible, the Soviets will not be able to collect the circulating currency and then demand enemy property in the Northeast. He said he is apprehensive and therefore cannot approve my proposal. Furthermore, he said that he is very pessimistic about the negotiations in the Northeast and urged me not to go back to Ch'ang-ch'un.

At noon, I called on Foreign Minister Wang Hsüeh-t'ing. He told me,

Yesterday I received from U.S. secretary of state Byrnes a dispatch saying, "Soviet rights in the Northeast must be restricted to those stipulated in the Sino-Soviet friendship treaty. Now we hear that China and the Soviet Union have been discussing control of the economy and industry of the Northeast. The United States government cannot acknowledge such control if it violates the principle of the Open Door. If reparations are involved in the Soviet demands then this should be settled by the Far Eastern Commission. We hope the Chinese government will continually keep the U.S. government informed about what goes on in these discussions."

Today the various newspapers published a report from Washington, D.C., on the twelfth, of comments by the U.S. secretary of state in response to questions from newspaper reporters:

President Chiang has indicated that China and the Soviet Union already are negotiating about the question of disposing of Japanese property and equipment in the Northeast. The United States requests that China continually keep it informed about the state of these negotiations. By now we already have received from China one report. We hold that this question should be discussed by the Far Eastern Commission (particularly by the Reparations Commission set up within that organization).

The publication of this news will further restrain our diplomatic authorities when dealing with Soviet demands for war booty, while those maintaining that we adopt a stiff attitude toward the Soviets will receive the impression that we can resist the Soviet Union by relying on American support. This will add further to the difficulty of negotiating.

FEBRUARY 15. At noon, Foreign Minister Wang Hsüeh-t'ing hosted a luncheon. Those who came were President Sun Fo of the Legislative Yuan, former Foreign Minister Wang Liang-ch'ou, Shao Li-tzu (the Political Consultative Conference), Ch'en Pu-lei [a very important figure in the Kuomintang and one close to Chiang Kai-shek], Wong Yung-ni, and Chiang Ching-kuo. First, the host gave a report on developments in the Sino-Soviet negotiations, as well as on the dispatch from the United States. President Sun of the Legislative Yuan spoke. He said that today's situation in the Northeast is comparable to that in Iran. Even if we present our case before the United Nations, nothing will come of it. Mr. Wang Liang-ch'ou said we still should continue with the discussions. Mr. Shao Li-tzu agreed. Mr. Ch'en Pu-lei said we must not take lightly the agitated feelings of the nationalists. Finally, the host said that we will decide on a policy after he goes to Nanking for President Chiang's instructions. What Mr. Ch'en Pu-lei meant by the nationalists were largely cadres of the Nationalist party. The viewpoint of these cadres is that a dangerous step is being taken by the Political Consultative Conference by including in future governmental organizations the Chinese Communists and various other parties to share in the political and military power. In the first place, it will be impossible for the Nationalist party to cooperate with the Chinese Communists; in the second place, Chinese communist participation in the government will lead to political unrest. Today, witnessing Chinese communist ambitions in the Northeast has added further to the indignation of the Nationalists. How this will explode really is worthy of attention.

FEBRUARY 16. In the morning I called on Wu Ta-ch'uan, chief of civil officials, to tell him about opinions from various quarters concerning Sino-Soviet negotiations, which I recently have learned of, as well as the conversation yesterday at Foreign Minister Wang's luncheon. Wu remarked that we should go as far as possible in publicizing the facts while at the same time continuing these negotiations. Otherwise, prolific speculations in various circles will merely add to misunderstanding.

Today, our northeastern compatriots in Chungking held a big rally to discuss the questions of recovering the Northeast and the tragic murder of Chang Hsing-fu. A great number of people attended, and Mr. Mo Liu-ts'un was invited to give a report on the situation in the Northeast. Of course, his report provoked sadness and indignation among the audience. After the rally everyone marched to the national government to present a petition. This is the first manifestation of popular dissatisfaction over negotiations in the Northeast. At the rally it was resolved to demand that (1) our government send to the Soviets a communication demanding a precise explanation of the real story of Chang Hsing-fu's murder, (2) the Soviet government make amends for the loss caused by Chang Hsing-fu's death, (3) the Soviet government apologize for the murder of Chang Hsing-fu, (4) the Soviet government guarantee that similar incidents will not reoccur, and (5) the Soviet Union withdraw its troops in accord with the scheduled date.

Another matter arousing resentment among cadres of the Nationalist party, especially among people from the Northeast belonging to the Nationalist party, are comments made by a spokesman of the Central Committee of the Chinese Communist Party on the fourteenth concerning the general situation in the Northeast and published in the *Liberation Daily* at Yen-an. His comments include the Chinese communist positions regarding the question of the Northeast: (1) Now, at various levels the national government's organizations for taking over the Northeast are being monopolized by one party, the Nationalist party. This is not in accord with the wishes of the people of the Northeast and the entire country. Therefore, all organizations, from the Northeast Headquarters and its Political and Economic commissions to the governments of the various provinces, should be reorganized. This reorganization should include as many as possible of the democratic people in the Northeast and people who belong to various parties as well as to no parties in our country. They must take part so that all democratic elements enjoy equal and effective representation. (2) The national government should recognize as well as reorganize the Anti-Japanese Democratic Forces now in the Northeast and let them, together with troops sent by the Nationalist government, jointly maintain local order, annihilating puppet troops and bandits and preventing military clashes. (3) The national government should recognize the democratic autonomous regimes in the various prefectures of the Northeast. In places where their foundations are not considered broad enough, the national government should take steps to reorganize them through consultation or hold new elections; it should not refuse to recognize these regimes or persist in the undemocratic practice of appointment, while opposing the democratic practice of a people's election. (4) At present, China and the Soviet Union are on friendly terms, the Nationalists and Communists have signed a cease-fire, the entire nation is demanding a reduction in the number of troops as well as repatriation, and, in the Northeast, there are local troops assisting in the maintenance of order. The national government should limit to a certain number the troops it sends into the Northeast for the purpose of restoring sovereignty. This will lighten the burden of the people and contribute to peace.

FEBRUARY 17.   Today, the editorial of the *Central Daily News* refuted Chinese communist demands, printed in yesterday's *Hsin-hua Daily*, with regard to the Northeast. In general, the editorial says, (1) At the time of the Japanese surrender, Chinese communist troops did not exist in the Northeast. Today, their self-styled armed force was manufactured by them after the Japanese surrender through recruiting soldiers and assembling the masses. Consequently, the independent troops and localities in the Northeast do not fall within the scope of issues to be settled by the Political Consultative Conference or through military mediation. (2) The question of the Northeast is a question of how the Sino-Soviet friendship treaty and its various appended documents should be implemented. The aim of the treaty is to achieve a 30-year peace between China and the Soviet Union. This differs fundamentally in nature from questions for political consultation.

In the afternoon I called on Odlum, Canadian ambassador to China, to ask about his view of the question of the Northeast. He said,

> I fear that Manchuria eventually will become a second Outer Mongolia. Because of current interests, President Chiang should personally hold a discussion with the president of the United States and the prime minister of Britain so that they mutually have a precise understanding about the way Britain and the United States should deal with the Soviets and help China, in case the Soviet Union disregards what is right and grabs the Northeast. As for how China should currently deal with the Soviet Union, it must on the one hand avoid frontal clashes while, on the other, not recognize unreasonable Soviet demands. If this means letting them occupy the Northeast by force, China should do this rather than make polite concessions. The question of the Northeast can await future settlement.

I was not in a position to tell him about the real state of Sino-Soviet negotiations. Furthermore, he did not know that the Soviets really do not plan to directly occupy the Northeast by force but to let the Chinese Communists occupy it. Nevertheless, we may as well adopt his advice that President Chiang personally have a discussion with U.S. and British authorities. But, at present, political consultation is going on and there are frequent clashes between Nationalist and communist troops. How can President Chiang find the time to go abroad?

FEBRUARY 18.   At eight o'clock in the evening Foreign Minister Wang Hsüeh-t'ing came to see me, having returned to Chungking after visiting President Chiang in Nanking. He brought a handwritten letter from the president, which says,

+   *Handwritten Letter from President Chiang Kai-shek*   +

February 17, 1946

Dear Kung-ch'uan:
   Hsüeh-t'ing [Hsüeh-t'ing is the alternative name for Wang Shih-chieh. In 1945–48 he was minister of Foreign Affairs in the national government. (*Biographical Dictionary of Republican China*, vol. 3, New York, Columbia University Press, 1970, p. 395).] has arrived in Nanking so I have learned about everything in detail. Please make a final effort to put into effect plans formulated by you and others. But under no circumstances add one more word; otherwise, not only will your trip have been in vain but also from now on the other side will further assume that we still have room to make concessions, which will more than double the difficulties we have had in the past. We must be determined that this is to be the final step. This is imperative.

Chung-Cheng

Hsüeh-t'ing also said that, in the president's opinion, measures for economic cooperation can be implemented only after the Soviets complete the withdrawal of their troops and we have taken over political power. Then, with Hsüeh-t'ing, I made a study of whether, in the final analysis, the phrase "the extent of the progress of the takeover" meant all prefectures in the Northeast or merely the provincial capitals. In the current situation, a takeover of all prefectures is likely to be impossible. If we merely take over the provincial capitals, then the takeover will be nominal. I said that, as a last resort, we could take over only the central places in each province and leave the rest for a political settlement.
   The Foreign Ministry forwarded a communication from the Soviet ambassador, signed and dispatched on February 16. It says,

In accord with stipulations in the Agreement Concerning Dairen and in the Paper of Agreement with Respect to the Agreement Concerning Dairen, signed on August 14, 1945, by China and the Soviet Union, the Soviet government considers that now is the suitable time to begin negotiations leading to the signing of an agreement concerning the following questions: rental to the Soviet Union of appropriate fortifications and equipment in the harbor of Dairen and the control of Dairen harbor.

In order to carry out such negotiations, the Soviet government proposes that each side send three representatives, to begin working in Dairen in the near future.

The ambassador will appreciate greatly Your Excellency's speedy reply to the above proposal of the Soviet government.

The Hsin-hua News Agency in Peiping issued a news item saying, "In order to attack the people's armed forces in the Liaotung plains, the nationalist New Sixth Army has entered the area of Kou-pang-tzu, Ta-hu-shan, and Hsin-min in Liaoning province. This is a violation of the cease-fire agreement." Clearly, the Chinese Communists already are indicating that they are prepared to fight battles with government troops sent into the Northeast to restore China's sovereignty.

Today in the afternoon [Tillman] Durdin, correspondent to the *New York Times*, came to visit me. He inquired about the state of negotiations in the Northeast. I really found it difficult to give him an answer. I only could answer in broad, general terms.

FEBRUARY 19.   Today at 5 P.M. Foreign Minister Wang invited the Soviet ambassador to the ministry and told him,

He [Foreign Minister Wang] already has made the greatest effort. We hope the Soviets soon will withdraw their troops. As for the economic question, Chairman Chang and Special Envoy Chiang will return to Ch'ang-ch'un for one more discussion with the Soviets. However, our counterplan already contains the greatest concessions we can make.

Again, the Soviet ambassador brought up the question of war booty. He said that this comprises the nub of the question, and if we do not settle this, nothing can be resolved. He then protested the anti-Soviet demonstration that took place a few days ago. (I presume he meant that during the demonstration held by northeastern compatriots, there were anti-Soviet slogans.)

Tung Pi-wu came to see me. He resolutely maintained that to take over political power without hindrance in the Northeast, we first must reorganize the Political Commission of the Northeast Headquarters. He meant that the central government must settle politically, not through the use of armed force, the question of Chinese communist armed forces in the Northeast.

Li-fu [Ch'en Li-fu] came to see me. I asked him to tell Chairman Hsiung that the Nationalist party headquarters should begin activities in the Northeast.

Because, together with Special Envoy Chiang, I will return to Ch'ang-ch'un tomorrow morning, I packed my luggage and forwarded it to the airport. At ten o'clock in the evening I suddenly received a long-distance call from President Chiang in Nanking. He asked me temporarily to postpone the trip.

FEBRUARY 20.   I presume that President Chiang called last night, asking me to temporarily postpone my trip, because he had received a call from Foreign Minister Wang reporting on his talk with the Soviet ambassador, who indicated that first the war booty question must be settled. I also learned that Special Envoy Chiang had asked Foreign Minister Wang whether we shouldn't agree to the Soviet demands; otherwise, he feared it would be difficult to reach an agreement. I presume that Minister Wang also has informed the president about these remarks and that as a result the president has had to reconsider. Therefore, there has been this change.

In the evening I received a copy of a wire from President Chiang, forwarded to me by Foreign Minister Wang. It says,

> To Foreign Minister Wang:
> Secretary Chou already has submitted for my knowledge the various points in your two telephone calls yesterday. Kung-ch'uan [here Chang Kia-ngau is referred to with a reverential form of address that does not have an equivalent in English] and Ching-kuo temporarily should remain in Chungking until my return in two or three days, so that we personally can discuss matters. Afterward, they can return to Ch'ang-ch'un. I urge you to please respectively notify them of this. Chung-cheng

Personally, I feel that although legally and rationally war booty is a necessity for the Soviets, already we have promised to replace it with a compensatory sum. Therefore, the discrepancy exists merely in words; in actual practice there is no difference. What really matters is the expansion of Chinese communist forces in the Northeast. Already, during the past month Chinese communist armed forces have acquired a foundation. Even if we can negotiate an agreement with the Soviets, we will have to resort to armed force to take over areas outside the various major cities. It follows from this that, although we have made great concessions to the Soviets, we still are unable to take over most areas. People in the Northeast and the so-called nationalists certainly will begin attacking us. Not only will they revile those in charge of the negotiations, but it certainly will be difficult to carry out the negotiations and reach an agreement. This is because a month ago, the northeastern question involved negotiating only with the Soviets, while today, military and political questions concerning the Chinese Communists have become part of the picture. Already, there has been created a situation which there is no way of settling.

FEBRUARY 21. Today I received a report saying that academic circles in Chungking are currently preparing to stage a big demonstration to protest the question of the Northeast.

Today Vice-Chief of Staff Tung talked with the Soviet chief of staff, demanding that the Soviets speedily hand over to our authorities the corpses of the tragically murdered Chang Hsing-fu, as well as the seven others, and speedily arrest the criminals and all offenders involved. Major General Trotsynko noted that since January 16 there have occurred in Mukden and Harbin as many as six incidents in which officers or soldiers of the Soviet Army were killed. I presume that these incidents were created by those opposed to the central government in order to alienate Chinese from Soviets.

FEBRUARY 22. From early morning today students from various middle schools and universities in Sha-p'ing-pa, numbering over thirty thousand, staged a big demonstration. Their slogans were (1) all Soviet troops withdraw from the Northeast, (2) China's territory must not be partitioned and China's sovereignty not impaired, (3) the Soviets must hand back looted material, (4) in the face of alien power, the entire nation must unanimously unite, (5) the Soviets must adhere strictly to the Sino-Soviet treaty, (6) the central government must eradicate all illegitimate local regimes, (7) the central government must eradicate all puppet governments, (8) we absolutely support our government in taking over the Northeast, (9) we request that our government thoroughly investigate the responsibility for the tragic case of Chang Hsing-fu, (10) we support our government adopting a stiff attitude toward the Soviets, (11) the Chinese Communists must love and cherish their fatherland, and (12) we support President Chiang's leadership in peacefully reconstructing our country and saving our compatriots in the Northeast. The demonstration was rather orderly. Moreover, the demonstrators were prevented from going to the Soviet embassy, the Foreign Ministry, or the national government. Fortunately no big incident occurred. However, the demonstrators held up various kinds of caricatures, including one depicting Stalin being stabbed by a knife. The same day, the site of the *Hsin-hua Daily* newspaper was demolished.

In the afternoon Mr. Mo Liu-ts'un came to visit. He remarked that he was deeply worried that today's demonstration might affect diplomatic relations between China and the Soviet Union, as well as recovery of the Northeast. In his opinion, it is necessary that President Chiang decide soon on an overall plan and as speedily as possible continue negotiations with the Soviets. Mo said the Soviet government always has stressed the practical; if there are prospects for a settlement on a practical level, perhaps we can retrieve an unfavorable situation.

FEBRUARY 23.   Special Envoy Chiang Ching-kuo came to visit and remarked that last night, following the big demonstration by students yesterday, no one from the Soviet side attended a banquet held by the Sino-Soviet Cultural Society to commemorate Red Army Day. He anticipates that the Soviet government certainly will make a gesture. The least may be a protest and the most, a mutual severance of diplomatic relations and recall of ambassadors. Both are possible. Our government soon must indicate that the student demonstration does not have anything to do with our government's attitude. I replied that since the question of the Northeast has developed in this way, it is necessary for President Chiang to state explicitly the attitude of our government and for the Foreign Ministry to make a gesture of sincerity so that relations between the two countries may take a slight turn for the better. Under present circumstances it will be absolutely futile for the two of us to return to Ch'ang-ch'un. He agreed.

Mr. Li You-ch'un of the Youth party came to visit. He said,

> From the vantage point of the Nationalist party's anticommunist strategy, yesterday's demonstration fulfilled a function. In terms of national strategy, it was unwise. Furthermore, it has placed President Chiang in a very difficult position. He [Li] also learned that certain people in the Nationalist party even are saying that if the problem of the Northeast can be exacerbated, it might provoke war between the United States and the Soviet Union, which perhaps will benefit China. This is even more absurd. [The last sentence in the quote may be a statement by Chang Kia-ngau.]

At twelve o'clock I went to the Soviet embassy to extend congratulations on Red Army Day. A great many people were there to extend congratulations.

At 6 P.M., accompanied by Mrs. Sun Yueh-chi, Mrs. Chang Hsing-fu came to say that she hopes she soon can have the remains of her husband. I told her that I already have received a wire from Vice-Chief of Staff Tung that he is actively negotiating with the Soviets about this matter.

FEBRUARY 24.   I received from Ch'ang-ch'un a report concerning the reception given in Ch'ang-ch'un yesterday by the Soviet Army general headquarters to commemorate Red Army Day. Thirty officials from our side were invited to attend. During the banquet Marshal Malinovsky made a speech. Generally, he said,

China and the Soviet Union really have a relationship forged by adversity. Their friendship was formed on the basis of blood shed in common. The two countries must not be swayed by the efforts of a third nation to provoke an estrangement between them. Right now, there is stretched between China and the Soviet Union the hand of a third party who wears suede gloves and has gold dollars in his pocket. Indeed, we must get rid of him by chopping off his hand. The Soviet Union will only cooperate with China and not with any third nation. The temperament of the Soviet people is true and pure, and they will maintain friendship even at the expense of shedding fresh blood. Recently, a certain party has created public opinion that accuses the Soviet Union of red imperialism and of plundering material from Manchuria. My economic counselor will reply concerning this matter.

Then Economic Counselor Sladkovsky made a speech. He said,

The Red Army is the oldest son of the Soviet Union. The Soviet Union expects the most of its oldest son and cherishes his achievements the most. It is all because of the blood shed by the Red Army that Manchuria has been liberated, and it is only because of this that there is an opportunity for China and the Soviet Union to enter into intimate economic cooperation. The Soviet Union never has raised demands detrimental to the interests of the sovereignty of the Chinese people. The Soviets only demand economic cooperation on an equal basis. Their aim is not money but national defense.

Major General Tevuchenkov, a member of the Soviet military commission, stood up and said, "The Red Army stationed in Manchuria is the vanguard defending Soviet territory. We will not allow encroachment from any direction." After the banquet, as we watched a play, Marshal Malinovsky, already half-drunk, again addressed Vice-Chief of Staff Tung, saying,

Other countries have assisted you, China, for the sake of their own interests, while we, the Soviets, assist China merely out of a genuine sense of righteousness. The leaders of your country are not clear in their thinking, and this also is your mistake. If other countries should try to rupture our friendly relations and encroach on our interests, together we should rise in resistance and teach them a lesson.

From the aforementioned speeches of various Soviet people, we can discern a general picture of the moods in their breasts: indignation at the frustration of their wish for economic cooperation, as well as suspicion of and jealousy toward the United States.

This morning Tung Pi-wu and Wang Jo-fei came to visit me. They asked whether, in the final analysis, the crux of the northeastern question lies in politics or economics. Tung thinks that we only need a democratic political situation and then the Soviets will give in, while Wang weighed over and over again various possibilities. I told them that the focal point was economics. If we do not settle this point, the Soviet Army still may not withdraw immediately. I also told them that before we can discuss political problems within our country, first all we must achieve internal unity in the face of alien power so that Soviet troops will withdraw and so that the central government definitely will not object to a political settlement. But in Tung and Wang's opinion, the Communists have already raised four big demands. If the Soviets do not withdraw their troops, then the communist armed forces will always be under the wing of the Soviets and unable to attain an independent status. As a result, Tung and Wang are very anxious to know the Soviet attitude. From this I gathered that the Soviets still have not indicated to the Chinese Communists the extent to which, in the final analysis, the Chinese Communists can have influence in the Northeast and the area they can occupy there.

FEBRUARY 25.   Today, at the weekly memorial service at the national government, President Chiang, having returned to Chungking from Nanking, stated explicitly our attitude toward the Soviets. His main points were the following: (1) He hopes the people of the entire country will believe in the government and that it certainly will reach a reasonable settlement concerning the question of the Northeast. They must not be misled by groundless speculations circulating outside the government and indulge in overly agitated speeches or activities. During the current Sino-Soviet discussions concerning economic cooperation, the government has instructed the Northeast Headquarters to adhere to the following principles: (a) the Soviets must conform with the laws and decrees of our country, (b) the Soviets must honor the Sino-Soviet Treaty of Friendship and Alliance, and (c) the Soviets must not abrogate general international agreements our country has signed with other countries. (2) Everyone must know that friendship between China and the Soviet Union is necessary not only to both China and the Soviet Union but also to peace and cooperation in the world.

Today's *Liberation Daily* printed an editorial published by the Chinese Communist Party entitled "The Chungking Incident and the Question of the Northeast."

After the weekly memorial service, President Chiang invited me to talk with him in a separate room. He asked me how people responded to the various points he had announced. I replied that conditions were good and secure. He then said that in his speech he mentioned that we will move Sino-Soviet negotiations to the central government to be dealt with. I told him that we can do this, but that, in order to avoid hurting the feelings of Soviet officials in Ch'ang-ch'un, we need not openly announce it. After I left him, I found that President Chiang had invited Mr. Ch'en Li-fu for a talk, during which President Chiang severely reprimanded him for arranging the student demonstration.

Today, together with Special Envoy Chiang Ching-kuo, I sent a wire to Vice-Chief of Staff Tung:

> Today, following his return to Chungking, His Excellency the president expressed the view that owing to various recent developments, it seems the two governments first should exchange opinions candidly before we return to Ch'ang-ch'un. Therefore, our date of departure has been postponed. Please convey this to Shu-jen, Chün-mai, Chieh-chen, Cho-an, and the various provincial governors.

Today the *Liberation Daily* in Yen-an published a lengthy editorial expressing opinions concerning the question of the Northeast and the student demonstration.

FEBRUARY 26.   In the morning I called on Foreign Minister Wang to present two points: (1) The government must send personnel to investigate thoroughly, with Soviet representatives, the case of Chang Hsing-fu. Otherwise, we will be reproved by public opinion. (2) On February 19, while meeting with the Soviet ambassador, Wang mentioned that I and Special Envoy Chiang in a few days would return to Ch'ang-ch'un. Because it has been decided that we postpone our trip and since President Chiang thinks that we should have Sino-Soviet negotiations handled by the central government, should I explain this situation to the Soviet ambassador or wire Ch'ang-ch'un to ask the Soviets to send their personnel to Chungking? Foreign Minister Wang thinks that, concerning my second point, we should ask for instructions from the president. Together we called on the president. The president's opinion was that temporarily we will not discuss the issue with the Soviets but see what the Soviet ambassador's attitude is when he comes to the ministry today and then decide on the next step. (The Soviet ambassador will come to the ministry some time in the afternoon.) Subsequently, I proposed to Ching-kuo that we not immediately return to Ch'ang-ch'un, and we decided to remain here.

At 6 P.M. Minister Wang Hsüeh-t'ing phoned to say that already he had seen the Soviet ambassador and also had received from him a personally delivered written protest. The contents are the following: (1) The big student demonstration was an organized activity. Moreover, they insulted the highest leader of the Soviets. The Chinese government must be held responsible.

(2) With respect to delays in the withdrawal of Soviet troops, the Soviets are not to blame; instead, there are various technical causes. (3) Chang Hsing-fu was killed by a mob.

FEBRUARY 27.   At 10 A.M. the Society of Engineers held a memorial service for Chang Hsing-fu. I went to mourn, as well as to give an account of what took place during the disaster.

Moscow has broadcast a defense by Trotsynko, chief of staff of the Soviet Army in Ch'ang-ch'un, concerning the delay in the withdrawal of Soviet troops. It includes this remark: "The withdrawal of Soviet troops from Manchuria will be completed whenever the U.S. Army withdraws from China. In any case, it will not be later than that date."

Furthermore, Vice-Chief of Staff Tung forwarded a wire to me from the TASS Agency, dated February 22 from Ch'ang-ch'un, which raved wildly about reactionary elements in China and enumerated a series of criminal activities in the Northeast.

Today, Vice-Chief of Staff Tung wrote a formal letter to the Soviet chief of staff pressing for an answer concerning the Chang Hsing-fu case:

> Now, in accord with my government's instructions, I wish to bring up the various following points:
>
> 1. That, within the shortest period, you must hand over to the authorities of our country, irrespective of their condition, the corpses of Chang Hsing-fu and the seven other tragically murdered men. The best course of action would be for your side to escort our personnel, dispatched by the mayor of Mukden and carrying coffins, to the place where these men were killed and where their corpses are. Our personnel will put the deceased into the coffins and transport them to Mukden.
> 2. That you adopt speedy and effective methods to continue investigating clearly the circumstances of the killing, as well as all matters pertinent to this case. You must arrest the criminals and all suspects involved. You must constantly send to our military delegation all data obtained from investigation of this case, so that I can transmit it to my government, which needs to know how the case is proceeding.

Today the Foreign Ministry sent a reply to the Soviet ambassador's communication of February 16, which had proposed that each side appoint three representatives to discuss the following issues: the renting to the Soviets of appropriate fortresses and equipment in Dairen harbor and the management of Dairen harbor. The Foreign Ministry replied, "The Chinese government already has asked Shen Yi, mayor of Dairen, to discuss and settle these matters with the Soviets when he takes over administration of the city."

FEBRUARY 28.   With respect to the case of Chang Hsing-fu, the Soviet chief of staff replied to Vice-Chief of Staff Tung's letter of yesterday. [The following is the letter written by Tung Yen-p'ing.]

To Chairman Chang Kung-ch'uan, Special Envoy Chiang Ching-kuo, Minister Hsü of the Ministry of Military Orders, and Minister Wang of Foreign Affairs: On *yi-kan-wei* [date], the broadcasting station of Ch'ang-ch'un reported a piece of news. The original text runs as follows:

Ch'ang-chun, wire of February 22, TASS Agency.
During the past few months, remnants of Japanese troops and puppet troops remaining in the Northeast have become very active. In the first few months after Japan's defeat only small groups of remnants of the Kwantung Army were active in the Northeast, defeated but unwilling to surrender. Frequently, these troops attacked Soviet troops, while at the same time disturbing and harming local inhabitants. At that time, the greater part of pro-Japanese elements went into hiding, biding time in order to engage in activities antagonistic to the Soviet Union. Since November of last year, these remnants of the Japanese invaders have become more active, and, moreover, their activities are larger in scale and better organized. They have carried out a propaganda campaign against the Soviet Union and summoned armed forces to attack Soviet troops, as well as individual soldiers of the Soviet Army. Later, it became evident that these remnants of Japanese troops in the Northeast, along with their running dogs, were receiving assistance and leadership from reactionary elements in China Proper. These reactionary elements dispatched their representatives directly into the Northeast to launch activities antagonistic to the Soviet Union. These reactionary elements engaged in anti-Soviet activities, along with defeated troops of the Kwantung Army and defeated Manchurian puppet troops. Circulars scattered in certain cities in the Northeast by the aforementioned bandit groups revealed they had summoned their armed forces to annihilate Soviet Army personnel as well as Chinese who cooperated with the Red Army. Beginning in the latter half of the month of November 1945, in many cities in the Northeast, Fengtien, Chia-mu-ssu, Lin-k'ou, etc., there occurred incidents in which Soviet troops and individual personnel of the Soviet Army were attacked. Moreover, many men of the Soviet Army were killed. In mid-January of this year around Sui-hua, a contingent of armed bandits, riding in a car, attacked troops of the Soviet Army. In February, in the city of Harbin, there were also several incidents in which bandits attacked Soviet Army personnel. These attacks resulted in the deaths of several Soviet officers and soldiers. The murder by bandits of engineer Chang Hsing-fu (Chinese) in early January of this year, while he and his retinue were

returning to Mukden from Fu-shun, apparently was aimed at creating a kind of provocation. Reactionary newspapers in China then made use of this provocation to carry on their anti-Soviet movement, while, on the basis of rumors circulated by these reactionary publications, the Chinese government also blamed the Red Army command for the murder of engineer Chang Hsing-fu and his retinue. To begin with, the bandit units are composed of Japanese and former Manchurian puppet officers and soldiers. Many bandits caught by the Soviet Army declared themselves to be members of the Nationalist party, saying they had joined the Nationalist party in the autumn of 1945. Those caught also declared that they had created these units for the purpose of waging a struggle against the Chinese Democratic Organization. Furthermore, they declared they were under orders from conspiratorial central leadership to disseminate anti-Soviet propaganda and organize attacks on Soviet troops and individual Soviet Army personnel. They also declared that this central leadership is expressly directing these criminal activities. Progressive elements in the Northeast are sincerely willing to consolidate the friendly relations between China and the Soviet Union and bitterly loathe the criminal activities of reactionary elements in China who carry on such activities in concert with remnants of Japanese troops.

And so forth. Respectfully, I submit this information.
Tung Yen-p'ing. *Ch'ou-kan-wu* [date]. Seal.

[The following is the Soviet chief of staff's letter, which was interrupted by the letter from Tung Yen-p'ing.]:

Concerning burial of the corpse of Chang Hsing-fu, now in Fu-shun, we will deliver the body to the mayor of Mukden through the Soviet regional commander of Mukden. But we were unable to find the corpses of those accompanying Chang Hsing-fu; the bandits burned all of them on the spot. I already have notified Your Excellency concerning this matter. Meanwhile, I wish respectfully to notify Your Excellency of the following: the Soviet Army command has taken measures to discover and arrest the criminals who killed Chang Hsing-fu and those with him, until now without success. We have not apprehended a single one of the bandits involved in this case. An examination of several Chinese, who some days ago were arrested because of this incident, resulted in their being found innocent of killing Chang Hsing-fu or his party. Now, all of them have been released. Already I have issued to the regional commander of Mukden the order to hand over the corpses.

Today I sent to my colleagues in Ch'ang-ch'un a wire, giving them detailed reasons why I have been so slow in returning to Ch'ang-ch'un:

To Yen-p'ing and Shu-jen and to be forwarded to Ching-yü and Chün-mai:

My present stay in Chungking is being prolonged for the following reasons: First, President Soong of the Executive Yuan was not in Chungking. Then, I decided to return to Ch'ang-ch'un around the fourteenth. But it happened that the president [Chiang Kai-shek] was going on an inspection tour. Before he left, he asked me not to leave until he returned. Subsequently, the U.S. State Department published various speeches that I feared would add further to the difficulty of negotiations with the Soviets. As a result, Foreign Minister Wang went to Nanking to ask for instructions. After he returned, I decided to go back north on the twentieth. Suddenly, students in Chungking staged a demonstration. It included provocative statements that also affected the negotiations in Ch'ang-ch'un. Because of this the president wired, asking me to postpone my departure. After returning to Chungking a few days ago, His Excellency the president made a speech, generally stating that we must enhance Sino-Soviet friendship and resolve the negotiations in the Northeast. With regard to the negotiations in Ch'ang-ch'un, he said they were carried out in accord with three big principles already stipulated by the central government: (1) that the Soviets must give full consideration to Chinese law, (2) that the Soviets must adhere to the spirit of the Sino-Soviet friendship agreement, and (3) that the Soviets must not violate international agreements. This somewhat mollified public opinion. However, yesterday the Soviet ambassador delivered to the Foreign Ministry a written protest having the following contents:

1. The students' demonstration was an organized activity. Moreover, they insulted the supreme leader of the Soviet Union. The Chinese government must take the responsibility.

2. The reason for the delay in withdrawing Soviet troops does not lie with the Soviet Union. Instead, it is the result of technical reasons.

3. Chang Hsing-fu was murdered by a mob.

His Excellency the president feels that it would be best to wait until Soviet misunderstandings somewhat dissipate before I return to Ch'ang-ch'un. Furthermore, since the Second Congress of the Nationalist party Central Committee soon will convene, the president asked me to return to Ch'ang-ch'un after the Congress. To sum up, during these twenty days there have occurred unfortunate incidents, one after another. First, there was the promulgation of the secret Yalta Agreement and the murder of Chang Hsing-fu. These were followed by the speech of the U.S. secretary of state and the Chinese Communist Party's four big demands concerning the Northeast. These culminated in the explosive student demonstration, creating the present situation. Fearing that my colleagues in Ch'ang-ch'un may feel uneasy, I have written this account. Please comfort them for me. Pray and constantly wire me concerning your worthy opinions.

I also sent to Chief Secretary Chang Ta-t'ung a wire:

Just now I sent a wire recounting in detail the reasons for my slow return. If my two secretaries, Keng Chieh-chih [apparently an alternative name for Keng K'uang] and Mi Hsin-min, see Counselor Sladkovsky, they may as well transmit to him the gist of my wire. In this way Sladkovsky will know that, in spite of my painful efforts, there have arisen complications beyond anyone's expectations. Keng and Mi can observe Sladkovsky's reactions. Then, with respect to the request of members of the Commission for the Formulation of Regulations for the Chinese–Ch'ang-ch'un Railroad that they hold their meetings in Chungking, this can be done.

In Chungking

Chang Kia-ngau remains in Chungking in March and April and communicates by telegram with his aide General Tung and the Northeast Commission's chairman, Hsiung Shih-hui. On March 1 the Second Congress of the Kuomintang (KMT) party's Central Committee commences. Chang Kia-ngau worries that the recent Republic of China (ROC) government's negotiations with the Soviet Union to recover Manchuria might be disrupted by KMT members publicly criticizing the ROC government and the Soviet Union. On March 2 Chang learns that Sladkovsky is expecting Chang to return early to Ch'ang-ch'un to resume negotiations on Sino-Soviet economic cooperation.

On March 5 Foreign Minister Wang reports to the Second KMT Congress on progress toward recovering Manchuria from the control of the Soviet Union. Wang tells the congress that the Soviets have several times broken their promises to withdraw from Manchuria and that the deadline for their most recent withdrawal has already passed. Wang reports that Soviet officials cite technical reasons for their inability to withdraw on time. Wang mentions that both sides have not agreed on the war booty issue and that the ROC government has demanded that all former Japanese assets in Manchuria be returned to China, whereas the Soviets still claim those assets as their rightful war booty. Wang's speech prompts many KMT members to demand that the Sino-Soviet treaty be revised immediately. The next day more KMT members react to the Wang report by demanding that the central government toughen its negotiations with the Soviet Union.

On March 6 Chang Kia-ngau learns that more Nationalist troops have arrived in Mukden and that as soon as all Soviet troops are out of that city those troops will take up its defense. But Chang also learns from a Ch'ang-ch'un newspaper that the Chinese Communists have just established their provincial government of Heilungkiang in northern Manchuria. Chang inter-prets this new development as one facilitated by Soviet troops and feels that after all Soviet troops have withdrawn from Manchuria, this new provincial government will then merge with the communist Eighth Route Army.

On March 7 Secretary of State James F. Byrnes issues a report on Soviet and Chinese economic cooperation. Byrnes states that the issue of war booty has stymied negotiations and prevented an agreement from being reached. Byrnes also admits that the United States has been concerned about any possible cooperation agreement between China and the Soviet Union, fear-ing that such an agreement would violate the principle of the Open Door for Americans who might want to develop industry in China's Northeast.

Chang Kia-ngau wires Hsiung Shih-hui in Chin-chou and asks him to closely observe the Soviet troops' activities and determine whether they will withdraw by the end of March. On March 10 Tung wires Chang Kia-ngau that Soviet troops are moving northward to Ch'ang-ch'un. On the next day Chang learns that Li Chao-lin, a Soviet supporter in Harbin, has been murdered. Li Chao-lin, who fought the Japanese after their troops had seized control of Manchuria and then escaped to the Soviet Union, re-entered Manchuria with Soviet troops in August 1945. Chang fears that the Soviet officials will blame the Nationalists for Li's murder.

Meanwhile, the KMT Second Congress continues to discuss the Manchu-rian problem, and criticisms increase about Chairman Hsiung's Northeast Commission. Many members strongly condemn Hsiung's personal behavior and urge the central government to disband Hsiung's commission.

Chang Kia-ngau is told by his secretary in Ch'ang-ch'un of Sladkovsky's reaction to Chang's previous message. Sladkovsky states that the Nationalist takeover of Mukden from Soviet troops went smoothly and that he now hopes that economic negotiations with Chang Kia-ngau can be soon finalized in Ch'ang-ch'un. But he emphasizes that economic negotiations must now be linked to negotiations of the Nationalist political takeover of Manchuria. Sladkovsky hopes that the Nationalist government will soon send officials to Ch'ang-chun to begin these negotiations.

On March 15 Chang Kia-ngau learns from sources in Manchuria that some twenty thousand troops are very near Harbin and might soon enter that city. Chang is asked to relay this information to President Chiang Kai-shek and to urge the ROC government to airlift troops to Harbin if the Soviets will permit it. Meanwhile, armed clashes between Nationalist and communist troops are already breaking out in various parts of Manchuria.

On March 16 Tung informs Chang Kia-ngau that Soviet troops have withdrawn from Ssu-p'ing and that ROC government troops should be rushed there as soon as possible. The next day Tung reports that bandits have taken over the airport at Ssu-p'ing and that the Nung-an county seat has fallen into enemy hands. Communications with Ssu-p'ing also have been cut.

On March 19 Chang Kia-ngau learns of an exchange between Tung and Major General Trotsynko. The Soviet general blames the Chinese for not sending troops northward much sooner to protect the Ch'ang-ch'un railway so that Soviet troops could speed up their withdrawal. Tung replies that the Soviets have never assisted the Nationalist troops' advance north of Mukden. The Nationalist government's Ministry of Foreign Affairs urges both Hsiung and Tung to negotiate with Soviet officials to help Chinese troops reach Ch'ang-ch'un as soon as possible.

To deal with this urgent military problem, President Chiang and Minister Wang ask Chang Kia-ngau to discuss with Sladkovsky whether the Soviets will confer with the Chinese before withdrawing their troops and will help transport Chinese troops to Ch'ang-ch'un. Chang immediately informs Tung and learns that Soviet officials have again complained of incidents in which Soviet citizens are being terrorized and of Chinese local authorities not protecting Soviet citizens in Manchuria. Chang Kia-ngau passes this new information to President Chiang. Chang Kia-ngau interprets these new Soviet activities as helping the armed irregular forces resist the Nationalist takeover of Manchuria and being unwilling to offer the Nationalists any assistance.

Discussions between Chinese and Soviet officials continue in Manchuria as to when Soviet troops will be withdrawn. But the Soviet officials complain that the Ch'ang-ch'un Railroad must first be made secure by Chinese troops and that Soviet citizens must be protected by local Chinese officials. Chinese officials respond that the Soviets are not assisting Chinese troop movements from Mukden to Ch'ang-ch'un and that they never inform the Chinese in advance of their departure plans. It appears that the railway and the communications system between Mukden and Ch'ang-ch'un have been disrupted and must be repaired before any Chinese troops can reach Ch'ang-ch'un.

On March 24 Chang Kia-ngau is informed by Tung that Sladkovsky still hopes Chang will return to Ch'ang-ch'un and that if such is not the case, Sladkovsky will be compelled to return to Moscow. Chiang Ching-kuo and Chang Kia-ngau discuss returning to Ch'ang-ch'un and decide to go only if the ROC and the Soviet Union can agree to continue discussions in Chungking. President Chiang Kai-shek is willing to continue these negotiations, but he first wants to notify the United States and observe Washington's reactions.

By March 26 the Soviets still have not begun withdrawing from Ch'ang-

ch'un, although Nationalist officials there learn that Soviet troops intend to complete their withdrawal from Manchuria by April 30. Soviet officials say that in areas north of Ch'ang-ch'un they will be forced to transfer areas under their control to the armed forces there. Chang Kia-ngau interprets this to mean that the Soviet Union hopes to retain a sphere of influence in northern Manchuria even if China and the Soviet Union cannot reach any agreement in their economic negotiations.

On March 27 Foreign Minister Wang summons Chang Kia-ngau. The Soviet ambassador then arrives to inform them that the Soviet Union is unwilling to give up those enterprises that it believes it deserves to control. Petrov lists the enterprises in Manchuria that both sides have agreed to jointly manage and then proposes that these be organized under a Sino-Soviet joint stock company, with the chairman designated from the Chinese representatives and the vice-chairman, from the Soviet representatives. The period for this arrangement would last 30 years, at which time these enterprises would revert to the Chinese government without compensation. Wang requests that Petrov ask his government to assist the Nationalist troops in reaching various cities in northern Manchuria.

Now Chang Kia-ngau fears that, even if Chungking agrees to these new economic cooperation terms with the Soviet Union, Nationalist troops still will not be able to replace the Soviet troops in northern Manchuria and that the ROC will have to compromise and form a "united government" with communist forces already there. Meanwhile, four truce mediation teams are to go to Manchuria to mediate the conflict already raging between the Communists and the Nationalists.

Chang Kia-ngau learns from the Foreign Ministry that the Soviets will pull out of Manchuria by the end of April. On March 30 Chang Kia-ngau confers with Chou En-lai and listens to Chou's interpretation of the Manchuria problem. Chou claims that Nationalist troops attacked communist troops and that truce teams have failed to reach an agreement. Chou urges the Nationalists and the Communists to reach an agreement and reorganize the Northeastern Political Committee rules so that both sides' troops can remain where they are in Manchuria. Chang Kia-ngau replies that the ROC government must first take over political power in Manchuria before considering any political consultation between the two sides.

On March 31 Tung wires Chang that Nationalist troops are encountering numerous obstacles in recovering the areas the Soviet troops have just evacuated: communist troops are attacking Nationalist trains; the Soviets have widened the railroad line gauge; Soviet troops often demand that Nationalist troops halt, using the pretext of inspecting troops for plague; and so forth. Chang Kia-ngau now worries whether the Nationalist troops can effectively replace the Soviet troops and establish adequate military defenses. He

*fears that the Soviet Union has successfully blocked Nationalist military
efforts to take over Manchuria while allowing the communist forces to enter
Manchuria and establish their networks of power and control.*

+ + + + + + +

MARCH 1.   At 9 A.M. the Second Congress of the Nationalist party Central
Committee convened. Therefore, from Sino-Soviet entanglement, America's
mouthing of empty words based on righteousness, unreasonable demands
raised by the Chinese Communists, and the anti-Soviet, anticommunist
stance of the nationalists, the question of the Northeast now will become a
political struggle within the party. This amply demonstrates that diplomacy on
the part of a weak nation invariably will lead to political upheavals within that
nation. On the other hand, positive assertions by a friendly nation that it will
act in accord with what is right not only cannot help solve the problem but will
intensify the dilemma of the weak nation. The situation in the Northeast is
becoming even darker.

MARCH 2.   In the morning, at the congress there was a report on party
affairs. In the afternoon, there was a critical examination of how party affairs
were conducted.
    I received from my secretary, Keng Chieh-chih, a wire:

Just now I saw Counselor Sladkovsky. I took the opportunity to tell him that
Your Excellency intends to return to Ch'ang-ch'un after you finish your
tasks at the congress. He remarked that Your Excellency has been away
from Ch'ang-ch'un for a long time and that since there is on the Chinese
side no one to take charge, all negotiations have come to a standstill. The
People's Congress of the Soviet Union has endowed Marshal Malinovsky
and Sladkovsky with full power to take charge of dealing with economic
negotiations. Soviet specialists already are here in full force. Therefore,
Sladkovsky is totally ignorant concerning newspaper reports about the negotiations being conducted separately at another place. Sladkovsky added that
after all, this matter must be settled. Furthermore, the time already has
arrived when it must be settled speedily. And so forth. I observed from his
attitude that he is not prejudiced against Your Excellency as a person. But,
concerning the negotiations, he did not reveal any intention at all of making
concessions. He went on to say that already the Soviets have sent many
additional persons to protect various industries and mines in the Northeast.
As for the Feng-man Hydroelectric Power Plant, last year the Japanese
plotted to destroy the dam during the seasonal thaw by sinking large quanti-
ties of wood in the river next to the dam. Now, with the seasonal thaw about
to arrive, the Soviets have discovered this and are in the process of trying to

remove the wood from the water. Finally, he brought up the students' demonstration. He indicated that this was an act organized by our government. His reasons are (1) the event took place in our wartime capital and (2) the students merely demanded that Soviet troops withdraw but made no mention of the United States Army.

MARCH 3.   I prepared a manuscript for a report I will make at the Second Congress of the party Central Committee.

MARCH 4.   I attended the weekly memorial service. President Chiang delivered a speech. Its gist was that in the party there are people reproving the government for being too dependent on foreigners and retrogressing to the behavior of several decades ago. They reprove our party for insincerely catering to various other parties and factions. This means that the strength of the party itself will be demolished by external forces. The President said that this kind of a viewpoint does not fit in with current trends. These people do not know that if we want our party to increase its own strength, we must make concessions to various other parties and factions. Furthermore, international cooperation has already become a worldwide trend, and it would be difficult for China to go against this trend. Finally, President Chiang held that we should adhere to the Five-Power Constitution.

At noon, Kuo T'ai-chi, Chinese ambassador to Britain, and Fu Ping-ch'ang, Chinese ambassador to the Soviet Union, came to my residence for lunch. Ambassador Fu remarked that the point mentioned in the agreement formulated by the three foreign ministers, to the effect that the Soviet Union withdraw its troops from the Northeast, was made solely for catering to the American people. From this I see that the United States and the Soviet Union really are not at all agreed in their opinions concerning the question of China. Furthermore, what the Americans fear most is being plunged into a war because of the China question.

MARCH 5.   In the morning, the congress critically examined the financial and economic report, with reproofs from all. Especially forceful were attacks on the Ministry of Economics. In the afternoon, Foreign Minister Wang reported on diplomacy. Concerning the question of the Northeast, he said:

> Originally, it was decided that Soviet troops would withdraw before December 3 of last year. This was three months after the date of Japan's surrender and in accord with the deadline, stipulated in the Sino-Soviet agreement for the withdrawal of Soviet troops. Later on our takeover suffered setbacks because China and the Soviet Union failed to reach an agreement concern-

ing the question of our landing troops at Dairen, while our takeover personnel were threatened by armed irregular forces at Ch'ang-ch'un, Mukden,
and other places. After twice-held discussions, China and the Soviet Union
decided on February 1 of this year as the date on which the Soviets would
complete the withdrawal of troops from the Northeast. Now the deadline is
past. Soviet troops still have not withdrawn. The Soviets have indicated that
technical difficulties have delayed the withdrawal of Soviet troops. Right
now, our government is continuing to press for an answer from the Soviets.
In January of this year, the Soviet government issued a statement to our
government saying that Japanese enterprises that had served the Kwantung
Army in the northeastern provinces should be regarded as war booty of the
Soviet Army. We, on the other hand, maintain that Japanese public and
private property in China all should be regarded as part of Japanese reparations to China. As a result, right up to the present, the Chinese and the
Soviets have not reached an accord on viewpoints concerning this question.
However, to begin with, in the agreement there was no condition attached
to the withdrawal of Soviet troops. Consequently, this dispute should not
constitute a reason for delaying the withdrawal of Soviet troops. Just as the
generalissimo of our party has stated, a friendly relationship between China
and the Soviet Union not only is necessary for our two countries but actually
is a prerequisite for the peace and security of the world. I deeply hope that
both sides, inspired by the spirit of friendship, will settle the question of
Soviet troops withdrawing.

At the end of Wang's report, many stood up to demand an answer or to
reprove him. There even were people who contended that the Sino-Soviet
agreement be revised.

Today's newspapers reported that, together with Chang Chih-chung,
Chou En-lai, and three members of the Executive Headquarters for military
mediation in Peiping, General Marshall went to Yen-an. Marshall indicated
that he desires to help China achieve a peaceful repatriation, and this is the
orientation of his efforts. Chang Chih-chung indicated that our government
has pledged to thoroughly implement the various agreements that it recently
signed. Mao Tse-Tung indicated that certainly the Chinese Communist
Party will do its utmost to carry out the three agreements.

MARCH 6.   In the morning the congress critically examined the diplomatic report. There was prolific objection to the Sino-Soviet friendship
treaty. Some maintained that we should submit the treaty to the Security
Council. Others said we should demand that the Soviets revise it. Concerning the question of the withdrawal of Soviet troops, Hu Chien-chung said
that we ought to find out whether, after all, the reason for the Soviets' failing
to withdraw troops is a matter of principle or of expediency. Liu Chien-ch'ün

said that we must hold fast to our position of sovereignty and the integrity of our territory. Toward the Soviets we should reach to the sky in demanding a price and descend to earth in repaying the money. Ku Cheng-kang said that we should launch a popular movement. Hsiao Chien said that we should request that the generalissimo dismiss the foreign minister or persuade him to resign. Someone raised the question of why, at the time the Sino-Soviet friendship treaty was being formulated, we did not enter into an agreement with the Soviet Union that China and the Soviet Union mutually would not station troops in Outer Mongolia.

In the evening, President Chiang invited me for supper. We discussed whether I should report on the Northeast. Yueh-chün [Chang Ch'ün] maintained that I need not give such a report. The president agreed.

Today, Chairman Hsiung sent to Vice-Chief of Staff Tung a wire:

> In response to personal instructions from the president, Special Envoy Chiang asks Vice-Chief of Staff Tung to make the following statement to Marshal Malinovsky: "Our government troops already have arrived in Mukden. As soon as the withdrawal of Soviet troops from Mukden is completed, we will be able to take over the defense of the city. As for taking over the defense of Ch'ang-ch'un, as soon as Soviet troops have withdrawn from that city our troops will enter and be stationed there."

Today, the *Ch'ang-ch'un New Daily*, the newspaper of the communist organization, suddenly resumed publication. It printed in a conspicuous place how the provincial government of Heilunkiang (the zone prior to the Mukden Incident) was established:

> Owing to the efforts of Yü T'ien-fang, Wang Chün, and Ch'en Lei, generals of the Anti-United [Anti-Japanese United Army], to carry out propaganda work and organize the people, a new People's Self-Defense Army has been expanded and established, based on the principles of that army, in Pei-an, Hai-lun, Sui-hua, Ai-hui, Nun-chiang, Na-ho, and other places. In early November a provincial government was formally established in Heilung-kiang, and the Maintenance Society ceased to exist. In succession new prefectural governments were set up in K'e-shan, K'e-tung, T'ung-pei, Te-tu, Pei-an, Hai-lun, Pai-ch'uen, Ming-shui, Sui-leng, Sui-hua, Wang-k'ui, Ch'ing-ch'eng, Nun-chiang, Sun-wu, and Ai-hui.

From the beginning I suspected that the Soviets would nurture in border areas a type of pro-Soviet armed force, directed by communist elements under the leadership of Moscow. This provincial government of Heilung-kung is merely a chesspiece in the Soviet scheme. Currently, this provincial government is still separate from the Eighth Route Army. If Soviet troops withdraw because China and the Soviets will not compromise, then this armed force will merge with the Eighth Route Army.

MARCH 7.   All day the congress critically examined the report of the Political Consultative Conference. There were prolific attacks on the Nationalist party for the failure of negotiations, as well as on the Chinese Communist Party for not keeping its word.

According to a report from Washington, today the U.S. State Department published Secretary of State Byrnes' communication of February 9, addressed to China and the Soviet Union: "The Soviet Union has declared that Japanese property in China's Northeast comprises legitimate war booty. It also has proposed that, following the Soviet Army's dismantling and expropriation of this war booty, remaining enterprises should be managed jointly by China and the Soviet Union." The State Department also published the Chinese government's reply:

In a memorandum to China, dated January 21 of this year, the Soviet government stated that the Soviet Union regards as war booty of the Soviet Army all Japanese enterprises serving the enemy Japanese army in the various northeastern provinces of China. The Chinese government regards this demand as a violation of the principle of war booty, with respect to the range of and dealing with this issue, as generally acknowledged by international law and international usage. Consequently, until today the two governments have been unable to reach, through discussion, an accord on pertinent basic principles. In another memorandum, to officials of the Northeast Headquarters in Ch'ang-ch'un, the Soviet government stated that the Soviets intend to hand over to China a number of Japanese enterprises, even though it regards these as war booty, while placing the rest of such enterprises (including designated coal mines and power plants as well as iron and steel industries, chemical industries, machine industries, and cement industries) under joint management of China and the Soviet Union. China decided against agreeing to this Soviet proposal because it goes beyond the stipulations of the Sino-Soviet agreement signed on August 14, 1945. Moreover, the proposal contradicts the Chinese government's position with regard to Japanese property and enterprises within Chinese territory.

The U.S. government sent its communication to the two countries because it learned that Chinese and Soviet officials were discussing matters concerning the disposal and control of industries in the Northeast. Byrnes remarked that the United States is quite concerned about remarks that

China and the Soviet Union are discussing the disposal of industries in the Northeast. In his communication Byrnes stated,

In current circumstances, people of other countries cannot freely go to China's northeastern region. Neither the people of the United States nor of other Allied countries have an equal opportunity to pursue economic development in China's Northeast. As a result, the U.S. government deeply feels that negotiations looking toward an agreement between the Chinese and Soviet governments concerning industry in the Northeast will violate the principle of the Open Door and may lead to obvious discrimination against Americans who want an opportunity to develop industry in the Northeast. Furthermore, when in the future China and the United States enter into trade relations in the Northeast, this may place American commercial interests in an exceedingly disadvantageous position.

Of course, the aforementioned communication aroused the attention of Allied nations as well as neutral nations but still has no relevance to the question of the Northeast itself.

I received from the Foreign Minister a copy of a wire from Wei [Wei Tao-ming], the Chinese ambassador to the United States:

Last night the U.S. secretary of state addressed to the Soviet government another communication concerning the question of the Northeast. Its contents are as follows:

(1) Until today the U.S. State Department has not received from the Soviet government a reply to its communication of February 9. But, according to the Chinese government's reply to our communication, the Soviet government regards as war booty of the Soviet Army all Japanese enterprises that met the needs of the Japanese army in the Northeast. The U.S. government cannot concur with this viewpoint. (2) The U.S. government regards all Japanese assets overseas as falling within the range of reparations so that their disposal should be settled jointly by the various victorious nations. (3) If in the future agreements signed between the Soviet and Chinese governments have monopolistic overtones, denying other countries an opportunity to participate, the U.S. government will consider such agreements in conflict with its principle of the Open Door and cannot acknowledge them.

Then, this morning the U.S. department received from the Soviet government a communication in reply. It made two major points: (1) Japanese enterprises in Manchuria that met the needs of the Japanese army should be regarded as war booty of the Soviet Army. (2) A number of Japanese assets in Manchuria already have been handed over to Chinese authorities. As for the rest, the Soviet government has proposed to the Chinese government that the two countries jointly manage them.

MARCH 8.   In the morning the congress listened to a political report and critically examined the report of the Political Consultative Conference. In the afternoon the congress critically examined the political report. T.V. Soong was absent; members of the congress demanded his presence. Naturally, after he arrived he was subjected to ferocious, relentless attacks. When replying Soong appeared very embarrassed.

MARCH 9.   The congress critically examined the report of the Ministry of Communications.
    At 11 I went to the Foreign Ministry. Foreign Minister Wang phoned to invite me for a talk. He told me,

On the seventh, the ministry sent to the Soviet ambassador a communication demanding to know the precise date of the withdrawal of Soviet troops. Yesterday the Soviet ambassador asked to see me. First he inquired how we are going to dispose of P'u-yi [this is the personal name of the last emperor of the Manchu dynasty, later appointed puppet emperor of Manchukuo by the Japanese]. His actual intention was to sound out our attitude. I [Foreign Minister Wang] told the ambassador that China is most willing to adhere sincerely to the Sino-Soviet treaty but that, currently, internal circumstances will thwart anyone advocating friendship between China and the Soviet Union. With respect to discussing economic cooperation, originally we intended to send Chang and Chiang back to Ch'ang-ch'un to continue discussions. But recently we received reports that the Soviets had dismantled and removed a large amount of machinery and equipment. Consequently, we really are unable to resume the discussions.

Foreign Minister Wang went on to discuss the U.S. State Department's reply from the Soviet Union to its communication, as well as the second communication addressed to the Soviet Union by the United States, largely the same as that published on the seventh by the U.S. State Department and reported by Ambassador Wei in his wire.
    I sent to Chairman Hsiung in Chin-chou a wire:

Hsüeh-t'ing asked me to tell you that the other day the Foreign Ministry sent to the Soviet ambassador a communication demanding that the Soviets fix a date for the withdrawal of their troops. I presume the Soviets will respond. Please ask our personnel in Mukden to pay close attention to movements of the other side and to do their best to maintain communications between Chin-chou and Mukden. Please wire to let me know if peculiar things occur.

I also sent to Vice-Chief of Staff Tung a wire:

The other day the Foreign Ministry presented the Soviet ambassador with a written demand that the Soviets fix a date for the withdrawal of their troops. I presume the Soviets will respond. Please pay close attention to movements of the other side. Furthermore, there has been news of Soviet troops withdrawing from Mukden. Does this mean that in various places the Self-Defense Army again will become active? If peculiar things occur, our central government personnel in Harbin can withdraw to Ch'ang-ch'un. Please deal with matters at all times as is expedient.

MARCH 10.   I received from Vice-Chief of Staff Tung a wire saying that during the last two days Soviet troops have been moving northward; along with these troops, tanks, artillery, heavy-duty vehicles, and so forth were being transported to Ch'ang-ch'un. In order to ask what really was happening, Tung tried to make an appointment to see Marshal Malinovsky. Malinovsky replied that he was too busy. Then Tung tried to make an appointment to see Major General Trotsynko but was given the answer that Trotsynko was away. Obviously, this indicates that Trotsynko deliberately left without giving us notice.

I sent to Secretary Keng Chieh-chih a wire:

Chinese and foreign public opinion are focused on the question of the withdrawal of Soviet troops. Recently, the Foreign Ministry submitted a written demand that the Soviets fix a date for the withdrawal of troops. However, our governing policy still aims at a satisfactory settlement and the maintenance of friendship. In my opinion, the current situation is decidedly different from a month ago. If, in the interests of lasting friendship, the Soviets can immediately fix a date for the withdrawal of troops and hand over political power to our central government before we discuss economic cooperation, perhaps I can return to Ch'ang-ch'un. If, as recently rumored, the Soviets are going to allow the People's Self-Defense Army to take over in places from which the Russians withdraw their troops, that will be tantamount to severing relations with China. Then, there will be no need for me to come back to Ch'ang-ch'un. Furthermore, do members of the committee for formulating regulations for the Chinese–Ch'ang-ch'un Railroad still intend to come to Chungking? Will Counselor Sladkovsky be willing to accompany them for an interview? Please find out about all this and send me a reply.

MARCH 11.　　At the weekly memorial service President Chiang delivered a speech. In general, he said that recently in their speeches party members have been attacking and abusing one another. Particularly noticeable were the abuse and reproach heaped on representatives of the Political Consultative Conference. The president feels that when mutual trust among comrades in the party is lost, this is tantamount to a loss of confidence in the party. Moreover, those not in responsible positions have been reproving those having responsibilities. This is tantamount to an ancient saying: The slovenly refuse to cultivate themselves but are jealous of those who do. During the Kwangtung period only one person was left in charge. Today, how can one person still take care of everything by himself? There must be a diffusion of responsibility to a number of persons. The current Political Consultative Conference resulted entirely from Chiang's decision. He added that in the future all problems must be settled politically and that this will be more difficult than resorting to arms. We must employ political deftness as well as forbearance. It seems that comrades in the party have not been able to thoroughly understand the purpose of his policy.

　　I received from Ch'ang-ch'un a wire saying that Li Chao-lin, who was supported by the Soviets, has been murdered. The atmosphere in Harbin is very tense. There is great fear that the Soviets will suspect this was instigated by anti-Soviet, anticommunist elements supporting our side in the Northeast.

　　Li Chao-lin, originally named Chang Shou-ch'ien, was a native of the prefecture of Liao-yang, in Liaoning province. After the Mukden Incident, together with Chao Shang-chih and others, he organized the Anti-Japanese United Army and later circuitously entered the Soviet Union. In company with the Soviet Army, he returned to the Northeast. He first became vice-governor of Pin-chiang province. On December 27 of last year I wired to Chairman Hsiung:

> Tomorrow I will go to Harbin. I intend to take the opportunity to inquire about Li Chao-lin, currently vice-governor of Pin-chiang province. If we do not find a position for this man we will encounter difficulties in administrative work at both the provincial and municipal levels. Li is supported by the Soviet Army and is not in agreement with Yen-an. He must be given a position before we can enlist the services of his troops for our central government. Please speedily tell me what type of title would be suitable for Li.

Subsequently, the matter was dropped because we failed to take over the provincial government. After we took over the city of Harbin, Li withdrew to become chairman of the Sino-Soviet Friendship Society in Harbin.

　　I received from Vice-Chief of Staff Tung a wire:

Today at 4 P.M. I talked with Major General Trotsynko. I asked him about the situation concerning the movement of Soviet troops in Mukden. He replied, "Soviet troops already have begun to withdraw from Mukden. On March 15 they will complete their withdrawal. Because of limited transportation facilities, they will not be able to withdraw directly to the national border and must be stationed temporarily in Ch'ang-ch'un and Harbin. Since both the municipal government and the police force of Mukden long ago have been taken over by our [the Chinese] side and since a number of our troops already are in the metropolitan area of Mukden, it would seem there is no need to implement formal procedures for the replacement of the defense." I found his attitude improved over what it was during several previous meetings.

I sent a wire to Vice-Chief of Staff Tung in Chin-chou:

I am deeply worried by the murder of Li Chao-lin. From now on there will be changes in the situation that cannot be predicted. I wonder whether our personnel remaining in Harbin, unable to take over the provincial government, shouldn't withdraw to Ch'ang-ch'un. With respect to the future movement of our personnel in Nun-chiang, Pin-chiang, and the Harbin municipal government, please constantly act in concert with Governors Kuan and P'eng, as well as Mayor Yang, to arrive at and implement decisions taking into consideration the circumstances. Concerning whether our personnel remaining in Ch'ang-ch'un should prepare for an emergency evacuation, please at all times request instructions from Chairman Hsiung. Furthermore, the ancient relics and old books from the Ch'ing Palace stored in the Bank of China that I found in the Ch'ing Palace, all are national treasures and hopefully can be shipped out.

MARCH 12.   Today, during the congress it was initially decided that Liu Wei-chang and I would attend the small-group meeting of the Central Committee for the Northeast. The time was set for 9 A.M. tomorrow. In the afternoon, the Central Committee for the Northeast, headed by committee member Ch'i Shih-ying, refused to allow the small-group meetings, contending that the report must be given to the whole congress. In his speech, member Ch'i's opposition to Chairman Hsiung already is evident. Originally, he intended to wait for Hsiung to attend the congress and then embarrass him. Now Hsiung has not returned to attend. Nevertheless, Ch'i insisted that the report be given at the big meeting.

I received from Secretary Keng a wire, sent on the eleventh:

This afternoon K'uang [Keng's first name] saw Counselor Sladkovsky and transmitted to him the various points communicated in Your Excellency's wire. He indicated his views as follows: (1) On the question of the withdrawal of Soviet troops, initially he said that the question was not within his jurisdiction. Then he said that it is not that the Soviets are unwilling to withdraw their troops. The problem is whether we are prepared to replace them as defenders of the Northeast. Suppose the Soviets decide to withdraw from a certain area on a certain date. If our troops fail to arrive in time to replace the Soviet defenders, nongovernment troops are likely to take advantage of this opportunity and encroach. Afterward, the Chinese will blame the Soviets, which does not seem reasonable. He also pressed for an answer as to why government troops are slow in arriving. (2) It is rumored that the Soviets will hand over to the People's Self-Defense Army administrative power in various places from which the Soviets withdraw troops. This is not true. He just returned to Ch'ang-ch'un from Mukden, where he witnessed how Soviet defenders were replaced and, together with Mayor Tung, transferred to our side various factories and Soviet organizations. Liaison between the troops and police on both sides was quite satisfactory. (3) He maintains that economic negotiations still be conducted in Ch'ang-ch'un and earnestly hopes that Your Excellency speedily will return to preside. Concerning conditions for cooperation in the management of industries and mines, he hinted that there is room for concessions. However, he is not interested in going to Chungking. To sum up the aforementioned points, I believe that in order to break the current deadlock we should adhere to the following principles: (1) Negotiations should proceed concurrently at the military, political, and economic levels, and economic negotiations should merely be one link. (2) On the basis of previous experience it seems that takeover procedure had best be as follows: military is the major step, political, next, and economic, third. We first should send to Ch'ang-ch'un a large number of military and political personnel to preside over the aforementioned steps. I entreat Your Excellency to take the time to consider this.

MARCH 13.   All day I prepared a report to be given at the congress tomorrow.

The Foreign Ministry forwarded to me a wire from Chargé d'Affaires Ch'en of our embassy in Moscow:

To vice-minister of the Ministry of Foreign Affairs:
The U.S. chargé d'affaires here personally told me that already, on March 4, the Soviets replied to the first U.S. dispatch concerning the question of enemy property in the Northeast. The Soviets stated generally that the Chinese and Soviets had discussed organizing a Sino-Soviet joint stock company for the purpose of developing a number of enterprises formerly serving the needs of the Japanese Kwantung Army. Since the Soviet Army defeated the Kwantung Army, the Soviet Union regards these enterprises as war booty. The Soviet government does not acknowledge that a discussion of this question between the Chinese and the Soviets has anything to

do with the matter of compensation, inasmuch as war booty and compensation are two separate issues. Since the aforementioned company is to develop a number of enterprises, certainly it cannot be regarded as discriminatory or harmful to the Open Door. And so forth. Then, in accord with instructions from the U.S. government, on March 9 the U.S. chargé d'affaires addressed another dispatch to the Soviet Foreign Ministry indicating that the U.S. government agrees with the viewpoint of the Chinese government concerning enemy property in the Northeast but does not agree with the Soviet government's opinion that such property be regarded as war booty. This dispatch also proposes that payment be assessed for goods shipped away by the Soviets. The U.S. government does not object to direct discussions between the Chinese and the Soviets, but it maintains that such discussions should be held after China has assumed control of administration in the Northeast. And so forth. The Soviets have not yet replied. Furthermore, on March 9 the U.S. chargé d'affaires addressed another letter to the Soviet Foreign Ministry stating that the U.S. government repeatedly has proposed to the Far Eastern Commission that there be set up a Japanese Reparations Commission for the purpose of disposing of enemy property. This proposal contains seven measures, and the U.S. government wishes first to discuss it informally with the Soviets. And so forth. The Soviets have not yet replied. I presume that the U.S. government also has brought up these seven measures with our government. In your employment, Ch'en Ting.

MARCH 14.   I attended the congress. Following Liu Wei-chang's military report concerning the Northeast, I made an economic report on the Northeast. I reported briefly on what transpired during the economic negotiations and the preparations for the northward advance of our government troops. I also reported on my personal thoughts and feelings. The most important was that we educate and change the thinking of people from the Northeast. In other words, cultivate among them a national consciousness. I finished about one o'clock. While I was making my report, a group of petitioners were shouting outside the hall. The Presidium had Ch'en Ch'eng and Ch'en Li-fu, two members, go out to deal with them. After I finished my report, Ch'en Ch'eng came forward to report on the demands of the petitioners concerning the question of the Northeast and their attacks on Chairman Hsiung. These included accusations that Hsiung had shipped 150 pieces of luggage from Ch'ang-ch'un and had carried out three treasures. This indicates that the attacks on Chairman Hsiung are personal and organized. In the afternoon the congress critically examined these reports. Those having the most to say were Chu Chi-ch'ing, Fu Ju-lin, Wang Hsing-chou, and Huang Yü-jen, all members of the congress. Before the end of the meeting the Congress scrutinized the military and economic reports. The *Central Daily News* printed the proceedings.

[In the original text the remaining portion of the page appears to have been blotted out by one long stroke. But since this blotting is incomplete, the translator cannot be sure that this part is meant to be deleted and has decided to retain it in the translation.] I received from Vice-Chief of Staff Tung a wire (of the fourteenth):

> Just now, Governor Liu of Liaopeh province phoned to say that on the night of the thirteenth Soviet troops in Ssu-p'ing totally withdrew and that order in the city was quite good. Wang, the head of the prefecture of K'ai-yüan, was captured by traitors and bandits, and the prefectural government of Ch'ang-t'u has been forced to withdraw to Ssu-p'ing.

I sent to Vice-Chief of Staff Tung a wire:

> I have read your wire of *han* [date, in code]. I am very concerned about whether there is sufficient armed force at Governor Liu's for protection. Can you spare a number of our troops arriving in Mukden and send them to Ssu-p'ing? Furthermore, please constantly give attention to the question of the safety of our personnel in various provinces and cities and seek Chairman Hsiung's instructions about how to deal with this question.

MARCH 15.   The congress discussed the report on the decision of the investigating committee. Concerning the report on the economic investigation, Hsiao Cheng rose and said in reproof that we should look into responsibility for neglect of duty in the Ministry of Economics. His aim was to make Minister Weng Yung-ni feel insecure about his position. The investigating committee's decision about the question of the Northeast indicated that Chairman Hsiung should be removed and replaced, that both the Political and Economic commissions should be abolished, and that negotiations should cease to be localized. Nothing but a series of personal attacks and, where issues are concerned, unrealistic talk.

I received from Governor Kuan of Pin-chiang province a wire (of the fifteenth):

> Just now I submitted to His Excellency the generalissimo a wire. The message is,
>
>> There have been discovered in the immediate suburbs of Harbin over twenty thousand armed men having no clear designation. They seem intent on taking advantage of the opportunity to enter and occupy the city. The situation has become even more serious since the murder of Li Chao-lin, the head of the Sino-Soviet Friendship Society. At any moment, a disaster could take place. We have merely four companies of the Peace Preservation Corps; we really are finding it difficult to

cope. Furthermore, the situation will become more perilous once Soviet troops withdraw; government troops still have not arrived. I beg of Your Excellency the following: (1) The urgent dispatch to Harbin of one division of government troops to take over the defense. (2) A request to the Soviets that, pending the arrival of our troops, they assume responsibility for maintaining local order. (3) A request that the Soviets first let us use the airport in Harbin to transport our government troops and liaison personnel. (4) Through diplomatic channels, a request that the Soviets effectively guarantee the safety of all our takeover personnel. I presume Your Excellency will look into this and issue orders of implementation. Pray also wire instructions. And so forth.

This is the situation: The city of Harbin comprises the focal point of northern Manchuria and is located in a strategic position. If they [presumably, the armed irregulars] occupy the city, this will have immeasurable consequences. You, honorable sir, loyally have the interests of the nation at heart and always have been most concerned about the Northeast. I earnestly pray that you transmit my message to His Excellency the generalissimo, as well as to Chairman Hsiung, and ask them speedily to consider these matters and issue orders of implementation. I also pray that you wire me a reply.

I also received from Chief Secretary Chang Ta-t'ung a wire of the same date, sent from Ch'ang-ch'un:

(1) Yesterday morning communist troops entered and occupied Nung-an. (2) In Harbin, since the death of Li [Li-Chao-lin], political commissar of the Anti-Japanese United Army, Chung Tzu-yün, has been declaring that the United Army intends to occupy the city of Harbin. (3) In Mukden, plague has been discovered. Already, 80 people have died. (4) The head of the Sino-Soviet Friendship Society in Ssu-p'ing also has been murdered. (5) South of Mukden clashes are occurring for control of hydroelectric power stations. (6) Our personnel in the two provinces of Ho and Lung will return to Ch'ang-ch'un tomorrow. (7) Vice-Chief of Staff Tung has urged that personnel not critically needed in various units be withdrawn first. The overall situation is not very promising. It seems that it would be best to take time to consider whether we should halt or advance.

MARCH 16.   Today, President Chiang personally attended the congress. First, we discussed the report on the Political Consultative Conference, with the result that it was passed without dissent. The report on the investigation of the constitution was handed over to the standing committee. The report on the investigation of diplomatic affairs also was passed without revision. With respect to the question of the Northeast, President Chiang personally gave an explanation. He said that, concerning the Soviets, we only can adhere to the Sino-Soviet treaty and settle any questions through diplomatic channels. We should strive for peace both for the sake of China and the world. He said that in dealing with matters, Chairman Hsiung and the others always have followed the instructions of the central government and that he personally must assume all responsibility. Chiang added that Chairman Hsiung's case should be handed over to the standing committee to be dealt with under his personal leadership. In the afternoon we elected members of the standing committee.

I received from Vice-Chief of Staff Tung a wire sent today from Ch'ang-ch'un:

On the night of the twelfth Soviet troops in Ssu-p'ing withdrew. Our armed force defending Ssu-p'ing consists of about six to seven thousand men and, hopefully, can hold out for a week. The vanguard of the underground troops of our government army long ago arrived in Fa-k'u. In case of an emergency, it would not be difficult for these troops to rush to the assistance of our garrison at Ssu-p'ing. (2) [there is no point 1] Our personnel in the two provinces of Hei and Ho will first return to Ch'ang-ch'un. As for important articles being kept in Ch'ang-ch'un and personnel in various units who do not need to remain in Ch'ang-ch'un, I already have obtained permission from Chairman Hsiung for them to board planes going to Peiping. This now is in the planning stage. With respect to Your Excellency's instructions concerning the ancient relics stored here and the old books from the Ch'ing Palace, naturally, I will transport them with special care. (3) Soviet troops who have withdrawn from Mukden largely remain in Ch'ang-ch'un. At present, conditions in the city of Ch'ang-ch'un are quite stable. (4) Since Li's murder the situation in northern Manchuria indeed merits our concern. However, until now it shows no sign of worsening. Naturally, I will give careful attention to assuring the safe movement of our personnel in the provinces and cities while at all times seeking instructions in making decisions. I wonder whether the Soviets have transmitted to our country the contents of their communication sent in reply to the U.S. State Department. Please instruct me about this.

MARCH 17.   I received from Vice-Chief of Staff Tung a wire of the sixteenth:

(1) Just now Governor Liu phoned to say that bandits have occupied the airport of Ssu-p'ing. The battle still is going on. Traitors and bandits are in the process of congregating around Ssu-p'ing in preparation for a large-scale attack. The situation is critically perilous. (2) On the fourteenth the county seat of Nung-an fell. Details have not yet been reported. (3) The burial of Li

Chao-lin has been scheduled for the twenty-fourth. Chou Pao-chung, as well as various other puppet leaders of the northern part of the Northeast, will attend the funeral service. They also have declared that Li was murdered as the result of a fascist conspiracy in China and have sworn to avenge his death. The various newspapers in Harbin have made a big thing of publicizing the aforementioned situation. The popular mood is exceedingly unsettled.

I also received from Vice-Chief of Staff Tung a wire of the seventeenth:

On the ninth and thirteenth of this month, at the former Railroad Bureau in Ch'ang-ch'un, a certain Soviet colonel convened a meeting of Chinese and Japanese Communists. He issued an important statement, to the effect that (1) In order to deal with the question of the Near East, the Soviet Army no longer will be able to station troops in China's Northeast. The question of the Northeast will be settled through diplomatic channels. (2) Besides the Sino-Soviet treaty, the Soviets also demand the right of joint control of power plants, iron and steel industries, mining enterprises, etc., in the Northeast. In the event that the United Nations adopts a stiff attitude, the Soviets also can withdraw these demands. (3) The Soviets hope that Chinese and Japanese Communists in the Northeast will maintain themselves by relying on their own efforts. The Soviets will not be able to give direct assistance. And so on. I think these disclosures are very important.

After his return to the United States, General Marshall issued a statement. He said the situation in the Northeast is perilous and hopes that the tripartite teams soon will arrive in Manchuria.

Today, the Second National Congress came to a close. The *Central Daily News* printed the decisions in the report on diplomacy: (1) that China will not be restricted by the secret agreements (indicating the Yalta Agreement), (2) that China will faithfully implement the Sino-Soviet treaty, and (3) that China must have priority in the distribution of Japanese reparations to the Allied nations.

The Chinese communist *Liberation Daily* printed that in various areas around Liaoning mass movements have been organized to attack reactionaries in the Nationalist party for the murder of Li Chao-lin. The paper also published a general outline of the Anti-Japanese United Army in the Northeast, proving that the army is already in possession of armed forces in the Northeast and is devoting its efforts to resisting the Japanese.

I received from Vice-Chief of Staff Tung a wire of today:

As of the morning of the seventeenth, electric communications and telephone service to and from Ssu-p'ing have been cut off. Conditions are unknown. I conclude that perhaps our garrison already has evacuated the city. (2) On the seventeenth administrative personnel in the two provinces of Hei and Ha, i.e., over one hundred people under Governors Han and Wu, arrived in Harbin from Ch'ang-ch'un. (3) I hear that Soviet Major General Karchakov in Harbin has been transferred and promoted to regional commander of Harbin. The vacancy will be filled by Lieutenant General Kovtun-Stankevich, formerly garrison commander at Mukden.

MARCH 18.   I received from Vice-Chief of Staff Tung a wire of today:

Today, I talked with Soviet major general Trotsynko. He expressed no objections either to our sending troops from Mukden toward Ch'ang-ch'un or to our transporting one division of troops by rail to Ch'ang-ch'un. On the occasion of Red Army Day, Marshal Malinovsky sent his regards to you, Chairman Chang. [Here, the mode of address in Chinese takes on a highly reverential form for which there is no English equivalent.] Today, before I parted from Major General Trotsynko, he also sent his regards both to you Chairman Chang and to Special Envoy Chiang. According to Yen-p'ing's [the sender of the wire] observations, the Soviets gradually are becoming tired of the northeastern question and say they are longing for you two honorable gentlemen to return to Ch'ang-ch'un. Respectfully, I am writing this for your consideration.

I sent a wire to Vice-Chief of Staff Tung:

I have read your wire of the sixteenth. (1) In their communication replying to the United States, the Soviets stated merely that they regard enemy industries in the Northeast as war booty but now are willing to hand back to China a number of these and place a number of others under joint Sino-Soviet management. And so forth. (2) Can reinforcing troops speedily reach northern Liaoning? Please attend to the safety of Governor Liu as well as of our colleagues in the provincial government. If there are dangers they will have to be evacuated. (3) During the recent congress, a number of comrades from the Northeast fiercely attacked Chairman Hsiung. This attack also was endorsed by the investigating committee. His Excellency the president stepped forward and took charge, saying that he alone assumed responsibility for everything. The endorsement was not passed.

I sent wires to Governor Kuan of Pin-chiang province and Mayor Yang of Harbin:

I have read respectfully your wire of the fifteenth. I am quite worried about the situation in northern Manchuria. I fear that for the time being it will not be easy for our government troops to reach areas north of Ch'ang-ch'un. The

Foreign Ministry already has proposed to the Soviet ambassador that the Soviets effectively protect our takeover personnel. In any event, please take care of yourselves.

MARCH 19.   In the morning, Foreign Minister Wang came to see me. He said the Soviets have indicated that, since we [the Chinese] have assumed responsibility for police protection of the Chinese–Ch'ang-ch'un Railroad, we are responsible for the current interruption of transportation along that railroad. Foreign Minister Wang asked me to draft, on his behalf, a statement.

The background of the aforementioned section is as follows: On the eighteenth, Vice-Chief of Staff Tung talked with Major General Trotsynko, who made a serious protest, saying,

> After Soviet troops withdrew from Mukden, rail communication between Port Arthur and Mukden was cut off because several rail yards and bridges were destroyed or else dynamite was planted underground. Furthermore, currently all of the coal produced at Fu-shun is being intercepted in Mukden and retained there, which has affected rail communication north of Mukden.
>
> Therefore, we expressly make a serious protest. According to the Sino-Soviet Treaty of Friendship and Alliance, responsibility for protecting the Chinese–Ch'ang-ch'un Railroad rests with the Chinese. We hope that your government will undertake to restore normal conditions along those sections of the Chinese–Ch'ang-ch'un Railroad from which Soviet troops have withdrawn.

Immediately, Vice-Chief of Staff Tung replied,

> Obstructions along the Chinese–Ch'ang-ch'un Railroad have resulted from destruction by armed irregular troops. In order to stop this we must have a certain type of specialized force. As for shipping coal from Fu-shun, if normal rail communication between Mukden and Ch'ang-ch'un can be restored, we will have the authorities in charge let coal pass as usual.

Trotsynko countered by remarking, "Your government should provide the type of force that Your Excellency mentions." Tung replied, "This is why you ought to assist our government troops to advance soon from Mukden northward."

Foreign Minister Wang also asked me to draft on his behalf and in the name of the president a wire to Chairman Hsiung and Vice-Chief of Staff Tung, asking them to negotiate with the Soviets the following points: that when they withdraw their troops the Soviets first confer with us and that they help our troops reach Ch'ang-ch'un. I immediately went to the Ministry of Military Orders, where I discussed with Vice-Minister Liu Wei-chang the tone of our negotiations with the Soviets. Next, I drafted the wire on behalf of Foreign Minister Wang. I affix in the following section the text of the wire.

At 9:30 P.M. President Chiang invited me for a talk. Also present was Foreign Minister Wang. The result of our discussion is that I am to sound out the Soviet economic counselor concerning whether the Soviets first will confer with us before withdrawing troops and help us transport our troops to Ch'ang-ch'un. [Here, the author's account is interrupted by the drafted wire to Chairman Hsiung.]

> To Chairman Hsiung in Chin-chou and Vice-Chief of Staff Tung in Ch'ang-ch'un:
> Secret. I respectfully have received from His Excellency the generalissimo handwritten instructions stating the following: The Chinese government deeply regrets that recently, when they withdrew their troops from Mukden, the Soviets did not notify us beforehand. Furthermore, with respect to police protection of the railroad between Mukden and Ch'ang-ch'un, they also did not discuss ahead of time procedures for replacing its defense. In order to maintain local order and ensure rail communications we must ask the Soviets to guarantee the following: (1) That the Soviets first notify us if they change the location where Soviet troops are stationed. (2) That in order for us to arrange for replacing the defense, the Soviets also must give us early notification of when they will withdraw their troops from various places and from along the Chinese–Ch'ang-ch'un rail line. (3) [Note that point 3 is not an imperative, like points 1 and 2.] We intend to transport our government troops to Ch'ang-ch'un by rail before the Soviets withdraw troops from that city. We hope the Soviets will assist us soon to begin transporting our troops. Please speedily wire Vice-Chief of Staff Tung and ask him immediately to raise these points with the Soviets, as instructed above, and request a reply. This is very important. I am expressly submitting this message to you. *Hao* [a date, in code].

[The following continues the author's account, interrupted by the drafted wire to Chairman Hsiung.] I immediately sent to Chief Secretary Chang Ta-t'ung a wire:

> Just now I received from Vice-Chief of Staff Tung a wire saying that Major General Trotsynko has asked about Ching-kuo and Ao (i.e., me), which seems to indicate a Soviet desire for us to return to Ch'ang-ch'un. Last time, Counselor Sladkovsky also indicated this. Since the Soviets are preparing to withdraw from Ch'ang-ch'un and Harbin, I very much hope that they will notify us about the date when, while withdrawing from Ch'ang-ch'un and Harbin, they will hand over these cities to us to defend. Furthermore, I

hope they really will assist us to transport our troops by rail to Ch'ang-ch'un. If this is the case, we immediately will return to Ch'ang-ch'un. Presumably, the Soviets understand the difficult situation we are in. Please ask Chi-chih [an alternative name for Keng K'uang] to transmit this message to Major General Trotsynko and Counselor Sladkovsky and wire me concerning their reactions.

MARCH 20.   I received from Chief Secretary Chang and Secretary Keng a wire of reply:

In keeping with Your Excellency's orders, K'uang saw Counselor Sladkovsky. He was unwilling to listen to the question of the withdrawal of Soviet troops, on the grounds that it is not in his jurisdiction, and asked me to discuss it directly with Major General Trotsynko. This is my plan: Vice-Chief of Staff Tung still will discuss the question with Major General Trotsynko. Then, I will wire to report the results. Furthermore, Counselor Sladkovsky told me that several days ago our troops in Mukden killed two staff members of a Soviet economic organization. There also have occurred incidents in which Soviet citizens were terrorized and robbed. Sladkovsky declared that Mayor Tung's declaration, made before the withdrawal of Soviet troops, that the Chinese will protect Soviet people, all have proved to be empty words. Sladkovsky said that he already has reported this situation to the Soviet government, requesting that it make a serious protest. And so forth. During his talk Sladkovsky was severe in both tone and countenance. We have no way of judging what the actual situation is.

I submitted this wire to the president. Judging from the aforementioned situation, already it is very clear that the Soviets are arranging for armed irregular forces to resist our takeover and are unwilling to give us any assistance.

I also received from Secretary Keng and Secretary Yang Hsiang-nien a joint wire:

1. Formerly, when Your Excellency was in Ch'ang-ch'un, together with Kalgin, Soviet vice-chairman of the board of directors of the Chinese–Ch'ang-ch'un Railroad, you decided on measures for transporting government troops by rail to Ch'ang-ch'un. This morning, Vice-Chief of Staff Tung submitted a letter requesting that the board of directors carry out the original proposal. At 3 P.M. Tung received a formal reply by letter. The Soviets refuse to allow us to transport our troops to Ch'ang-ch'un. Their reasons are (a) Because of the incidence of plague between Mukden and Ch'ang-ch'un, they are under orders from the Soviet Army command to stop communications. (b) Since the incident at Ssu-p'ing took place, rail communications have been cut off and the iron

bridge near Mukden also has been bombed. (c) Because the supply of coal from Fu-shun has been cut off, the railroad is extraordinarily short of coal.

2. Tomorrow at 3 P.M. Vice-Chief of Staff Tung plans to again negotiate with Major General Trotsynko about transporting our troops by rail to Ch'ang-ch'un and to reiterate the gist of Your Excellency's wire of the nineteenth.

3. It is rumored that one trainload of the Soviet Army's main force has withdrawn northward. Starting tomorrow, there will be no more passenger traffic between Harbin and Ch'ang-ch'un.

4. Today at 6 P.M. somebody phoned the board of directors from the Ssu-p'ing railroad station. The person called himself Governor Liu of Liaopeh province. He asked the office to transmit to Vice-Chief of Staff Tung this message: speedily try to negotiate sending a train to take him and other personnel back to Ch'ang-ch'un.

Judging from the current situation, the total withdrawal of Soviet troops is imminent. Yet, until today the Soviets have not notified us that they are ready to assist in transporting our troops. We fear they may be insincere and that prospects are dim.

I received a wire from Vice-Chief of Staff Tung, reporting that the board of directors of the Chinese–Ch'ang-ch'un Railroad has refused to assist in transporting our government troops. Their reasons on the whole are the same as in the wire from Secretaries Chang and Yang. I affix in the following section the text of the wire.

I also received from Vice-Chief of Staff Tung a wire stating that he had received from Liaopeh a phone call saying, "The Ssu-p'ing battle has ended. Governor Liu as well as all of his staff members are safe. Please send a train to take them back to Ch'ang-ch'un."

MARCH 21.   [Here is inserted the text of the wire from Tung Yen-p'ing.]

To Minister Hsü of the Ministry of Military Orders, Chairman Chang Kung-ch'uan and Special Envoy Chiang Ching-kuo:
Secret. Concerning the question of our transporting our troops by rail from Mukden to Ch'ang-ch'un on *yin-hao* [a date, in code, the twentieth?], I had sent a letter raising this question with the board of directors of the Chinese–Ch'ang-ch'un Railroad. Now, I have received from Kalgin, Soviet vice-chairman of the board of directors, a letter of reply, stating generally that in principle this is all right and that, previously, he had asked the Railroad Bureau to act accordingly. But there exist the following problems: (1) In order to prevent the spread of the plague in Mukden and Ssu-p'ing, the Soviet Army general headquarters has issued orders that in various places within the plague-stricken region all passenger and freight transportation

will be stopped. (2) From *yin-hsi* [the sixteenth] to *yin-hao* [date?] rail communication was sabotaged. On orders from Chinese government troops stationed in Mukden, the Nan-huen-ho iron bridge in Mukden was bombed and destroyed so that coal produced in Fu-shun could not be shipped northward. Coal stored at the station of Huang-ku-t'un was totally drained. The twelve locomotives in storage, belonging to the Chinese–Ch'ang-ch'un Railroad, were sent to Mukden and other sections of the Pei-Ning Railroad. Then, the water supply was cut off. In Ssu-p'ing the same situation exists. (3) Soviet railroad personnel in the Mukden region have been subjected to every kind of oppression, illegal arrest, and humiliation. In fact, these personnel already have been rendered incapable of maintaining order in that region. Chinese troops have not provided assistance or ensured conditions for restoring normal rail communication. Repeatedly, technicians sent by the Chinese–Ch'ang-ch'un Railroad to repair and restore rail communications have been fired at by Chinese government troops. A locomotive has been riddled with sixteen holes and a passenger coach, with ten. Fortunately, there were no casualties. Until all of this stops the Soviets will find it difficult to assist in transporting Chinese troops. And so forth. At present, I am continuing to negotiate and using reason to argue against these Soviet contentions. But I fear there will be no results. Respectfully, I first am wiring to you this information. Tung Yen-p'ing. *Yin-k'e-shu* [a date, in code?]. Seal.

I received a wire from Chairman Hsiung reporting on conditions surrounding the withdrawal of Soviet troops northward from Ch'ang-ch'un. I sent a wire to Chief Secretary Chang and Secretary Keng:

I have read your wire of the twentieth. (1) Concerning the incident of Soviet citizens being killed in Mukden, please immediately wire Mayor Tung to inquire whether this is fact or an excuse for the Soviets to act in Mukden. For the last two or three months, Ao [the author] has tried to promote friendship between China and the Soviet Union. Unexpectedly, the outcome more often has been unfavorable rather than favorable. Judging from Counselor Sladkovsky's tone, the situation will reach a stage where nothing can be done. This is very regrettable for the interests of both sides. When convenient, please convey to Sladkovsky my thoughts. (2) If, after the majority of our personnel have been evacuated, circumstances still are unfavorable, you can go to Mukden and work with committee member Wang. As for Chi-chih, please discuss matters with Directors Liu and Wan and remain there or leave with them. As for electric communications personnel, aside from retaining necessary persons, the rest can be evacuated to Mukden.

I received from Vice-Chief of Staff Tung four wires dated the twenty-first: A report on his interview today with Major General Trotsynko during which

he delivered to Trotsynko the Chinese communication to Marshal Malinovsky. In the communication, we requested (1) that the Soviets first must notify
us when they move their troops. (2) When they withdraw their troops from
various places the Soviets must, at an early date, formally notify us as well as
comply with procedures for our replacing the defense. Otherwise, we will find
it difficult to assume responsibility for Soviet emigrés. (3) In order to prevent
the destruction or obstruction of railroads as they withdraw, Soviet troops
must hand over to Chinese troops the places for them to defend. (4) We
intend, before the Soviets withdraw troops from Ch'ang-ch'un, to transport
Chinese troops there by rail. We ask the Soviets to assist us. Major General
Trotsynko's reply to the aforementioned communication is (1) the Soviets are
not responsible for the failure immediately to replace with Nationalist troops
the Soviet troops defending Mukden and the Chinese–Ch'ang-ch'un Railroad. Long ago the Soviets notified us about the withdrawal of Soviet troops
from Mukden. Moreover, long ago our troops arrived in Mukden. Soviet
troops in Ch'ang-ch'un already have begun to withdraw. But, since coal produced in Fu-shun cannot be shipped northward, the Soviets have no way of
determining the date when they will complete their withdrawal. (2) Major
General Trotsynko told Tung that the Chinese–Ch'ang-ch'un Railroad already
has agreed to send our troops northward by rail from Mukden. Our troops all
have been inoculated. Major General Trotsynko insisted that after our troops
arrive in Kung-chu-ling, they must remain for ten days and only can proceed
after an examination by both sides has shown there is no plague. Tung requested that Major General Trotsynko dispatch liaison officials to accompany
Tung to Ssu-p'ing so that he can transport back to Ch'ang-ch'un our personnel
in the provincial government. After repeated negotiations he [Trotsynko]
promised to give Tung a reply some other day. Tung then personally went to
the Chinese–Ch'ang-ch'un Railroad Bureau to phone Ssu-p'ing. Because communist troops there were very powerful, he was unable to communicate with
Ssu-p'ing. (4) Tung personally asked Major General Trotsynko whether in the
future the military delegation is to leave or remain. Trotsynko replied that,
naturally, it should move with the Soviet Army, and he also promised to notify
us about Soviet troop movements one week in advance.

MARCH 22.   Early in the morning, I received from Foreign Minister
Wang Hsüeh-t'ing a phone call saying that in the afternoon the Soviet ambassador will come to the ministry. After seeing the Soviet ambassador, Minister Wang again phoned to say that the Soviet ambassador had stated,

> Actually, Soviet troops could have completed their withdrawal earlier. How-
> ever, they were obliged to procrastinate, first, because of our demands and
> then because of the shortage of coal in winter. But now that the cold season

is over, they can speed up their withdrawal. They intend to make the end of April the deadline.

On the whole, all Soviet arrangements have been completed. But I wonder how much resistance our troops will encounter before they can gain control of the Chinese–Ch'ang-ch'un Railroad, much less beyond the rail lines. Furthermore, I fear the armed irregulars will not let our troops advance to Harbin. By now Soviet troops are withdrawing. It seems that we first must wait for the Soviets to withdraw troops before discussing economic cooperation. On the other hand, it still is very uncertain whether we can take over the Northeast. My heart churns with worry.

[The following section contains the four wires from Vice-Chief of Staff Tung.]

One: To Minister Hsü of the Ministry of Military Orders, Chairman Chang Kung-ch'uan, and Special Envoy Chiang Ching-kuo: Secret.

1. Concerning the question of the withdrawal of Soviet troops and the replacement of the defense, in keeping with handwritten orders of His Excellency the generalissimo, forwarded to me by Chairman Chang Kung-ch'uan, and handwritten instructions of Chairman Hsiung, as well as instructions in the coded telegram of *yin-hao* [a date, in code], I wrote a letter to Marshal Malinovsky and during our interview personally delivered it to Major General Trotsynko on *yin-ma* [date, in code]. Major General Trotsynko indicated that the Soviets are unwilling to assume responsibility for the failure to replace immediately the Russians defending Mukden and the Chinese–Ch'ang-ch'un Railroad with Nationalist troops. He said that the Soviets already have formally notified us that, begining from *tzu-shan* [a date, in code], they will withdraw from Mukden. Furthermore, Chinese troops arrived long ago in Mukden. As for Soviet troops in Ch'ang-ch'un, indeed already they have begun to withdraw. But because coal produced in Fu-shun cannot be shipped northward, they have no way of determining a date for completing their withdrawal.

2. I told him that the Chinese–Ch'ang-ch'un Railroad Bureau already has agreed to our troops advancing northward from Mukden by rail but has stated that our troops all must be inoculated. He insisted that, after arriving in Kung-chu-ling, the Chinese army must stay for ten days and advance only after doctors from both sides examine our troops and conclude that they have no symptoms of plague. I promised that I would ask for my government's instructions and insisted that after our troops arrive in Kung-chu-ling the two sides still must formally replace the Soviet defense with our own. He indicated nothing.

Allow me to report the rest subsequently. In your employment, Tung Yen-p'ing. *Yin-ma-vou-yi* [a date in code, with parts of it denoting the month and the hour]. Secret. Seal.

Two: To Chairman Chang Kung-ch'uan and Special Envoy Chiang Ching-kuo:
Secret. The original text of the four points, which on *yin-ma* [date] I brought up with Marshal Malinovsky, is as follows: (1) If the Soviets change the location where their troops are stationed, they please first must notify the military delegation dispatched by the Chinese government. (2) When the Soviets withdraw their troops from various places in the Northeast, they please must formally notify our military delegation well in advance, as well as comply with procedures for the replacement of Russian defenders with our troops. Otherwise, there is social chaos at the local level, and I fear it will be difficult for the Chinese government to fulfill its responsibility to protect Soviet emigrés. (3) The Chinese–Ch'ang-ch'un Railroad is under the joint management of the Chinese and the Soviets. According to the treaty, China is responsible for protecting the railroad. When Soviet troops withdraw, they please must really hand over the railroad to Chinese troops to defend. Otherwise, if the railroad is damaged or communication hindered, both sides will suffer losses. We intend, before Soviet troops withdraw from Ch'ang-ch'un, to transport Chinese troops by rail to Ch'ang-ch'un. We request that the Soviets at an early date assist us in transporting our troops. And so forth. Respectfully, I submit this information. Tung Yen-p'ing. *Yin-ma-wu* [a date in code, with the third character denoting the hour]. Seal.

Three: To Chairman Chang Kung-ch'uan and Special Envoy Chiang Ching-kuo:
Secret. On *yin-ma* [date] I personally asked Major General Trotsynko to send liaison officials to accompany me to Ssu-p'ing to transport back to Ch'ang-ch'un our personnel in the provincial government. After repeated negotiations he promised to give me a reply at some later date. After our talk I personally went to the Chinese–Ch'ang-ch'un Railroad Bureau to telephone Ssu-p'ing to establish liaison. Because communist troops were very powerful, I failed to establish communication. Respectfully, I submit this information. In your employment, Tung Yen-p'ing. *Yin-ke-hai* [a date in code, with the third character denoting the hour]. Secret. Seal.

Four: To Chairman Chang Kung-ch'uan and Special Envoy Chiang Ching-kuo:
Secret. On *yin-ma* I personally asked Major General Trotsynko whether in the future the military delegation is to leave or stay. He replied that naturally it should move with the Soviet Army. He also promised to notify us about Soviet troop movements one week in advance. Respectfully, I submit

this information. In your employment, Tung Yen-p'ing. *Yin-ke-shu* [again, a date in code]. Seal.

I sent a wire to Vice-Chief of Staff Tung and Chairman Hsiung: "Just now the Soviet ambassador notified the Foreign Ministry that the Soviet Army is in the process of gradually withdrawing from the Northeast. It intends to complete withdrawal by the end of April."

I received from Vice-Chief of Staff Tung a wire addressed to me and Special Envoy Chiang:

> Yesterday, when I saw Major General Trotsynko, I told him about Chairman Chang Kung-ch'uan's gratitude to Marshal Malinovsky and Major General Trotsynko for their fond thoughts. I also said that if Their Excellencies Messrs. Chang and Chiang can know the specific date when Soviet troops will withdraw from Ch'ang-ch'un, they intend to return to Ch'ang-ch'un if time permits. I added that, presumably, the Soviets also understand the difficult situation Your Excellencies are in. Major General Trotsynko expressed his thanks and will report my message to Marshal Malinovsky. Currently, Soviet troops in Ch'ang-ch'un have begun to withdraw. But, since he has promised one week before the Soviet Army command leaves to notify our military delegation so that it can leave with the Soviet command and also has expressed a wish that our troops stop for ten days in Kung-chu-ling, it would appear that Soviet troops will not complete their withdrawal in ten days or so. Please take into consideration every aspect of conditions and decide whether to make the trip.
>
> Trotsynko's attitude was quite good. Pray wire and instruct me about what your plans are.

I sent back a wire:

> I have read your wire. The atmosphere this side of the Great Wall cannot be imagined by the Soviets. In my previous wire, I hoped the Soviet Army would indicate the date of its withdrawal from Ch'ang-ch'un and Harbin, arrange in advance procedures for replacing defense of those cities, and help our troops reach Ch'ang-ch'un. I hoped that these might improve the atmosphere so that we could return to Ch'ang-ch'un. Now, the Soviets have indicated that they will complete withdrawal by the end of April. But they have not specified a date for our taking over the defense of Ch'ang-ch'un and Harbin. Furthermore, their requirement that our troops stay for ten days in Kung-chu-ling makes it difficult to dispel suspicion. I sincerely hope that the Soviets take into consideration the current situation of our central government and, in the interests of a lasting friendship between the two countries, alter the overall situation. We always are willing to make the greatest effort to improve the friendly relationship between China and the Soviet

Union. With respect to the issue raised by Counselor Sladkovsky, that Soviet staff members were killed in Mukden, I already have wired our authorities to thoroughly investigate. Will Hsin-min, et al., please transmit this message to Sladkovsky?

I received from Vice-Chief of Staff Tung a wire replying to mine inquiring about conditions surrounding the transportation of our troops northward from Mukden:

> I have read Your Excellency's wire. Kalgin has agreed to issue orders to assist in transporting our troops by rail.
> Apparently, if the railroad between Mukden and Ch'ang-ch'un can be swiftly repaired in time, communication restored, and the problems of locomotives and coal supply are resolved without hindrance, we can transport our troops by rail along that entire section. Our troops already have reached several stations beyond Mukden, but we have not yet received precise reports. We estimate that at present probably they still are south of T'ieh-ling.

Today's newspaper (the *Liberation Daily*) printed a talk by Chou En-lai. He said that the resolutions of the Second Congress of the Nationalist party Central Committee contradict the decisions made by the Political Consultative Conference.

MARCH 23. Mr. Mo Liu-ts'un came to talk. In his opinion, we should invite General Li Tu, who is anti-Japanese, to return to the Northeast because he is a former acquaintance of Chou Pao-chung, Li Yen-lu, and others who can relieve the central government of a part of its work. My feeling is that now already there is rivalry between the Nationalists and the Communists; personal relationships are out of the question. In an article about the true history of the northeastern question, which appeared in the *Liberation Daily* on the eighteenth of this month, it was mentioned that Li Tu is a former acquaintance of Hsia Yün-chieh, commander of the Seventh Army of the Anti-Japanese United Army; Tai Hung-pin, divisional commander subordinate to Hsia Yün-chieh; and Li Hua-ta, commander of the Ninth Army of the Anti-Japanese United Army. There still is no way to determine exactly how strong his forces are.

Today's *Liberation Daily* printed that Chou Pao-chung took the lead in signing a circular telegram demanding that the National government punish the criminals responsible for the murder of Li Chao-lin, recognize the People's Self-Defense Army in the Northeast, and allow troops of the People's Self-Defense Army to enter Ch'ang-ch'un, Harbin, and other places, as well as guarantee the safety of those troops.

MARCH 24.   I received from Vice-Chief of Staff Tung a wire replying to mine of the twenty-second:

(1) On the twenty-third, Secretary Mi Hsin-min tactfully transmitted to Counselor Sladkovsky Your Excellency's opinions. Sladkovsky was congenial and still expressed the wish that Your Excellency return to Ch'ang-ch'un. He added that if Mr. Chang [Chang Kia-ngau] does not come back to Ch'ang-ch'un then I [Sladkovsky] will have nothing to do and can only return to Moscow. And so forth. (2) As for transferring our electric communications and finance personnel to Chin-chou and Mukden, I already have wired Chairman Hsiung for a decision. (3) Concerning the antiquities and old books, I have received from Chairman Hsiung instructions that these are to be temporarily secretly kept in the storehouse. I intend to wait until there are planes available when I will discuss with the air force having these articles shipped out of Ch'ang-ch'un.

I received a wire from Vice-Chief of Staff Tung:

Several times I have negotiated with the Soviet Army command and the Soviet vice-chairman of the board of directors of the Chinese–Ch'ang-ch'un Railroad the question of bringing back to Ch'ang-ch'un Governor Liu of Liaopeh province and the others. The Soviets promised to have a special train with Soviet railroad personnel accompany me to Ssu-p'ing to bring back these people. On *mei-jih* [a date, in code] at ten o'clock we left the Ch'ang-ch'un station. When the train reached the station at Liu-fang-tzu, we were held up because of the plague blockade. We arrived in Ssu-p'ing only this morning.

MARCH 25.   At approximately noon Foreign Minister Wang Hsüeh-t'ing called to say that just now the Soviet ambassador came to the ministry for an interview. He [the Soviet ambassador] stated,

On March 11, Chairman Chang sent Secretary Keng to see Counselor Sladkovsky to inquire whether he was willing to come to Chungking because the Chinese hope to continue the discussions in Chungking. Now, the Soviets have agreed to do this and the ambassador asked that the Chinese immediately discuss the matter with Counselor Sladkovsky.

Ching-kuo came to see me. I discussed with him whether we should return to Ch'ang-ch'un. We both agreed that if the two countries decide to continue the discussions in Chungking, then we may return to Ch'ang-ch'un, as an expression of goodwill toward the Soviets.

In the evening, President Chiang invited me for supper. We decided that we will carry on discussions with the Soviets in Chungking, presided over by the central government. But we intend first to notify the United States and observe its reaction. We [Chang Kia-ngau and Chiang Ching-kuo] are to wait until our Foreign Ministry has replied to the Soviet ambassador before returning to Ch'ang-ch'un.

MARCH 26. Today, Vice-Chief of Staff Tung met with Major General Trotsynko to discuss and ask about our request that when Soviet troops withdraw from various places they must formally hand them over to us so that we can replace the Soviet defenders. In his reply, Major General Trotsynko deliberately evaded the issue. He said that if Tung meant handing over barracks we only have to specify the troops or organization to take over and naturally they will be handed over. Tung then told Trotsynko that by replacing their defenders we meant assuming the duty of defending social order. Moreover, Tung told him that, until our side has sufficient real strength, we are unable to replace Soviet defenders, implying a wish that the Soviets assist us. Trotsynko replied that, concerning this point, the Soviets are unable to assist us. Finally, he raised three points:

1. Because of current conditions affecting rail transportation, it will require from ten to twelve days for the Soviets to transport troops from Ch'ang-ch'un to the Soviet national border. The Soviets already have received orders to complete the withdrawal before April 30.

2. On April 25, at the latest, and irrespective of conditions affecting rail communication, Soviet troops in the Ch'ang-ch'un area will complete their withdrawal.

3. Trotsynko solemnly stated,

In regions north of Ch'ang-ch'un, garrisoned by the Soviets, our troops cannot wait for regular Chinese government troops to replace the defenders. Instead, we can only hand over our duties to whatever armed force currently exists. If regular Chinese government troops cannot hurry in time, we cannot, on that account, stop the scheduled withdrawal. Your side please will give special attention to this.

I find his third point extraordinarily important because, since negotiations began, I have felt that the Soviet Union retains its old outlook with respect to northern Manchuria. In other words, it constitutes a Soviet sphere of influence. Consequently, even if China and the Soviet Union can reach an agreement in their negotiations, he certainly will see to it that the Soviet Union covertly possesses the power to control northern Manchuria. If the Chinese Communists prevail, the Soviets certainly will secretly nurture a kind of force that can manipulate the situation in the Northeast.

I received a report saying that, along the railroad from Man-chou-li to

Sui-fen-he, the standard gauge of the rails (1.435 meters, equal to 4.85 feet) already has been altered to the wide gauge rails of Soviet railroads (1.524 meters, equal to 5.2 feet). Consequently, even if our government troops reach Harbin, how can we obtain coaches to transport the troops both east-ward and westward?

I received from Vice-Chief of Staff Tung a wire saying that Governor Liu of Liaopeh province, Secretary Hsü Nai, and their group of fourteen people have arrived safely in Ch'ang-ch'un. There has been no repetition of the Chang Hsing-fu incident, and this has calmed my heart somewhat.

MARCH 27.   At 4:30 P.M. Foreign Minister Wang invited me for a talk. The Soviet ambassador happened to be there to see him and delivered a summary. [The following account is very confusing with respect to which party is related to what action. The translation may not be totally accurate.] Largely on the basis of my repeated discussions with Counselor Sladkovsky in January and my talk with Marshal Malinovsky on February 1, the sum-mary proposed a minimal number of enterprises for economic cooperation, along with those which, except for the Fu-shun coal mines, the Soviets anticipate we may agree on. The Soviets are unwilling "to lose the enter-prises that they may have obtained for joint management simply because the withdrawal of their troops is not accompanied by the formal replacement of the defense." They anticipate that, when the Communists have been de-feated by us, the Soviets still can continue to negotiate with us and reach an agreement. I really admire their far-sightedness. (In the following section, I affix the text of the Soviet proposal.)

Strictly secret [this phrase is placed on the margin of the paper and precedes the text proper.]

Proposal that Soviet Ambassador Petrov
Personally Delivered to the Foreign Minister
when He Came to the Ministry March 27, 1946, at 5:30 P.M.

A. The governments of China and the Soviet Union have agreed to jointly manage various formerly Japanese enterprises in Manchuria, as follows:

1. Coal mine enterprises: Mi-shan, Fu-shun, Chi-hsi, Heng-shan, Cha-lai-no-erh, and He-kang

2. The An-shan Iron-making Metals Complex, which includes the steel-tempering plant, the Liao-yang Iron Mine, the An-shan Fire Brick Factory, and the Kobe Mechanism Factory of An-shan

3. The Dairen Oil Refinery (in the original text the plural form is used)

4. The cement factory at Dairen and Harbin

5. The T'ien-chih-ch'uan Power Plant (in the original text the plural form is used) of Dairen

6. The salt flat (in the original text, the plural form is used) on the Liaotung Peninsula

7. The airports in Dairen, Mukden, Ch'ang-ch'un, Harbin, Ch'i-ch'i-ha-erh, Hailar, Mu-tan-chiang, and Chia-mu-ssu. The above-listed airports are to be managed by the Sino-Soviet Civil Aviation Company.

B. For the purpose of managing the above-listed enterprises, and in accord with the principle of equality, there will be organized the Sino-Soviet Joint Stock Company (in the original text, the plural form is used) for Joint Management. The chairman of the board of trustees of the Sino-Soviet Joint Stock Company for Joint Management will be chosen from among Chinese representatives. The vice-chairman of the board of directors will be chosen from among Soviet representatives.

In the various companies, executive duties will be handed over to a manager designated by the Soviets and an assistant manager designated by the Chinese.

The term of management by the Sino-Soviet Joint Stock Company for Joint Management will be 30 years. Upon the expiration of this term, all the above-listed enterprises will revert to the Chinese government without compensation. March 27, 1946, in Chungking.

Meanwhile, Foreign Minister Wang requested this of the Soviet ambassador: "Before Soviet troops withdraw, we must reach various places in the Northeast. According to the Sino-Soviet agreement, the Soviets must assist us and discuss everything with our Northeast Headquarters." The Soviet ambassador promised immediately to report the matter to the Soviet government. At once, I wired Chairman Hsiung and Vice-Chief of Staff Tung to notify them about this. (In the following section I affix a copied record of Wang's talk.)

I received from Vice-Chief of Staff Tung a wire, at the end of which he made these remarks: "Apparently, in their desires and inclinations the Soviets cherish an ulterior motive with respect to the five provinces in the northern part of the Northeast." This is a very wise observation and coincides with mine. It follows that, even if we agree to the conditions for cooperation proposed by the Soviet ambassador, our troops can only go as far as Harbin. As for our taking over the five provinces in the northern part of the Northeast, we are bound to be obstructed. Circumstances even may compel us to compromise with armed forces in the locality and form a united government. (In the following section I affix the text of the wire.)

Concerning mediation, Nationalist, communist, and American representatives have reached an agreement. They will dispatch to the Northeast four teams, under the following conditions:

1. Their task is restricted merely to mediation.

2. The teams must work only in regions where there are government troops and Chinese communist troops.

3. The teams must proceed to places where there are military clashes or where government and communist troops are in close proximity to make them end their clashes and to conduct necessary and fair mediation.

MARCH 28.   Liang Shu-ming has just returned from Yen-an. I invited him for supper. He said Mao Tse-tung told him that the Chinese Communists must alter their conduct. But what Mao wants is that the change not be accompanied by chaos. Liang wonders whether by change Mao was indicating the New Democracy, intending to use this to alleviate the people's dread of communism. Liang also said that he witnessed the confession movement in which those involved openly criticized one another. He went on to say that none of the public servants (at Ye-nan) drew a salary and that they planted vegetables and raised chickens while the state provided these public servants with clothing and food. All of this is gradually having an effect. As for the northeastern question, he [here, the author's account of his conversation with Liang Shu-ming is interrupted by the text of Foreign Minister Wang's talk with the Soviet Ambassador, followed by the wire from Tung Yen-p'ing].

Concerning the notice from the Soviet government that Soviet troops in the Northeaast will complete withdrawal by the end of April of this year, we already have replied that we can approve.

At present, there still is more than a month before the date when Soviet troops will complete withdrawal. Moreover, the Northeast has a multitude of convenient railroads and communications. Therefore, before the Soviet withdrawal, Chinese government troops certainly will be able to reach all regions from which Soviet troops are about to withdraw.

The Chinese government now requests that the Soviet government wire the Soviet Army command in the Northeast, asking that, in accord with the spirit of the Sino-Soviet Treaty of Friendship and Alliance, it speedily discuss and formulate with Major General Tung Yen-p'ing of our military delegation measures for replacing the defense in various places so that, when Chinese government troops replace that defense, they will be able to obtain Soviet assistance. March 27, 1946.

[A very dark bottom section of the sheet has rendered several characters undecipherable. The translator has tried to be as accurate as possible.] To Chairman Chang Kung-ch'uan and for submission to Generalissimo Chiang: Secret. On *yin-you* [a date, in code] I met with Major General Trotsynko and solemnly brought up for negotiation the question of our replacing the defense in various places in the Northeast. Instead of giving me a direct reply, he first evaded the question in all kinds of ways. Subsequently, after repeated questioning, he revealed his real thoughts. He said that, since he has received orders to complete the withdrawal before *mao-sa* [date], all he knows is that he must follow orders and complete the task. There is no time to take care of other matters. He also stated that in regions north of Ch'ang-ch'un garrisoned by the Soviets, the Soviet Army cannot wait for Chinese government troops to replace the defense. Instead, it can only hand over the defense to armed forces currently existing in the locality. If Chinese troops cannot arrive in time, the Soviet troops cannot, on this account, stop their withdrawal. And so forth. As for the deadline for the withdrawal from Ch'ang-ch'un, he said that their withdrawal can be completed on *mao-you* [April 25], at the latest, or from *mao-shan* [April 15] to *mao-hao* [April 20], at the earliest. Chinese government troops can enter the metropolitan district of Ch'ang-ch'un before Soviet troops complete their withdrawal. When Chinese troops enter the vicinity of Ch'ang-ch'un, they still must halt to be examined for plague. This need not be restricted to Kung-chu-ling. It also can take place in an area north of the ridge. I then raised the point that since, along the railroad from Man-chou-li to Sui-fen-he, the gauge of the rails has been widened, how are we to deal with the question of coaches needed by our troops on that section or, in other words, the question of transporting our troops to replace the defense? He said that coaches will be supplied by the Soviet government but control will belong to the authorities of the Chinese–Ch'ang-ch'un Railroad. Subsequently, we decided that, in order to speedily settle the question, both sides will report to their governments. And so forth. On the basis of my general observations of Soviet desires and inclinations, it seems that they cherish an ulterior motive toward the five provinces in the northern part of the Northeast. The matter is very urgent. Respectfully, I submit it for your consideration. In your employment, Tung Yen-p'ing. *Yin-kan-tzu* [presumably, the month, day, and hour in code]. Secret. Seal.

[The following continues the author's conversation with Liang Shu-ming, interrupted by the above two texts.] said that he heard nothing about it in Ye-nan.

MARCH 29.   General Li Tu came to see me. I told him that I already had
talked with President Chiang and that we have to wait awhile to ascertain
whether we can invite him to go to the Northeast. He said that, among his
former subordinates, those whom he can talk with are Chou Pao-chung and
Li Yen-lu.

Shen Ch'eng-chang [another name for Shen Hung-lieh] came to talk. I
told him that General Li Tu is willing to go to the Northeast and work there.
He [Shen] did not quite approve of this, saying he feared this will not have
much effect. He added that with respect to the northeastern question, the
Soviet Union still is the most important element: we first must reach an
agreement with the Soviets before entering into consultations with the Chinese Communists. He also said that in the future, perhaps we can allow
Chinese communist armed forces to be stationed in a number of regions in
the Northeast. I told him that already it will be difficult to reach a satisfactory
agreement with the Soviet Union. If in the future we must let Chinese
communist armed forces be stationed in certain regions in the Northeast, the
locality should be north of Harbin. I only hope that the mediation teams can
have an effect.

MARCH 30.   In the morning, Foreign Minister Wang invited me for a
talk. He told me,

> I intend to propose to the Soviet ambassador that the Soviet Army assist our
> troops as they enter various places north of Mukden. I also intend to protest
> against the armed irregular forces receiving Soviet assistance and, there-
> fore, being helped in their endeavors. Furthermore, I intend to ask the
> Soviet ambassador to explain the term "have reached an agreement" con-
> tained in the summary that the Soviet ambassador delivered to us on the
> twenty-seventh.

Foreign Minister Wang's opinion is that we should temporarily maintain the
position of an observer and wait for the Security Council to convene to see
whether the U.S. government's policy toward the Soviet Union changes,
before replying to the summary of the Soviet ambassador. My feelings are
that no matter what policy the U.S. government adopts in the Security
Council, it will have no effect on the Soviets.

In the afternoon, Chou En-lai came to see me. He said that the northeastern problem is rooted in the following missteps: first, in early December,
central government troops attacked communist troops in Jehol. Moreover,
they went further and attacked communist troops southwest of Mukden.
Next, in early January, the tripartite truce team failed to reach an agreement, with the result that in February and March there occurred anti-

Soviet, anticommunist movements. Now, the Communists, hearing that large numbers of Nationalist troops are marching northward, have had to adopt a defensive strategy. Consequently, already Nationalist troops advancing northward have been obstructed at T'ieh-ling. He feared they will be further obstructed at Ssu-p'ing. Chou went on to say that at present the only path to a solution is to seek a speedy and simultaneous resolution, both politically and militarily: politically, to reorganize the Northeast Political Commission and add to it participants from various parties and factions, while militarily, speedily making regulations governing the locations where troops from both sides are to be stationed, as well as plans for army reorganization. The Peace Preservation Corps in the various provinces also are to be included in these regulations. As for diplomacy, this still will be the responsibility of the central government. My reply was that the central government first must take over political power in the various places before considering political consultation.

The *Liberation Daily* printed that the Northeast Democratic United Army has issued a statement saying that government troops have advanced along the route to Ch'ang-ch'un to attack it and that the Nationalist party must bear all responsibility for the consequences.

MARCH 31.   I received from Vice-Chief of Staff Tung a wire, which I also forwarded to Foreign Minister Wang:

Our troops have encountered serious obstacles as they try to occupy various places in the Northeast following the withdrawal of Soviet troops: (1) Communications have been cut along the Mukden-Ch'ang-ch'un section of the Chinese-Ch'ang-ch'un Railroad. Furthermore, along that line there are communist troops intercepting and attacking trains. Consequently, we still are unable to transport government troops northward without hindrance. (2) The Soviet Army already has widened the gauge of the rails along the line from Harbin to Sui-fen-he and Man-chou-li. Consequently, we are unable to use coaches of the Chinese-Ch'ang-ch'un and Pei-Ning railroads. (3) Except for those that have been destroyed or dismantled, all railroads except the Chinese-Ch'ang-ch'un Railroad secretly are being used by communist troops. (4) Under the pretext of imposing an examination for plague, the Soviets have demanded that our troops still must halt for a number of days south of Ch'ang-ch'un. (5) The Soviet Army has notified us that on April 25, at the latest, they will complete their withdrawal from Ch'ang-ch'un. I fear this also will impede transporting our troops along the rail section from Ch'ang-ch'un to Harbin. Among the five aforementioned points, points 4 and 5 are particularly important. If these cannot be settled, it really will be difficult to formulate a feasible plan for replacing the defense in the Northeast. While Yen-p'ing [the sender of the wire] will try his best to achieve a diplomatic breakthrough in negotiations with the Soviets, it would seem that Your Excellency still should report the situation to the Foreign Ministry and ask that, in order to obtain a basic solution, it please enter into detailed discussions with the Soviet government.

This wire already indicates that, although the Soviets have promised to withdraw their troops, there still remains the question of whether we can replace the defense. Therefore, apparently the Foreign Ministry's negotiations concerning the withdrawal of Soviet troops already have borne fruit. Does not the Foreign Ministry realize that long ago the Soviets made arrangements not to let us take over the defense of the Northeast without obstruction? I sent to Vice-Chief of Staff Tung a wire in reply:

I have read your wire. Already, Foreign Minister Wang twice has raised with the Soviet ambassador that when Soviet troops withdraw, they must hand over to us the places they are garrisoning so that we can defend them. The Soviet ambassador replied that he already had wired Moscow. Please transmit this to the Soviets. Originally, there were no local armed irregular forces along the rail line between Mukden and Ch'ang-ch'un. Near Ch'ang-ch'un these forces also long ago disappeared. Consequently, we must blame the failure of the Soviets to assist us, in accord with the Sino-Soviet agreement, for current obstructions along the rail line and, possibly, the future occupation of Ch'ang-ch'un by communist troops. If our troops can reach Ch'ang-ch'un, this could alter the atmosphere this side of the Great Wall. You still can continue to work for friendly relations. The Soviets should be able to appreciate this. Please tactfully transmit this message to the Soviets.

From Chungking to Shanghai

On April 1 Major General Trotsynko informs Chinese officials in Ch'ang-ch'un that Soviet officials will let them know by April 3 when Soviet troops will withdraw from Manchuria. He appeals to the Chinese to have their troops ready to occupy Ch'ang-ch'un by mid-April. Malinovsky's headquarters in Ch'ang-ch'un will decamp for the Soviet Union between April 10 and 15. Tung Yen-p'ing believes that the Soviet troops, by avoiding contact with the Chinese and by trying to prevent the Chinese troops from moving northward, will be free to act as they choose in northern Manchuria.

On April 3 Tung wires Chang Kia-ngau to express his concern about Nationalist troops arriving soon enough to establish suitable defenses in Manchuria's major cities. Tung also worries that the railway gauge from Harbin to the Soviet border has been widened by Soviet work crews and that the Nationalists will have to ask Soviet officials to help transport their troops. Tung further states that Trotsynko has not firmly promised to help the Nationalists bring their troops into northern Manchuria.

On April 3 Chang Kia-ngau receives a wire from Chairman Hsiung reporting numerous Soviet official complaints that Soviet citizens are being killed and terrorized. Chang immediately wires Tung about this and asks him to tell Trotsynko that Chungking has learned from the Soviet embassy that Soviet troops will transfer former Manchukuo monarch P'u-yi to the Chinese authorities. Therefore, would General Trotsynko please transfer

P'u-yi to Nationalist officials in either Mukden or Ch'ang-ch'un? Chang also informs Tung that he has learned from Hsiung of Soviet troops destroying public buildings and warehouses near the Ch'ang-ch'un airport; would Tung check on these reports so that officials in Chungking could make a formal protest to the Soviet embassy?

Tung replies that on April 6 Malinovsky's headquarters in Ch'ang-ch'un will leave for the Soviet Union, that by mid-April Soviet troops will have left Ch'ang-ch'un, that on April 25 Soviet troops will complete their withdrawal from Harbin, and that by the end of April their troops will be entirely out of Manchuria.

The next day Chang Kia-ngau meets with President Chiang Kai-shek and other officials. President Chiang suggests that the time might be ripe for resuming economic cooperation talks with the Soviet Union. That same evening Chang Kia-ngau expresses his wish to leave politics, but the president disapproves.

On April 5 Chang Kia-ngau and Chiang Ching-kuo wire Marshal Malinovsky their farewell, their apology for not seeing him off, and their regards to M. I. Sladkovsky.

On April 6 Chinese officials in Ch'ang-ch'un give Malinovsky a farewell banquet. Malinovsky tells his hosts that he would like the Chinese military delegation in Ch'ang-ch'un to accompany him to Harbin and that Chungking should now negotiate directly with Moscow about when Chinese troops can occupy Ch'ang-ch'un and Harbin. Representatives of both sides make speeches and avoid criticizing each other's behavior.

Chang Kia-ngau interprets Malinovsky's departure as a move to await the outcome of further Sino-Soviet negotiations on economic cooperation. If these negotiations are successfully concluded, Soviet officials will not prevent Nationalist troops from taking over northern Manchuria, but if the negotiations fail, the Soviets will allow and even help communist troops to attack Nationalist troops.

Chang immediately drafts a new list of enterprises to be managed jointly by China and the Soviet Union. On April 7 Chang goes to the Foreign Ministry to consult with Minister Wang. Wang asks Chang to wire Tung to request that Soviet officials provide assistance to repair the Ch'ang-ch'un railway and not to request that Soviet troops remain to defend Ch'ang-ch'un until Nationalist troops arrive because Wang fears that might give the Soviets another excuse to delay their troop withdrawal. Chang immediately wires Tung and instructs him to request the Soviets' assistance in restoring the Ch'ang-ch'un Railroad and to tell them not to allow Chinese communist troops to occupy any areas as they did at Ssu-p'ing; such action will violate the spirit of the Sino-Soviet friendship treaty.

By April 8 Chang has completed his alternative plan for resuming Sino-

Soviet economic cooperation negotiations. He gives the plan to Minister Wang. Wang states that only after the Soviets assist the Nationalist troops in establishing their defenses in northern Manchuria should there be any discussions with Soviet officials. Chang Kia-ngau later confides to his diary that the Foreign Minister still does not realize that the key to eliciting Soviet help is obtaining an agreement on Sino-Soviet economic cooperation. Chang realizes that negotiations on this issue have shifted to other officials in the central government and that he now has little influence on their outcome.

On April 9 Chang Kia-ngau again confers with President Chiang Kai-shek and other leading officials. President Chiang suggests that the Chinese side quickly begin negotiations with the Soviet Union but that Minister Wang maintain his tough stand. Chang Kia-ngau urges that negotiations begin but that they be linked to a Soviet commitment to help the Nationalists quickly recover northern Manchuria. At the end of the meeting President Chiang instructs the Foreign Ministry and the Economics Ministry to assign their vice-ministers to take up these negotiations and tells Chang Kia-ngau to assist both vice-ministers in these negotiations.

Meanwhile, Tung continues to keep Chang Kia-ngau informed about the gradual Soviet troop withdrawal. On April 12 Chang Kia-ngau joins with the two vice-ministers to discuss how to initiate negotations on Sino-Soviet economic cooperation. But now Chang learns from other government officials that negotiations are already taking place with the Chinese Communists about the Nationalist troop takeover of Ch'ang-ch'un. Chang fears that it is now too late to work out any agreement with the Soviets because the Chinese Communists are too well established in Manchuria and their forces greatly expanded in number. He further worries that communist troops might occupy Ch'ang-ch'un before Nationalist troops are able to do so.

Chang learns that Tung has moved to Harbin with General Trotsynko. Tung brings him up to date on the developments in northern Manchuria. The former emperor, P'u-yi, is supposed to be turned over to the Chinese in Harbin very soon, and a plane is being sent to Harbin to receive him from Soviet officials.

On April 13 the Chinese foreign minister informs the Soviet embassy of China's desire to begin economic cooperation discussions. But the Soviet ambassador cannot approve the new principle in the Chinese proposal that all former Japanese property must be used to compensate China's wartime losses. Both sides continue to disagree, and there is no progress.

On April 14 President Chiang Kai-shek tells Chang Kia-ngau that no more concessions will be made to the Communists in Manchuria and that Chang should delay his return to Ch'ang-ch'un. That same day Chang wires Tung to tell Sladkovsky and Malinovsky that efforts are under way in Chungking to reopen economic cooperation negotiations; Chang hopes an agree-

ment will be reached before Soviet troops withdraw. Chang urgently desires that Soviet troops help Nationalist forces reach Ch'ang-ch'un quickly.

On April 15 Chang Kia-ngau learns that Chinese communist troops are pressing closer to Ch'ang-ch'un. Chang now fears that war between the Nationalists and the Communists will decide the fate of Manchuria and that the Soviets will help the Communists in order to maintain Soviet influence in Manchuria. Chang also predicts that the outcome of such a conflict will be in the Communists' favor because of the central government's great difficulty in supplying its troops so far from China Proper. Therefore, Chang regrets the lack of an economic cooperation agreement between China and the Soviet Union, for had there been one, the tragic events in Manchuria might not have occurred.

Tung then notifies Chang Kia-ngau that he has learned that Lin Piao's communist troops will try to occupy Harbin after Soviet forces withdraw. Tung outlines some possible scenarios of Nationalist-communist conflict that might take place in the near future.

On April 17 Chang Kia-ngau visits Soviet ambassador Petrov and urges that greater efforts be made to reach an economic cooperation settlement between the two countries. Petrov repeats the familiar Soviet position and suggests that the joint management on civil aviation also be included in the agreement. Petrov then insists that both sides agree on some basic principles to conclude the economic cooperation agreement. Chang replies that the Nationalist government is most concerned about the takeover of Ch'ang-ch'un and Harbin and that if those cities cannot be recovered by Nationalist forces, then economic negotiations with the Soviet Union might be impossible.

Chang Kia-ngau interprets Petrov's position as one of the Soviets allowing the Nationalist troops to recover Ch'ang-ch'un and Harbin, but Chang fears that the Chinese communist forces will have grown so large in the interim that they will demand that the Nationalists establish a united government with them in Manchuria.

Chairman Hsiung then notifies Chang Kia-ngau of Malinovsky's recent accusation that some Chinese military police killed a Soviet engineer of the Chinese–Ch'ang-ch'un Railroad and wounded another staff member. Malinovsky follows up that accusation by saying Soviet troops cannot help Chinese troops replace their defense of Ch'ang-ch'un but hopes Chang Kia-ngau and Chiang Ching-kuo will meet with him in Harbin before April 24. Chang also learns that Ch'ang-ch'un has come under attack by communist troops.

On April 18 Foreign Minister Wang summons Chang Kia-ngau for a talk and tells him that economic negotiations cannot be undertaken until the Soviet side responds to recent Chinese demands. Wang believes that the Soviet Union has no intention of helping the Nationalists take over Ch'ang-ch'un. Chang is surprised that Minister Wang does not want him to go to

Harbin and even more surprised to learn that Minister Wang wants President Chiang Kai-shek to negotiate with the Communists to help the Nationalist troops take over Ch'ang-ch'un and Harbin. Chang Kia-ngau surmises that the Communists will now realize that the Soviet Union is rejecting the Nationalists and thus will not make any concessions to the central government in these new negotiations.

On April 19 Chang Kia-ngau learns from the communist press that communist troops have entered Ch'ang-ch'un and set up an autonomous government. Chang worries for the safety of his former colleagues. He becomes more depressed about the recent turn of events in Manchuria and wonders if the policies pursued by the Republic of China (ROC) leaders in the past five months will produce a disaster or a favorable outcome for the country. Furthermore, because Sino-Soviet negotiations have become politicized since the Second Kuomintang Congress and because the Soviets were enraged by Chinese criticisms, Chang fears that a calamity will soon befall the central government over the problem of recovering Manchuria. Chang further speculates on how the Soviet Union will react to the new situation in Manchuria and predicts that Soviet officials will become more hostile to the Nationalist government and more supportive of the Communists.

On April 21 Tung wires Chang that Soviet officials have informed him that they will turn P'u-yi over to the Nationalists in Vladivostok and that Tung can still take P'u-yi into custody. On the twenty-second Chang learns that the Chinese communist representative of the truce mediation committee demanded a settlement of major questions pertaining to Manchuria or else the communist side would not nominate members for the National government. General Marshall calls Chou En-lai in to discuss how to resolve this new problem.

Tung wires Chang Kia-ngau and urges him to dissuade the central government from negotiating with the Communists about transporting Nationalist personnel from Ch'ang-ch'un. Tung insists that the central government ought to arrange for Soviet officials in Ch'ang-ch'un to confer with the Communists and arrange for the escort of Nationalist personnel to Harbin. Tung also states that on the twenty-fourth and twenty-fifth of April all Nationalist personnel in Harbin will leave under Soviet protection for the Soviet border.

Chang learns that General Marshall has insisted that both the Nationalists and the Communists cease fighting in Manchuria and not send any more troops into that region. On April 25 Marshall meets with Chang Kia-ngau's brother, Chang Chün-mai, and Lo Lung-chi to tell them that China is now at a crisis stage. Marshall admits that the Chinese Communists violated the truce agreement and prevented Nationalist troops from entering Manchuria but says that the central government also made some mistakes. Chang Kia-

ngau learns from Chou En-lai that members of Chang's delegation in Ch'ang-ch'un are safe. On April 28 Marshall again meets with Chang Chün-mai and Lo Lung-chi; both men suggest to Marshall some steps to bring peace to Manchuria, steps that Marshall approves but that are contingent on the response of President Chiang Kai-shek.

President Chiang approves Chang Kia-ngau's request that he be allowed to return to Chekiang to bury his recently deceased wife. On April 30 Chang leaves for Shanghai by train. In the remaining few pages of the diary Chang Kia-ngau reviews the events of the preceding six months that have produced the current debacle in Manchuria. The Nationalist government still does not have control of Manchuria, and now it confronts a powerful armed, established communist force that has already extended its control over large sections of Manchuria. Chang fears that if the ROC government loses Manchuria, China's fate will be sealed.

+ + + + + + +

APRIL 1.   I received two wires from the vice-chief of staff:

One: Today Tung met with Major General Trotsynko and requested that the Soviets assist us in replacing the defense in the Northeast. Trotsynko replied, "I hope we meet again on the third. By then I will be able to inform you of the specific dates on which Soviet troops will withdraw from Ch'ang-ch'un, Harbin, and various other places. But, since Soviet troops are withdrawing on a large scale, we also fear being attacked en route. Therefore, we really cannot postpone the dates when our troops will withdraw from Ch'ang-ch'un, Harbin, and other places. I hope that Chinese troops will speedily reach the various places in time. By the middle of April the number of Soviet troops in Ch'ang-ch'un will be reduced to a minimum, and we will not be able to maintain an effective force. We hope that by that time a considerable force of Chinese troops already will have occupied Ch'ang-ch'un."

Two: Concerning the future movements of our military delegation, Major General Trotsynko stated, "Your military delegation need not withdraw with the Soviet Army general headquarters beyond the national border. Marshal Malinovsky's headquarters has decided to leave Ch'ang-ch'un and return home between the tenth and the fifteenth. In the course of the journey, liaison will be difficult; we can discuss and decide upon all unsettled matters when we meet on the third." Trotsynko's views are diametrically opposed to those he indicated on March 20. Major General Trotsynko also told Tung, "After Marshal Malinovsky's headquarters leaves Ch'ang-ch'un, you can discuss military matters with Lieutenant General Karlov and political matters with Political Counselor Baluleichëv. Lieutenant General Karlov will be the last to leave Ch'ang-ch'un." Yen-p'ing [the sender of the wire] speculates that after ten days the Soviets will avoid direct contact with us, as well as refuse to let our military delegation move northward so that they will have freedom of action in the various provinces in the northern part of the Northeast.

At noon, I invited for lunch Shih Chien, chairman of the party headquarters of Kirin province, and Li K'e-chen, chairman of the party headquarters of Liaoning province. Both of them expressed hope that I will assign positions to party affairs personnel and give them employment. When the general situation has reached such a stage, that these people still should be discussing such questions, demonstrates how alienated from one another are the party and those in government administration.

APRIL 2.   All day I rested. By chance I thought of the many great figures the province of Szechwan has produced. For example, among men there was Ta Yü and among women, Shan Wen-chün, Ch'in Liang-yü, Hsüeh T'ao, etc. In the face of such a great catastrophe, can Szechwan produce one or two great figures to save the people from disaster?

APRIL 3.   I received from Vice-Chief of Staff Tung a wire saying that today he saw Major General Trotsynko and raised three points concerning the question of replacing the defense in the Northeast: (1) Tung fears that under the current conditions, when rail communication is obstructed, it will be difficult for our troops to arrive on schedule at various places to replace the defense. Tung wonders whether, in keeping with repeated Soviet statements that they will assist our National government in establishing political power in the Northeast, we can ask the Soviet Army, so long as this does not affect its overall plan for withdrawal, to keep, as appropriate, a small number of troops in various major cities and temporarily take responsibility for maintaining social order, withdrawing only after the arrival of our troops. (2) Along the railroad from Mukden to Harbin we can use, for the transportation of troops, coaches of the Chinese–Ch'ang-ch'un Railroad or Pei-Ning Railroad. But the gauge of the rails along the line from Harbin to Man-chou-li and Sui-fen-he has been widened. Consequently, we must ask the Soviets to fully assist us by supplying the coaches we will need. (3) In order to facilitate early replacement of the defense from one side to the other we can, when necessary, airlift troops to Ch'ang-ch'un, Harbin, Ch'i-ch'i-ha-erh, etc. Trotsynko said,

We cannot alter our plans for withdrawing. If, before the withdrawal of our troops, Chinese troops can arrive, naturally we will use every means to hand over the defense. Otherwise, we cannot wait. As for keeping, as appropriate, a small number of troops in various major cities, regrettably, we find it difficult to comply. This is because it will take fifteen days from Ch'ang-ch'un to the national border, and I fear complying with your request will affect the deadline for the withdrawal of all Soviet troops. Moreover, on the basis of previous Soviet experience in Mukden, a small number of troops face great threats. Neither are we willing to repeat a past mistake. As for the question of the wider gauge of rails along the line from Harbin to Man-chou-li and Sui-fen-he, already on April 1 I sought my government's instructions but have not yet received a reply.

Today, the Foreign Ministry sent to Chairman Hsiung by express mail in lieu of telegram the communication presented by the Soviet ambassador on April 1, which listed a series of complaints related to attacks on Soviet citizens and destruction of their property.

I sent a wire to Vice-Chief of Staff Tung:

(1) Recently, the Soviet ambassador protested the killing of Soviet emigrés in Mukden and insults to Soviet employees of the railroad, etc. (2) Today the Soviet ambassador replied to our communication, saying that they certainly will notify us before Soviet troops withdraw and that within the limits possible will assist us in replacing the defense. (3) The tripartite team already has arrived in Mukden to work. For the time being, it will not go to regions from which Soviet troops have not withdrawn. When you meet with Major General Trotsynko, please mention this to him, as an informal notice. (4) The Soviets have promised to hand P'u-yi over to our Foreign Ministry. I intend to tell the Soviets that it would be best to hand him over in Mukden. Otherwise, they can hand him over right in Ch'ang-ch'un. If our troops have not yet arrived in Ch'ang-ch'un, they can hand him over to our military delegation. Immediately after, have a plane ready to send him to Chin-chou, where he will be handed over to Chairman Hsiung. (5) Chairman Hsiung has reported to the Foreign Ministry that in Ch'ang-ch'un Soviet troops set fire to the University of Law and Politics, destroying it. They also used bombs to destroy the warehouses near the airport. Please wire and let me know the actual situation, so that we can protest.

I received a wire from Vice-Chief of Staff Tung saying that today Major General Trotsynko invited him for a talk. Trotsynko said that he had been ordered to announce the following dates when Soviet troops will withdraw from various places.

1. On the sixth, Marshal Malinovsky's headquarters and all of his subordinates will leave Ch'ang-ch'un for home.

2. On the fourteenth or the fifteenth, Soviet troops will complete their withdrawal from Ch'ang-ch'un. Garrison Commander Karlov will

be the last to leave Ch'ang-ch'un. No later than the tenth, quarantine stations will be withdrawn from the suburbs. Likewise, on the tenth, Soviet army planes will withdraw from the airport.

3. On the twenty-fifth, Soviet troops will complete their withdrawal from Harbin.

4. Between the thirteenth and the sixteenth, Soviet troops will complete their withdrawal from the city of Kirin.

5. On the twenty-fourth or the twenty-seventh, Soviet troops will complete their withdrawal from Ch'i-ch'i-ha-erh.

6. On the twenty-eighth or twenty-ninth, Soviet troops will complete their withdrawal from Mu-tan-chiang.

7. Before the tenth, Soviet troops will complete their withdrawal from Pei-an, Chia-mu-ssu, Khabarovsk, and various places north of these.

According to the above plan, by the thirtieth of this month Soviet troops will have been totally withdrawn to the Soviet national border.

General Ma Chan-shan came to see me. He expressed a desire to go back to the Northeast to work.

APRIL 4.   At noon, President Chiang invited me for lunch. Also present were Foreign Minister Wang, Yueh-chün [Chang Yueh-chün], Ling Yü-chíu, and Shao Ts'ung-en [a few characters in these names are not clear]. After lunch we discussed the question of the Northeast. Because, according to Vice-Chief of Staff Tung's wire, the Soviets already have fixed dates for the withdrawal and because Marshal Malinovsky will be leaving Ch'ang-ch'un on the sixth, President Chiang thinks that perhaps we should immediately indicate to the Soviets that we are willing to discuss the question of economic cooperation. On this same afternoon, Foreign Minister Wang invited the Soviet ambassador to the Foreign Ministry and told him that the Chinese government is willing to immediately discuss the plan for economic cooperation proposed by the Soviets. Wang added that we will begin discussions as soon as both sides have appointed appropriate persons. But Wang hopes that, in order to prevent another deterioration of public opinion in China, what happened in Ssu-p'ing will not be repeated in Ch'ang-ch'un or Harbin.

In the evening, President Chiang hosted a banquet for Wang Pao-ta of Annam. I was also invited. After dinner, President Chiang invited me to stay as his guest at Ling Yuan. He solicited my opinion concerning various aspects of the northeastern question and the political situation. While talking with him I indicated a desire to leave politics in favor of an involvement in social concerns. He did not approve.

I received a wire from Vice-Chief of Staff Tung:

On the third I talked with Major General Trotsynko and discussed with him in person the question of future movements of our military delegation. I said that the task of our military delegation is to station itself with the Soviet Army to maintain liaison. In the coming month both the Soviet Army and our army will face numerous concerns replacing the defense of the Northeast; thus, that time really will be an important stage in implementing the liaison duties of our delegation. After the Soviet Army headquarters withdraws on the sixth, whom should we regard as our counterpart in the negotiations? And so forth. Trotsynko replied that, after the sixth, we should maintain liaison with Karlov concerning military questions and with Counselor Baluleichëv about political questions. After the fifteenth, when Karlov leaves Ch'ang-ch'un, we can communicate with Commander Kovtun-Stankevich in Harbin, where he will remain until the twenty-fifth, while Counselor Baluleichëv will remain in Ch'ang-ch'un indefinitely. I then said that whether our military delegation leaves or remains will have to wait until I have sought my government's instructions and must be postponed. Trotsynko then replied that this is not a question he can settle and must be decided by his government, and so forth. Respectfully, I report. Please consider and send me instructions.

Also, the same day I received a wire from the vice-chief of staff:

On the third, when we talked, Major General Trotsynko said that on the tenth Soviet Army planes will be withdrawn from the Ch'ang-ch'un airport, while civilian planes still will continue to use it. He also said that he has already reached an understanding with Chairman Chang concerning the matter of civilian aviation. And so forth. Since he mentioned this casually, Yen [Tung Yen-p'ing] did not consider it appropriate to give an immediate reply. Subsequently, I asked Secretary Mi Hsin-min to indicate to Counselor Sladkovsky our denial.

From the point about civil aviation we can see that the Soviets still hope to reach an agreement concerning economic cooperation. We also can infer that the Soviets still are prepared to have us control regions south of Harbin. In other words, the National government still will remain an object of Soviet diplomatic concern, while they will let the Political Consultative Conference settle to whom political power belongs in various places in northern Manchuria.

APRIL 5.   President Chiang breakfasted with Wang Pao-ta of Annam and his entourage. I also was invited to attend. After the guests left I talked some with the president. He hopes that we soon reach an agreement with the Soviets and asked me continually to confer with Foreign Minister Wang.

Together with Special Envoy Chiang, I sent Marshal Malinovsky a wire to say farewell:

To His Excellency Marshal Malinovsky:
Hearing that Your Excellency will leave Ch'ang-ch'un on the sixth, we regret that duties prevent us from hurrying there to see you off. We dare to trust that, although physically Your Excellency will have left Ch'ang-ch'un, the spirit of lasting friendship between China and the Soviet Union, which you have cherished, will remain in China. Kia-ngau and Ching-kuo still wish to strive persistently for friendly relations between China and the Soviet Union. We respectfully express our highest esteem for Your Excellency and give our regards to Counselor Sladkovsky. Chang. Chiang.

I sent a wire to Vice-Chief of Staff Tung: "Yesterday, Foreign Minister Wang personally brought up with the Soviet ambassador that what happened at Ssu-p'ing must not be repeated in Ch'ang-ch'un or Harbin. The Soviet ambassador promised immediately to wire Marshal Malinovsky."

I received from Vice-Chief of Staff Tung a wire of the fourth: "Marshal Malinovsky is scheduled to leave Ch'ang-ch'un for home on the sixth. Our military delegation already has arranged to host a farewell banquet at the Central Bank on the evening of the fifth. Twenty-eight persons from the Soviet side will attend."

I also received from Vice-Chief of Staff Tung a wire of the fifth:

Today, I talked with Major General Trotsynko. Yen-p'ing [the sender of the wire] personally told him that in the Soviet ambassador's reply to our communication, made on the third, he said he will instruct Soviet troops stationed in the Northeast to assist us, within the limits possible, in replacing the defense. (I) asked His Excellency Trotsynko to please take note. And so forth. Trotsynko replied that, concerning the question of replacing the defense, he had nothing to say in reply other than what he had said when we talked on the third. Nor has he received any new instructions from his government.

This indicates that in discussions between our Foreign Ministry and the Soviet ambassador, as well as in the responses of the Soviet ambassador, the Soviets have merely employed diplomatic jargon and that real power rests with Marshal Malinovsky. Consequently, whether what happened at Ssu-p'ing will not reoccur still hinges on whether the two sides can reach an agreement regarding economic cooperation.

APRIL 6.   I received a wire from Vice-Chief of Staff Tung reporting on the farewell banquet for Marshal Malinovsky given last night by our military delegation. On the Soviet side, in addition to Marshal Malinovsky, over twenty people under him attended; on our side, there were over thirty of our military and political personnel. The banquet was staged on the fourth floor of the Central Bank. Marshal Malinovsky responded with a speech in which he stressed that, instead of being pressured by provocative and damaging forces from outside, China and the Soviet Union certainly can cooperate permanently. He was implying that China and the Soviet Union have been unable to reach an accord because of the provocative and damaging influence of the Americans. (In the following section I affix the text of the wire.)

This same day Vice-Chief of Staff Tung sent me another wire reporting that Karlov had transmitted to him by telephone these thoughts of Marshal Malinovsky: (1) The Soviet Army general headquarters intends to remain for a few more days in Harbin. Since there will be important matters to communicate and ask us about, Malinovsky wonders whether our entire military delegation can accompany them to Harbin. (2) While taking his leave at the railroad station, Malinovsky remarked that, although the Soviet Army has set the end of April as the date for completing its withdrawal, we can bring up, specifically, any needs we may have. For example, our government can negotiate directly with Moscow about the date when our troops can reach Ch'ang-ch'un and Harbin, as well as the date when it will be necessary for Soviet troops to withdraw from these cities and, certainly, will be able to receive a satisfactory answer. He added that he does not want any misunderstanding to arise to the effect that the Soviet Army is handing over to Chinese communist troops political power in various parts of the Northeast. (3) Major General Trotsynko noted that he has already received instructions from Moscow indicating that the Soviet Army should continue to maintain liaison with our military delegation. (In the following section I affix the text of the wire.)

I received a wire from Chief Secretary Chang Ta-t'ung:

This morning the Soviet liaison official indicated to Yang Tsuo-jen that Marshal Malinovsky will leave for Harbin at noon today but must remain there for a number of days. Originally, our military delegation planned to send many persons there for liaison purposes, and he asked whether this plan is now being implemented. Yang replied that he will seek instructions from Tung [Tung Yen-p'ing]. Soon afterwards, Tung decided that our military delegation should accompany Marshal Malinovsky to Harbin. First, Yang Tsuo-jen and Chang P'ei-cheh will accompany Malinovsky, while Tung and Mi Hsin-min will go there a few days later [here the author's account is interrupted by the text of the wires received from Tung Yen-p'ing].

Wire received.

To Chairman Chang Kung-ch'uan.
On mao-wei [the fifth] at 1800 hours our military delegation hosted a banquet for Marshal Malinovsky. Altogether the hosts and guests numbered

over fifty people. During the banquet I made a speech. The gist of it was (1) I commended Marshal Malinovsky and his subordinates for their contributions to the defeat of Germany and the recovery of the Northeast. (2) Recalling briefly the five months of liaison work between our military delegation and the Soviet Army, I expressed my gratitude to Marshal Malinovsky for his assistance to us in various ways. (3) I expressed a hope that, after Marshal Malinovsky leaves Ch'ang-ch'un, his representative here, in keeping with the harmonious spirit of the past, still will discuss and settle with us all issues so that the Chinese government troops can soon arrive and replace the defense at various places and so that all talks between our two sides can turn out satisfactorily. And so forth. Marshal Malinovsky then made a speech expressing his thanks. In general, he said that the Soviet Army came to the Northeast to liberate the people there and has not assumed the posture of a victor. He believed that, under the leadership of Generalissimo Chiang and Marshal Stalin, the two great nations of China and the Soviet Union certainly can cooperate permanently and will not be affected by provocative and damaging forces from outside. He hoped that the personnel of our central government would try to create democratic political conditions and deeply trusts that China will have a great future. And so forth. He repeatedly stressed the point about provocative and damaging forces from outside. The atmosphere at the banquet was rather pleasant and harmonious. I will make a separate copy of the entire text of the speeches of Yen-p'ing and Marshal Malinovsky and submit it by air mail for your consideration. Respectfully, I submit this information. In your employment, Tung Yen-p'ing. *Mao-yü*. Seal.

To Chairman Chang Kung-ch'uan, and please forward to the Foreign Ministry.
Secret. On *mao-yü-ch'en* [the third character in this code presumably stands for an hour] Karlov transmitted to me by telephone the opinions of Marshal Malinovsky, saying that the Soviet Army general headquarters intends to remain in Harbin a few more days and that since, inevitably, there will be important matters to maintain liaison about, he wonders whether our entire military delegation can accompany them to Harbin. And so forth. Because of this sudden change in his [Malinovsky's] attitude, Yen [Tung Yen-p'ing] is unclear about Malinovsky's intentions and inclinations. I then replied that we can, in addition, have Chang P'ei-cheh and Yang Tsuo-jen go there first, while Yen-p'ing, et al., will go soon afterward. At noon that same day, I went to the station to see Malinovsky off. Marshal Malinovsky and I stood talking for about an hour. He asked for the specific meaning of my remarks concerning the question of our replacing the defense, made in Your Excellency's [Tung Yen-p'ing's] speech at the banquet yesterday, as well as what kinds of assistance we would need from the Soviets. Yen-p'ing then replied that we hope your Soviet Army can leave behind, as appropriate, a small number of troops to help our government

troops quickly reach various places. After that, we can carry out procedures for replacing the defense. He replied that, in keeping with the Soviet government's order that Soviet troops complete their withdrawal by the end of April, the Soviet Army, separately, has already fixed dates for its withdrawal from various places in the Northeast; however, your [the Chinese] side can bring up any specific needs you may have and let Chungking negotiate with Moscow about them. For example, the date when your Chinese army will require that the Soviet army withdraw from Ch'angch'un, Harbin, and other places and the date when your army can arrive to replace the defense. Certainly you will be able to obtain a satisfactory reply. It has been the consistent hope of the Soviets to hand over the Northeast to troops of the National government. Originally, our army decided to withdraw from the Northeast on *hai-chiang* [apparently, a date in code] of last year. But, because your Northeast Headquarters had left Ch'ang-ch'un and there was no way to negotiate, we temporarily decided to postpone our withdrawal so that your government troops could replace the defense. Subsequently, because we had to delay a very long time, there arose in foreign circles numerous misunderstandings, making it necessary that we withdraw our troops as soon as possible. But the current situation makes me deeply apprehensive lest there be a misunderstanding to the effect that the Soviet Army is handing over to Chinese communist troops political power in various parts of the Northeast. We hold that cooperation between China and the Soviet Union is a necessity for both sides; we really do not want there to occur today any further misunderstandings that would bring about an unhappy end to our relationship. Malinovsky also hoped that our military delegation can accompany him to Harbin to maintain liaison. He is moving to Harbin and will remain for two weeks, during which all issues between the two sides can be settled through discussion. And so forth. In my opinion, his intentions seem very sincere. After our talk Major General Trotsynko told me that, following the banquet last night, Malinovsky received from Moscow a wire instructing the Soviet Army to continue to maintain liaison with our military delegation. And so forth. I presume that the sudden change in Marshal Malinovsky's intentions and inclinations is the result of the change in Moscow's diplomatic policy toward us. Within a few days, Yen-p'ing intends to go to Harbin, along with Ch'iu Nan and Chu Hsin-min, to continue negotiations. As for the question of replacing the defense, it seems that, in order to reach a fundamental settlement, we should ask the Foreign Ministry to immediately discuss this question specifically with the Soviet ambassador. Respectfully, I wire this information for you to please consider. In your employment, Tung Yen-p'ing. *Mao-yü-shen*. Secret.

[The following is a continuation of the author's account, interrupted by the text of the two wires from Tung Yen-p'ing.] These are my speculations:

1. Malinovsky still has to make arrangements in Harbin concerning northern Manchuria; this is bound to postpone the end of April as the date for the withdrawal of Soviet troops.

2. The Soviets may create another incident similar to that at Ssu-p'ing as an excuse for delaying the withdrawal of their troops.

I infer from Marshal Malinovsky's indications that what he will be waiting for in Harbin is the outcome of the negotiations in Chungking concerning economic cooperation. If the outcome of these negotiations is positive, then, irrespective of any obstructions created by the communist army between Ch'ang-ch'un and Harbin, the Soviets still will allow our troops to arrive and replace the defense. Otherwise, they will let the communist troops obstruct us and even may secretly assist them.

Today I drafted an alternative to the list of various enterprises to be managed cooperatively as proposed by the Soviet Union:

1. Basic conditions
2. Enterprises to be jointly managed
3. Opinions concerning joint management of the salt flats on the Liaotung Peninsula
4. Concerning the organization of the Civil Aviation Company

Because we will soon be meeting with the Soviets to discuss the question of economic cooperation, the aforementioned draft will be for reference in the discussions. I was unable to finish the draft today; let me continue it tomorrow.

Today's *Liberation Daily* published a statement issued by Chou En-lai:

The Nationalist party is in the process of enlarging the civil war in the Northeast. We resolutely oppose the continued dispatch of Nationalist reinforcements to the Northeast. We ask that a peaceful settlement be speedily sought, through political consultation . . . Already the Nationalists have increased their troops sent into the Northeast from two armies to seven armies [only six are listed] (the Thirteenth, the Fifty-second, the Ninety-fourth, the Seventy-first, the New First, the New Sixth). The total number of men is 285,000. Now, in addition, the Nationalists are sending there eight more armies. The total number of troops sent there will reach fifteen armies, and the total number of men, 512,000.

APRIL 7.   In the morning I went to the Foreign Ministry because Foreign Minister Wang regarded as inappropriate Vice-Chief of Staff Tung's request, mentioned in his wire, that the Soviets leave behind, as appropriate, a small number of troops to await the arrival of our government troops. Fearing that the Soviets again may use this as an excuse to delay the withdrawal of troops, he asked me to wire Tung and tell him not to mention this again. Moreover, in order to facilitate transporting our government troops to the Northeast, Wang wants me to ask Tung to request that at an early date the Soviets assist in repairing and restoring communication on the Chinese–Ch'ang-ch'un Railroad. Simultaneously, the Foreign Ministry will submit this proposal to the Soviet ambassador.

[Chang then wired Tung Yen-p'ing the following.]

> With respect to the question of the replacing of the defense, Foreign Minister Wang thinks that since the Soviets already have announced dates for the withdrawal of their troops from various places, we must not again request that they leave behind, as appropriate, a small number of troops in various places. This is what we are demanding from the Soviets today: (1) The Soviets must speedily try to repair and restore the Chinese–Ch'ang-ch'un Railroad. (2) To ensure that before Soviet troops withdraw our government troops can arrive in time to replace the defense, the Soviets must use every possible method to assist in eliminating obstructions along the Chinese–Ch'ang-ch'un Railroad as well as in various other places. If the Soviets let communist troops occupy the various places from which Soviet troops have withdrawn, repeating what happened at Ssu-p'ing, then we must regard this as a Soviet violation of the spirit of the Sino-Soviet friendship treaty. Foreign Minister Wang will immediately notify the Soviet ambassador about the aforementioned points. Please, just as frankly, inform the Soviets and ask them to please do their best, for the sake of future Sino-Soviet friendly relations.

APRIL 8.   I finished the draft of the alternative plan for the negotiations about Sino-Soviet economic cooperation, as well as my opinions concerning the question of the salt flats on the Liaotung Peninsula and the Civil Aviation Company. At 5 P.M. I went to Foreign Minister Wang's and gave them to him to study. He insists that we should begin discussions with the Soviets only after we receive a reply concerning whether they will assist our troops to advance northward to replace the defense. He does not know that the key to whether the Soviets will assist our troops to advance northward to replace this defense is whether or not an agreement is reached on economic cooperation. Moreover, long ago the Soviets already completed arrangements for obstructing, in a variety of ways, the northward advance of our troops. Now, they are quietly awaiting the outcome of the negotiations about economic cooperation and will manipulate the situation accordingly. Foreign Minister Wang still does not perceive this. I really am deeply worried about the future of our country. Today, the negotiations having been placed under the charge of the central government, what have I to say about the issue? The *Liberation Daily* printed this news item issued by the Communists: "Nationalist troops have ferociously invaded An-shan, Pen-hsi-hu, and other places. They were defeated by our troops."

APRIL 9.   At 11 President Chiang invited me for a talk. Also present were Chief of Civil Officials Wu Ta-ch'uan, Foreign Minister Wang, President Chang Yueh-chün, and Chiang Meng-lin, chief secretary of the Executive Yuan (he was for a long time president of Peking University), and others. President Chiang maintained that, in order to quickly replace the garrison along the Chinese–Ch'ang-ch'un line, we should soon begin talks with the Soviets. But Foreign Minister Wang thought we should wait, on the one hand, for Vice-President of the Executive Yuan Wong's return to Chungking and, on the other, for the Soviet ambassador's reply concerning the question of the Soviets' assisting us in replacing the defense of the Northeast. My view was that we may as well soon begin talks and discuss simultaneously economic cooperation and the Soviets' assisting us in replacing the defense of the Northeast. In this way, both matters can proceed. In the end, President Chiang instructed the ministries of Foreign Affairs and Economics to each assign one vice-minister to take up the negotiations. He also instructed me to assist them from the sidelines. On this very day, President Chiang's handwritten instructions were delivered to me. The message is as follows:

> To Foreign Minister Wang, Minister of Economics Wong, and Chairman Chang:
> Concerning the question of economic cooperation between China and the Soviet Union in the Northeast, the ministries of Foreign Affairs and Economics each will assign one vice-minister to begin discussions with the Soviets. I also will assign Chairman Chang Kung-ch'uan of the Northeast Headquarters to assist the two ministries in their planning of everything. Chung-cheng, April 9, 1946.

Today, in Mukden, Chairman Hsiung and my superior Tu Yü-ming hosted a reception for the tripartite truce team. Communist representative Jao Shu-shih delivered a speech. He said that the people in the Northeast long for peace and that the dispute between the Nationalists and Communists must be settled peacefully. On this day Hsiung and Tu did not attend the reception. They were represented by P'eng Pi-sheng. The American representative also delivered a speech. He said that if the question of the Northeast is not settled, it will affect the entire Chinese question. According to reports, the American representative had flown to visit Lin Piao at his command. (The location should be in Chia-mu-ssu.)

I received a wire from Vice-Chief of Staff Tung: "At noon on the ninth, fourteen [according to the Chinese way of counting, the fourteen should include Tung Yen-p'ing] officers and soldiers of our military delegation under Yen-p'ing, in your employment, left Ch'ang-ch'un by special train for Harbin. The Soviet Army dispatched one liaison official and three body-guards to accompany us.

Vice-Chief of Staff Tung and I have been colleagues for nearly six months. Concerning his personality, he is prudent, fair, and uncompromisingly straight and uncorrupt. In his dealings with the Soviets he demonstrates appropriate moderation [literally, neither arrogant nor humble]. Today his mission is almost concluded, but the prospects for a solution to the question of the Northeast are dark. Can this be the working out of the nation's destiny?

APRIL 10.   I received four wires from Vice-Chief of Staff Tung:

One: Reporting that, through discussions with the Soviet garrison commander in Harbin, Yang Tso-jen and Chang P'ei-cheh have arranged that our ground personnel, who will use the airport at Harbin, immediately can go to Harbin to set up radio stations. Until their arrival, the Soviets will be in charge of the airport.

Two: Reporting on a meeting between Yang, Chang, and Major General Trotsynko concerning the railroad coaches, we need to transport our troops owing to widening of the gauge of the rails along the railroad from Harbin to Sui-fen-he and Man-chou-li. Trotsynko's reply was that we can directly confer with the Soviet directors of the Chinese–Ch'ang-ch'un Railroad.

Three: Reporting on a discussion between Yang, Chang, and Major General Trotsynko, as well as the Soviet head of the Chinese–Ch'ang-ch'un Railroad Bureau, about ensuring rail communication, Major General Trotsynko was of the opinion that, in order for our troops to enter major locations along the rail line at appropriate moments and thus ensure communications, we had best have powerful troops advance closely in the wake of the last trains evacuating Soviet troops from Ch'ang-ch'un. Bureau Head Ju of the Railroad Bureau proposed that railroad employees be armed to protect the railroad by sections. He also guaranteed that these employees immediately will be disarmed upon arrival of our government troops. Tung thought this proposal could only benefit us and would seek instructions about whether he could act on it.

Four: With respect to the question of the security of Harbin, the Soviet garrison commander of Harbin has promised immediately to issue orders for the approximately twelve thousand men of the armed, irregular forces who had entered the metropolitan district of Harbin, to withdraw within two days to areas more than ten kilometers from the metropolitan district.

The *Liberation Daily* printed the news that government troops in the Northeast have suffered setbacks while attacking communist troops.

Vice-President of the Executive Yuan and Minister of Economics Wong returned to Chungking. I called on them to report about recent developments.

APRIL 11.   I received six wires from Vice-Chief of Staff Tung:

One: Reporting that he had received a wire from Ch'en Ch'ia-chen, a member of our military delegation in Ch'ang-ch'un, saying that at 5 A.M. on April 9 Chiu-t'ai fell to an attack by armed irregular troops.

Two: Major General Trotsynko personally told him that he has no objections if our administrative personnel in provinces and cities already taken over by us must accompany evacuating Soviet troops. But he hopes that we will provide the Soviets with the number of persons to be evacuated, a list of names of these persons, weight of goods accompanying these people, the route of their journey, and the length of time they intend to stay in Soviet territory.

Three: Bureau Head Ju of the Chinese–Ch'ang-ch'un Railroad personally told Chu Hsin-min and Chang P'ei-choh that the Railroad Bureau intends to ask personnel of the division of engineering and the various railroad sections temporarily to take up garrison duty along the railroad. The minimum requirement is that these men must do their utmost to maintain important structures along the rail line, such as big bridges, railway tunnels, and factories. Therefore, the Railroad Bureau considers it necessary to arm a suitable number of railroad employees. This railroad protection team will consist of workers from the engineering division and supervising foremen and will be placed under the unified command of the bureau heads of the various branch bureaus. As for clothing, these railroad workers still will wear the railroad uniform. These workers will be disarmed as soon as, acting in accord with the Sino-Soviet agreement, our government troops replace the defense. Bureau Head Ju also sent a list of structures that must be protected, as well as the number of persons and weapons needed. Structures: nineteen bridges, five mountain caves, the Chinese–Ch'ang-ch'un Railroad Bureau and its repair shop. Number of persons: six hundred, to be largely Chinese. Weapons: the Soviet Army will provide five hundred rifles and ten machine guns. He hopes we will provide five hundred rifles and twenty machine guns. He hopes that we speedily will reply, so that before the fourteenth they can begin to organize the team.

Bureau Head Ju also stated that, with respect to the damaged bridge at Kung-chu-ling, personnel sent by the Soviets to speedily repair it found their way obstructed by armed irregular troops and had to return. Meanwhile he also hopes that the two coal mines of Fu-shun and Hsi-an continuously will provide needed coal.

Four: Tung talked with Major General Trotsynko and reached the following understanding with respect to the question of transporting our troops: (1) Concerning the railroad from Ch'ang-ch'un to Ssu-p'ing, if there is armed protection for it, naturally he can ask the Chinese–Ch'ang-ch'un Railroad authorities to make repairs and restore communications along it. (2) Concerning the issue of transporting Chinese government troops along the two rail lines now having wider-gauge rails, from Harbin to Man-chou-li and from Harbin to Sui-fen-he, already Moscow has wired back its approval. If necessary, the Soviet Army command can assist us in every way. (3) The Soviets have no objection to our airlifting our troops to Harbin, Ch'i-ch'i-ha-erh, and other places. Moreover, they can help us.

Five: Trotsynko said that he has received from his government instructions to hand P'u-yi over to our military delegation. He hopes that this can be done in Harbin or Ch'ang-ch'un before Soviet troops withdraw. After conferring, we decided to have him handed over in Harbin.

Six: Major General Trotsynko told Tung that he has received from his government, by wire, instructions that the Chinese military delegation can withdraw to Khabarovsk along with the Soviet Army general headquarters. Trotsynko then asked Tung whether in Khabarovsk the Chinese military delegation can stay in the Chinese consulate there, what type of vehicles we hope to use, and which route we wish to take. We can notify the Soviet Army command about these matters.

APRIL 12.   In the morning, Foreign Minister Wang invited the following persons to discuss an alternative plan for a number of industrial and mining enterprises that the Soviets demand be jointly managed with us: Vice-President Wong of the Executive Yuan, Vice-Minister Ho Ts'ui-lien of the Ministry of Economics, and Vice-Minister Liu K'ai of the Foreign Ministry. We only adjourned at twelve o'clock. What was discussed fell roughly into three categories: (1) statement of principles, (2) conditions for joint management, and (3) range of enterprises to be jointly managed.

At noon I invited for lunch and an exchange of opinions on the northeastern question the following executive secretaries of the Society for Political Reconstruction of the Northeast: Ning Meng-yen, Yen Yü-heng, Wang Hui-po, Liu Wu-hsuan, Lu Kuang-sheng, Chou Wei-lu, etc. Yesterday, they interviewed Minister of National Defense Ch'en Ch'eng and today visited the Democratic League and Chou En-lai. They expressed the demand that Nationalist and communist armies cease fighting and that communist troops not occupy Ch'ang-ch'un. From their remarks about troops not occupying Ch'ang-ch'un, it would appear that Chou En-lai is leaving room for concessions. Upon hearing their words, I felt that already the central government is in a disadvantageous position. Certainly, if earlier we had reached an agreement with the Soviets, we would not be in today's situation.

In the afternoon, I called on Vice-Minister Liu Wei-chang of the Ministry of Military Affairs to ask about the conditions surrounding the advance of our government troops. He said that our troops still are over forty *li* [Chinese mile, 1,890 feet] from Ssu-p'ing and that their advance has slowed somewhat because of the need to reinforce troops behind them. He then said that the number of government troops sent into the Northeast already comprises six armies. [It is uncertain whether the following statement is made by Liu or by the author.] So the Soviet Army command long ago evacuated, but our troops advance slowly. How are we going to prevent Communist troops from occupying Ch'ang-ch'un? Aren't we already in a disadvantageous position?

I received from Vice-Chief of Staff Tung a wire of the eleventh, reporting on his first conference with Major General Trotsynko after arriving in Harbin. Major General Trotsynko indicated the following:

1. That our military delegation can accompany the Soviet Army general headquarters to Khabarovsk.

2. That, when necessary, our administrative personnel can withdraw into Soviet territory.

3. That, provided its personnel are protected by armed force, the Railroad Bureau will assume responsibility for repairing and restoring communications along the Mukden–Ch'ang-Ch'un section of the Chinese–Ch'ang-ch'un Railroad (by armed force Trotsynko meant armed forces from our side). On the other hand, Soviet staff members of the Railroad Bureau will protect important bridges and railway tunnels along the Ch'ang-ch'un–Harbin section, the Harbin–Man-chou-li section, and the Harbin–Sui-fen-he section of the railroad. (In other words, those bridges and tunnels proposed by the Soviet head of the Railroad Bureau.)

4. That, with respect to transporting our government troops along

the rail lines between Harbin and Man-chou-li and between Harbin and Sui-fen-he, where the gauge of the rails has been widened, the Soviets will provide coaches and fuel, as well as assist us in other ways.

5. That at any time we can airlift troops to Harbin and Ch'i-ch'i-ha-erh.

6. That P'u-yi will be extradited in Harbin.

7. That, on the twenty-seventh, the Soviets will hand over to our provincial government the three thousand Chinese POWs in Ch'i-ch'i-ha-erh.

8. That the Soviets have issued orders for armed irregular forces in Harbin, Ch'i-ch'i-ha-erh, and other places to withdraw more than ten kilometers from these cities. Trotsynko also indicated that the Soviets will guarantee the safety of our personnel before Soviet troops withdraw.

9. That the Soviets have no interest in the tripartite truce team.

10. Tung was very dissatisfied about the delay in our airplanes going to Harbin. He wants me to ask the government to punish the personnel responsible.

I received a wire from Vice-Chief of Staff Tung sent today. He reported that the TASS Agency was spreading malicious propaganda based on his statement to Major General Trotsynko of April 3, expressing a hope that the Soviets will leave behind in various major cities a small number of troops, as appropriate, to temporarily take charge of garrison duty there so that our government troops can speedily replace the defense. Tung said that already our Central News Agency has released a news item to correct this.

I wired Vice-Chief of Staff Tung in reply:

Concerning points 1, 2, 3, 4, and 7, there is no problem. Concerning point 5, for the time being I fear it will be difficult to achieve. Concerning point 6, I already have wired asking Chairman Hsiung to dispatch an airplane from nearby to get P'u-yi. Concerning point 10, I fear that our airplanes did not go to Harbin because the Aviation Commission feels that, before beginning scheduled flights, we first must send ground personnel there to set up stations. Concerning this, I already have wired Chairman Hsiung asking him to confer with the nearby Soviet regional commander. Furthermore, owing to the need to reinforce their strength, recently government troops have slowed somewhat their advance from Mukden toward Ch'ang-ch'un. As for negotiations between the Nationalists and Communists, no agreement has yet been reached because the Chinese Communists hold that there must be an immediate cease-fire in the Northeast, while the government holds that government troops must reach Ch'ang-ch'un before there can be a cease-fire.

APRIL 13.   In the morning, the Soviet embassy sent a counselor to tell our Foreign Ministry that the Soviets will do their best to assist in repairing the railroad and restoring communications and that, naturally, they will give attention to our hope that the Soviets give us every possible assistance in replacing the defense of the Northeast.

In the afternoon, Foreign Minister Wang invited the Soviet ambassador for a meeting. He told the ambassador that the Chinese government already has appointed as representatives the vice-ministers of the ministries of Foreign Affairs and Economics and has decided to begin discussions with the Soviets next Monday (today is Saturday). Wang also informed the ambassador about the princples and agenda we have proposed for the discussions. The Soviet ambassador indicated that he cannot approve of the following two points included in the principles formulated by our Foreign Ministry: that all enemy property must be used to compensate for China's wartime losses and that stocks in the jointly managed enterprises held by the Soviets are to be regarded as concessions from the Chinese. He stated that Stalin repeatedly stressed this when Special Envoy Chiang Ching-kuo talked with him during a recent visit to Russia. Then the ambassador asked why we cannot immediately discuss with the Soviets the question of civil aviation. Finally, Foreign Minister Wang stressed that what had happened at Ssu-p'ing must not be repeated in Ch'ang-ch'un.

In the evening, President Chiang invited me, together with Yüeh-chün and Ta-ch'uan, up the hill to his residence and invited me to stay the night at his official residence. Before dinner we discussed somewhat the question of the Northeast. He asked me whether the Soviets will slightly alter their attitude if we begin discussing with them the question of economic cooperation. After dinner the president discussed with Yüeh-chün and Ta-ch'uan how to implement the resolutions of the Political Consultative Conference. It was decided that tomorrow President Chiang will invite to a tea party representatives from various parties and factions and urge them to proceed.

APRIL 14.   At 11 A.M. President Chiang came to my residence to talk. This is his view:

> Concerning the question of the Northeast, we must not make any more concessions to the Communists. Before there can be a cease-fire, the Communists must withdraw 30 kilometers from either side of the railroad. Otherwise, the government will become a puppet of puppets. As for your returning to Ch'ang-ch'un, you may as well delay somewhat.

From his words I could see that his heart churns with worry. Certainly, his viewpoint with respect to the question of the Northeast is more profound than that of any other responsible authority in the government. But what can one do when those in charge of our diplomacy are totally inflexible and not versed in expediency? This has resulted in the current situation in which the Communists occupy an advantageous position. Furthermore, with these people still bent on their inflexible ways, even though today we face a crisis and imminent peril, the overall situation has become immeasurably foreboding.

I sent a wire to Vice-Chief of Staff Tung:

> Extremely secret. Please ask Hsin-min to have a talk with Counselor Sladkovsky and, adopting the following tone, ask him to politely transmit the following message to Marshal Malinovsky. Generally, let him tell Sladkovsky that already, yesterday, Foreign Minister Wang personally gave the Soviet ambassador a general view of our opinions concerning the economic question and that we have decided to enter into detailed discussions with the Soviets beginning tomorrow, in the hope that we can reach a satisfactory settlement. At present, the most urgent issue is that our government troops reach Ch'ang-ch'un soon and, before Soviet troops withdraw, reach Harbin. Meanwhile, the central government already solemnly has declared to the Communists that their troops must withdraw 30 kilometers from both sides of the Chinese–Ch'ang-ch'un Railroad. In this way, we not only can be spared a catastrophic war but also can avoid losses to the Chinese–Ch'ang-ch'un Railroad as well as to industrial and mining enterprises, while, at the same time, establishing on solid ground a friendly relationship between China and the Soviet Union. We hope the Soviets speedily will help our government troops reach Ch'ang-ch'un, so that the work of building friendly relations can begin soon. Ao [the author] very much hopes that before Malinovsky's departure, Ching-kuo and I can return to Ch'ang-ch'un so that we can come to Harbin to bid him farewell. And so forth. Please keep the above conversation strictly secret. Then, with regard to the Soviets' offer to arm Soviet employees of the Railroad Bureau and have them protect the railroad, this can be done. But we hope the Soviets will state in writing that as soon as our government troops notify us of their arrival, such armed personnel immediately will withdraw.

I also sent to Chairman Hsiung a wire:

> Extremely secret. Concerning economic negotiations, already, yesterday, Foreign Minister Wang and the Soviet ambassador met and talked for the first time. Beginning tomorrow we will enter into detailed discussions. Presumably, the Soviets' attitude will improve. Concerning the Chinese communist demand for a cease-fire, the president has insisted that first they must back off 30 kilometers from either side of the Chinese–Ch'ang-ch'un Railroad. This is still being urged. With respect to the Chinese–Ch'ang-ch'un Railroad, the Soviets already have promised to protect communica-

tions between Ch'ang-ch'un and Harbin as well as to send employees to Mukden to assist in repairs. With respect to air communication between Mukden, Ch'ang-ch'un, and Harbin, I hope it can begin speedily. After attending the meetings once or twice, Ao will be able to decide on a date for returning north.

On successive days the *Liberation Daily* has printed news of our army losing battles. A news dispatch of the thirteenth said that our government troops failed in their offensive on Ssu-p'ing, suffering rather heavy losses. Another news dispatch of the fourteenth said that our government troops were seriously mauled in a campaign against areas north of Pen-hsi-hu and Ch'ang-t'u and that more than one thousand officers and soldiers of the Nationalist Army were unwilling to wage a civil war and laid down their weapons. The newspaper also publicized their new plans in the Northeast, saying that the Central Bureau of the Chinese Communist Party in the Northeast has issued instructions to launch a mass production movement having agriculture as its base while, at the same time, restoring industrial production there. Furthermore, they will stage democratic elections and have people's representatives elect democratic governments. They also will set up a provisional senate and have upright people from various strata of society continuously elected to the government parliament. Such propaganda indicates that the Chinese Communists are making both military and political advances.

APRIL 15. Received from Chief Secretary Chang Ta-t'ung a wire sent at ten o'clock this morning from Ch'ang-ch'un saying, "Communist troops are pressing close on Ch'ang-ch'un. The Central Bank is in imminent peril."

I received a wire from Vice-Chief of Staff Tung from Harbin:

On the afternoon of the fifteenth Ch'en Chia-chen in Ch'ang-ch'un phoned. Beginning on the morning of the fourteenth, Ch'ang-ch'un was subjected to large-scale encircling attack by superior bandit forces. The attack still continues. The bandits already have occupied the airport. In the suburbs their attack has reached our inner defense line.

Note: Ch'en Ch'ia-chen was appointed the defense commander of Ch'ang-ch'un. He commands the second and fourth general contingents of the security maintenance corps of the Northeast Headquarters, as well as the security maintenance corps of the provincial government of Kirin. This situation indicates that there is no other way of settling the northeastern question except through an armed duel between Nationalists and Communists. In order to maintain their influence in the Northeast the Soviets are bound to help the Chinese Communists and enable them to win a victory so that the Chinese Communists must rely on the Soviet Union. Consequently, this armed duel is a struggle between the Nationalist Army and the Chinese Communists and the Soviet Union. It is not difficult to predict the outcome of such a battle, given the topography of the Northeast, the difficulty of maintaining lines of supply for government troops there, fatigue of the government's troops because of the long distances they must travel, and the exigencies of the cold northerly climate. This is why I was so earnest when, initially, I reported to our government authorities on the situation in the Northeast and firmly held that we must reach an agreement with the Soviets.

[Here the author's account is interrupted by the text of a wire from Tung Yen-p'ing.]

To Chairman Chang Kung-ch'uan and Special Envoy Chiang Ching-kuo: Secret. Movements of the communist party are (1) the headquarters of the communist army has received from Lin Piao secret orders to the effect that communist troops will enter and occupy the city of Harbin upon the withdrawal of Soviet troops. If a small number of central troops reach Harbin, communist forces immediately will defeat them by means of scattered attacks. However, if large numbers of central troops reach the city, communist forces will avoid a conflict by evacuating Harbin. They are scheduled to begin taking action on *hao-jih* [a date, in code]. (2) The Communists have divided their order of battle into four stages: south of Ssu-p'ing comprises the first stage; the vicinity of Ch'ang-ch'un comprises the second stage; the vicinity of Te-hui and T'ao-lai-chao, as well as river fighting along the Sungari River, comprises the third stage; and the immediate suburbs of Harbin and the vicinity of Lan-ling comprise the fourth stage. After completing these four stages, communist troops will evacuate to places like Mu-tan-chiang, Chia-mu-ssu, and Yen-chi, but they have sworn never to surrender. (3) Cadres of the communist party, such as Chung Tze-yun and others, already have evacuated the city of Harbin and are in the process of transferring and deploying their troops. They are very annoyed and angry about the Soviet Army ordering communist troops to withdraw ten kilometers from the city of Harbin. (4) Important elements of the communist party in Harbin have indicated that a large-scale conflict between Nationalist and communist armies in the Northeast no longer can be avoided; the communist army will fight to the end, even to the last man. Respectfully, I submit this information. In your employment, Tung Yen-p'ing. *Mao-hsien-shu* [probably, the month, date, and hour in code. Beside the character *hsien* is the word *sixteenth*].

APRIL 16.   I sent a wire to Vice-Chief of Staff Tung:

Today, representatives of the ministries of Foreign Affairs and Economics held the first discussion with the Soviets on the economic question. I hope that after several discussions we can reach a settlement. However, if Ch'ang-ch'un should be occupied by armed irregular forces that certainly will cause the atmosphere within our government to deteriorate, which, in turn, will affect discussions about the economic question. Please ask Hsin-min, as well as Vice-Chairman Kalgin of the board of directors of the Chinese–Ch'ang-ch'un Railroad and President Kan Yü-p'ei of the Sino-Soviet Friendship Society, to persuade the armed irregular forces to back off from the city of Ch'ang-ch'un this very day. Also, please constantly wire and let me know the day-to-day situation in Ch'ang-ch'un.

I am well aware that this wire will be ineffectual but, nevertheless, still am making the effort in the hope that the situation can be turned around, however miniscule the possibility of success.

I received a wire from Vice-Chief of Staff Tung reporting on aims of the communist army. (In the following section I affix the text of the wire.) [Here the author is probably referring to the wire of Tung Yen-p'ing that appears before the April 16 entry.]

The Liberation Daily printed a news dispatch, dated the fifteenth, saying that the following persons have arrived in Mukden: Major General Ch'in Te-chun and Major General Ch'en Shih-liang, our representatives in the Northeast to the military tripartite truce team, and General Gilliem, the U.S. representative. The following persons also have arrived in Mukden: Cheng Chieh-min, the government representative to the military mediation headquarters; Luo Jui-ch'ing, the Chinese communist representative (and deputy for Yeh Chien-ying) and [Walter] Robertson, the U.S. representative. Our government representative to the Mukden team is Chao Chia-hsiang; the Chinese communist representative, Jao Shu-shih; and the U.S. representative, Tedlum.

In Chungking Chou En-lai issued a statement: "Pending settlement of the question of a cease-fire in the Northeast, as well as that of a draft revision of the Constitution reorganizing the government and guaranteeing human rights, the Chinese Communists will not take part in the National Congress."

APRIL 17.   At 5:30 P.M. I went to see Soviet ambassador Petrov. I told him that I already have devoted several months to trying to retrieve the situation in the Northeast and hope he also will make great efforts to retrieve the situation there. He replied,

Concerning the points brought up in the Chinese proposal, that enemy property in the Northeast should be used to compensate China for its

wartime losses and that Soviet stock in jointly managed companies should
be regarded as a concession by the Chinese, why should the Chinese be so
demanding of the Soviets when, in addition to already having indicated a
willingness to relinquish their demand that all industrial and mining enterprises serving the Kwangtung Army be regarded as Soviet war booty, the
Soviets likewise already have promised that in the future, upon expiration of
the period of joint management, these assets still will be handed back to
China? They can let us omit the Fu-shun coal mines from the list of jointly
managed enterprises but hope we can replace them with the Hui-ch'un
Coal Mine.

Petrov placed particular emphasis on the joint management of civil aviation,
expressing a hope that we first discuss pertinent principles. I answered, "My
government lays great emphasis on replacing the defense of Ch'ang-ch'un
and Harbin. If the current situation in Ch'ang-ch'un continues, it will be
difficult to continue discussions about the economic question on a satisfactory
basis." Then, Petrov asked whether, upon arriving in the Northeast, the
tripartite truce team can help settle problems there and why the Nationalists
and Communists cannot reach an accord.

Judging from the aforementioned tone of the Soviet ambassador's remarks, if we immediately settle the economic question with the Soviets, the
situation in Ch'ang-ch'un may well be retrieved by dint of the tripartite truce
team. My observations suggest that in Ch'ang-ch'un and Harbin the Soviets
still are inclined to let us replace the defense. But, owing to their growing
armed strength, the Chinese Communists are liable to demand a united
regime. However, from the beginning I have held that the Soviet Union
cherishes different views with regard to southern and northern Manchuria.
In southern Manchuria, it still accepts our government as the host, while in
northern Manchuria it is letting Chinese Communists from Yen-an, as well
as communist elements nurtured by the Soviets, share political power.

I received a copy of a wire sent to Chairman Hsiung by Vice-Chief of
Staff Tung:

> In his wire of April 14 Chairman Chang Kung-ch'uan asked me to politely
> transmit to Marshal Malinovsky a request that he assist us in replacing the
> defense of the Northeast. In the wire Chairman Chang also said he plans to
> return to Ch'ang-ch'un and then come to Harbin to bid farewell to the
> marshal. In the wire Chairman Chang asked me to sound out the marshal's
> intentions and inclinations. Consequently, at noon on the sixteenth I called
> on Marshal Malinovsky at the Soviet Army general headquarters in Harbin.
> In a grave and solemn tone he told me the following: (1) In Ch'ang-ch'un,
> Chinese military policemen shot to death a Soviet engineer of the Chinese–
> Ch'ang-ch'un Railroad and wounded Soviet staff members of the railroad.

They also deliberately wounded Dzhidzhyn, Soviet representative to the railroad and Soviet vice-consul in Ch'ang-ch'un. Dzhidzhyn is in critical condition. Moreover, these military policemen used bayonets to stab a portrait of Stalin as well as the national flag of the Soviet Union. The Soviet Union never has similarly insulted the leader of China or its national flag. What friendship is there to speak of when Chinese military policemen have behaved in this way? (2) With respect to Chinese troops replacing the defense, since for several months these troops have not been able to arrive in the Northeast, Malinovsky deeply regrets that the Soviets cannot give them further effective assistance. (3) Unfortunate incidents have occurred wherever Soviet troops withdrew. Chinese officials have failed to prevent or circumscribe these incidents while, everywhere, Americans are receiving your considerate protection. Does this mean you are meting out unequal treatment to citizens of other Allied nations? And so forth. After Yen-p'ing defended and explained, item by item, our position, Malinovsky's tone gradually softened. He then remarked that Messrs. Chang and Chiang please can come to Harbin for a meeting with him before the twenty-fourth. And so forth.

I received in succession reports, forwarded by Vice-Chief of Staff Tung in Harbin, from Ch'en Chia-chen in Ch'ang-ch'un. Ch'ang-ch'un is going to fall.

A wire on the morning of the fifteenth from Ch'en Chia-chen says (1) throughout the night, communist troops attacked us. Their artillery fire was especially fierce. By eight o'clock on the morning of the fifteenth they were approaching our outer defense line from every direction. At Ching-ma-ch'ang our fourteenth regiment has been encircled by the Communists. A number of communist troops have infiltrated the city from the South Ch'ang-ch'un Railroad Station and rapidly are advancing toward Hsin-huang-kung. (2) The Continental Science Academy in Nan Ling has been burned down. (3) Beginning at daybreak today, the number of communist troops to the northeast of the railroad station suddenly increased to over three thousand men. They are intensifying their pressure on us. Furthermore, the size of their rear guard is continually increasing.

Moreover, on the evening of the seventeenth Ch'en wired to say (1) all around Ch'ang-ch'un heavy fire from communist troops still is very fierce. Particularly intense is their artillery fire. Since our various defense forces all were able to retain their original positions, the Communists did not achieve their objective. At noon, the fighting slackened somewhat. After a counterattack by our reserve troops, communist troops that had invaded from the South Ch'ang-ch'un Railroad Station retreated to the vicinity of the station. Beginning at three o'clock in the afternoon, under the protection of superior artillery fire, communist troops to both the north and the west carried out large-scale attacks on our outer defense perimeter. Many conspicuous targets were subjected to bombardment by ferocious artillery fire. There were heavy casualties. (2) At one o'clock part of the thirteenth regiment, defending the airport, withdrew into the city. The commander of that regiment, together with its main force, now is in the vicinity of Ta-t'ung and is in the process of establishing liaison with underground troops hoping to get relief. [The following remarks are attached to the end of Ch'en Chia-chen's message. Apparently they are remarks made by the author.] Today a wire, from Ch'ang-ch'un expressed hope that troop reinforcements speedily will reach that city or that the tripartite truce team speedily will arrive there.

I received from Vice-Chief of Staff Tung a wire in reply to mine of the sixteenth:

> Currently, Kalgin and Kan Yü-p'ei both are in Ch'ang-ch'un. Hsin-min already has revealed Your Excellency's opinions to the head of the Railroad Bureau, Zhuravliev, and Tso-jen has done the same with respect to Lieutenant General Kovtun-Stankevich. Beginning on the morning of the seventeenth, liaison between here and the radio station at Ch'ang-ch'un was cut off, so that what goes on in Ch'ang-ch'un is not known. But we speculate that this has been caused by a rupture of electric lines.

APRIL 18.　　　In the morning, Foreign Minister Wang invited me for a talk. In his opinion, the situation in Ch'ang-ch'un indicates that the Soviets really have no sincere desire to assist us in replacing the defense of the Northeast. With respect to negotiations about economic cooperation, he thinks we should wait until the Soviets have given us a specific reply concerning the point we raised, i.e., what happened at Ssu-p'ing still is being repeated with respect to their assisting us to replace the defense in Ch'ang-ch'un and Harbin. With respect to the question of civil aviation, Wang is even more unwilling to discuss it with the Soviets at this time. He revealed slightly his personal opinions: he would rather negotiate with the Chinese Communists. Moreover, he said President Chiang should boldly discuss matters with the Chinese Communists. As for the idea of my returning to Harbin, he feels there is no need for this. I was deeply astonished at hearing his remarks. If now we are going to discuss with the Chinese Communists the question of the Northeast, why didn't we do so at an earlier date? By now the Chinese Communists know that the Soviet Union already has rejected us while giving them assistance. Certainly they will not make concessions to us.

In the evening, I wired Vice-Chief of Staff Tung to tell him that, with the situation in Ch'ang-ch'un worsening, my coming there will not help matters. I also asked him to try to remove to Harbin our personnel still remaining in Ch'ang-ch'un.

Today communication by wire to and from Ch'ang-ch'un was cut off. Presumably, Ch'ang-ch'un has fallen.

Today's *Liberation Daily* printed a wire of the fourteenth from the Northeast: "The Central Bureau of the Chinese Communist Party in the Northeast has issued instructions to confiscate land formerly belonging to the enemy and their puppets, to be redistributed to the peasantry. The people's legitimate right to the land and property must not be encroached upon." Also, a news dispatch of the eighteenth says: "Nationalist troops, attacking Pen-hsi-hu and other places, suffered sad defeat. This demonstrates the bankruptcy of their civil war policy."

APRIL 19. All day there has been no wire from Ch'ang-ch'un. No doubt, the city must have fallen. I inquired of Vice-Minister Liu Wei-chang of the Ministry of Military Orders. He replied that our troops have not yet passed Ssu-p'ing. I fear there still will be a fierce battle there.

The *Liberation Daily* printed a news dispatch of the eighteenth from Ch'ang-ch'un: "In compliance with the people's request, the Democratic United Army, which has eradicated remnants of enemy and puppet troops, has entered Ch'ang-ch'un and has established a local autonomous government."

APRIL 20. I received from Vice-Chief of Staff Tung the various following wires:

One: He saw Major General Trotsynko and inquired about the date on which P'u-yi will be handed over to us. Trotsynko replied that he has not yet received instructions from Moscow. He indicated that he also would like this matter settled soon and that, in any case, he expects to have P'u-yi handed over before Soviet troops leave Harbin.

Two: Major General Trotsynko personally told him the following: that on the twenty-fourth of this month our military delegation will board a Soviet army train and proceed directly to Khabarovsk by way of Sui-fen-he; that on the twenty-fourth or the twenty-third our provincial and municipal administrative personnel will board a special train and, under the protection of the Soviet Army, proceed directly to Vladivostok; as for our personnel for Nunkiang province, he hopes that before the twenty-fourth they will arrive in Harbin, to depart together with the Soviet Army. And so forth. Yen-p'ing proposed that our provincial and municipal personnel depart on the same day as our military delegation, but several hours before it, and that the Soviets please take charge of providing coaches from Ch'i-ch'i-ha-erh to Harbin. He promised to act accordingly.

Three: Tung negotiated this with Major General Trotsynko: by now we have concluded that already the Ch'ang-ch'un airport no longer is guarded by our army. Consequently, if the Soviets should send an airplane to Ch'ang-ch'un to bring back to Harbin Soviet vice-consul Dzhidzhyn, then, if convenient, will they please try to let Directors Liu Che and Wan I, as well as others, board the plane and come to Harbin. He replied that, the current situation at the Ch'ang-ch'un airport being unknown, he does not know whether Soviet airplanes can land there. Therefore he cannot promise that they can send an airplane to Ch'ang-ch'un.

The *Liberation Daily* printed this news dispatch: "During the communist army's battle in defense of Pen-hsi-hu, two divisions of the Nationalist Army (the twenty-fifth division of the Fifty-Second Army and the fourteenth division of the New Sixth Army) were totally defeated. Their casualties amounted to over two thousand men. We captured a great number of weapons."

The *Hsin-hua Daily News* in Chungking published an editorial entitled "Celebrating the Victory of Ch'ang-ch'un." The newspaper also mentioned that Ssu-p'ing still is in the hands of communist troops.

What I am worried about is the safety of my subordinates still in Ch'ang-ch'un. I must try to rescue them from that city. Only then can my heart rest.

For more than five months, I earnestly and with great anxiety have trotted back and forth between Chungking and Ch'ang-ch'un. In the snowbound Northeast or in the high-flying airplanes, I gave up thinking about my own life. Yet I have achieved a result like this! I do not know whether the policy adhered to by our authorities in charge presages disaster or good fortune. Add to this the spectacle of the Second Congress, where the nationalists flaunted their biased, narrow viewpoints, while others chimed in, taking advantage of the situation to wage personal vendettas. This has created today's irretrievable situation. Will the result be darkness or light? So, now I know that great affairs of state really are like a heavy weight hanging by a single hair. I fear that, instead of examining themselves introspectively, those responsible for the current situation still pride themselves on having settled on a correct policy.

Meanwhile, as for Soviet interests, it would appear that at present the Soviets have obtained in the Northeast a regime obedient to their commands and so can fulfill their ambition of monopolizing the Northeast. But there also are many points disadvantageous to the Soviets: (1) By failing to implement the Sino-Soviet friendship treaty, the Soviets have left the northeastern question suspended. Even if they can obtain rights and status from a communist regime in the Northeast, such rights and status cannot be legitimized. (2) The Nationalists and Communists will continue to fight, and the Northeast will continue to be in a state of war. Consequently, the political situation there cannot be stabilized, nor can the economy there develop. (3) Because of its disregard for the Sino-Soviet friendship treaty, as well as for what is right, and its plots to invade the Northeast, the Soviet Union will be reproved by world opinion. From this I infer that, having these three kinds of apprehensions in the future, the Soviets will adopt the following policies: (1) At a moment when Nationalist and communist armies are locked in battle, the Soviets will offer themselves as mediators to settle the problem through consultation, in accord with resolutions of the Political Consultative Conference. (2) They will become uncompromisingly hostile to the national government, step up assistance to Chinese communist armed forces in the Northeast, and will obstruct the advance of our government troops northward. Furthermore, on this side of the Great Wall they will try to make the Chinese Communists sever their ties with the national government and wage all-out warfare against the national government so that the central government will be unable simultaneously to concern itself with the Northeast and even must compromise with the Chinese Communists. For the time being, let me wipe my eyes and see what happens.

APRIL 21.   I received a wire from Vice-Chief of Staff Tung from Harbin:

> Major General Trotsynko personally told me that there is not enough time for the Soviets to send P'u-yi in custody to Harbin and there hand him over to us. After a discussion it was decided that this will be done in Vladivostok at a future time and that he still will be handed over to Yen-p'ing. Then, along with me in my ship, he will be sent in custody back to our delegation.

At noon I invited Major General Ch'in Te-chun for a talk. I asked him about conditions in Mukden since his arrival there. He said that, after the tripartite truce team arrived in Mukden, it sent representatives to Ch'ang-t'u and Pen-hsi-hu. The team sent to Ch'ang-t'u had no success because at that very time there was intense fighting there, and Army Commander Liang Hua-sheng was unwilling to inform the team about the deployment of Nationalist military strength. Moreover, Liang did not allow the communist representative to use his army's communications equipment. The work of the team sent to Pen-hsi-hu also was fruitless because communist troops there were carrying out an inspection, so there was nothing the representatives could do after arriving. I then asked him about the state of our government troops in battle. He said that at Ssu-p'ing and Pen-hsi-hu government troops suffered severely and that approximately two divisions were mauled. He gave the reasons for the defeat: (1) The soldiers lacked combat experience. (2) There was difficulty in supplying them with ammunition. (3) It was not easy for the army to obtain grain. According to his observations, it will not be easy for government troops to advance beyond Ssu-p'ing. And so forth. This situation, in which our government troops have suffered severely right at the beginning of the battles, will tend to affect the morale of the soldiers. We have reason to be concerned about the future.

The *Liberation Daily* printed this news dispatch:

> The East Manchurian Railroad Control Bureau has formally been established. Under it are set up five branch bureaus: (1) the Mei-he-k'ou (southwest of Hai-lung) Branch Bureau, (2) the T'ung-hua Branch Bureau, (3) the Kirin Branch Bureau, (4) the T'i-fa Branch Bureau, and (5) the Chao-yang (near Yen-chi) Branch Bureau. These branch bureaus will have under their jurisdiction sections of the railroad from Fu-shun to Kirin, from Mei-he-k'ou to Chi-an, from Ssu-p'ing to Mei-he-k'ou, from Ch'ang-ch'un to Tumen, from La-fa to Harbin, and from Tumen to Mu-tan-chiang. Altogether these railroad sections comprise three thousand kilometers.

APRIL 22.   Today, the Chinese communist representative to the military mediation headquarters addressed a letter to the government representative to the same organization stating that there must be an overall settlement of all questions between the two sides and that the Communists are unwilling to participate in the national congress, which will nominate candidates for members of the national government. They appear ready to sever their ties with the Nationalists. General Marshall invited Chou En-lai in and talked with him for three hours.

I received several wires from Vice-Chief of Staff Tung:

> One: Tung again negotiated with the Chinese–Ch'ang-ch'un Railroad Bureau concerning the issue of bringing directors Liu and Wan, as well as other personnel of the central government, from Ch'ang-ch'un to Harbin. Bureau Head Ju generously promised to dispatch coaches for this purpose. But, fearing there may be unexpected incidents along the way, he dared not take the responsibility for the safety of these people.

> Two: Today at five o'clock Tung communicated with Director Liu Che in Ch'ang-ch'un, using the railroad telephone. Liu described the situation in Ch'ang-ch'un as follows: (1) Commander Ch'en Chia-chen was wounded in battle and currently is staying at the Red Cross Hospital. Vice-Chief of the General Contingent Liu Te-p'u was killed in action. Casualties among our officers and soldiers amount to over four thousand men. The remainder of these troops have withdrawn from the city. Casualties among citizens amount to over two thousand men. (2) The Communists have detained at Lü-kung-kuan Mayor Chao Chün-mai, Chief Secretary Chang Ta-t'ung, and Section Head Ts'ao Chih-hu, as well as others, along with over thirty employees of various organizations of the Northeast Headquarters. In the build-

ing of the board of directors, seventeen persons under directors Liu and Wan [wording does not make it clear whether Liu and Wan were among the seventeen persons] are being protected by armed Soviet staff members.

Three: Director Liu Che has requested that our government propose to Chou En-lai that we dispatch three airplanes to Ch'ang-ch'un, to take away our personnel there.

Today's *Liberation Daily* printed this news dispatch: "Kao Ts'ung-min has assumed the post of governor of Antung province. In Ch'ang-ch'un order has been restored. The Nationalist Army and Air Force fiercely attacked Ssu-p'ing."

APRIL 23.   Today, Chou En-lai again met with General Marshall. Afterward I learned that Chou told Marshall,

The Chinese Communists do not intend to one-sidedly favor the Soviet Union. They wish instead to constitute a bridge between the United States and the Soviet Union. Moreover, the Chinese Communists really do not wish to monopolize the Northeast but do not want the Northeast to become a Kuomintang base for anticommunist, anti-Soviet activities.

I sent to Vice-Chief of Staff Tung, in reply, a wire:

I have read your wires of yesterday. I fear that if you immediately enter into negotiations with the Chinese Communists concerning transporting our personnel from Ch'ang-ch'un it will be a circuitous, time-consuming process. Can you have Bureau Head Ju ask Vice-Chairman Kalgin of the board of directors to confer with the communist army, requesting that it guarantee the safety of our personnel en route and also have the Railroad Bureau dispatch armed Soviet staff members to escort them to Harbin. Furthermore, as early as the sixteenth I sent to Chou En-lai a list of names, Messrs. Liu, Wan, Chao, and Chang, asking Chou to send a wire notifying communist authorities at the front that these persons really must be protected. If you communicate by phone with Director Liu, please convey to him my consolations.

I received a wire from Vice-Chief of Staff Tung:

Yesterday, Major General Trotsynko personally told me: "On the night of the twenty-fourth or the morning of the twenty-fifth, under protection of the Soviet Army the Chinese military delegation and Chinese personnel belonging to the three provinces and cities of Sung-chiang, Nunkiang, and Harbin will board the same train to the city of Voroshilov, beyond the

Soviet border. After arriving there, the personnel of the provinces and cities immediately will change trains right there and leave for Vladivostok, while personnel of the military delegation will leave directly for Khabarovsk. On the morning of the twenty-fourth, Marshal Malinovsky and Major General Trotsynko will leave Harbin by plane. Major General Trotsynko will go to Khabarovsk and there wait in order to continue maintaining liaison with our military delegation. As for how the personnel of the aforementioned provinces and cities are to return to their own country, following their arrival in Vladivostok, the two governments should decide the following: whether these personnel are to take a commercial steamship, whether the Soviets are to dispatch a steamship to send them back under escort, or whether the Chinese themselves are to dispatch a warship for the same purpose.

I sent a wire to Vice-Chief of Staff Tung:

I presume you have received the wire I just sent. As long as there exist ways to evacuate the personnel of our provincial and municipal governments and as long as our personnel remaining in Ch'ang-ch'un are part of the personnel of our central government, naturally they should receive the same treatment. In order to avoid being unfair, I urge you to confer with the Soviets about sending these personnel, under Soviet escort, to Harbin for simultaneous evacuation. Please reply.

The *Liberation Daily* printed this news dispatch: "The Central Bureau of the Chinese Communist Party in the Northeast instructed both its troops and organizations to plunge into productive activities."

APRIL 24.   Today, Chou En-lai again talked with General Marshall. Afterward, I learned that Marshall proposed the following conditions: (1) That the fighting must stop immediately. (2) That army reorganization must begin immediately. (3) That, except for the two Nationalist Armies currently being transported into the Northeast, no more troops must be sent there. (4) That, from now on, both sides should notify the tripartite truce teams about the transfer of troops. If the central government has agreed to these four points, then this suggests that it has discarded its former condition that it must take over Ch'ang-ch'un before it stops fighting.

Today, President Chiang invited to a tea party representatives from the various parties and factions. I also learned that it was decided to postpone the date for convening the national congress.

I received from Vice-Chief of Staff Tung three wires:

One: Respectfully, I have read your wire of yesterday. Now, time does not permit carrying out Your Excellency's instructions. Moreover, since Ch'ang-ch'un constitutes a zone from which Soviet troops already have withdrawn, I fear it will be difficult to negotiate with the Soviets on this issue. On the other hand, Director Liu already has wired the president, asking him to propose to Chou En-lai that we dispatch airplanes to Ch'ang-ch'un to take away our personnel there. Perhaps this can have specific results. Since Your Excellency is close to the president, will you please urge this?

Two: On the twenty-fourth, Major General Trotsynko gave Tung a reply concerning our previous inquiry about the amount of bank notes issued by the Red Army in the Northeast. He said that he has received from his government a wire instructing that, pending complete withdrawal of Soviet troops from the Northeast, the Soviets are unable to assess the total figure of bank notes issued and that, in accord with the financial agreement signed on December 11 of last year, the Soviet government must wait until Soviet troops have completed their withdrawal from the Northeast before notifying the Chinese government.

Three: On the morning of the twenty-third Governor P'eng of Nunkiang province and 30 personnel of the Nunkiang provincial government arrived in Harbin. At noon, four of our airplanes arrived in Harbin to take back to Mukden over 70 of the personnel of our various organizations stationed in Harbin. This is the last flight of our airplanes to Harbin. Tonight, 8 persons under Directors Liu and Wan and Supervisor Kao of the Chinese–Ch'ang-ch'un Railroad [it is not clear whether Liu, Wan, and Kao were among the 8 persons] arrived in Harbin by special train.

APRIL 25.   Today, I received from Vice-Chief of Staff Tung a wire reporting his departure from Harbin:

At 11 A.M. the following persons, 70 in all, separately boarded three coaches and, accompanying Major General Trotsynko and other personnel of the Soviet Army general headquarters, safely evacuated the city of Harbin; 15 persons of the military delegation under Yen-p'ing [It is uncertain whether Tung Yen-p'ing was among the 15. The same is true of the ensuing list of persons.], 14 persons under Governor Kuan of the Sung-chiang provincial government, 31 persons under Governor P'eng of the Nunkiang provincial government, 12 persons under Mayor Yang of the municipal government of Harbin, and 8 persons under Director Liu of the board of directors of the Chinese–Ch'ang-ch'un Railroad.

Today, General Marshall invited for an interview representatives of the Democratic League; my brother, Chün-mai; and Lo Lung-chi. Marshall stated that currently the situation in China is one of dire peril and that there must be peace. He then asked what, in the final analysis, the Chinese

Communists want. In his opinion, although the Chinese Communists acted wrongly by violating the truce agreement and obstructing Nationalist troops from entering the Northeast, the central government also has committed many mistakes.

Chou En-lai asked my brother, Chün-mai, to transmit to me this message: with respect to my hope that the Chinese Communists will allow airplanes to take away our personnel remaining in Ch'ang-ch'un, he already has received a wire of reply saying that these personnel all are safe. Only then did I feel relieved.

Today's *Liberation Daily* printed this news dispatch: "Six divisions of the Nationalist Army fiercely attacked Ssu-p'ing." It also printed this: "A certain American correspondent reported that if, in addition, the Soviets are involved in the mediation effort, it would be more effective."

APRIL 26.   Today, General Marshall continued to confer with representatives of the Democratic League and the Chinese Communist Party.

For the past five or six days I have been consumed with worry about the safety of central government personnel in the Northeast and my small number of subordinates there, seeking their rescue. Now that they all are safe and uninjured, my work in the Northeast is concluded.

APRIL 27.   For the entire day I rested.

According to the *Liberation Daily*, Chou En-lai has reiterated that there must be an unconditional cease-fire in the Northeast.

APRIL 28.   Today, General Marshall again talked with my brother, Chün-mai, and Lo Lung-chi. The two of them proposed that there be set up a three-man commission to go to the Northeast and investigate actual conditions there. They also proposed the following points: (1) That the Nationalist and communist armies speedily end their clashes. (2) That the Nationalist and communist armies withdraw to a distance of several kilometers from one another. (3) That communications be restored. (4) That the political power of the central government be restored in various cities in the Northeast. (5) That political organizations in the Northeast be reorganized. Upon hearing this, Marshall thoroughly approved. He intends to wait until President Chiang returns from Ch'eng-tu, when he will confer with the president and then give them a reply.

APRIL 29.   Chief of Civil Officials Wu Ta-ch'uan told me that he has informed the president, on my behalf, about my plan to return to my native place to arrange for the burial of my deceased wife. Today, he saw the president and got his permission.

According to the *Liberation Daily*, "Communist troops firmly are defending Ssu-p'ing. In the First District of Ning-an the redistribution of land already has been completed. In Ning-an and Mu-tan-chiang there were farewell rallies for the Red Army."

APRIL 30.   At 7:15 A.M. I took a train to return to Shanghai.

According to the *Liberation Daily*, "The Democratic United Army entered Harbin."

Because of the deadline for the withdrawal of Soviet troops, negotiations in the Northeast between China and the Soviet Union took place over a short period of time. Although the period was prolonged owing to postponement of the deadline for that withdrawal, it lasted only a little more than six months. During this period, chances for cooperation or estrangement from one another constantly cropped up and often tended to disappear at the slightest oversight. Initially, because of the Soviets' pretending that Dairen was a free port and consequently not allowing our troops to land there, it almost became impossible for us to initiate negotiations with them. Then, after negotiations began, we were greatly disappointed by the demanding nature of the conditions raised by the other side. Subsequently, after slight concessions by the other side, there seemed to be a ray of hope. But then, in the hope of establishing a pro-Soviet buffer zone, the Soviets tried to have the communist forces they had created on the northern Manchurian border endorse the united government that the Chinese Communists attempted to promote during the peace talks between the Communists and the Nationalists. This led to objections on the part of radicals in the Nationalist party, who stirred up a crazy, anticommunist, anti-Soviet movement, which eventually resulted in the breakdown of Sino-Soviet negotiations. I recall a remark that a weak nation has no diplomatic leverage. After these negotiations, I know that although a country without sufficient military power or wealth is not equal to conducting diplomatic negotiations with a strong nation, the weak country is in still less of a position to engage in diplomatic talks with a strong neighbor when its political organization is weak and, at the top, lacks an effective policymaking organ while, at the bottom, there is no disciplined, unified public opinion. In addition, while the negotiations were going on, there were differences of opinion within the ruling party. Furthermore, people exposed and attacked one another. The administrative departments responsible were apprehensive about assuming their responsibilities, so that in making each decision they relied solely on the highest authority. However, then, while the decision was being made, it was restricted by the dominant opinion within the party. This reveals fully the weaknesses of its administrative organization. In the end, we resorted to military force. At the time the climate, topography, and situation of the Northeast all were disadvantageous to our side. Once we lose, this certainly will affect our entire situation. Can there be a greater peril?

Index

HOOVER ARCHIVAL DOCUMENTARIES
General editors: Milorad M. Drachkovitch (1976–83)
Robert Hessen (1983–   )

The documents reproduced in this series (unless otherwise indicated) are deposited in the archives of the Hoover Institution on War, Revolution and Peace at Stanford University. The purpose of their publication is to shed new light on some important events concerning the United States or the general history of the twentieth century.

Last Chance
in Manchuria

THE DIARY OF CHANG KIA-NGAU

This diary offers an important new perspective on the critical events leading to the end of the Chinese civil war. From September 1945 to April 1946, Chang Kia-ngau kept a daily log in the negotiations between Nationalist China and the Soviet Union to recover Manchuria from Soviet military occupation. The diary reveals that the Russians actively sought Nationalist China's cooperation in rehabilitating and operating the huge industrial complex that the Japanese had built in Manchuria during the 1930s and 1940s. The Russians were willing to let Chiang Kai-shek's government take control over Manchuria if the Nationalists would pledge that only Russia would be able to exert foreign influence in Manchuria.

If the Nationalists had not relied so heavily on the goodwill of the United States, they might have been able to reach an accord with the Soviets. Instead, they refused to accept the Soviet proposal to jointly manage Manchuria's industries, mines, and railroads. In reaction, the Soviet Union turned over Japanese weapons and supplies to the Chinese Communists, which helped them gain a strategic foothold in Manchuria where they could ultimately engage the Nationalist army on an equal basis.

The failure of the Nationalists to recover Manchuria led to intense factional struggles in the Kuomintang, thereby weakening it. Moreover, when American envoy General George C. Marshall imposed a truce in January 1946, it not only delayed the Nationalist advance into Manchuria but also legitimatized the Chinese communist presence there. By April, when Stalin realized that it was impossible to reach an accord with Chiang Kai-shek, the Chinese civil war already had spread into Manchuria—and it was in Manchuria that the civil war was ultimately lost.

Chang Kia-ngau's diary is an eyewitness account of how Manchuria, one of the world's greatest industrial sites, fell to the control of the Chinese Red Army and thus led to the communist victory over Chiang Kai-shek. This book will interest students of cold war rivalry, U.S. foreign policy, Soviet diplomacy, and Chinese history alike.